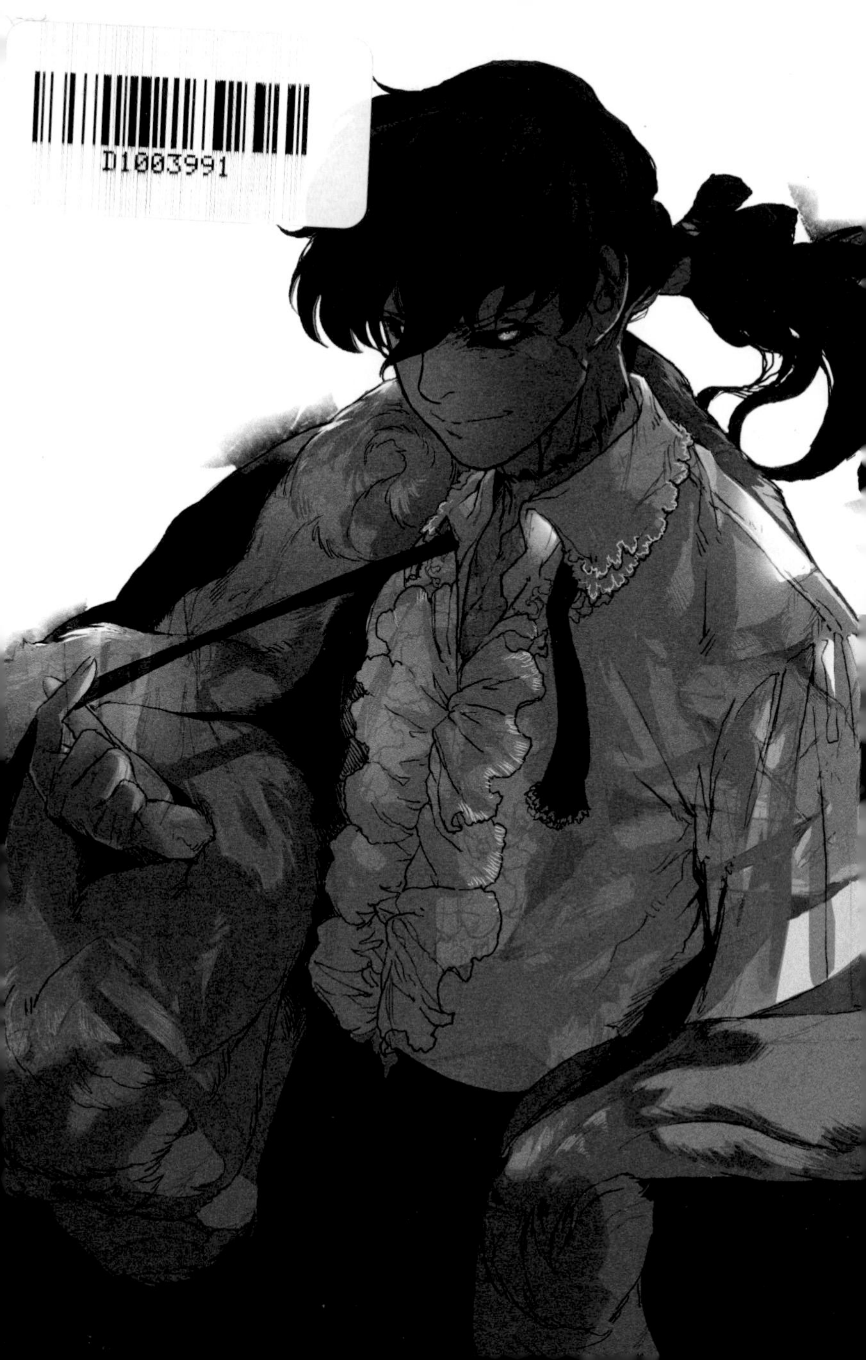

Contents

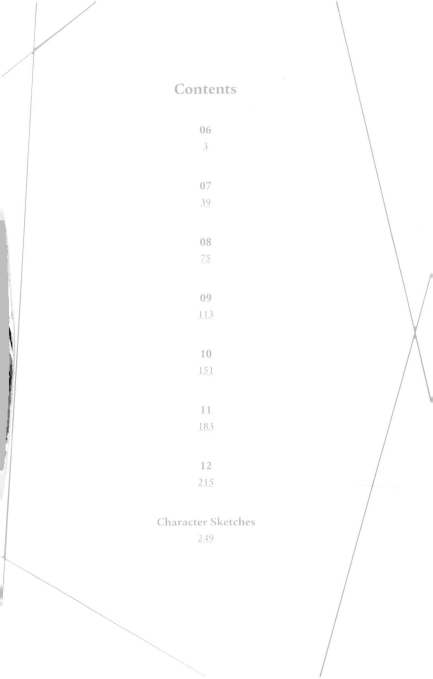

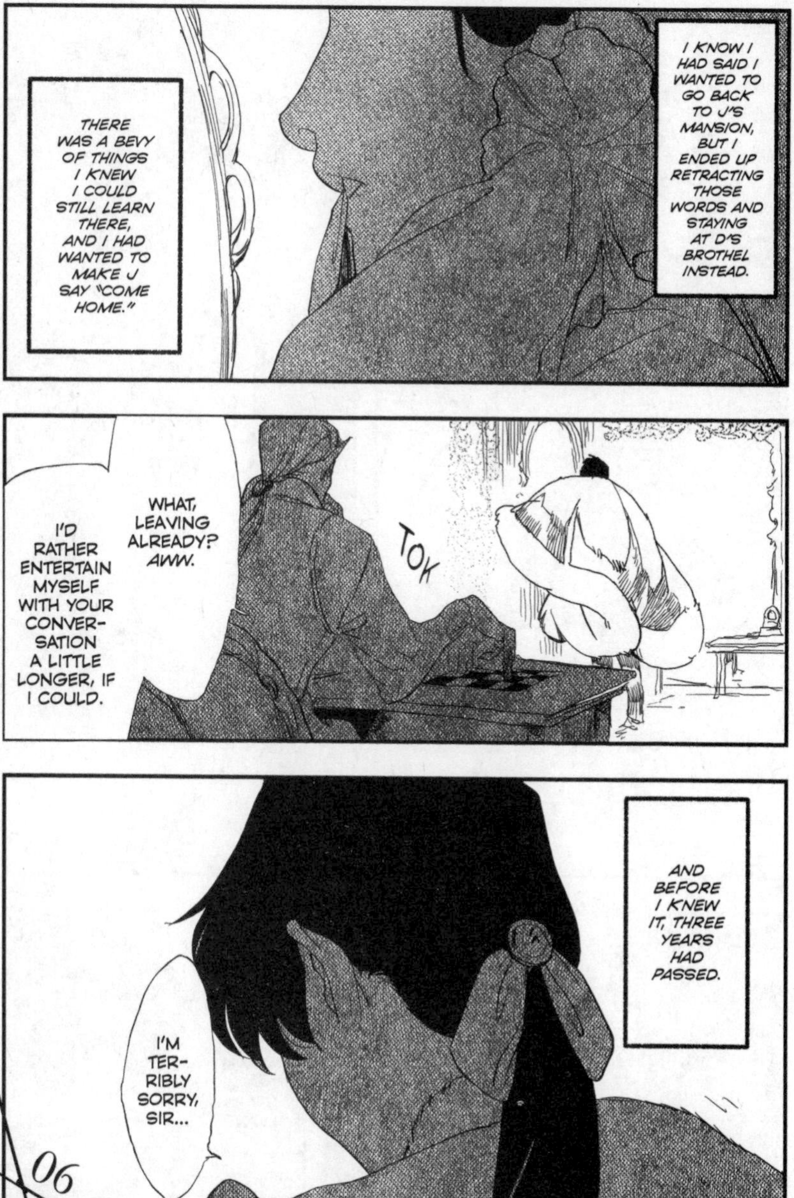
I KNOW I HAD SAID I WANTED TO GO BACK TO J'S MANSION, BUT I ENDED UP RETRACTING THOSE WORDS AND STAYING AT D'S BROTHEL INSTEAD.
THERE WAS A BEVY OF THINGS I KNEW I COULD STILL LEARN THERE, AND I HAD WANTED TO MAKE J SAY "COME HOME."
TOK
WHAT, LEAVING ALREADY? AWW.
I'D RATHER ENTERTAIN MYSELF WITH YOUR CONVER-SATION A LITTLE LONGER, IF I COULD.
AND BEFORE I KNEW IT, THREE YEARS HAD PASSED.
I'M TER-RIBLY SORRY, SIR...

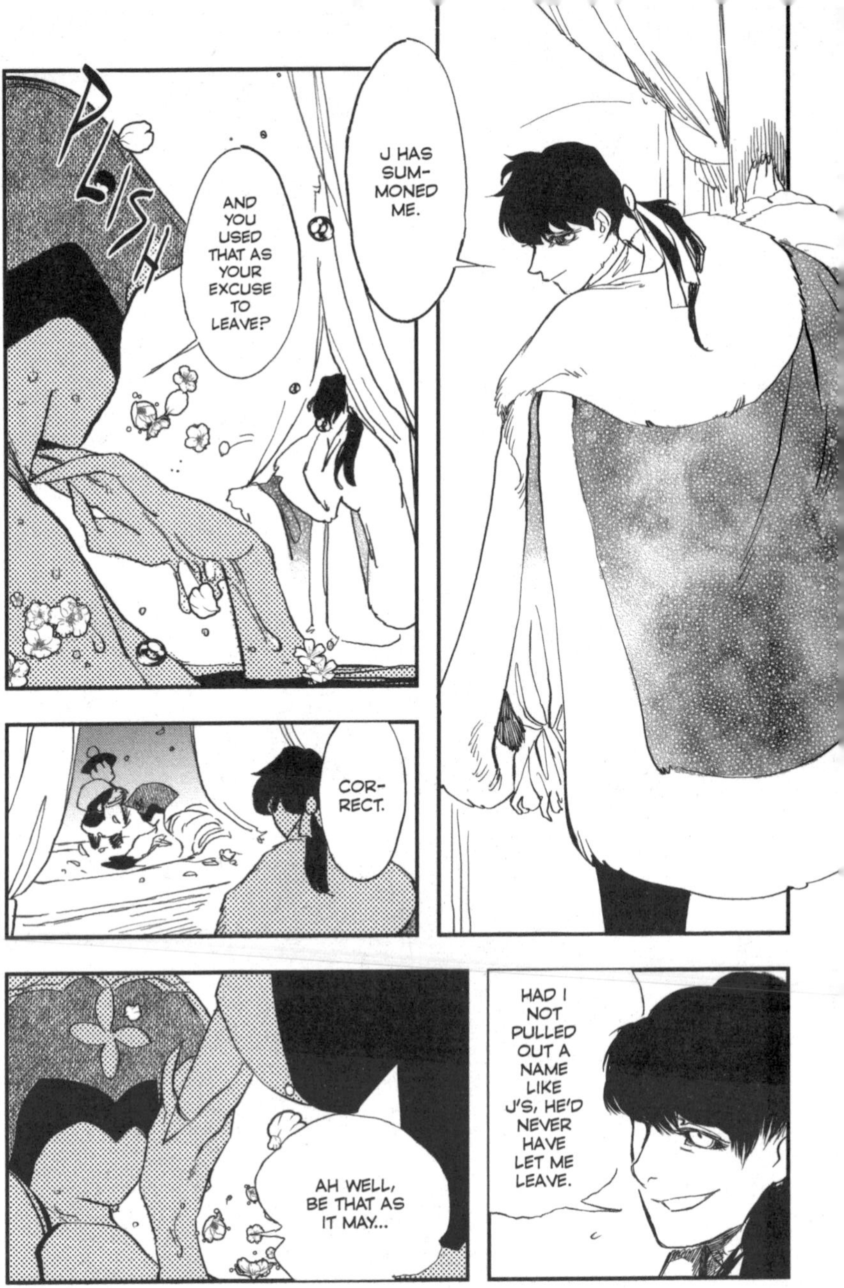
J HAS SUMMONED ME.
PLISH
AND YOU USED THAT AS YOUR EXCUSE TO LEAVE?
CORRECT.
HAD I NOT PULLED OUT A NAME LIKE J'S, HE'D NEVER HAVE LET ME LEAVE.
AH WELL, BE THAT AS IT MAY...

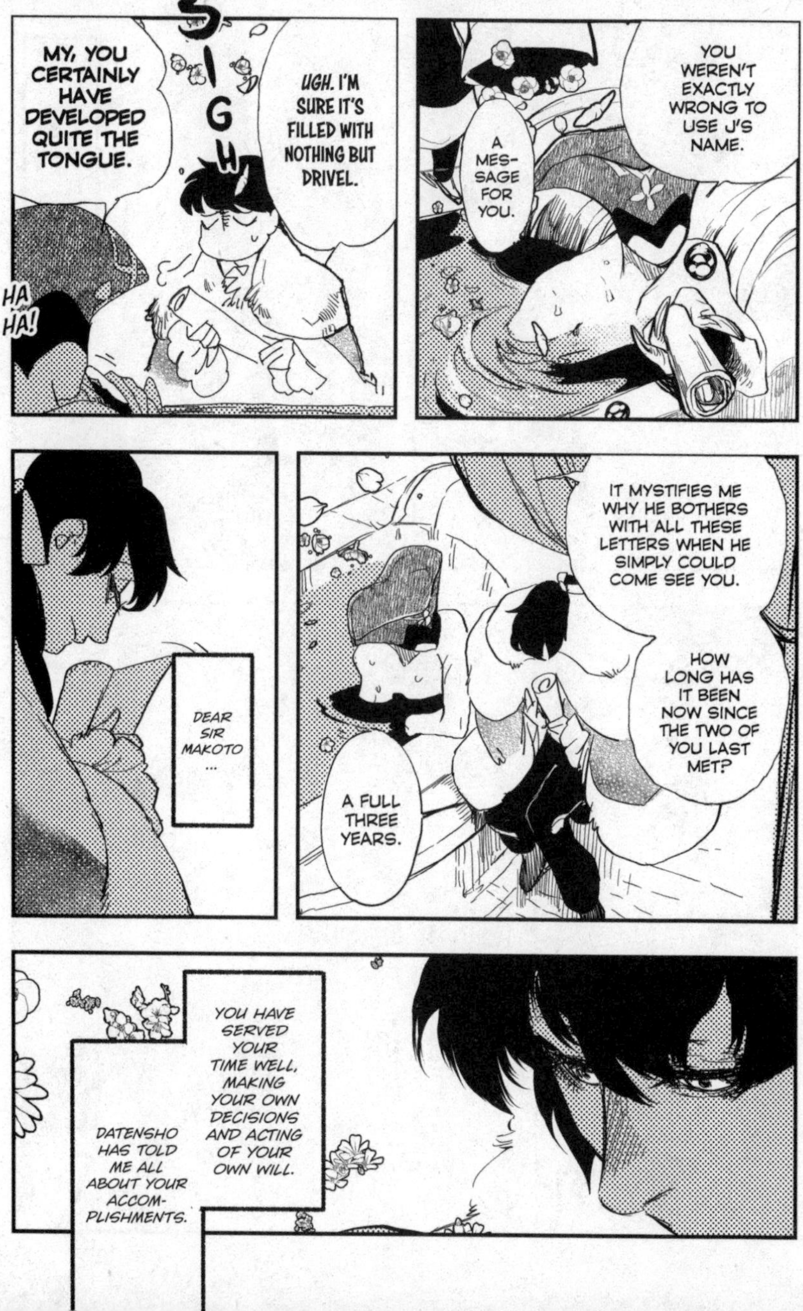
YOU WEREN'T EXACTLY WRONG TO USE J'S NAME.
A MES-SAGE FOR YOU.
UGH. I'M SURE IT'S FILLED WITH NOTHING BUT DRIVEL.
SIGH
MY, YOU CERTAINLY HAVE DEVELOPED QUITE THE TONGUE.
HA HA!
IT MYSTIFIES ME WHY HE BOTHERS WITH ALL THESE LETTERS WHEN HE SIMPLY COULD COME SEE YOU.
HOW LONG HAS IT BEEN NOW SINCE THE TWO OF YOU LAST MET?
A FULL THREE YEARS.
DEAR SIR MAKOTO ...
YOU HAVE SERVED YOUR TIME WELL, MAKING YOUR OWN DECISIONS AND ACTING OF YOUR OWN WILL.
DATENSHO HAS TOLD ME ALL ABOUT YOUR ACCOM-PLISHMENTS.

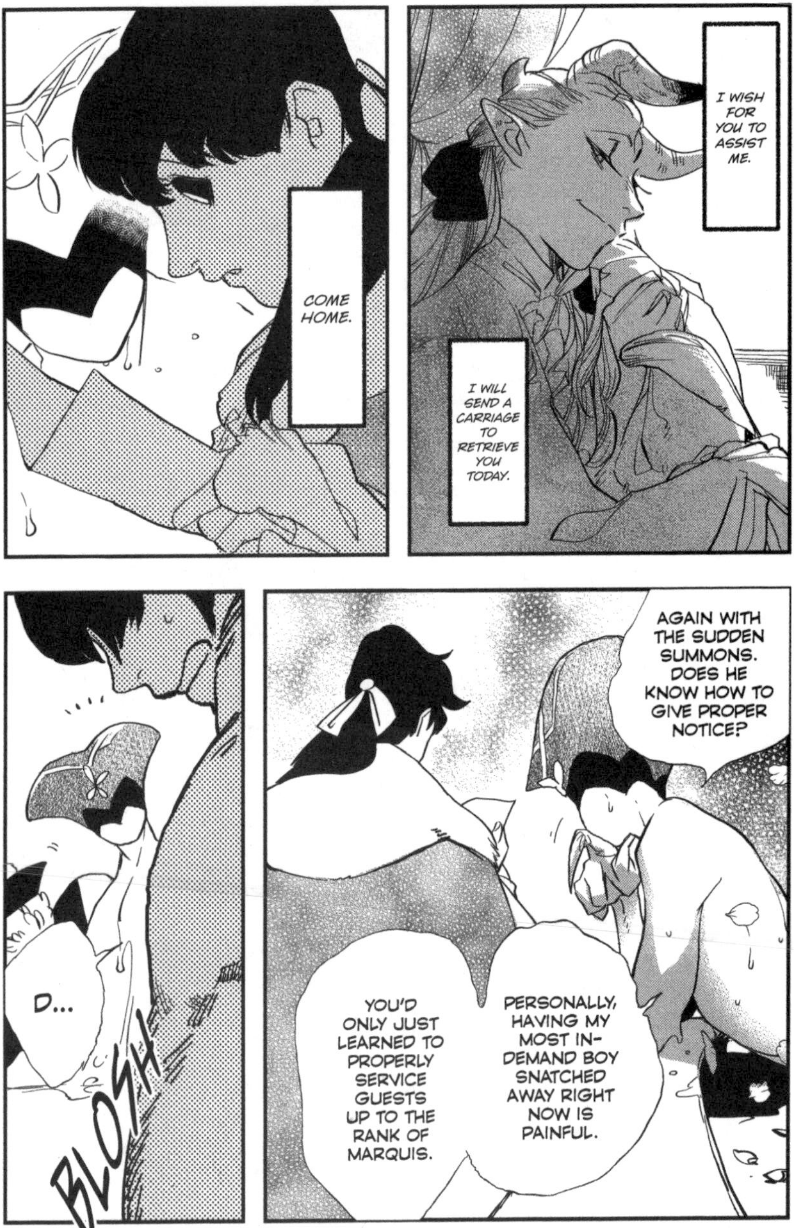
I WISH FOR YOU TO ASSIST ME.
I WILL SEND A CARRIAGE TO RETRIEVE YOU TODAY.
COME HOME.
AGAIN WITH THE SUDDEN SUMMONS. DOES HE KNOW HOW TO GIVE PROPER NOTICE?
PERSONALLY, HAVING MY MOST IN-DEMAND BOY SNATCHED AWAY RIGHT NOW IS PAINFUL.
YOU'D ONLY JUST LEARNED TO PROPERLY SERVICE GUESTS UP TO THE RANK OF MARQUIS.
...
D...
BLOSH

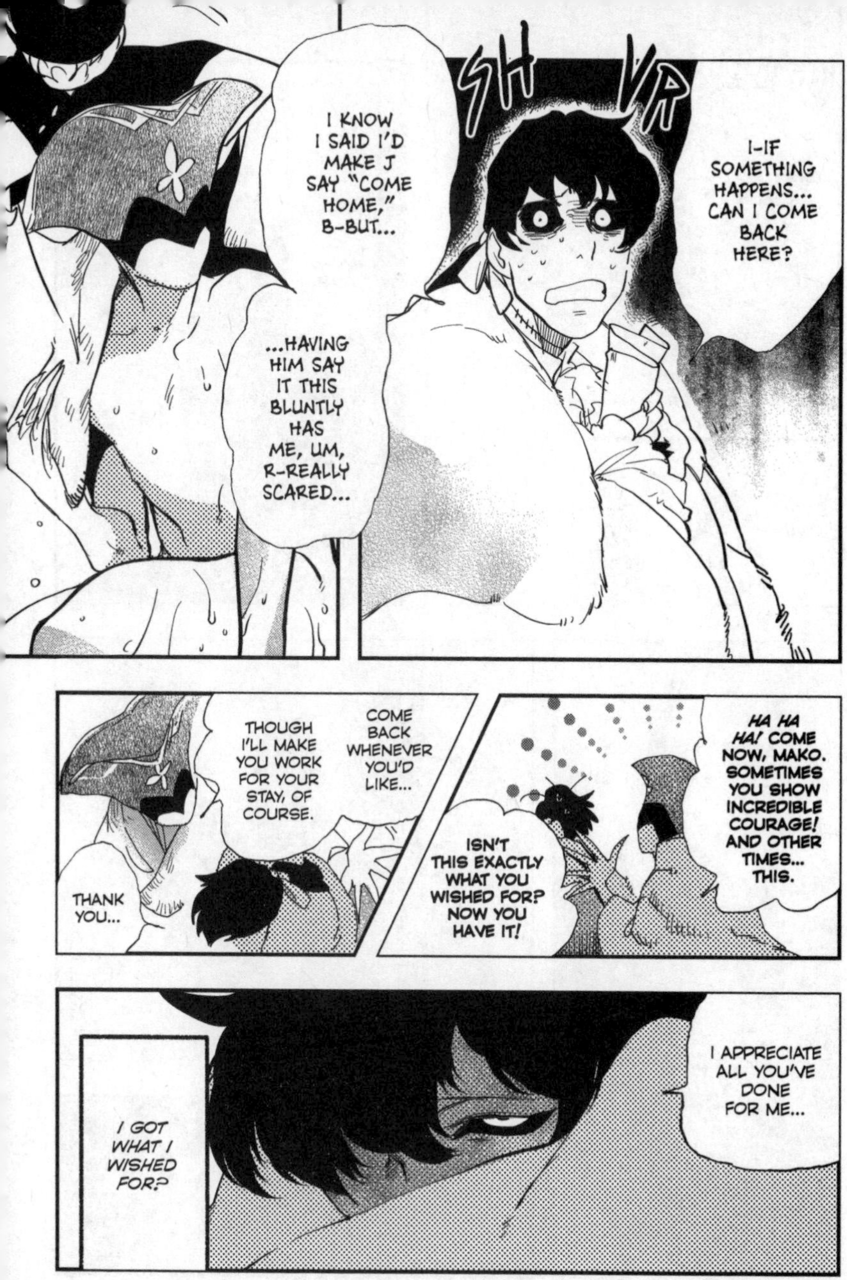
SH VR
I-IF SOMETHING HAPPENS... CAN I COME BACK HERE?
I KNOW I SAID I'D MAKE J SAY "COME HOME," B-BUT...
...HAVING HIM SAY IT THIS BLUNTLY HAS ME, UM, R-REALLY SCARED...
HA HA HA! COME NOW, MAKO. SOMETIMES YOU SHOW INCREDIBLE COURAGE! AND OTHER TIMES... THIS.
ISN'T THIS EXACTLY WHAT YOU WISHED FOR? NOW YOU HAVE IT!
COME BACK WHENEVER YOU'D LIKE...
THOUGH I'LL MAKE YOU WORK FOR YOUR STAY, OF COURSE.
THANK YOU...
I APPRECIATE ALL YOU'VE DONE FOR ME...
I GOT WHAT I WISHED FOR?

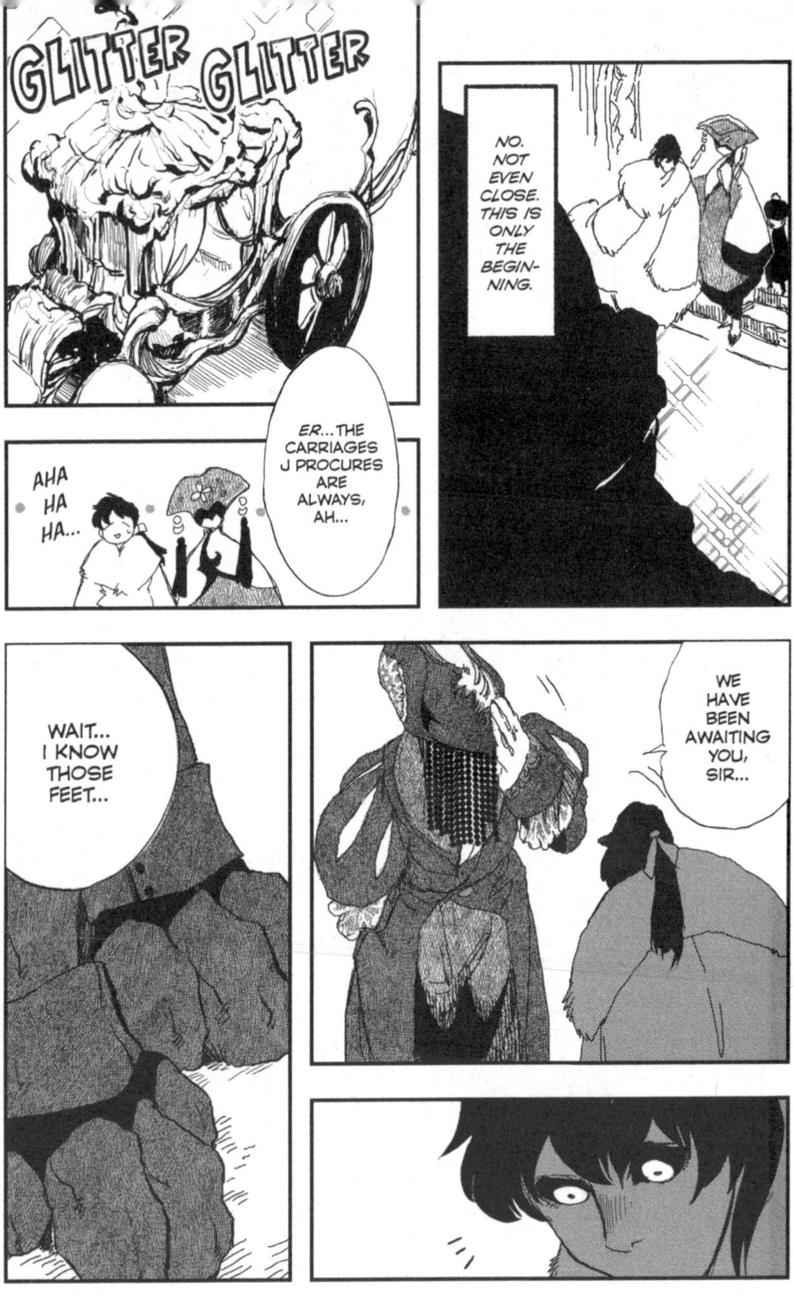
NO. NOT EVEN CLOSE. THIS IS ONLY THE BEGIN-NING.
GLITTER GLITTER
ER... THE CARRIAGES J PROCURES ARE ALWAYS, AH...
AHA HA HA...
WE HAVE BEEN AWAITING YOU, SIR...
WAIT... I KNOW THOSE FEET...

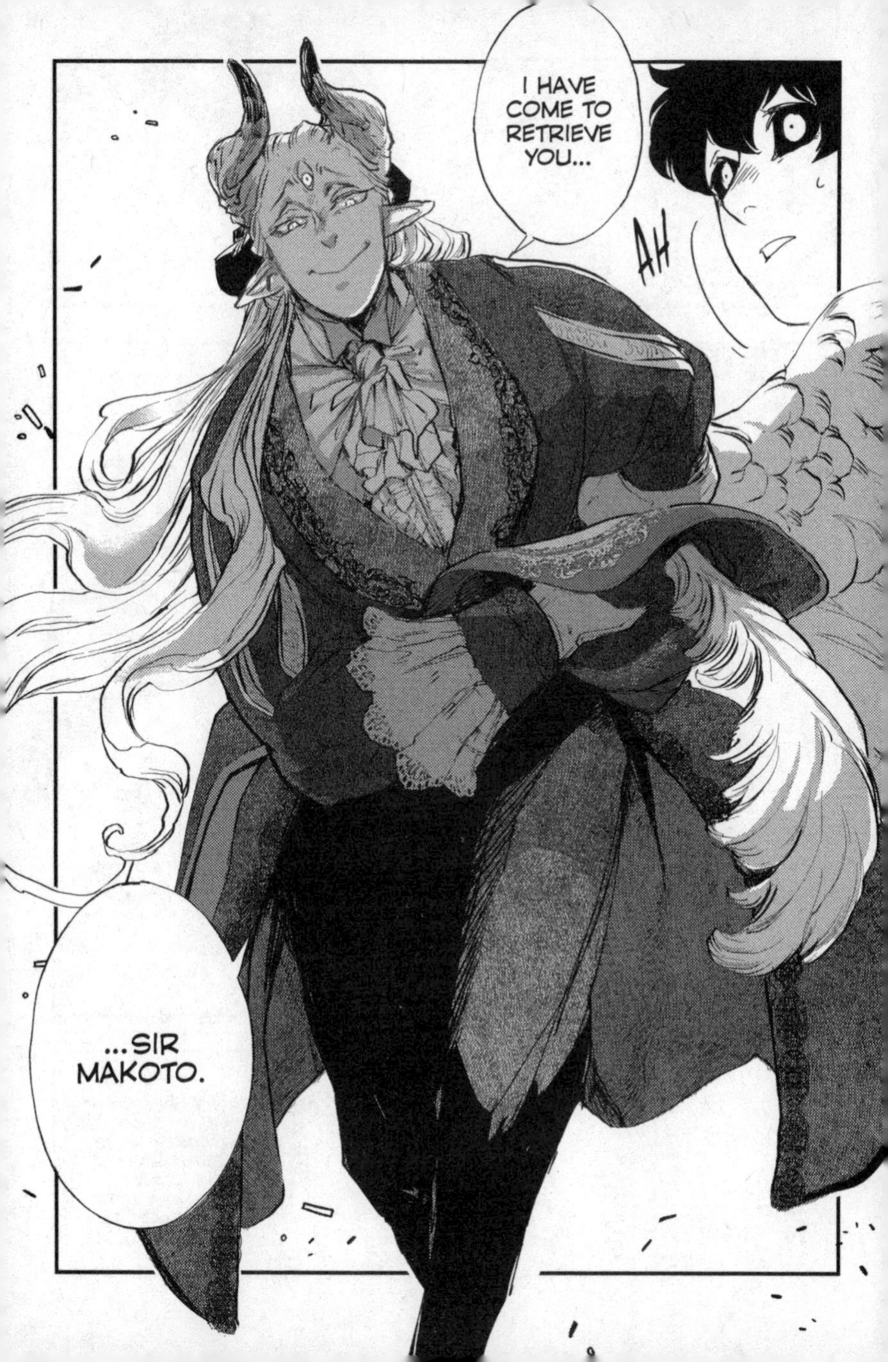
I HAVE COME TO RETRIEVE YOU...
AH
...SIR MAKOTO.

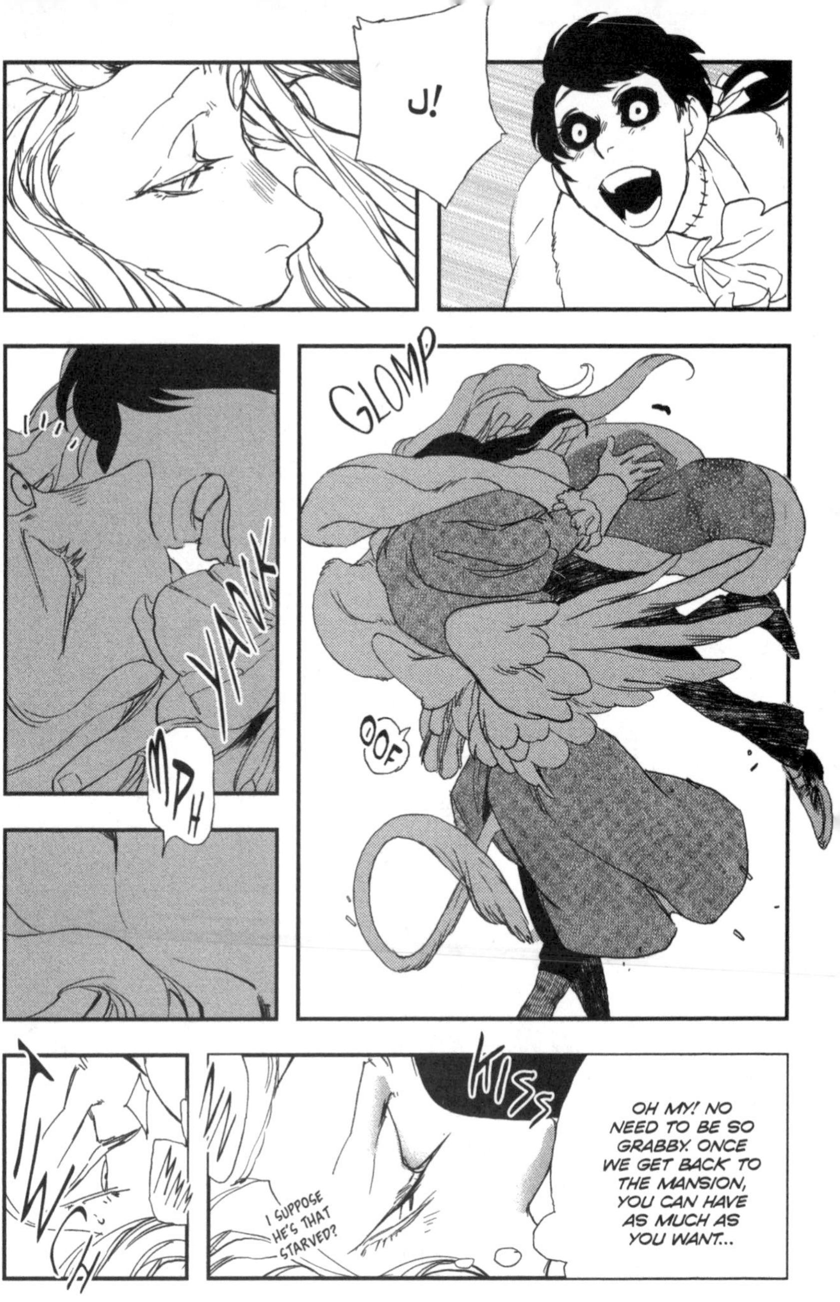
J!
GLOMP
OOF
YANK
MPH
KISS
OH MY! NO NEED TO BE SO GRABBY. ONCE WE GET BACK TO THE MANSION, YOU CAN HAVE AS MUCH AS YOU WANT...
I SUPPOSE HE'S THAT STARVED?
MMM

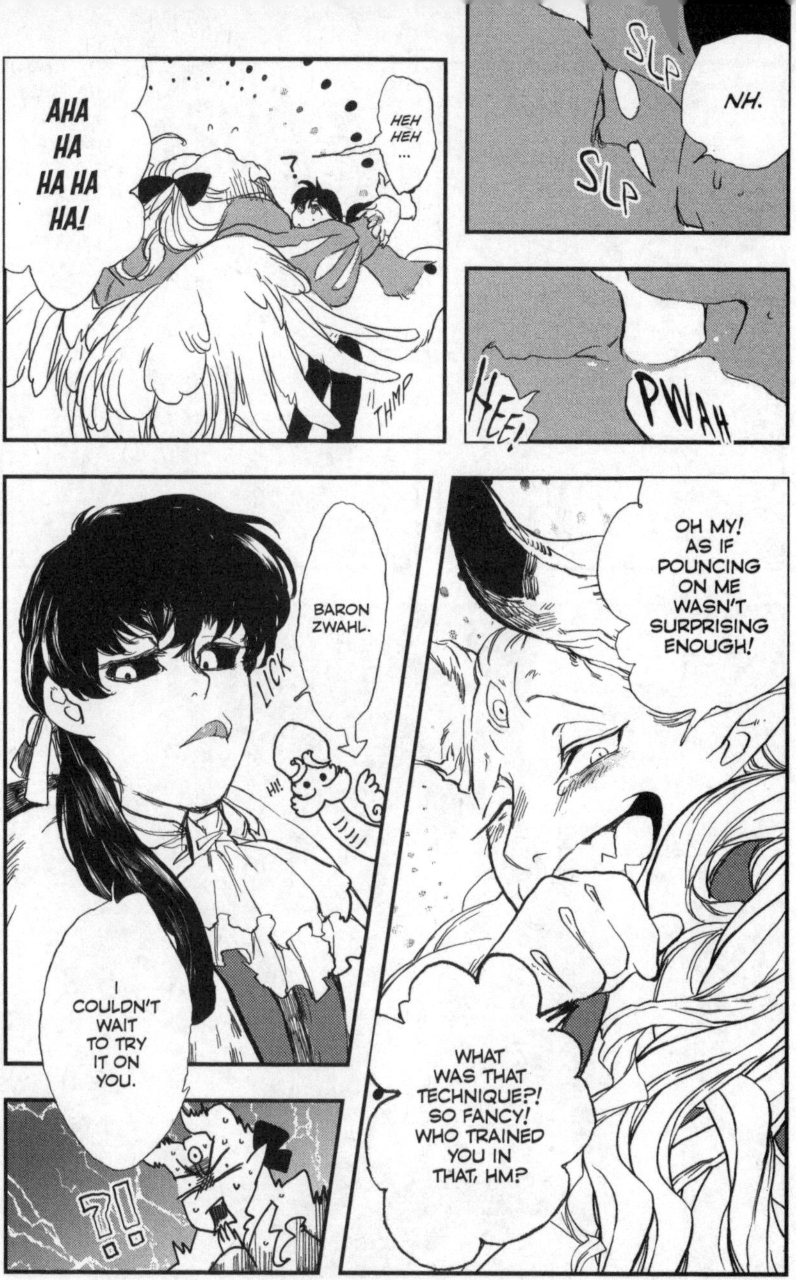
SLP
SLP
NH.
PWAH
HEE!
HEH HEH ...
?
AHA HA HA HA HA!
THMP
OH MY! AS IF POUNCING ON ME WASN'T SURPRISING ENOUGH!
WHAT WAS THAT TECHNIQUE?! SO FANCY! WHO TRAINED YOU IN THAT, HM?
BARON ZWAHL.
LICK
HI!
I COULDN'T WAIT TO TRY IT ON YOU.
?!

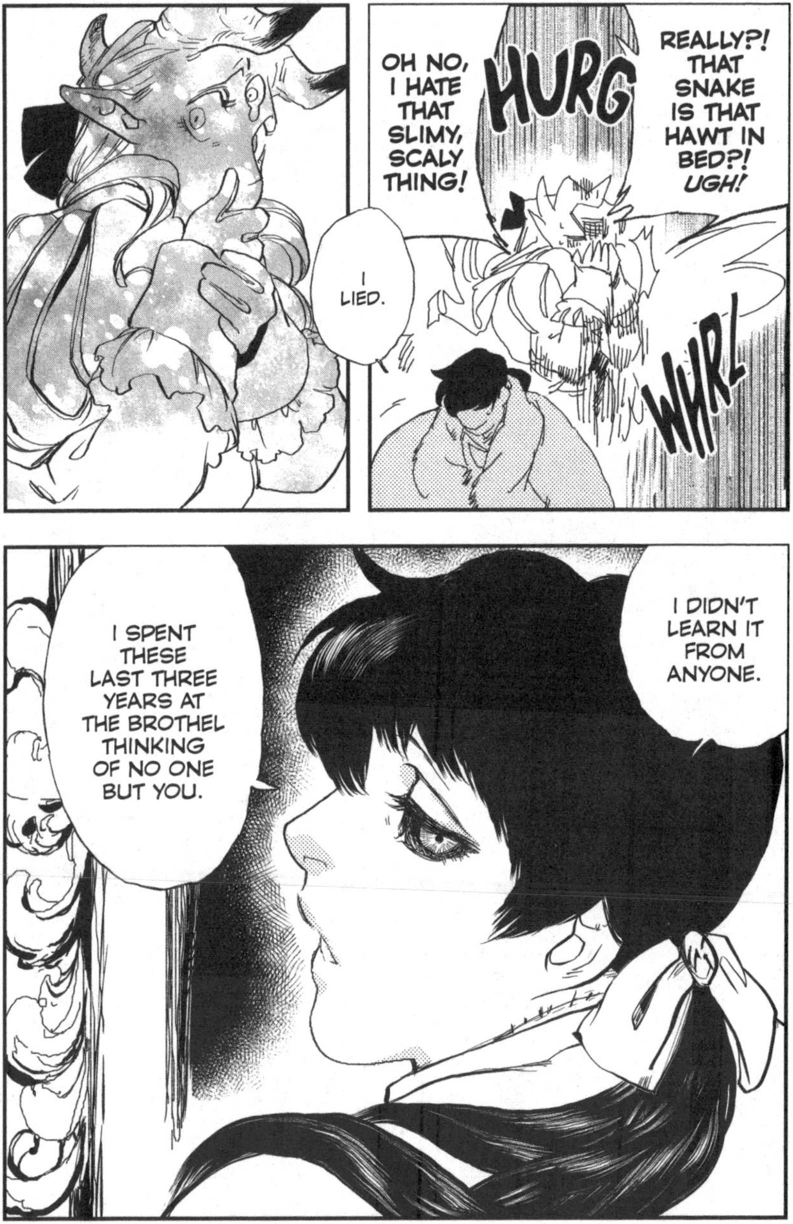
REALLY?! THAT SNAKE IS THAT HAWT IN BED?! UGH!
HURG
OH NO, I HATE THAT SLIMY, SCALY THING!
WHRL
I LIED.
I DIDN'T LEARN IT FROM ANYONE.
I SPENT THESE LAST THREE YEARS AT THE BROTHEL THINKING OF NO ONE BUT YOU.

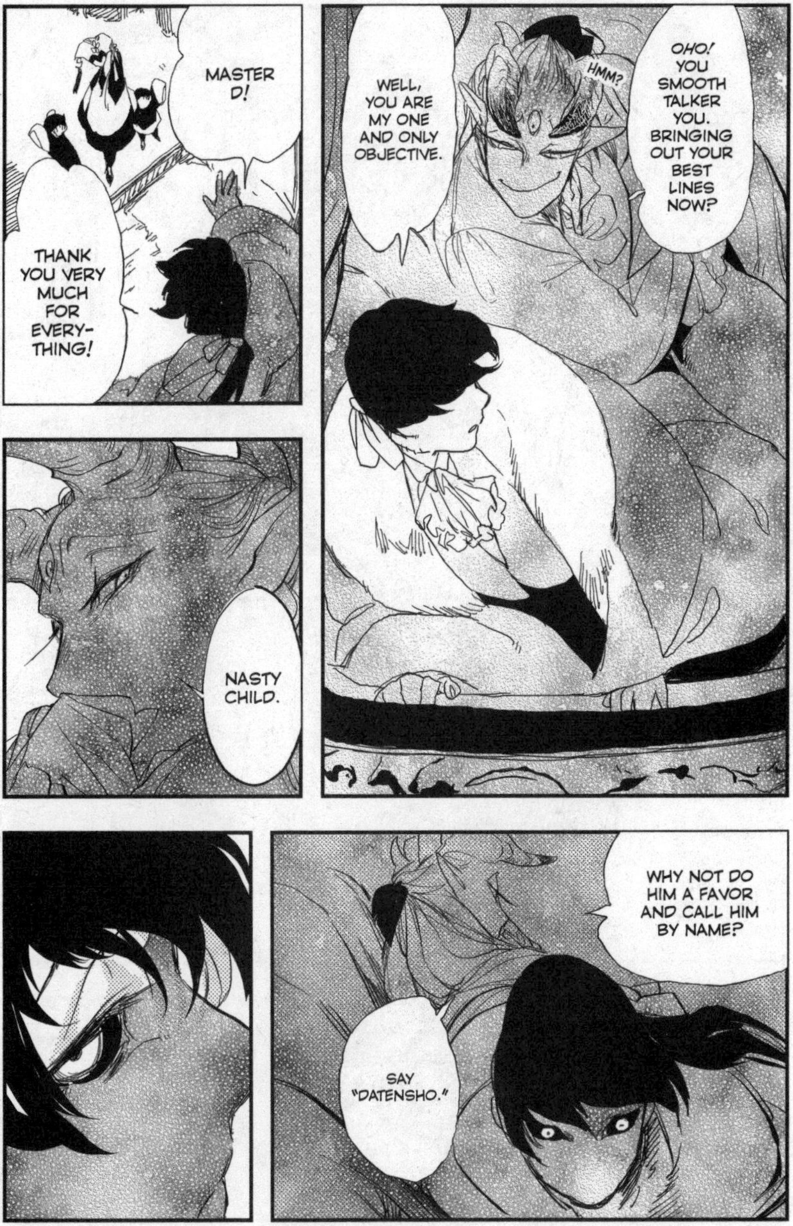
OHO! YOU SMOOTH TALKER YOU. BRINGING OUT YOUR BEST LINES NOW?
HMM?
WELL, YOU ARE MY ONE AND ONLY OBJECTIVE.
MASTER D!
THANK YOU VERY MUCH FOR EVERY-THING!
NASTY CHILD.
WHY NOT DO HIM A FAVOR AND CALL HIM BY NAME?
SAY "DATENSHO."

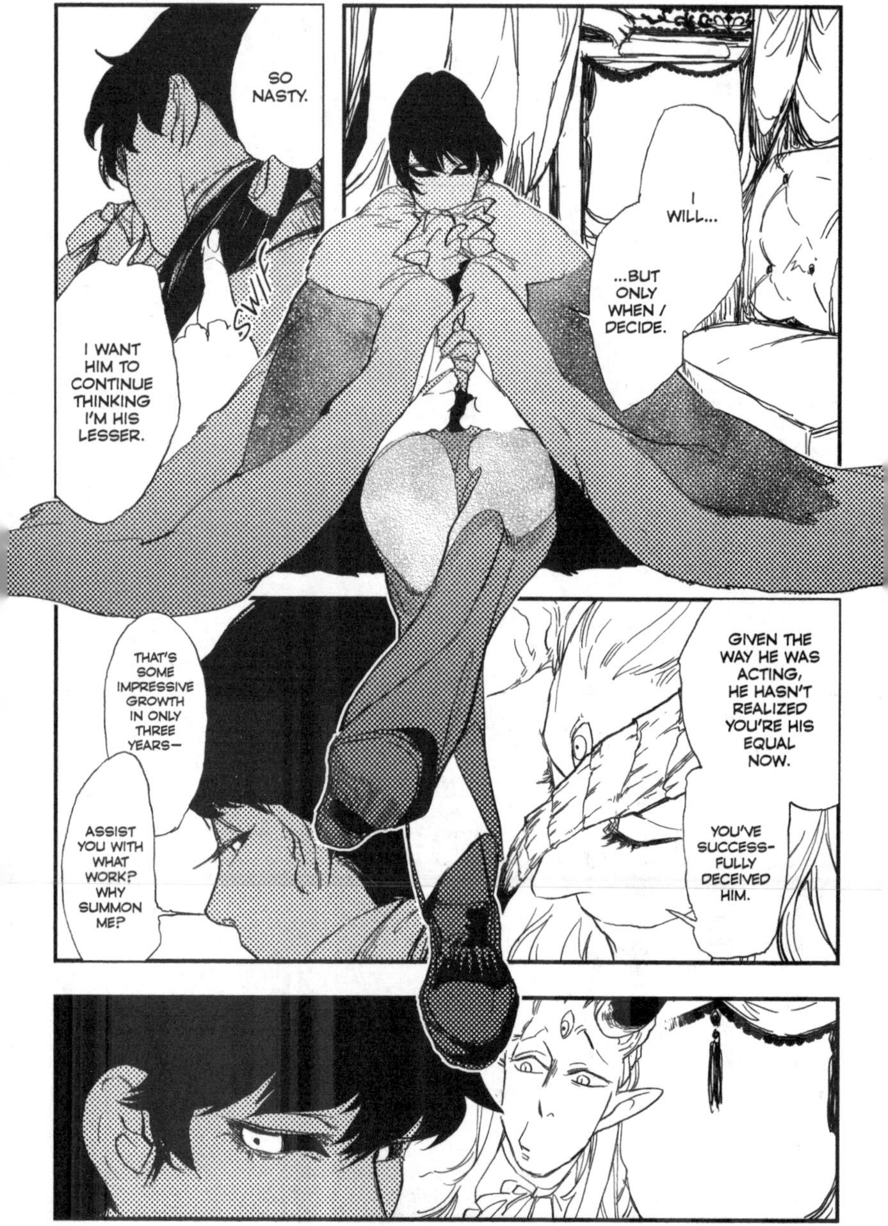
I WILL...
...BUT ONLY WHEN I DECIDE.
SO NASTY.
SWIF
I WANT HIM TO CONTINUE THINKING I'M HIS LESSER.
GIVEN THE WAY HE WAS ACTING, HE HASN'T REALIZED YOU'RE HIS EQUAL NOW.
YOU'VE SUCCESSFULLY DECEIVED HIM.
THAT'S SOME IMPRESSIVE GROWTH IN ONLY THREE YEARS—
ASSIST YOU WITH WHAT WORK? WHY SUMMON ME?

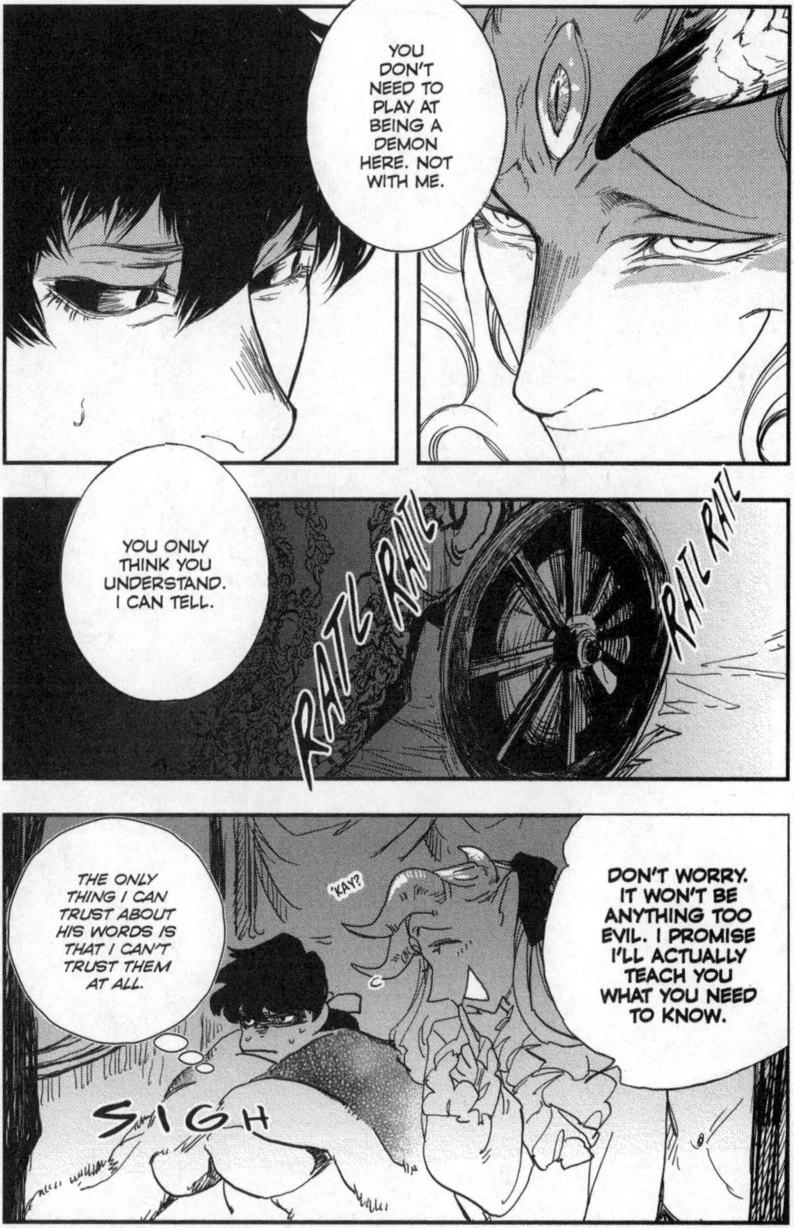
YOU DON'T NEED TO PLAY AT BEING A DEMON HERE. NOT WITH ME.
RATL RATL
YOU ONLY THINK YOU UNDERSTAND. I CAN TELL.
RATL RATL
DON'T WORRY. IT WON'T BE ANYTHING TOO EVIL. I PROMISE I'LL ACTUALLY TEACH YOU WHAT YOU NEED TO KNOW.
'KAY?
THE ONLY THING I CAN TRUST ABOUT HIS WORDS IS THAT I CAN'T TRUST THEM AT ALL.
SIGH

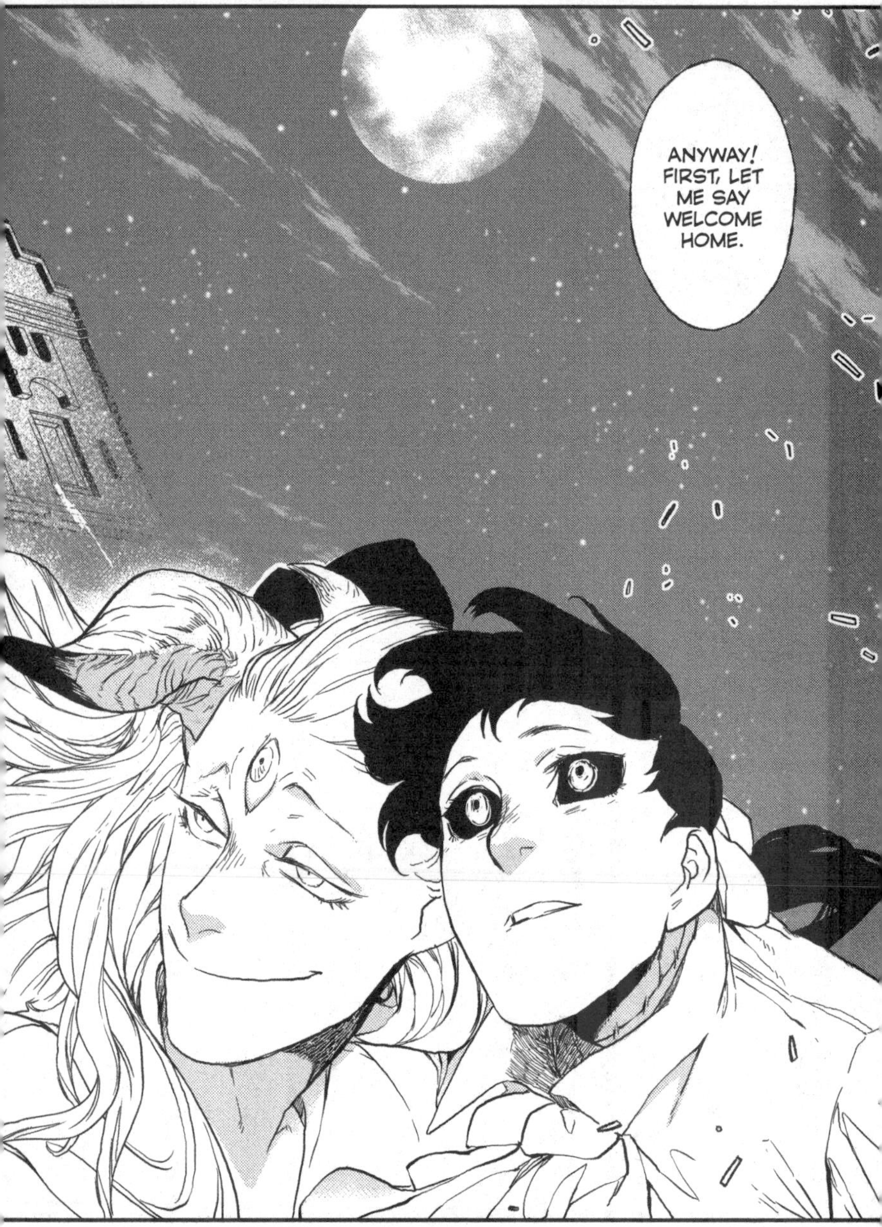
ANYWAY! FIRST, LET ME SAY WELCOME HOME.

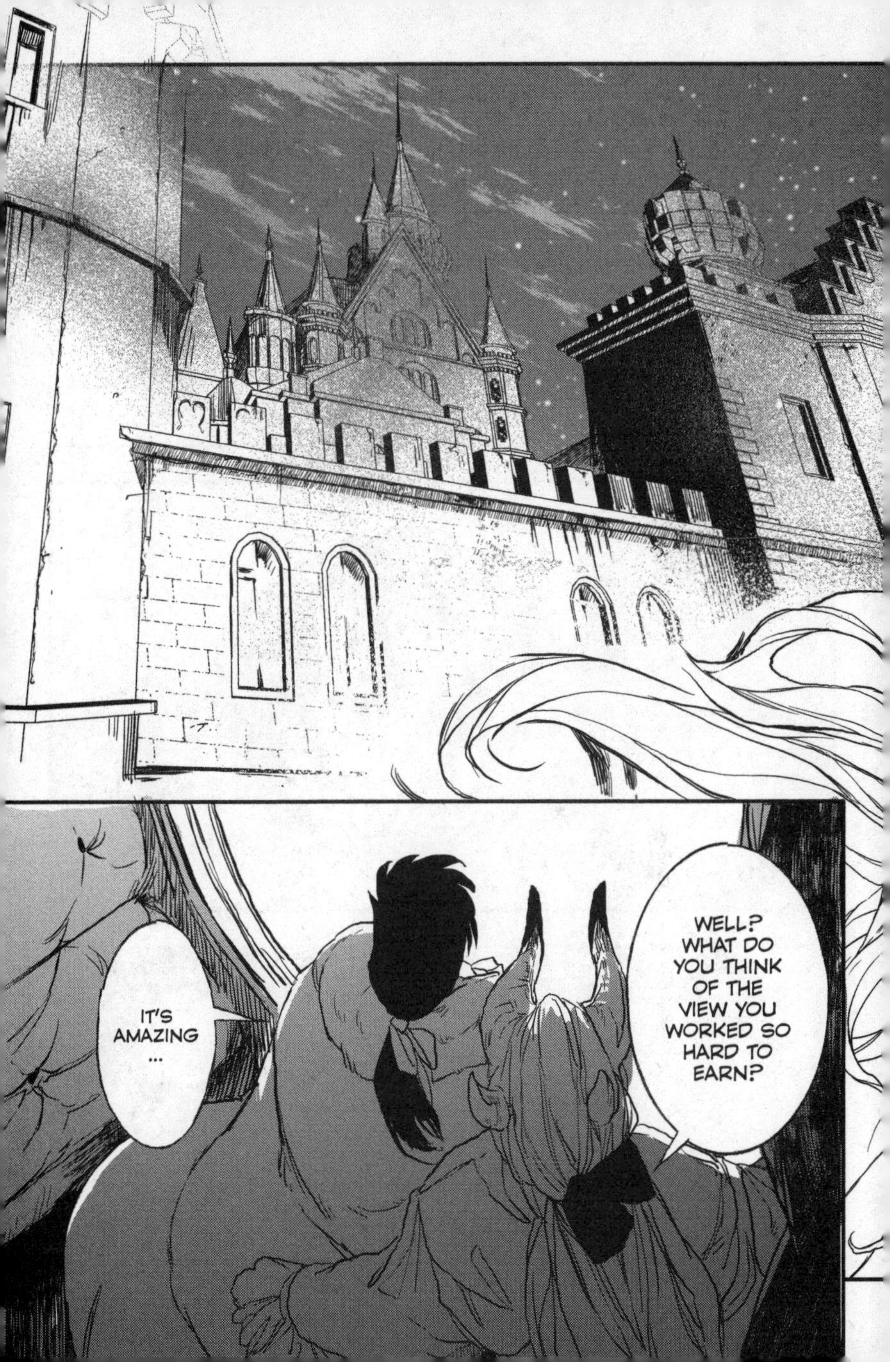
WELL? WHAT DO YOU THINK OF THE VIEW YOU WORKED SO HARD TO EARN?
IT'S AMAZING ...

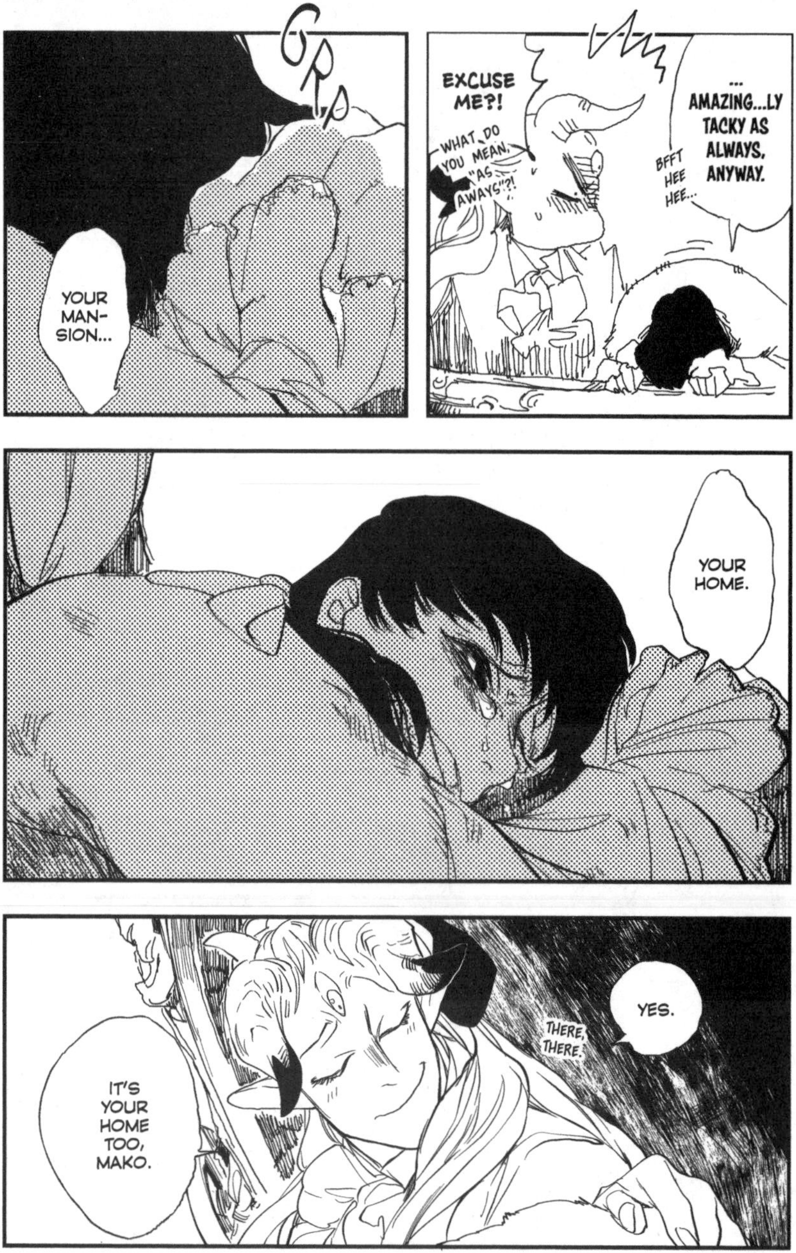

VAM
...AMAZING...LY TACKY AS ALWAYS, ANYWAY.
BFFT HEE HEE...
EXCUSE ME?!
WHAT DO YOU MEAN, "AS AWAYS"?!
GRP
YOUR MAN-SION...
YOUR HOME.
YES.
THERE, THERE.
IT'S YOUR HOME TOO, MAKO.

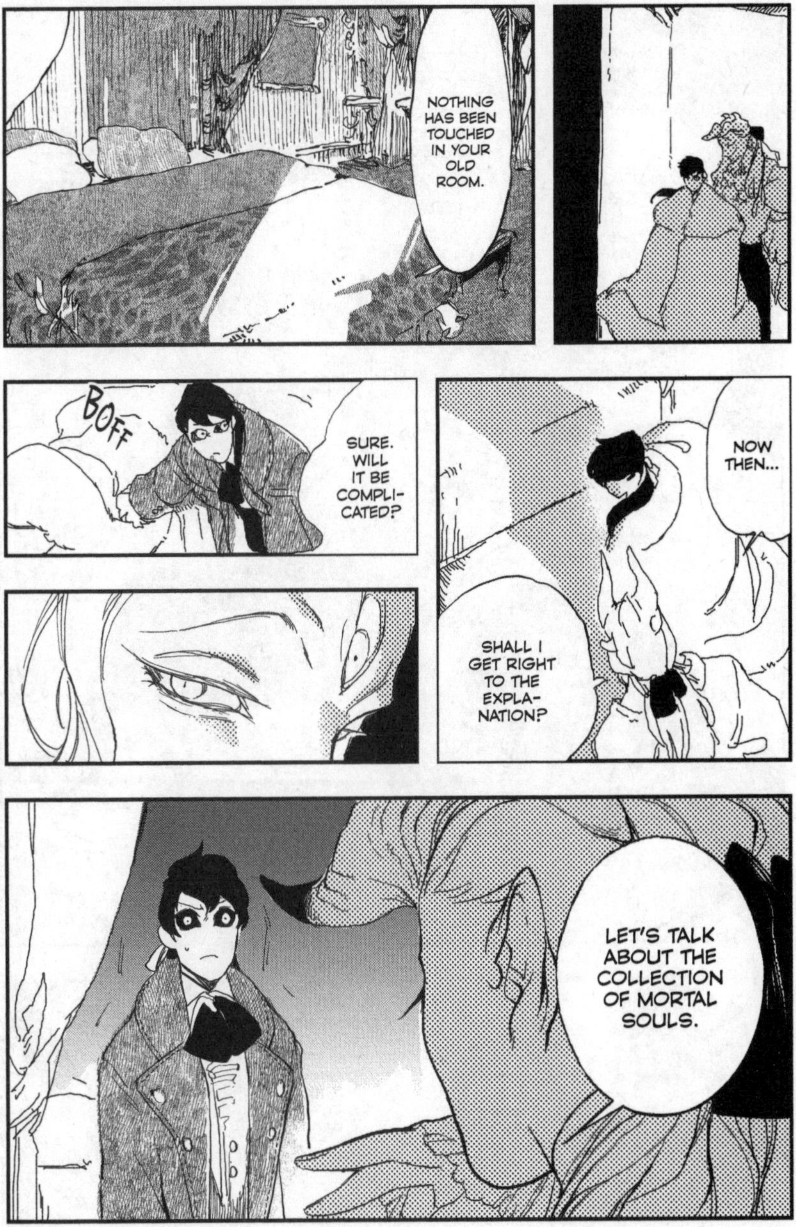
NOTHING HAS BEEN TOUCHED IN YOUR OLD ROOM.
NOW THEN...
SHALL I GET RIGHT TO THE EXPLA-NATION?
BOFF
SURE. WILL IT BE COMPLI-CATED?
LET'S TALK ABOUT THE COLLECTION OF MORTAL SOULS.

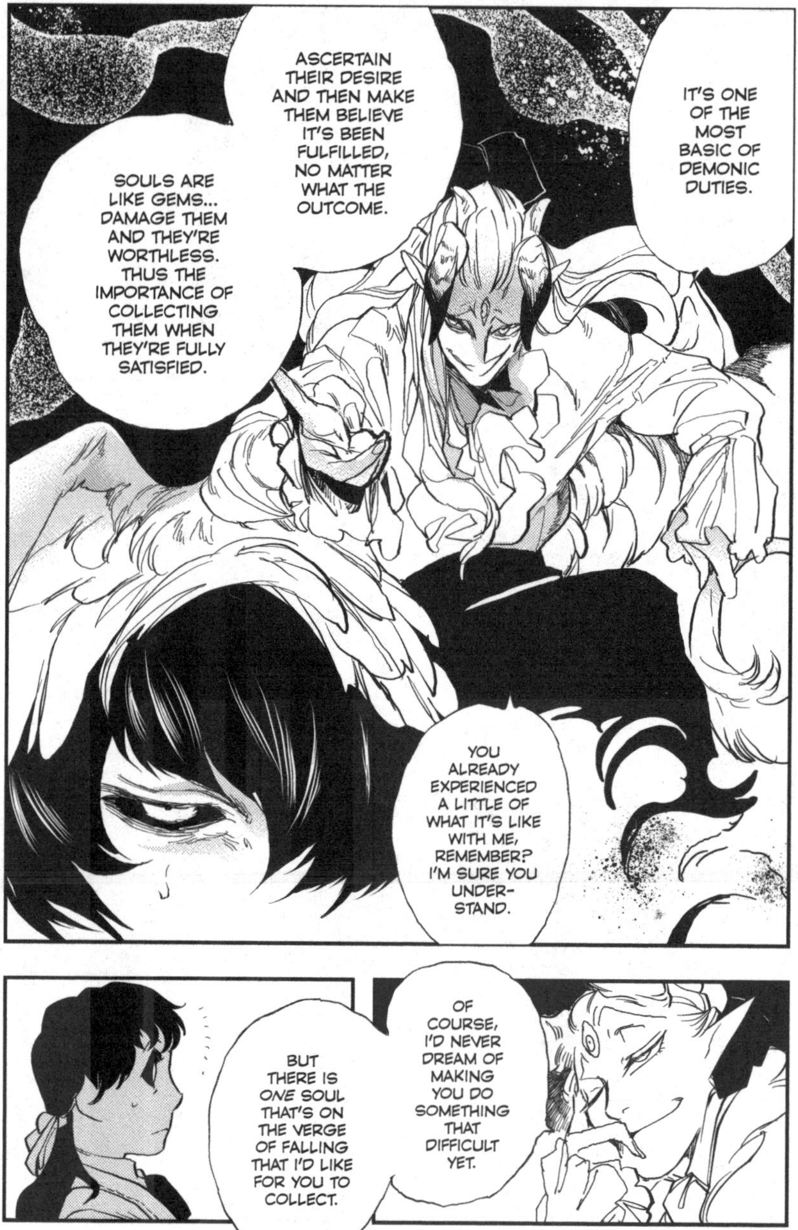
IT'S ONE OF THE MOST BASIC OF DEMONIC DUTIES.
ASCERTAIN THEIR DESIRE AND THEN MAKE THEM BELIEVE IT'S BEEN FULFILLED, NO MATTER WHAT THE OUTCOME.
SOULS ARE LIKE GEMS... DAMAGE THEM AND THEY'RE WORTHLESS. THUS THE IMPORTANCE OF COLLECTING THEM WHEN THEY'RE FULLY SATISFIED.
YOU ALREADY EXPERIENCED A LITTLE OF WHAT IT'S LIKE WITH ME, REMEMBER? I'M SURE YOU UNDER-STAND.
OF COURSE, I'D NEVER DREAM OF MAKING YOU DO SOMETHING THAT DIFFICULT YET.
BUT THERE IS *ONE* SOUL THAT'S ON THE VERGE OF FALLING THAT I'D LIKE FOR YOU TO COLLECT.

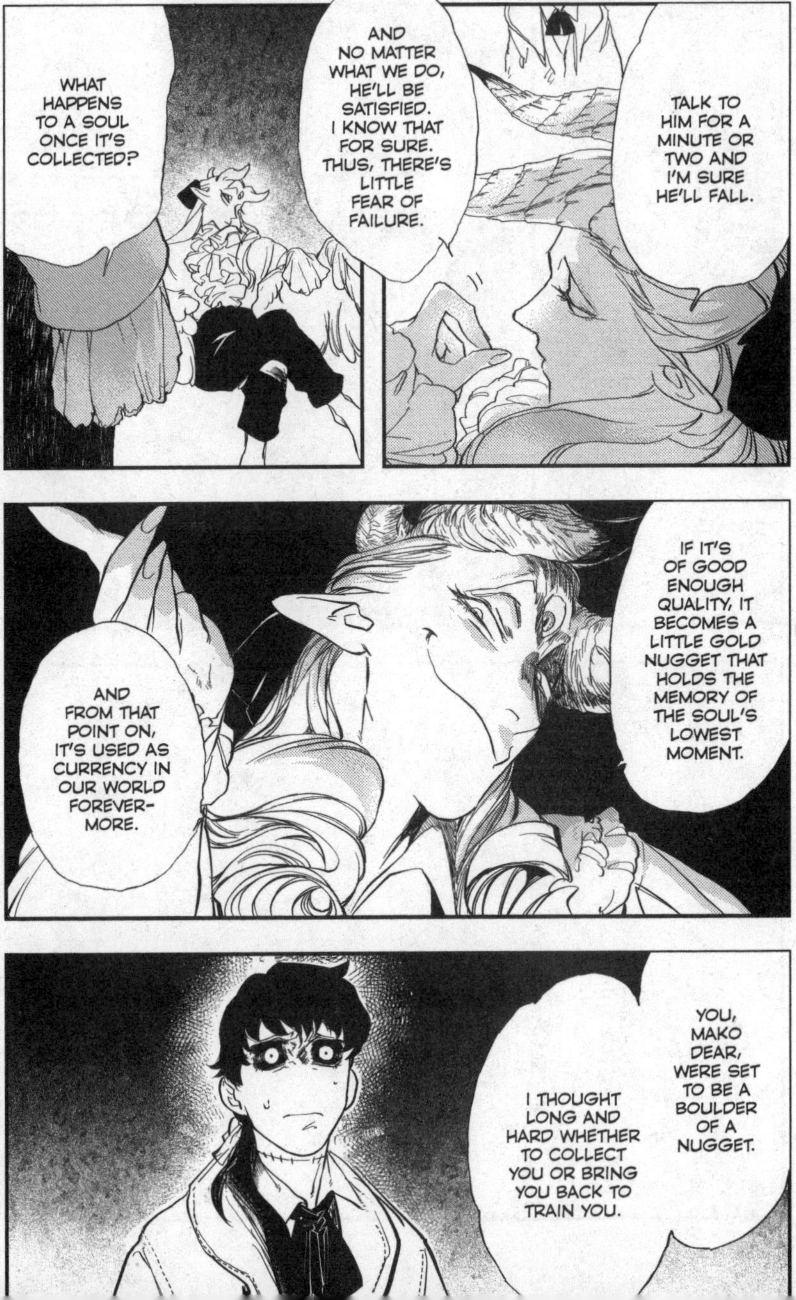
TALK TO HIM FOR A MINUTE OR TWO AND I'M SURE HE'LL FALL.
AND NO MATTER WHAT WE DO, HE'LL BE SATISFIED. I KNOW THAT FOR SURE. THUS, THERE'S LITTLE FEAR OF FAILURE.
WHAT HAPPENS TO A SOUL ONCE IT'S COLLECTED?
IF IT'S OF GOOD ENOUGH QUALITY, IT BECOMES A LITTLE GOLD NUGGET THAT HOLDS THE MEMORY OF THE SOUL'S LOWEST MOMENT.
AND FROM THAT POINT ON, IT'S USED AS CURRENCY IN OUR WORLD FOREVER-MORE.
YOU, MAKO DEAR, WERE SET TO BE A BOULDER OF A NUGGET.
I THOUGHT LONG AND HARD WHETHER TO COLLECT YOU OR BRING YOU BACK TO TRAIN YOU.

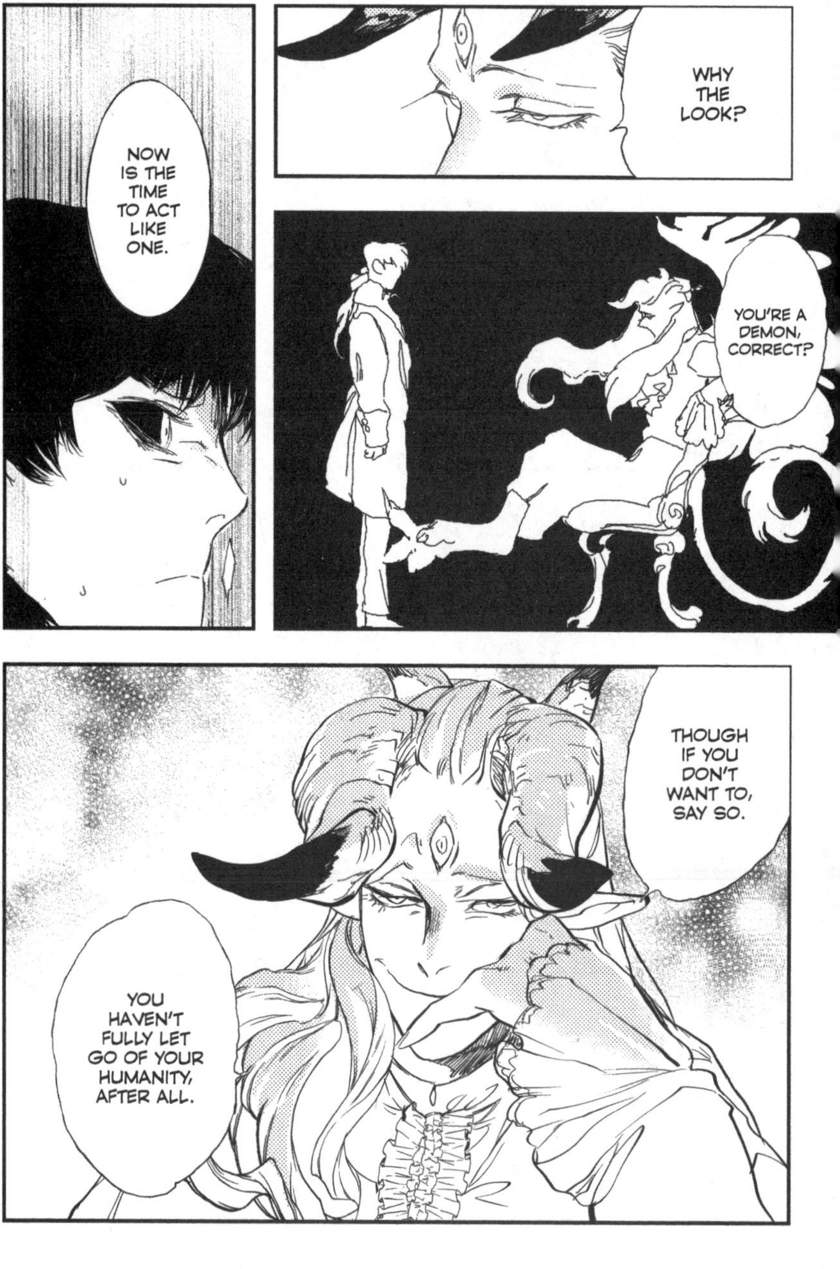
WHY THE LOOK?
YOU'RE A DEMON, CORRECT?
NOW IS THE TIME TO ACT LIKE ONE.
THOUGH IF YOU DON'T WANT TO, SAY SO.
YOU HAVEN'T FULLY LET GO OF YOUR HUMANITY, AFTER ALL.

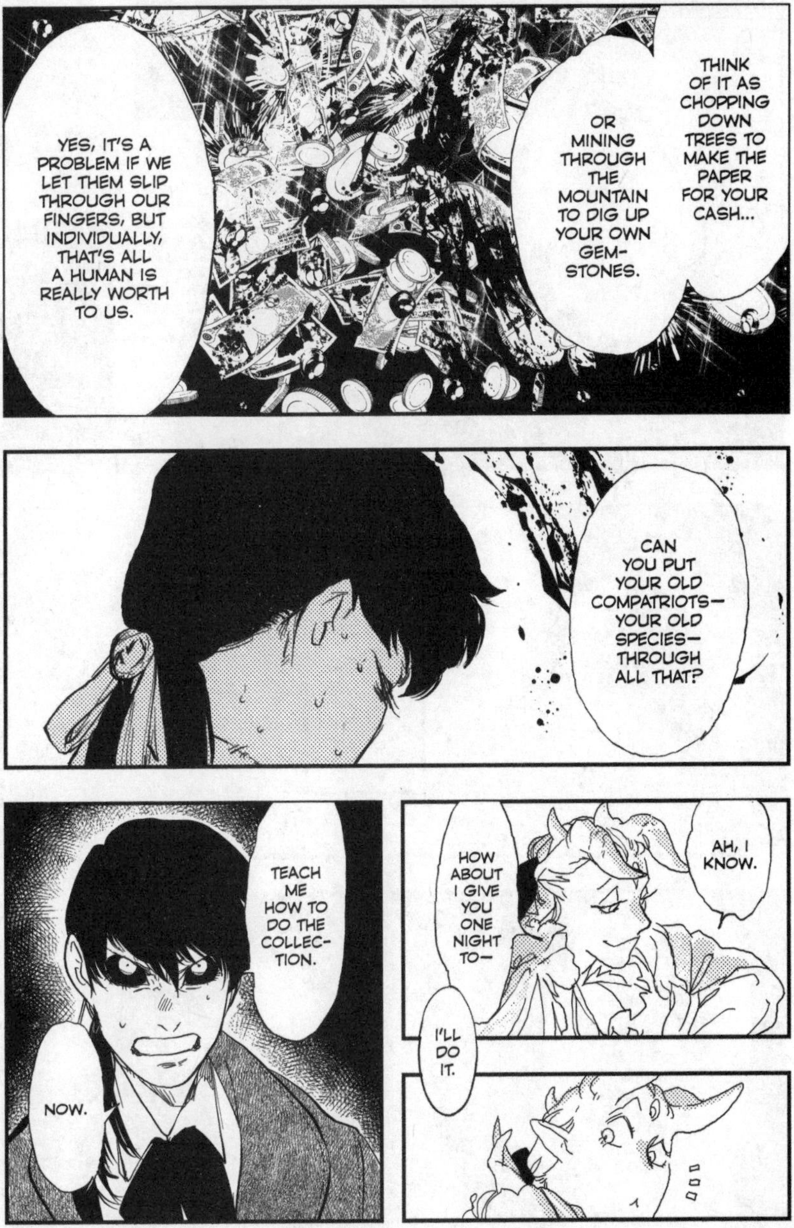
THINK OF IT AS CHOPPING DOWN TREES TO MAKE THE PAPER FOR YOUR CASH...
OR MINING THROUGH THE MOUNTAIN TO DIG UP YOUR OWN GEM-STONES.
YES, IT'S A PROBLEM IF WE LET THEM SLIP THROUGH OUR FINGERS, BUT INDIVIDUALLY, THAT'S ALL A HUMAN IS REALLY WORTH TO US.
CAN YOU PUT YOUR OLD COMPATRIOTS— YOUR OLD SPECIES— THROUGH ALL THAT?
AH, I KNOW.
HOW ABOUT I GIVE YOU ONE NIGHT TO—
I'LL DO IT.
TEACH ME HOW TO DO THE COLLEC-TION.
NOW.

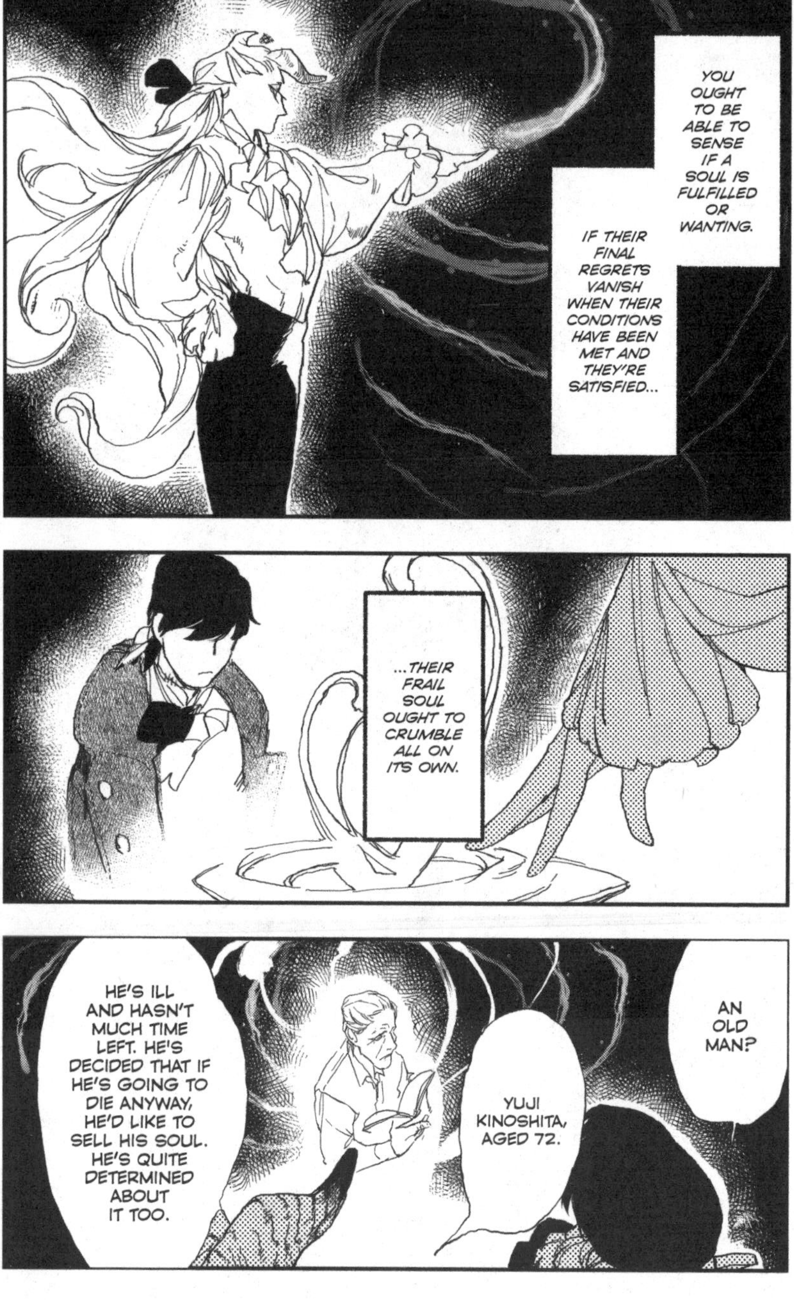
YOU OUGHT TO BE ABLE TO SENSE IF A SOUL IS FULFILLED OR WANTING.
IF THEIR FINAL REGRETS VANISH WHEN THEIR CONDITIONS HAVE BEEN MET AND THEY'RE SATISFIED...
...THEIR FRAIL SOUL OUGHT TO CRUMBLE ALL ON ITS OWN.
AN OLD MAN?
YUJI KINOSHITA, AGED 72.
HE'S ILL AND HASN'T MUCH TIME LEFT. HE'S DECIDED THAT IF HE'S GOING TO DIE ANYWAY, HE'D LIKE TO SELL HIS SOUL. HE'S QUITE DETERMINED ABOUT IT TOO.

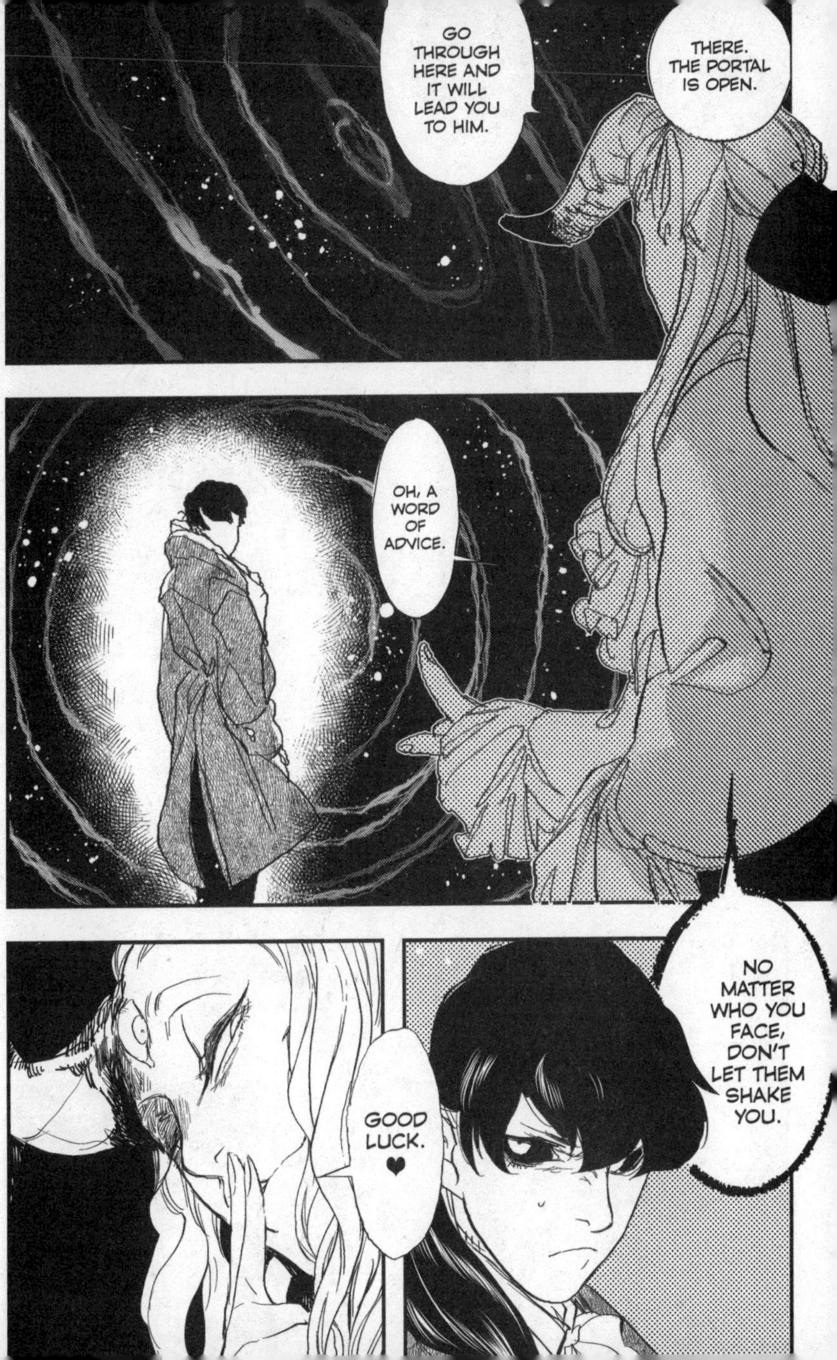
THERE. THE PORTAL IS OPEN.
GO THROUGH HERE AND IT WILL LEAD YOU TO HIM.
OH, A WORD OF ADVICE.
NO MATTER WHO YOU FACE, DON'T LET THEM SHAKE YOU.
GOOD LUCK. ♥

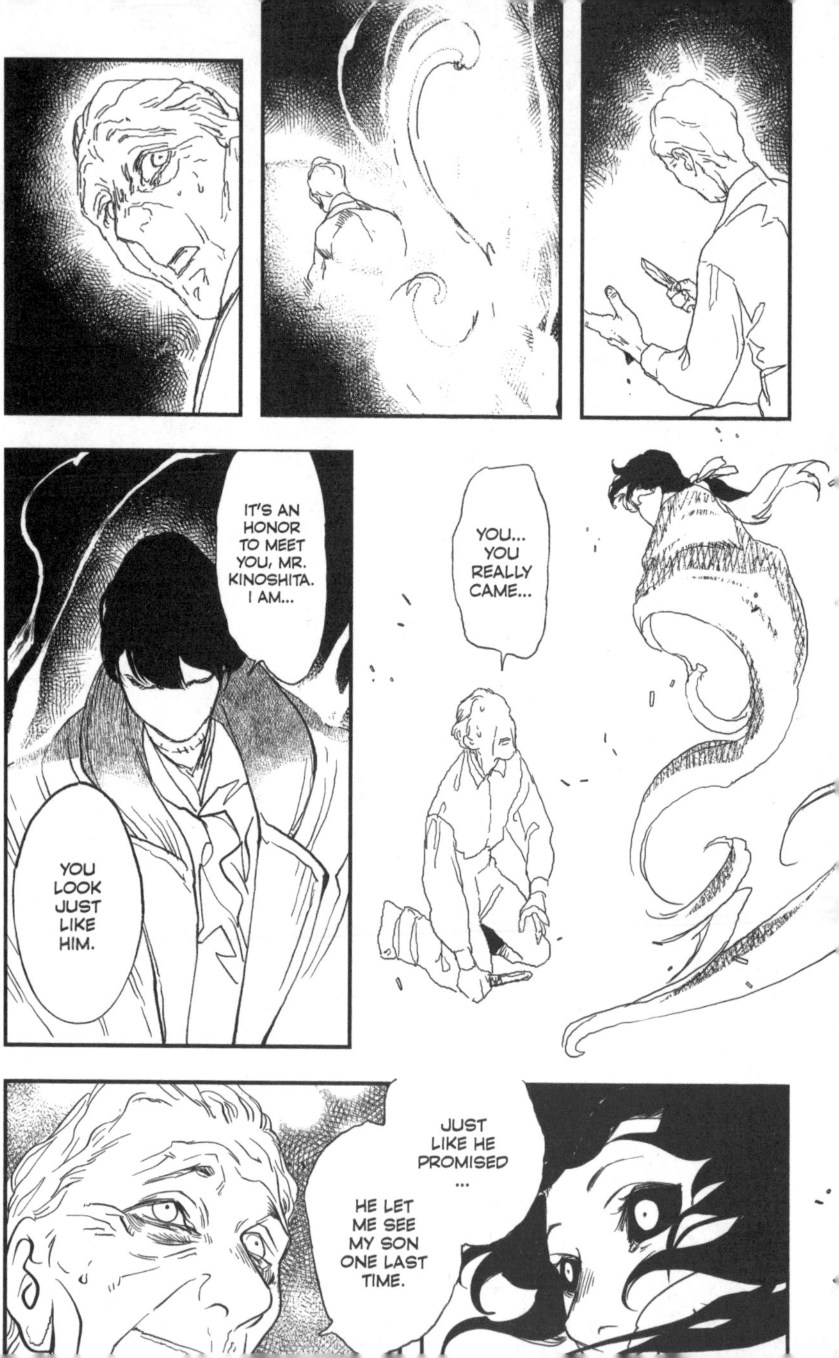
YOU... YOU REALLY CAME...
IT'S AN HONOR TO MEET YOU, MR. KINOSHITA. I AM...
YOU LOOK JUST LIKE HIM.
JUST LIKE HE PROMISED...
HE LET ME SEE MY SON ONE LAST TIME.

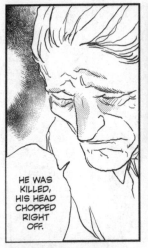

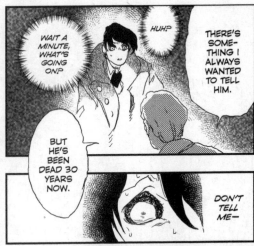

THERE'S SOME-THING I ALWAYS WANTED TO TELL HIM.
HUH?
WAIT A MINUTE, WHAT'S GOING ON?
BUT HE'S BEEN DEAD 30 YEARS NOW.
DON'T TELL ME—
HE WAS KILLED, HIS HEAD CHOPPED RIGHT OFF.
THIRTY YEARS?!
HIS CORPSE WAS FOUND SURROUNDED BY BOOKS ON CULTS AS WELL AS SPLATTERS OF HIS OWN SEMEN...
...AND THE BLOOD OF SOME OTHER MAN.
THE POLICE SAID IT WAS PROBABLY SOME DEVIANT SEX ACT BETWEEN TWO HOMOSEXUAL CULT FANATICS!
WHATEVER IT WAS, DID YOU HAVE TO DIE IN OUR HOME?!
COULDN'T YOU HAVE GONE SOME-WHERE ELSE TO GET YOUR HEAD LOPPED OFF?!

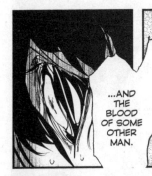

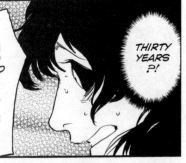

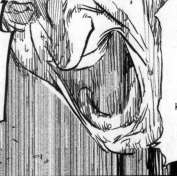

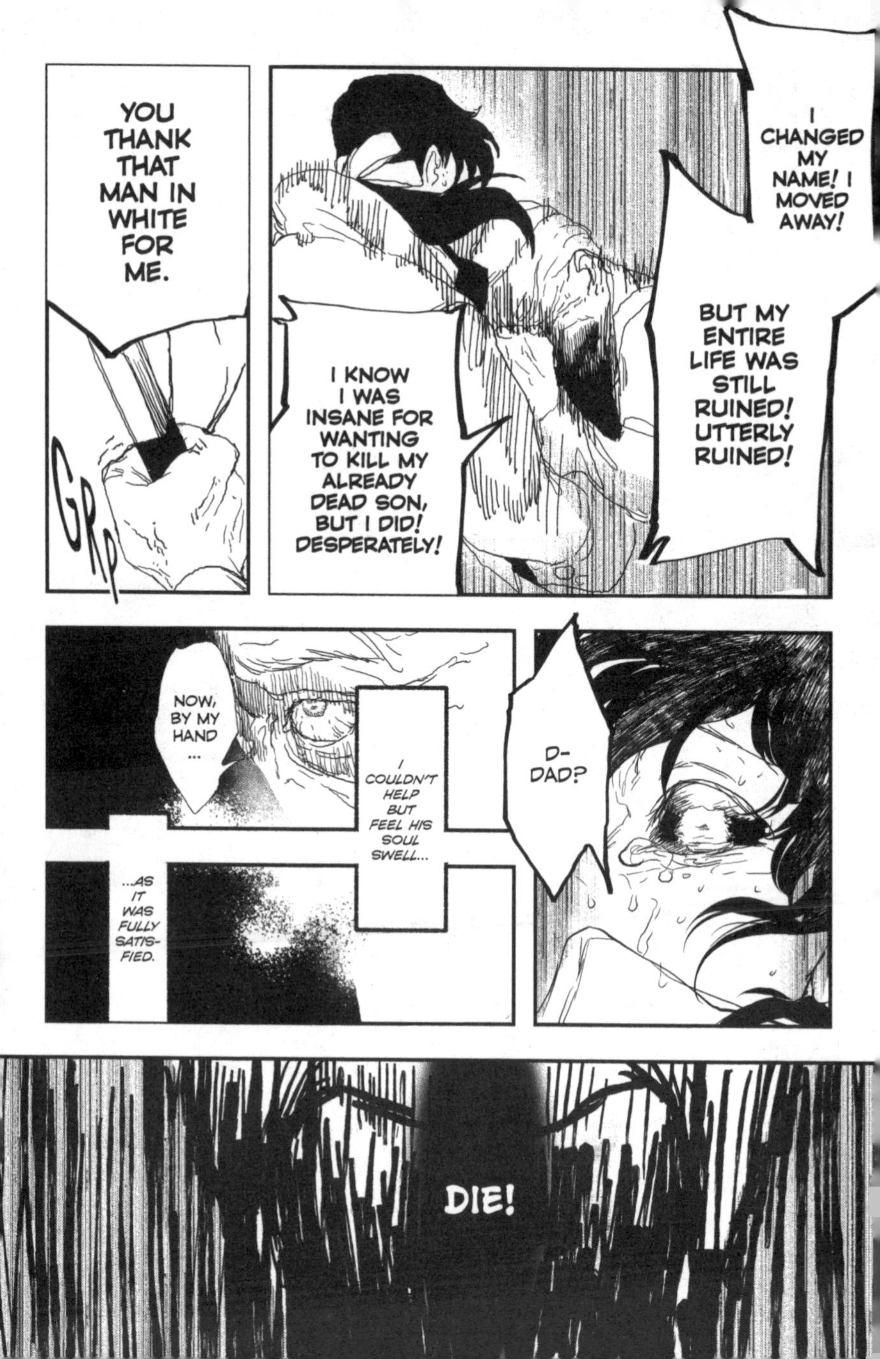
I CHANGED MY NAME! I MOVED AWAY!
BUT MY ENTIRE LIFE WAS STILL RUINED! UTTERLY RUINED!
I KNOW I WAS INSANE FOR WANTING TO KILL MY ALREADY DEAD SON, BUT I DID! DESPERATELY!
YOU THANK THAT MAN IN WHITE FOR ME.
GRP
D-DAD?
NOW, BY MY HAND...
I COULDN'T HELP BUT FEEL HIS SOUL SWELL...
...AS IT WAS FULLY SATIS-FIED.
DIE!

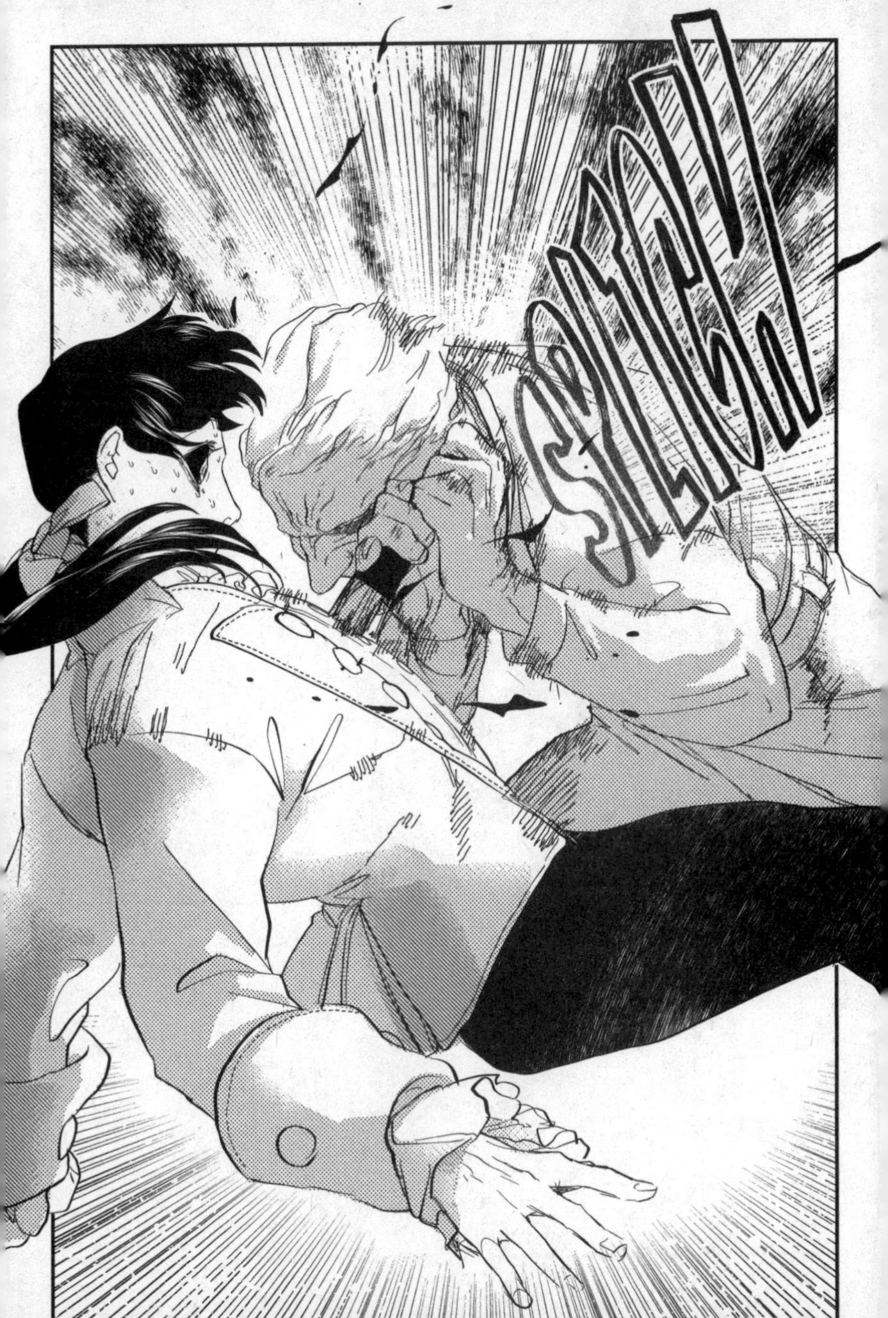

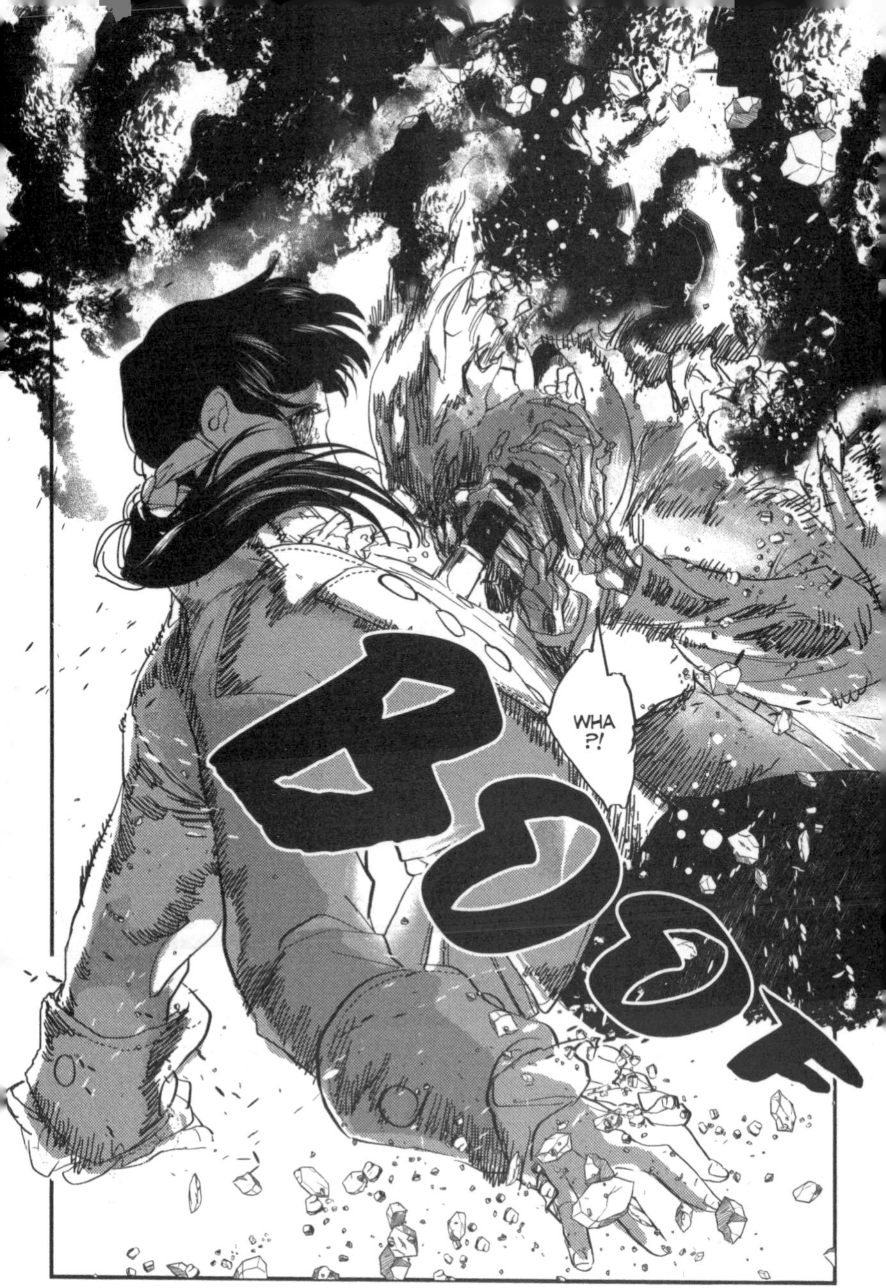
WHA?!

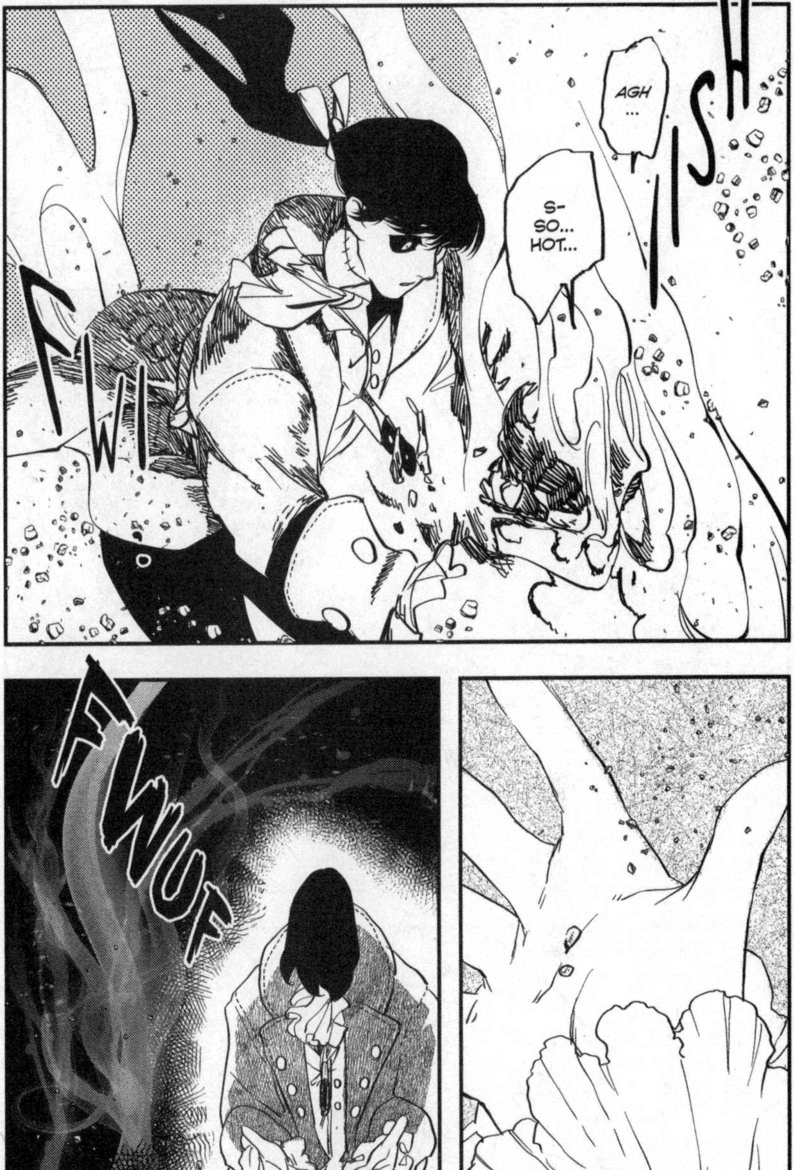

ISH
AGH ...
S- SO... HOT...
FWI
FWUF

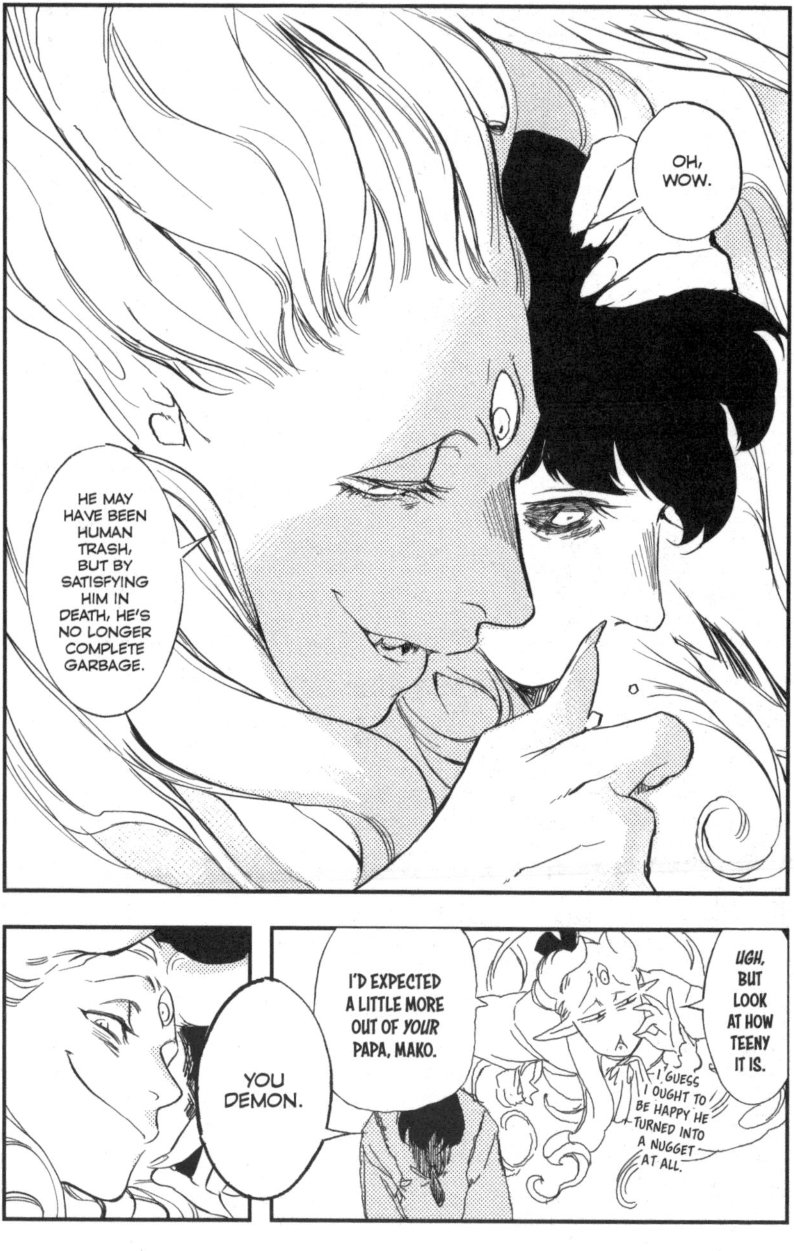
OH, WOW.
HE MAY HAVE BEEN HUMAN TRASH, BUT BY SATISFYING HIM IN DEATH, HE'S NO LONGER COMPLETE GARBAGE.
UGH, BUT LOOK AT HOW TEENY IT IS.
I'D EXPECTED A LITTLE MORE OUT OF *YOUR* PAPA, MAKO.
I GUESS I OUGHT TO BE HAPPY HE TURNED INTO A NUGGET AT ALL.
YOU DEMON.

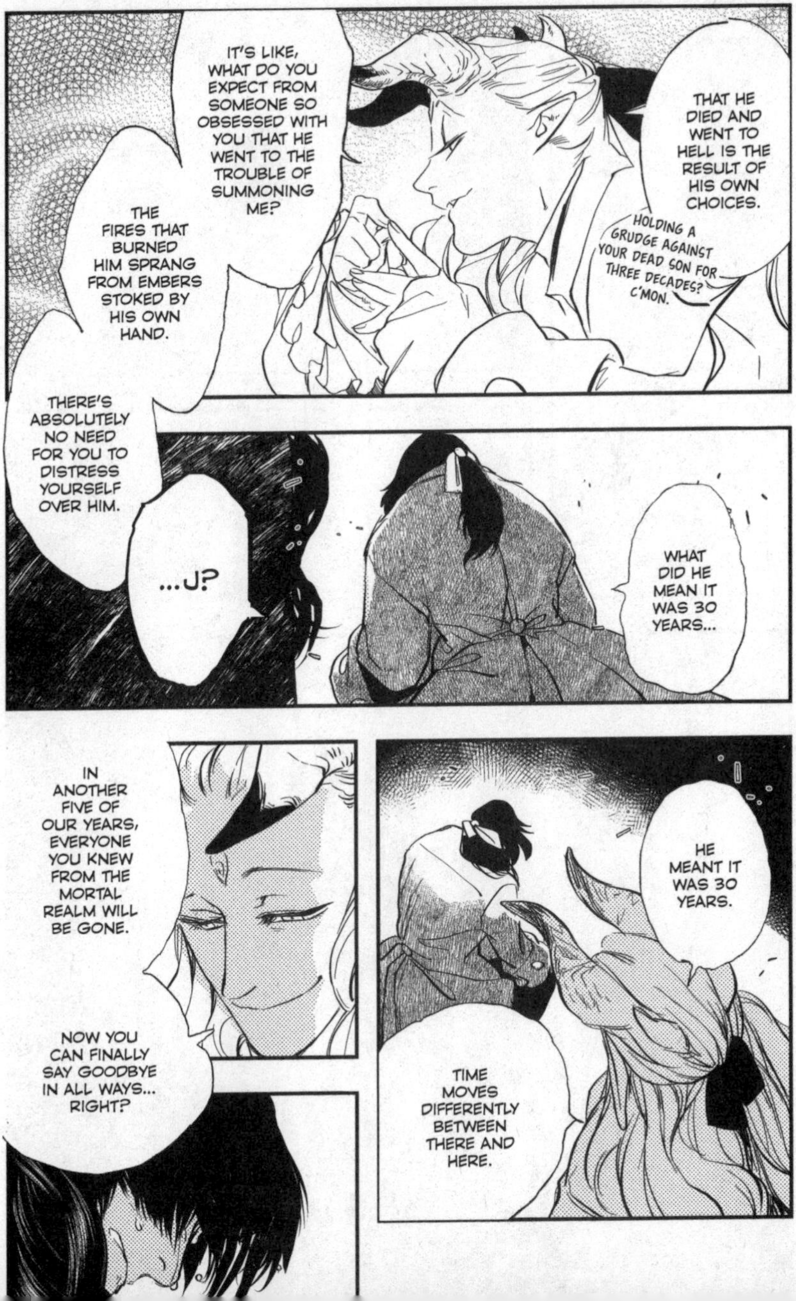
THAT HE DIED AND WENT TO HELL IS THE RESULT OF HIS OWN CHOICES.
HOLDING A GRUDGE AGAINST YOUR DEAD SON FOR THREE DECADES? C'MON.
IT'S LIKE, WHAT DO YOU EXPECT FROM SOMEONE SO OBSESSED WITH YOU THAT HE WENT TO THE TROUBLE OF SUMMONING ME?
THE FIRES THAT BURNED HIM SPRANG FROM EMBERS STOKED BY HIS OWN HAND.
THERE'S ABSOLUTELY NO NEED FOR YOU TO DISTRESS YOURSELF OVER HIM.
WHAT DID HE MEAN IT WAS 30 YEARS...
...J?
HE MEANT IT WAS 30 YEARS.
TIME MOVES DIFFERENTLY BETWEEN THERE AND HERE.
IN ANOTHER FIVE OF OUR YEARS, EVERYONE YOU KNEW FROM THE MORTAL REALM WILL BE GONE.
NOW YOU CAN FINALLY SAY GOODBYE IN ALL WAYS... RIGHT?

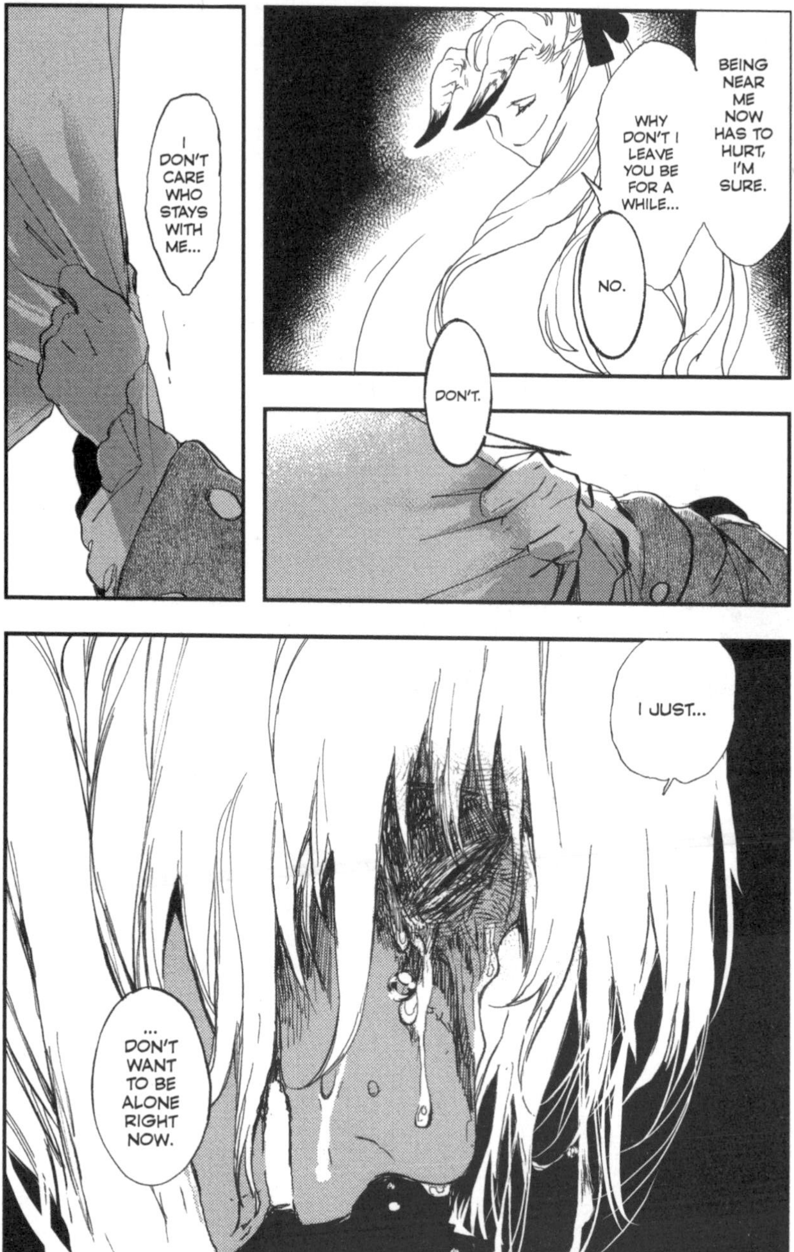
BEING NEAR ME NOW HAS TO HURT, I'M SURE.
WHY DON'T I LEAVE YOU BE FOR A WHILE...
NO.
DON'T.
I DON'T CARE WHO STAYS WITH ME...
I JUST...
...DON'T WANT TO BE ALONE RIGHT NOW.

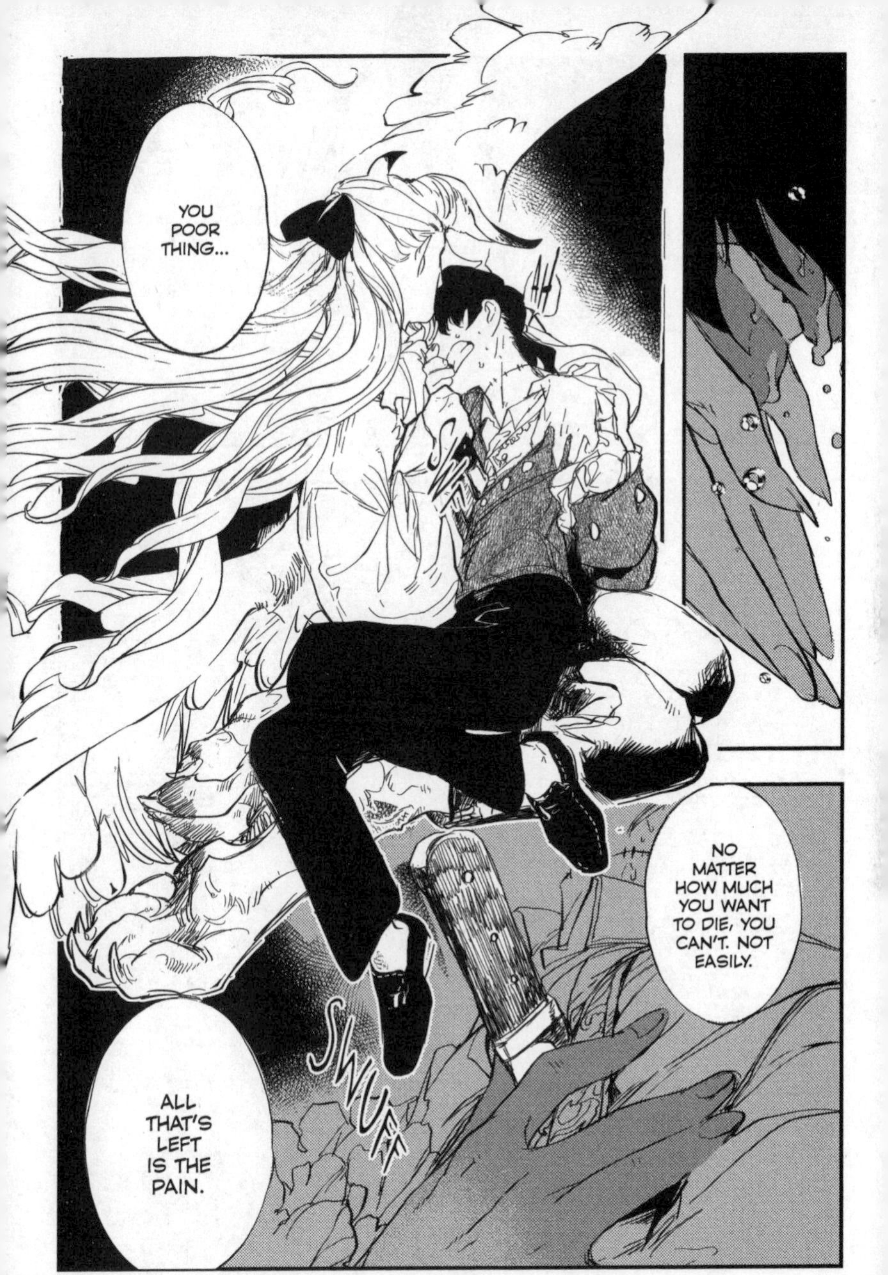
AH
YOU POOR THING...
NO MATTER HOW MUCH YOU WANT TO DIE, YOU CAN'T. NOT EASILY.
SWUFF
ALL THAT'S LEFT IS THE PAIN.

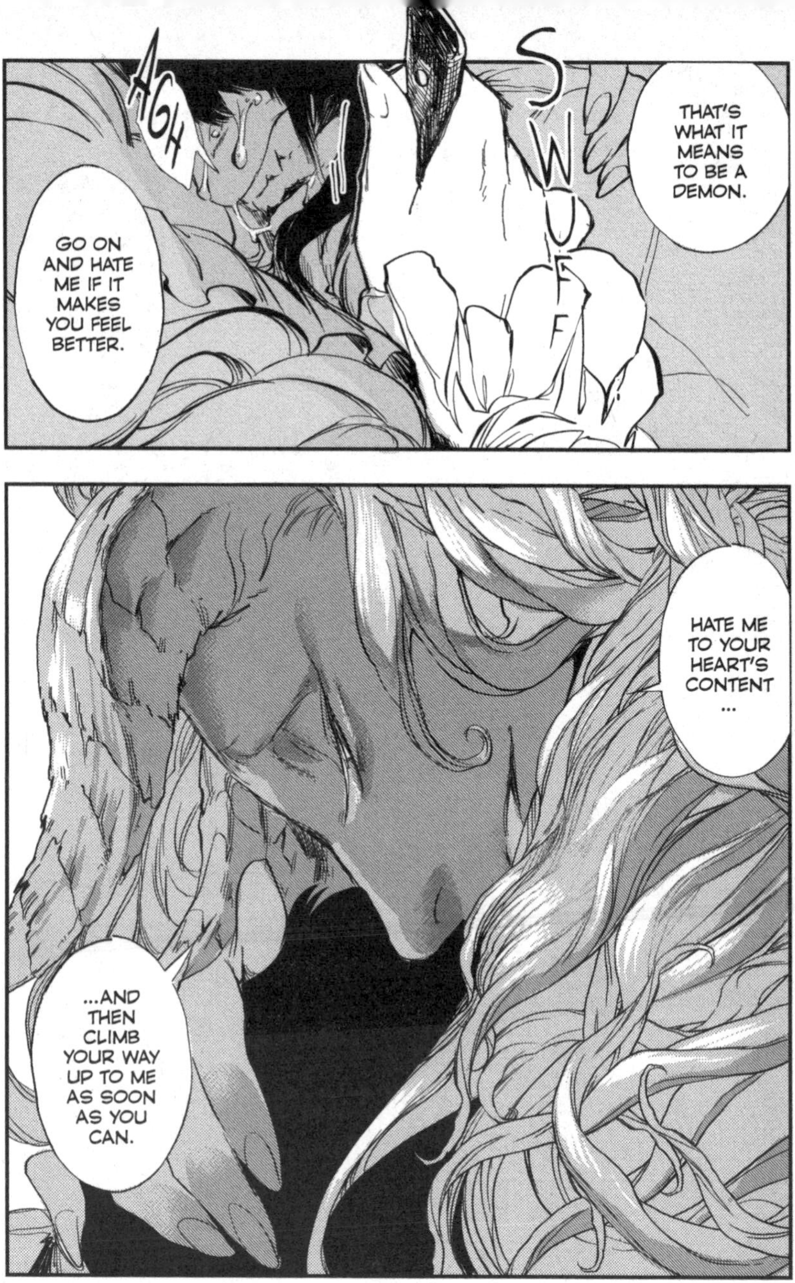
THAT'S WHAT IT MEANS TO BE A DEMON.
SWUFF
AGH
GO ON AND HATE ME IF IT MAKES YOU FEEL BETTER.
HATE ME TO YOUR HEART'S CONTENT ...
...AND THEN CLIMB YOUR WAY UP TO ME AS SOON AS YOU CAN.

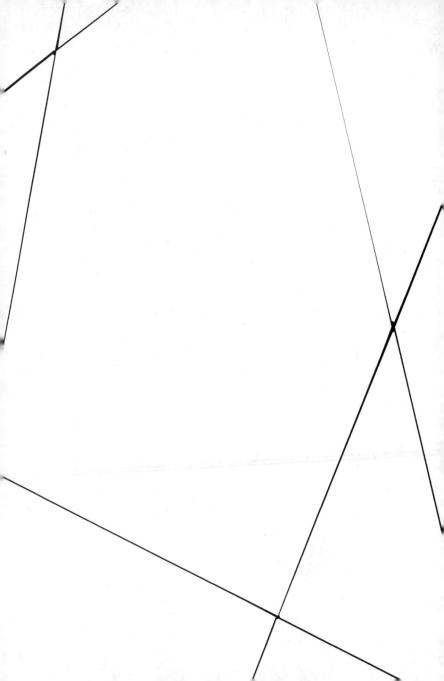

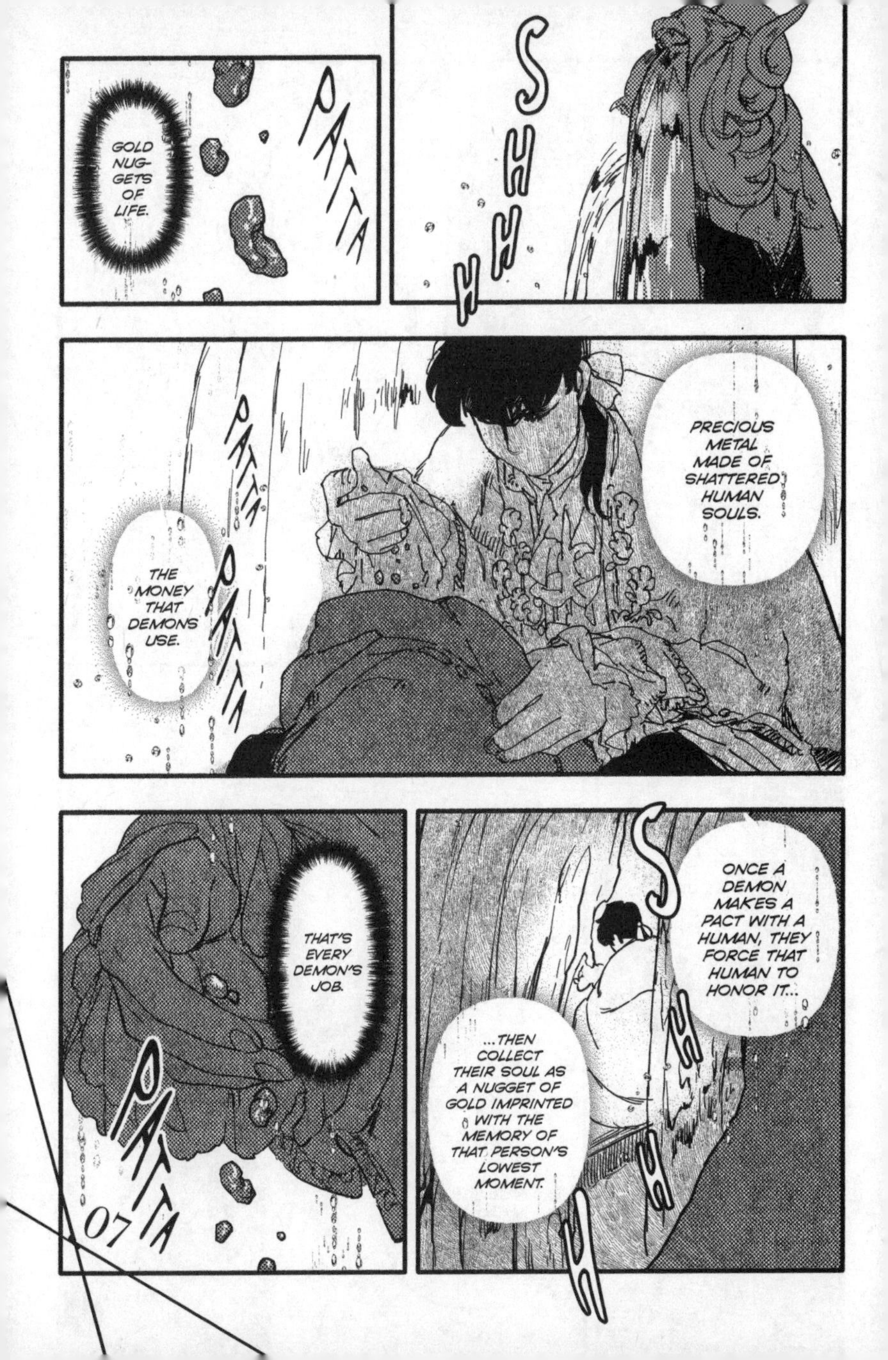
SHHHH
PATTA
GOLD NUGGETS OF LIFE.
PRECIOUS METAL MADE OF SHATTERED HUMAN SOULS.
PATTA
PATTA
THE MONEY THAT DEMONS USE.
SHHHH
ONCE A DEMON MAKES A PACT WITH A HUMAN, THEY FORCE THAT HUMAN TO HONOR IT...
...THEN COLLECT THEIR SOUL AS A NUGGET OF GOLD IMPRINTED WITH THE MEMORY OF THAT PERSON'S LOWEST MOMENT.
THAT'S EVERY DEMON'S JOB.
PATTA
07

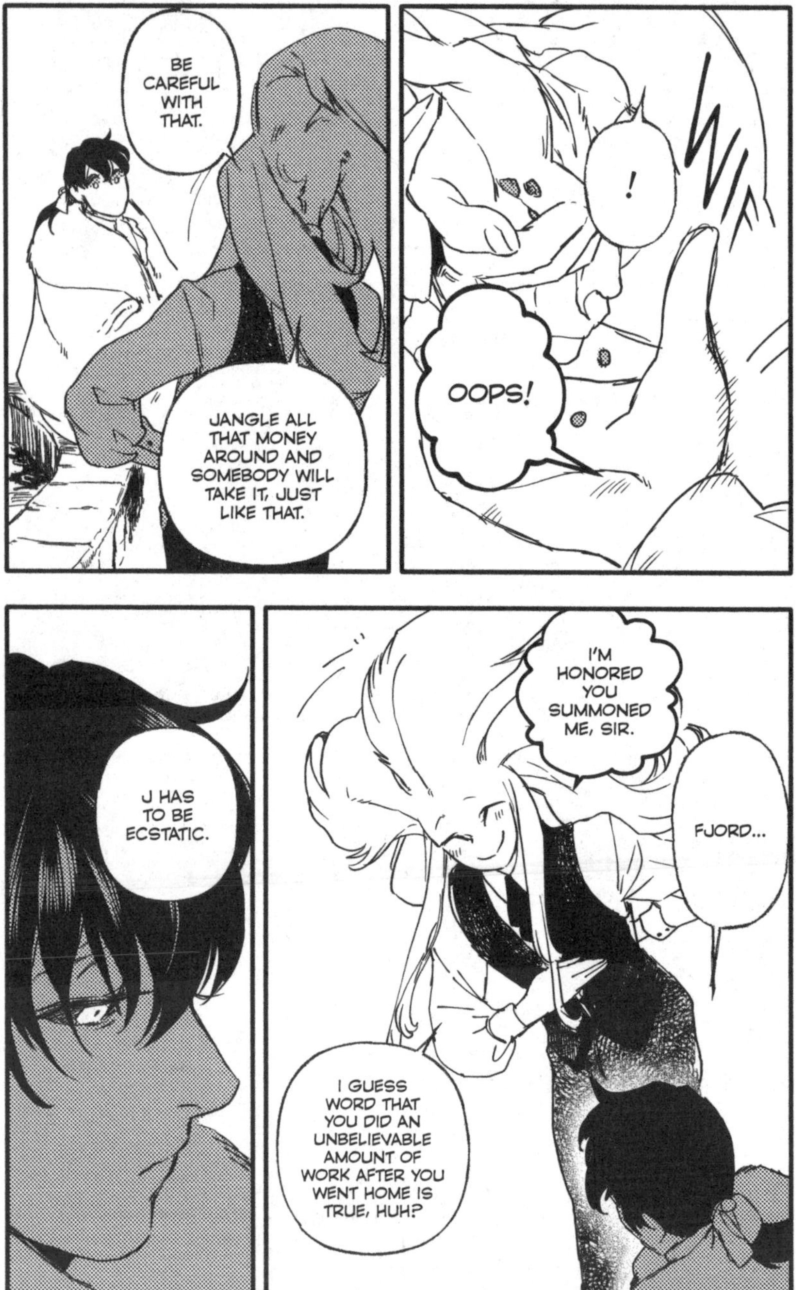
!
OOPS!
BE CAREFUL WITH THAT.
JANGLE ALL THAT MONEY AROUND AND SOMEBODY WILL TAKE IT, JUST LIKE THAT.
I'M HONORED YOU SUMMONED ME, SIR.
FJORD...
I GUESS WORD THAT YOU DID AN UNBELIEVABLE AMOUNT OF WORK AFTER YOU WENT HOME IS TRUE, HUH?
J HAS TO BE ECSTATIC.

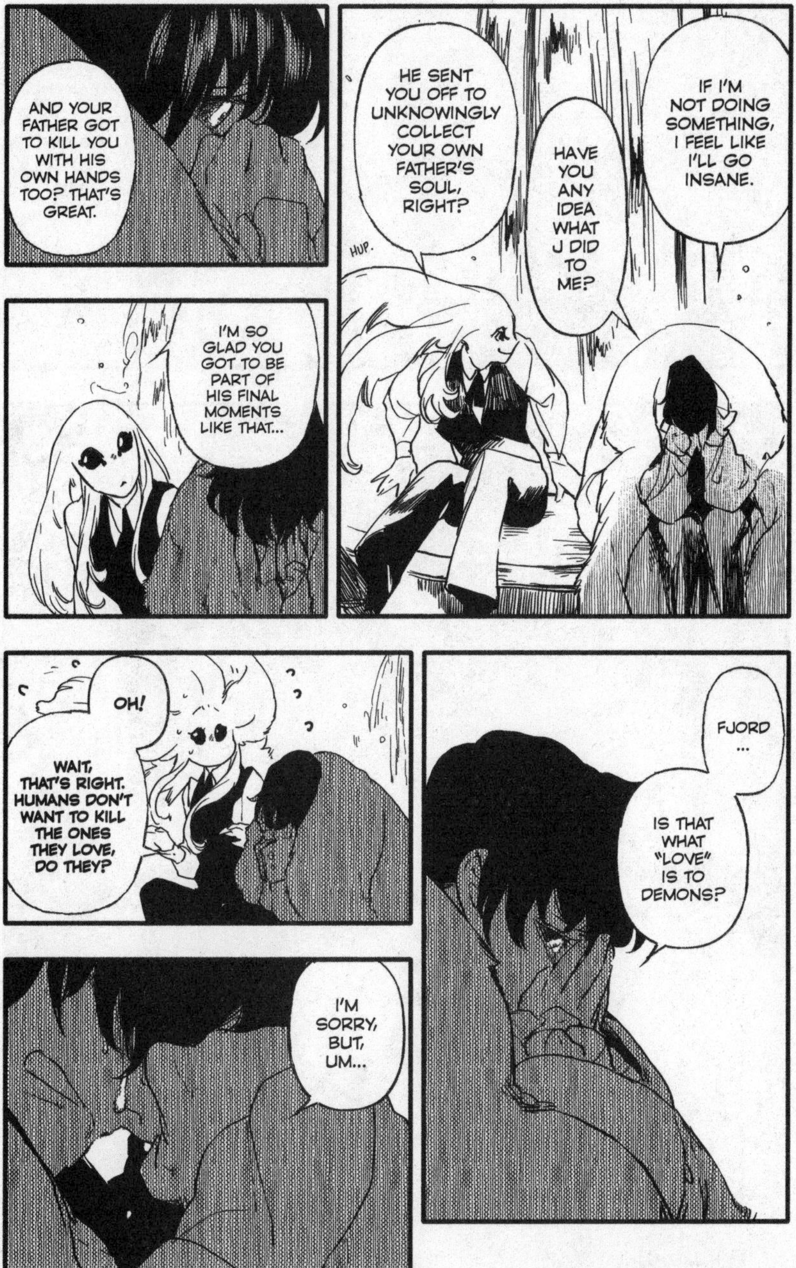
IF I'M NOT DOING SOMETHING, I FEEL LIKE I'LL GO INSANE.
HAVE YOU ANY IDEA WHAT J DID TO ME?
HE SENT YOU OFF TO UNKNOWINGLY COLLECT YOUR OWN FATHER'S SOUL, RIGHT?
HUP.
AND YOUR FATHER GOT TO KILL YOU WITH HIS OWN HANDS TOO? THAT'S GREAT.
I'M SO GLAD YOU GOT TO BE PART OF HIS FINAL MOMENTS LIKE THAT...
FJORD ...
IS THAT WHAT "LOVE" IS TO DEMONS?
OH!
WAIT, THAT'S RIGHT. HUMANS DON'T WANT TO KILL THE ONES THEY LOVE, DO THEY?
I'M SORRY, BUT, UM...

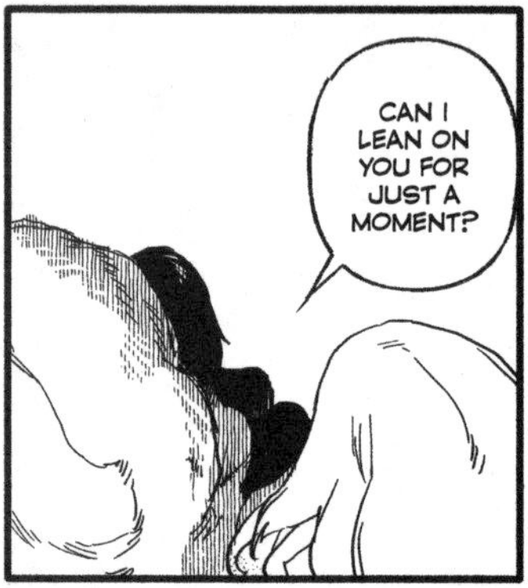
CAN I LEAN ON YOU FOR JUST A MOMENT?

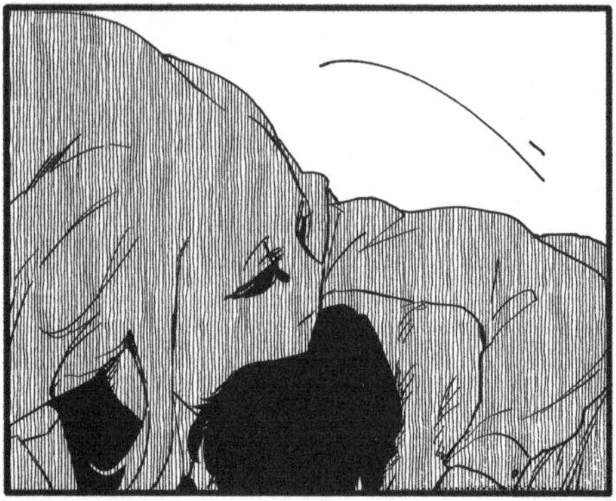

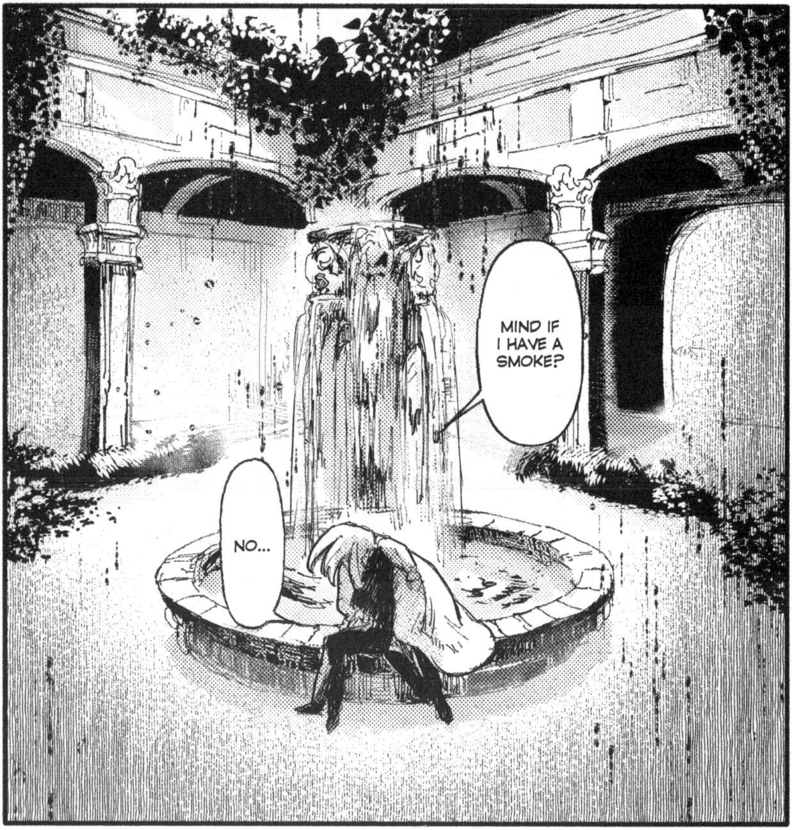
MIND IF I HAVE A SMOKE?
NO...

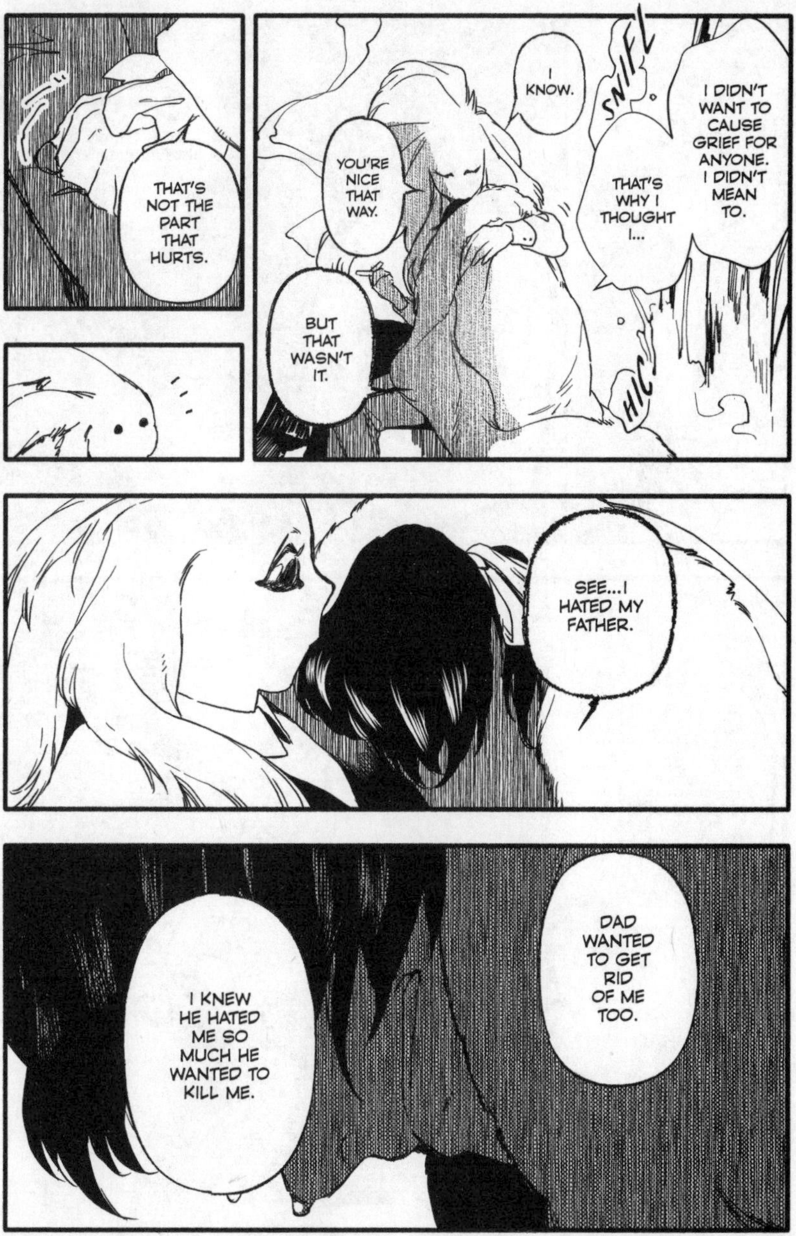
I DIDN'T WANT TO CAUSE GRIEF FOR ANYONE. I DIDN'T MEAN TO.
SNIFL
THAT'S WHY I THOUGHT I...
I KNOW.
HIC
YOU'RE NICE THAT WAY.
BUT THAT WASN'T IT.
THAT'S NOT THE PART THAT HURTS.
SEE...I HATED MY FATHER.
DAD WANTED TO GET RID OF ME TOO.
I KNEW HE HATED ME SO MUCH HE WANTED TO KILL ME.

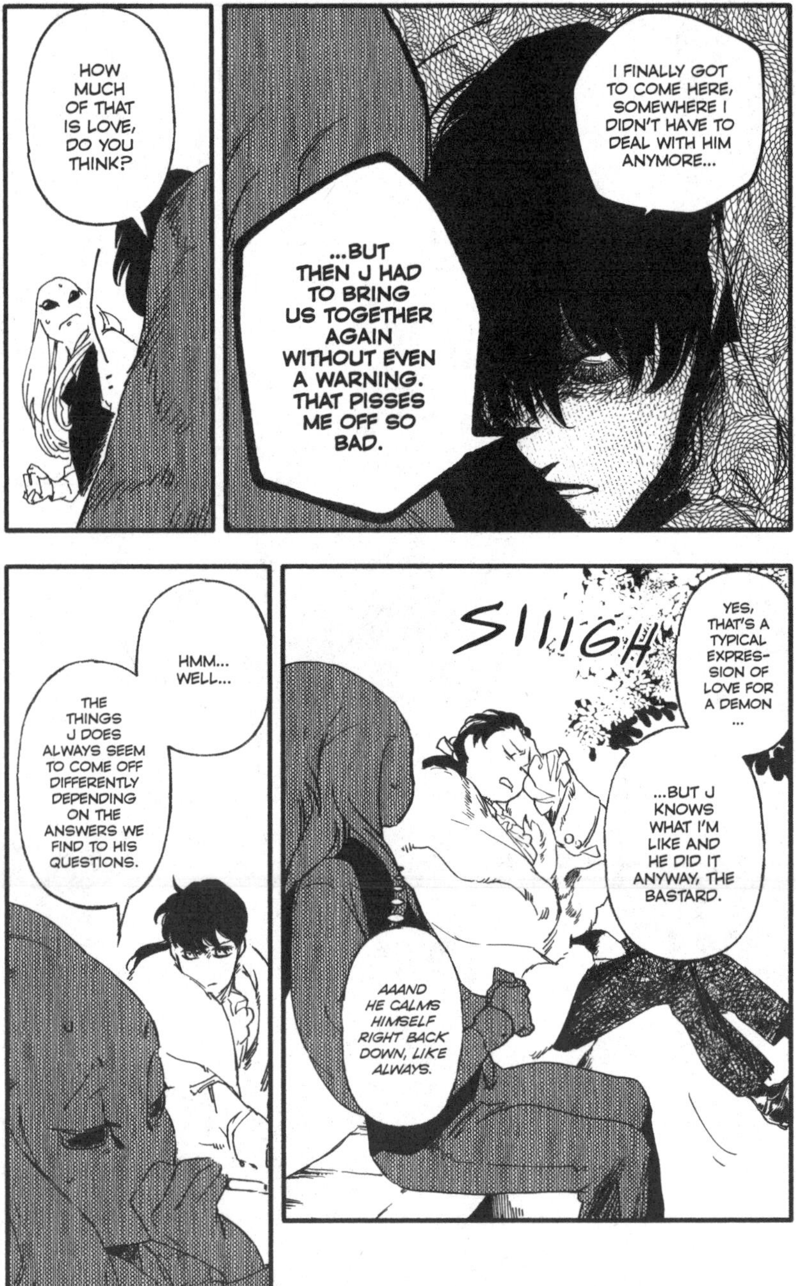
I FINALLY GOT TO COME HERE, SOMEWHERE I DIDN'T HAVE TO DEAL WITH HIM ANYMORE...
...BUT THEN J HAD TO BRING US TOGETHER AGAIN WITHOUT EVEN A WARNING. THAT PISSES ME OFF SO BAD.
HOW MUCH OF THAT IS LOVE, DO YOU THINK?
SIIIGH
YES, THAT'S A TYPICAL EXPRESSION OF LOVE FOR A DEMON...
...BUT J KNOWS WHAT I'M LIKE AND HE DID IT ANYWAY, THE BASTARD.
AAAND HE CALMS HIMSELF RIGHT BACK DOWN, LIKE ALWAYS.
HMM... WELL...
THE THINGS J DOES ALWAYS SEEM TO COME OFF DIFFERENTLY DEPENDING ON THE ANSWERS WE FIND TO HIS QUESTIONS.

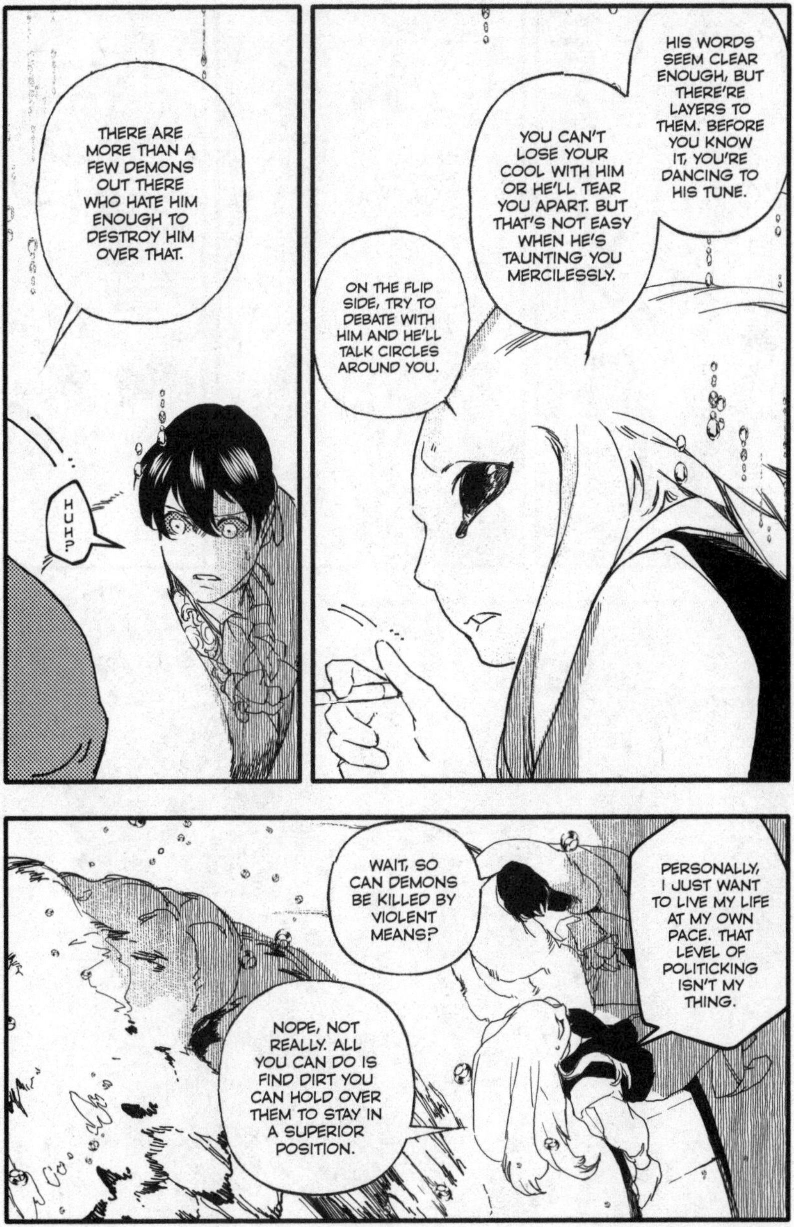
HIS WORDS SEEM CLEAR ENOUGH, BUT THERE'RE LAYERS TO THEM. BEFORE YOU KNOW IT, YOU'RE DANCING TO HIS TUNE.
YOU CAN'T LOSE YOUR COOL WITH HIM OR HE'LL TEAR YOU APART. BUT THAT'S NOT EASY WHEN HE'S TAUNTING YOU MERCILESSLY.
ON THE FLIP SIDE, TRY TO DEBATE WITH HIM AND HE'LL TALK CIRCLES AROUND YOU.
THERE ARE MORE THAN A FEW DEMONS OUT THERE WHO HATE HIM ENOUGH TO DESTROY HIM OVER THAT.
HUH?
PERSONALLY, I JUST WANT TO LIVE MY LIFE AT MY OWN PACE. THAT LEVEL OF POLITICKING ISN'T MY THING.
WAIT, SO CAN DEMONS BE KILLED BY VIOLENT MEANS?
NOPE, NOT REALLY. ALL YOU CAN DO IS FIND DIRT YOU CAN HOLD OVER THEM TO STAY IN A SUPERIOR POSITION.

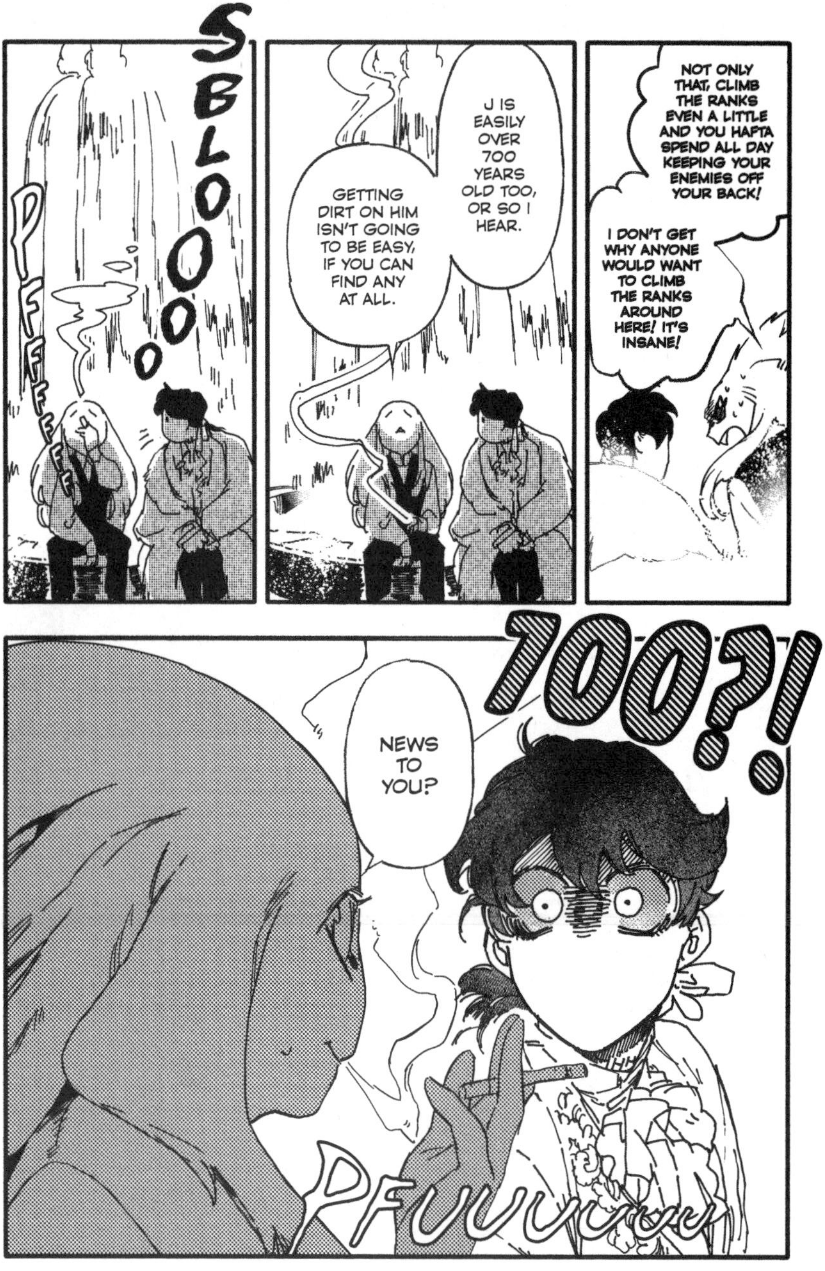
NOT ONLY THAT, CLIMB THE RANKS EVEN A LITTLE AND YOU HAFTA SPEND ALL DAY KEEPING YOUR ENEMIES OFF YOUR BACK!
I DON'T GET WHY ANYONE WOULD WANT TO CLIMB THE RANKS AROUND HERE! IT'S INSANE!
J IS EASILY OVER 700 YEARS OLD TOO, OR SO I HEAR.
GETTING DIRT ON HIM ISN'T GOING TO BE EASY, IF YOU CAN FIND ANY AT ALL.
SBLOOOOO
PFFFFFFF
700?!
NEWS TO YOU?
PFUUUUUU

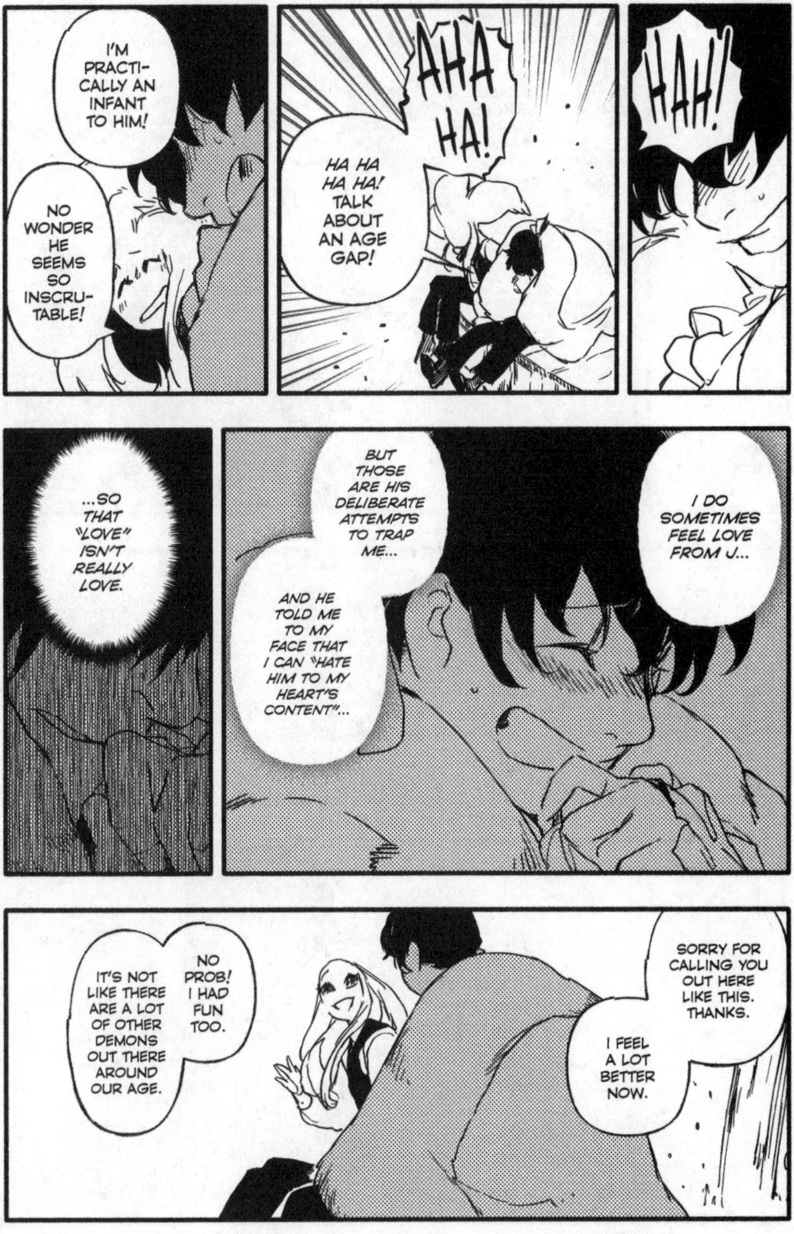
HAH!
AHA HA!
HA HA HA HA! TALK ABOUT AN AGE GAP!
I'M PRACTICALLY AN INFANT TO HIM!
NO WONDER HE SEEMS SO INSCRUTABLE!
I DO SOMETIMES FEEL LOVE FROM J...
BUT THOSE ARE HIS DELIBERATE ATTEMPTS TO TRAP ME...
AND HE TOLD ME TO MY FACE THAT I CAN "HATE HIM TO MY HEART'S CONTENT"...
...SO THAT "LOVE" ISN'T REALLY LOVE.
SORRY FOR CALLING YOU OUT HERE LIKE THIS. THANKS.
I FEEL A LOT BETTER NOW.
NO PROB! I HAD FUN TOO.
IT'S NOT LIKE THERE ARE A LOT OF OTHER DEMONS OUT THERE AROUND OUR AGE.

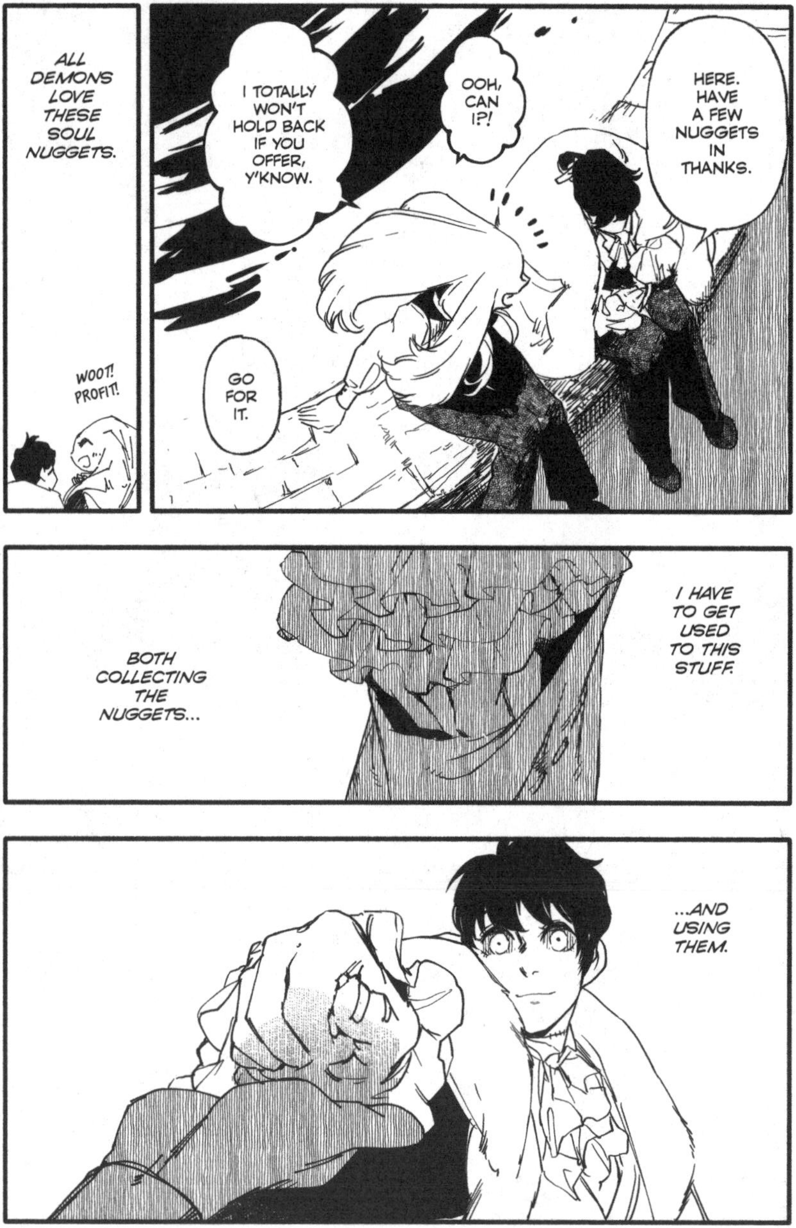
HERE. HAVE A FEW NUGGETS IN THANKS.
OOH, CAN I?!
I TOTALLY WON'T HOLD BACK IF YOU OFFER, Y'KNOW.
GO FOR IT.
ALL DEMONS LOVE THESE SOUL NUGGETS.
WOOT! PROFIT!
I HAVE TO GET USED TO THIS STUFF.
BOTH COLLECTING THE NUGGETS...
...AND USING THEM.

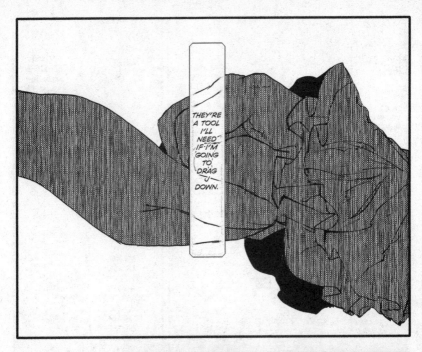

THEY'RE A TOOL I'LL NEED IF I'M GOING TO DRAG J DOWN.

WELCOME HOME.

YOU'RE LATER THAN I EXPECTED.

NOK NOK

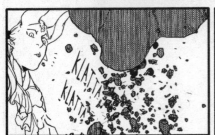

KLATTA KLATTA

SWF

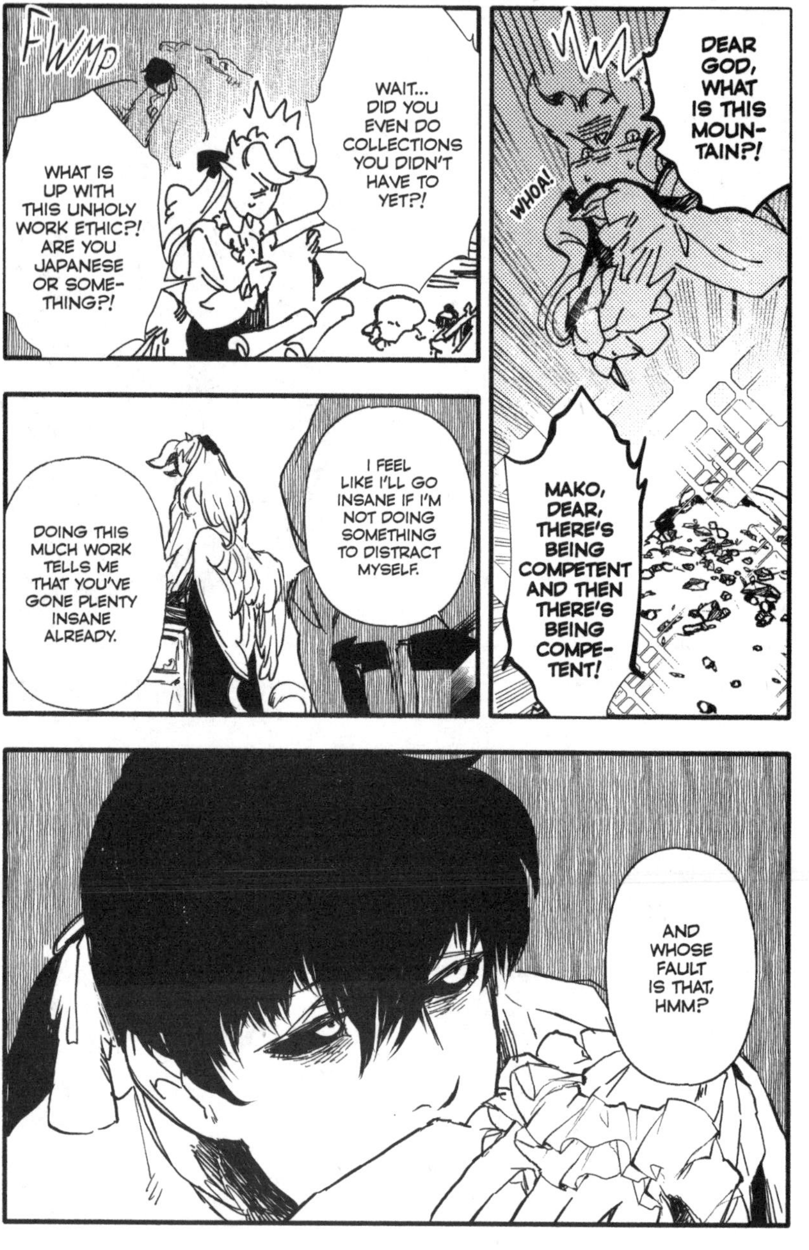
DEAR GOD, WHAT IS THIS MOUN-TAIN?!
WHOA!
MAKO, DEAR, THERE'S BEING COMPETENT AND THEN THERE'S BEING COMPE-TENT!
WAIT... DID YOU EVEN DO COLLECTIONS YOU DIDN'T HAVE TO YET?!
FWMP
WHAT IS UP WITH THIS UNHOLY WORK ETHIC?! ARE YOU JAPANESE OR SOME-THING?!
I FEEL LIKE I'LL GO INSANE IF I'M NOT DOING SOMETHING TO DISTRACT MYSELF.
DOING THIS MUCH WORK TELLS ME THAT YOU'VE GONE PLENTY INSANE ALREADY.
AND WHOSE FAULT IS THAT, HMM?

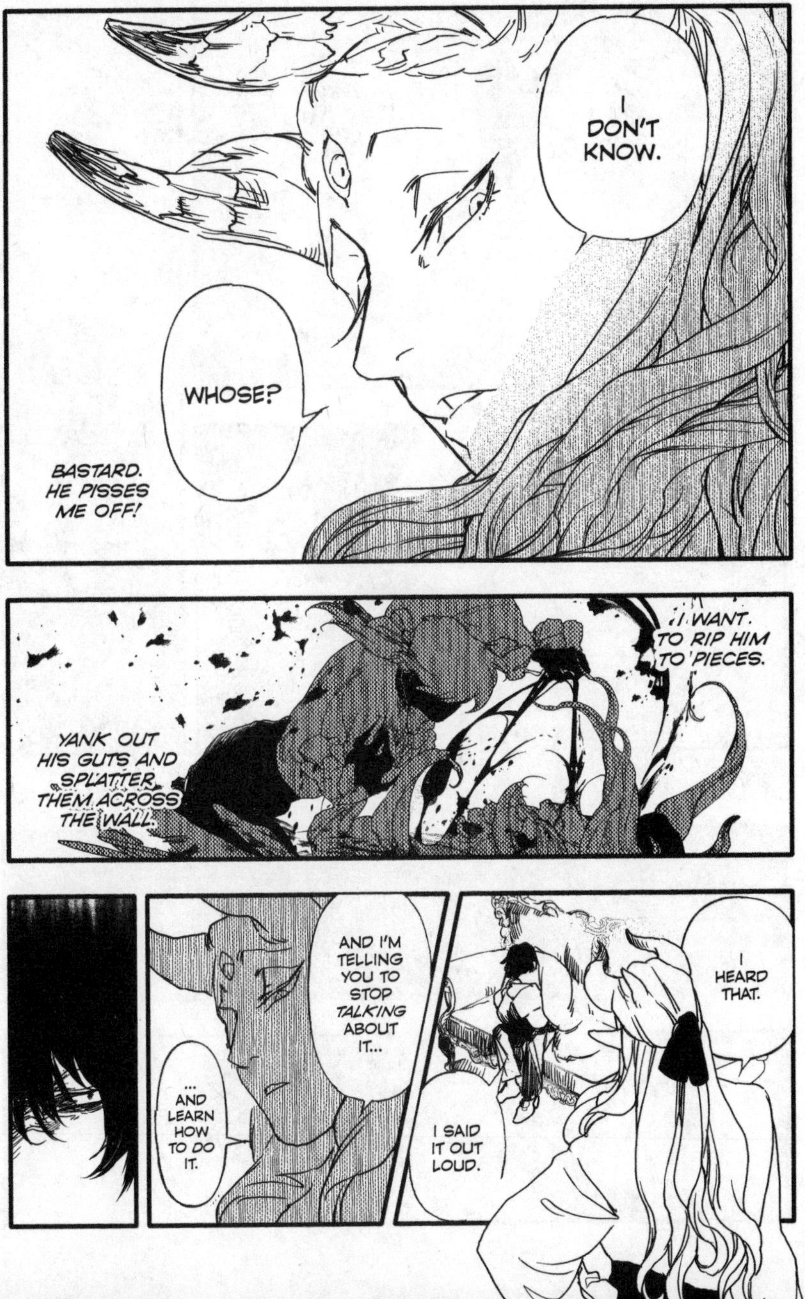
I DON'T KNOW.
WHOSE?
BASTARD. HE PISSES ME OFF!
I WANT TO RIP HIM TO PIECES.
YANK OUT HIS GUTS AND SPLATTER THEM ACROSS THE WALL.
I HEARD THAT.
I SAID IT OUT LOUD.
AND I'M TELLING YOU TO STOP *TALKING* ABOUT IT...
...AND LEARN HOW TO *DO* IT.

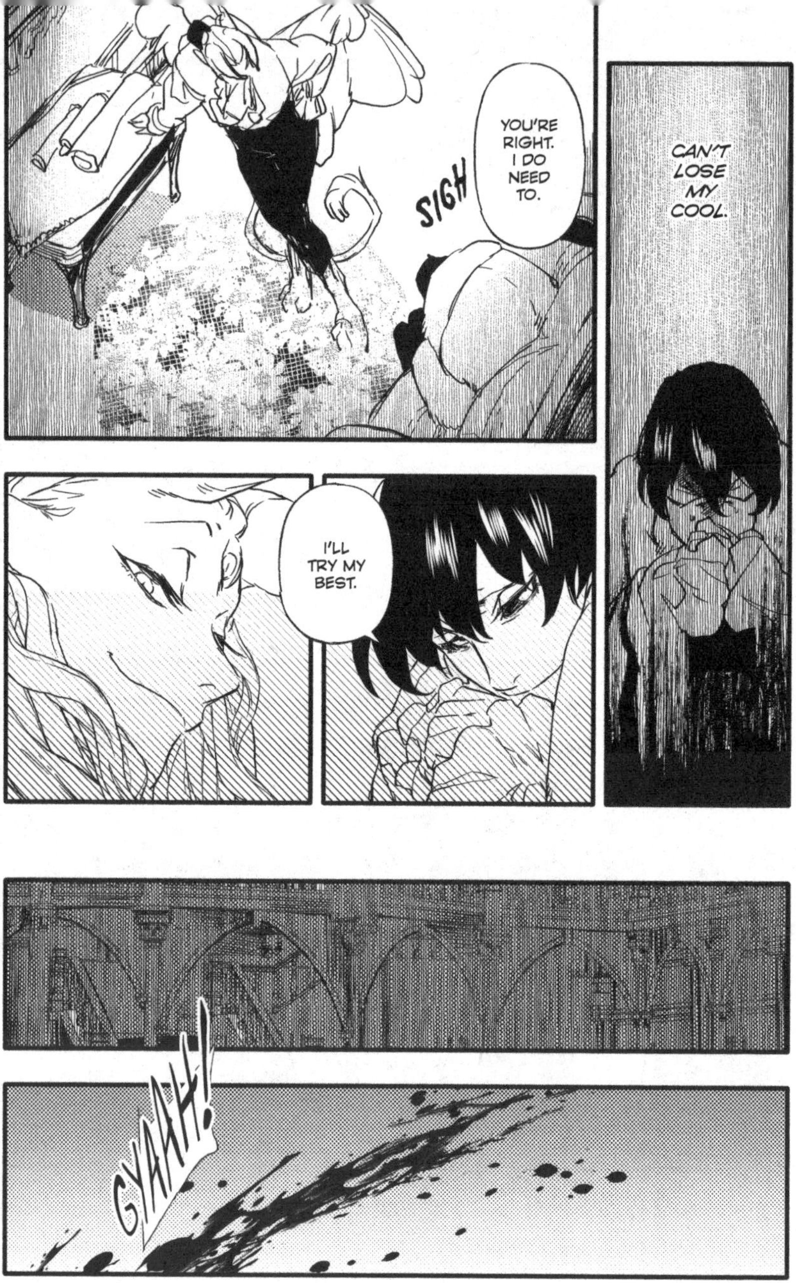
CAN'T LOSE MY COOL.
YOU'RE RIGHT. I DO NEED TO.
SIGH
I'LL TRY MY BEST.
GYAHH!

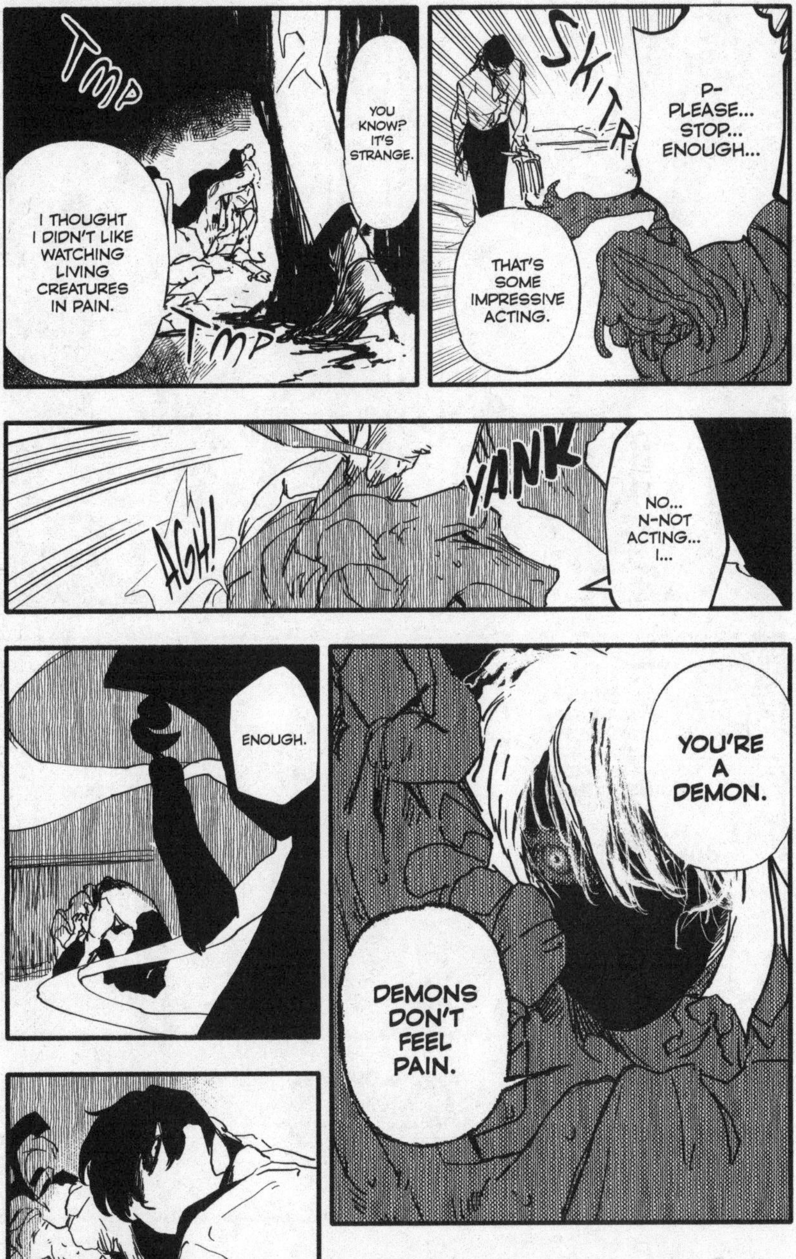
SKTR
P- PLEASE... STOP... ENOUGH...
THAT'S SOME IMPRESSIVE ACTING.
YOU KNOW? IT'S STRANGE.
I THOUGHT I DIDN'T LIKE WATCHING LIVING CREATURES IN PAIN.
TMP
TMP
NO... N-NOT ACTING... I...
YANK
AGH!
YOU'RE A DEMON.
DEMONS DON'T FEEL PAIN.
ENOUGH.

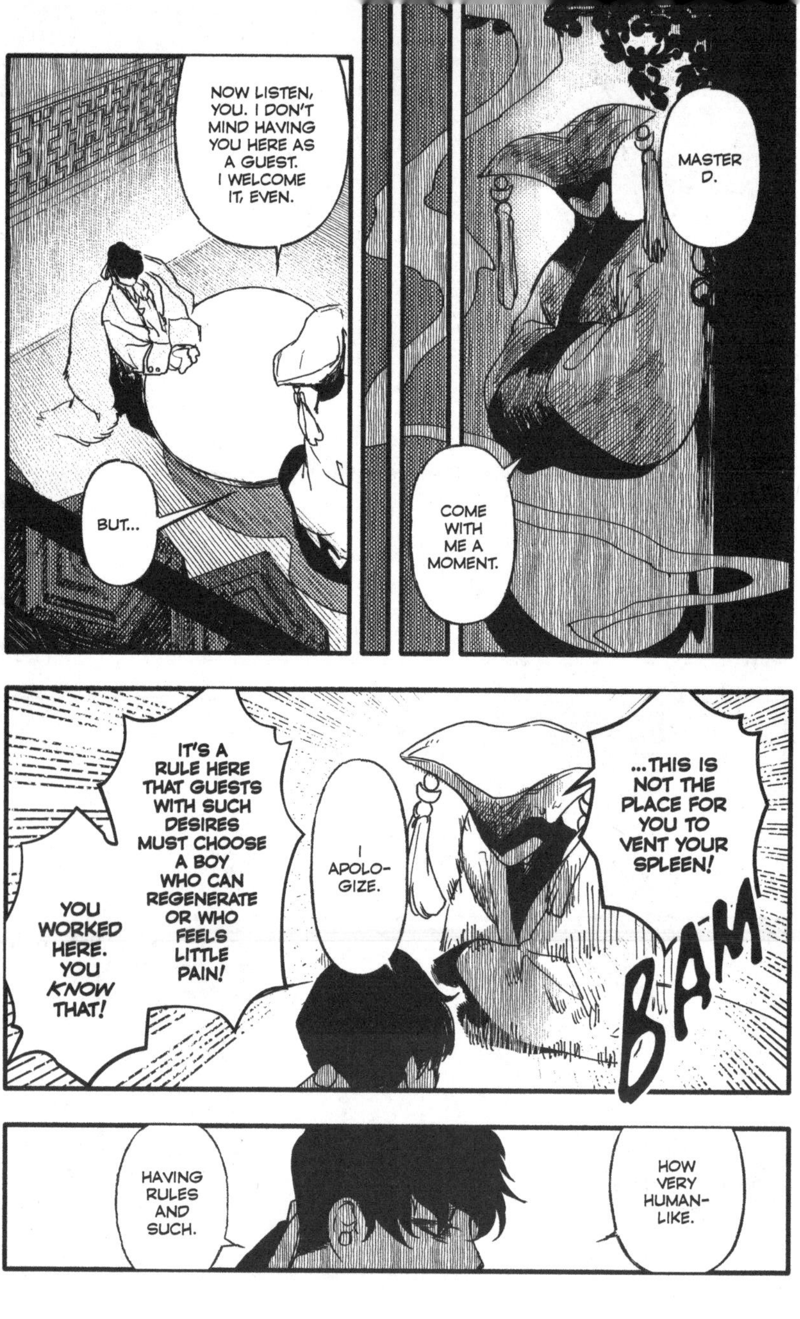
MASTER D.
COME WITH ME A MOMENT.
NOW LISTEN, YOU. I DON'T MIND HAVING YOU HERE AS A GUEST. I WELCOME IT, EVEN.
BUT...
...THIS IS NOT THE PLACE FOR YOU TO VENT YOUR SPLEEN!
BAM
I APOLOGIZE.
IT'S A RULE HERE THAT GUESTS WITH SUCH DESIRES MUST CHOOSE A BOY WHO CAN REGENERATE OR WHO FEELS LITTLE PAIN!
YOU WORKED HERE. YOU *KNOW* THAT!
HOW VERY HUMAN-LIKE.
HAVING RULES AND SUCH.

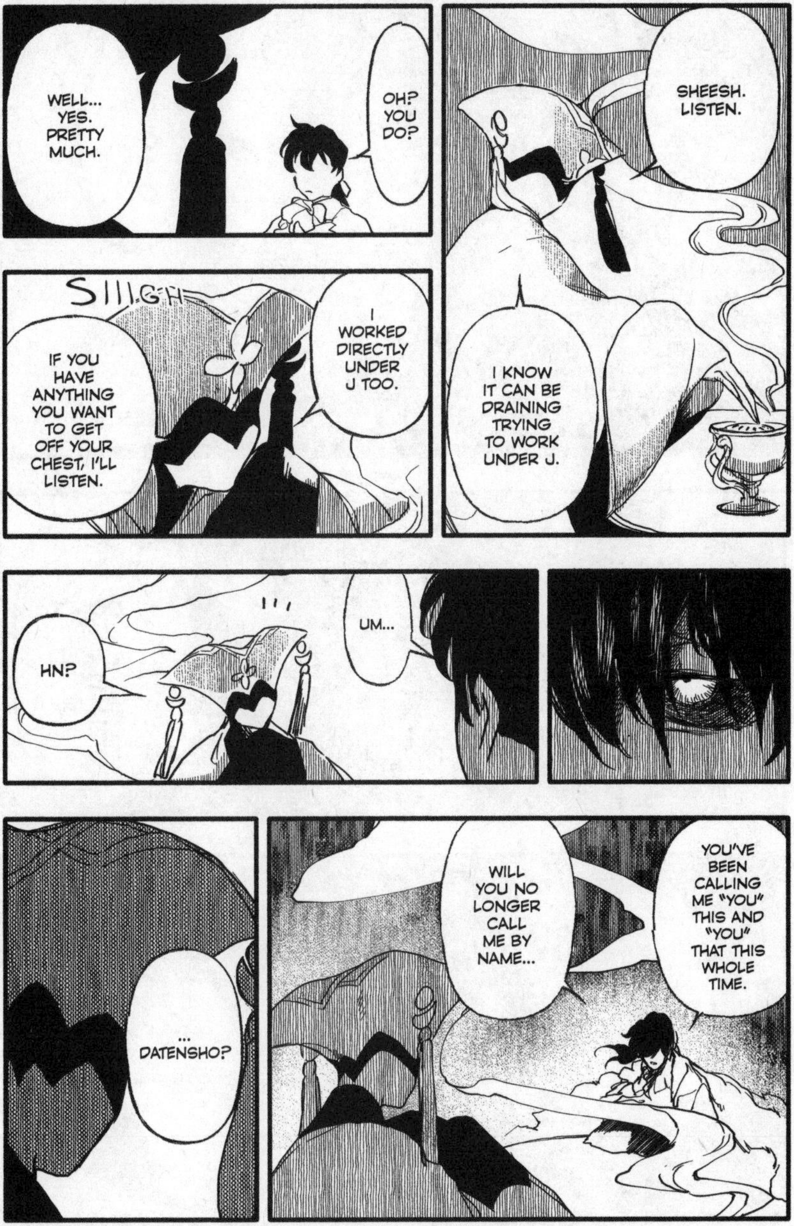

SHEESH. LISTEN.
I KNOW IT CAN BE DRAINING TRYING TO WORK UNDER J.
OH? YOU DO?
WELL... YES. PRETTY MUCH.
I WORKED DIRECTLY UNDER J TOO.
SIIIGH
IF YOU HAVE ANYTHING YOU WANT TO GET OFF YOUR CHEST, I'LL LISTEN.
UM...
HN?
YOU'VE BEEN CALLING ME "YOU" THIS AND "YOU" THAT THIS WHOLE TIME.
WILL YOU NO LONGER CALL ME BY NAME...
... DATENSHO?

MAKOTO.

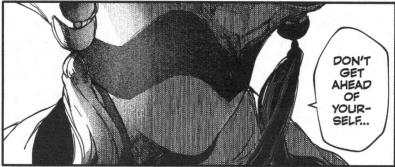

DON'T GET AHEAD OF YOUR-SELF...

...BOY.

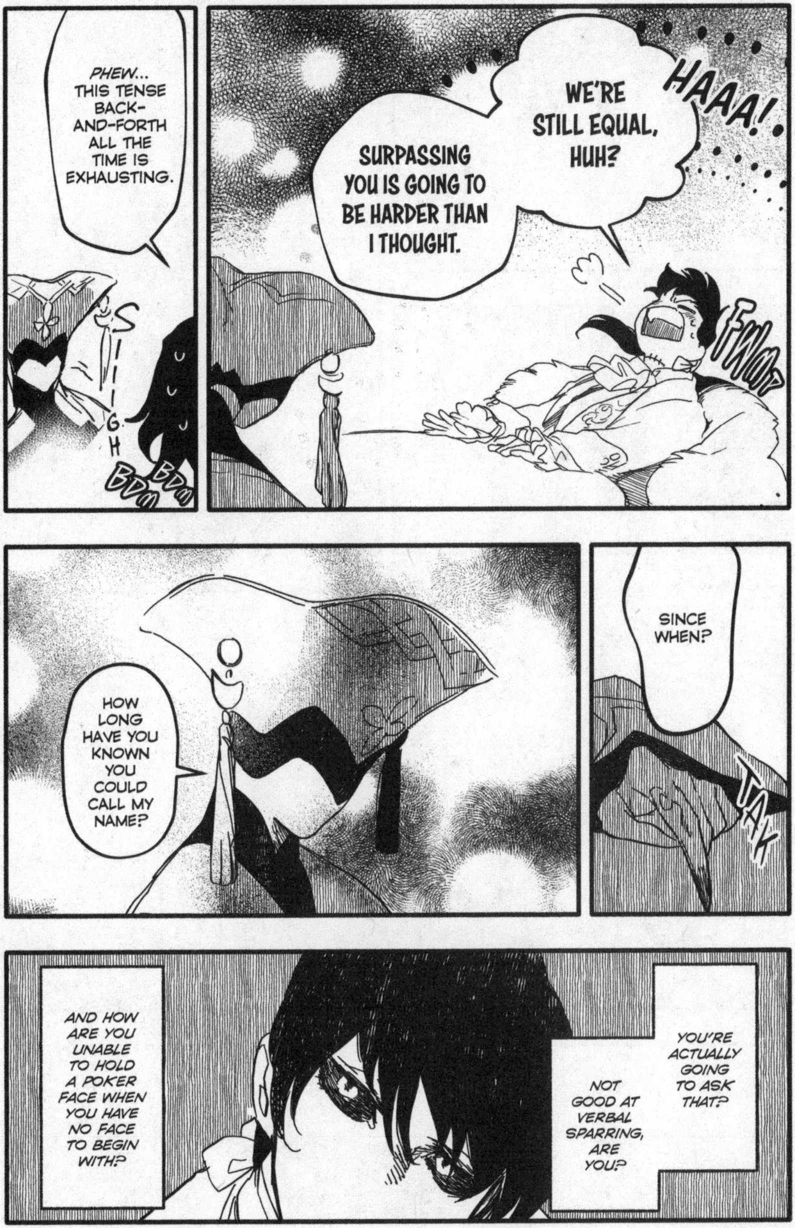
WE'RE STILL EQUAL, HUH?
SURPASSING YOU IS GOING TO BE HARDER THAN I THOUGHT.
HAAAA!
PHEW... THIS TENSE BACK-AND-FORTH ALL THE TIME IS EXHAUSTING.
SIIIGH
BDM BDM
SINCE WHEN?
TAK
HOW LONG HAVE YOU KNOWN YOU COULD CALL MY NAME?
YOU'RE ACTUALLY GOING TO ASK THAT?
NOT GOOD AT VERBAL SPARRING, ARE YOU?
AND HOW ARE YOU UNABLE TO HOLD A POKER FACE WHEN YOU HAVE NO FACE TO BEGIN WITH?

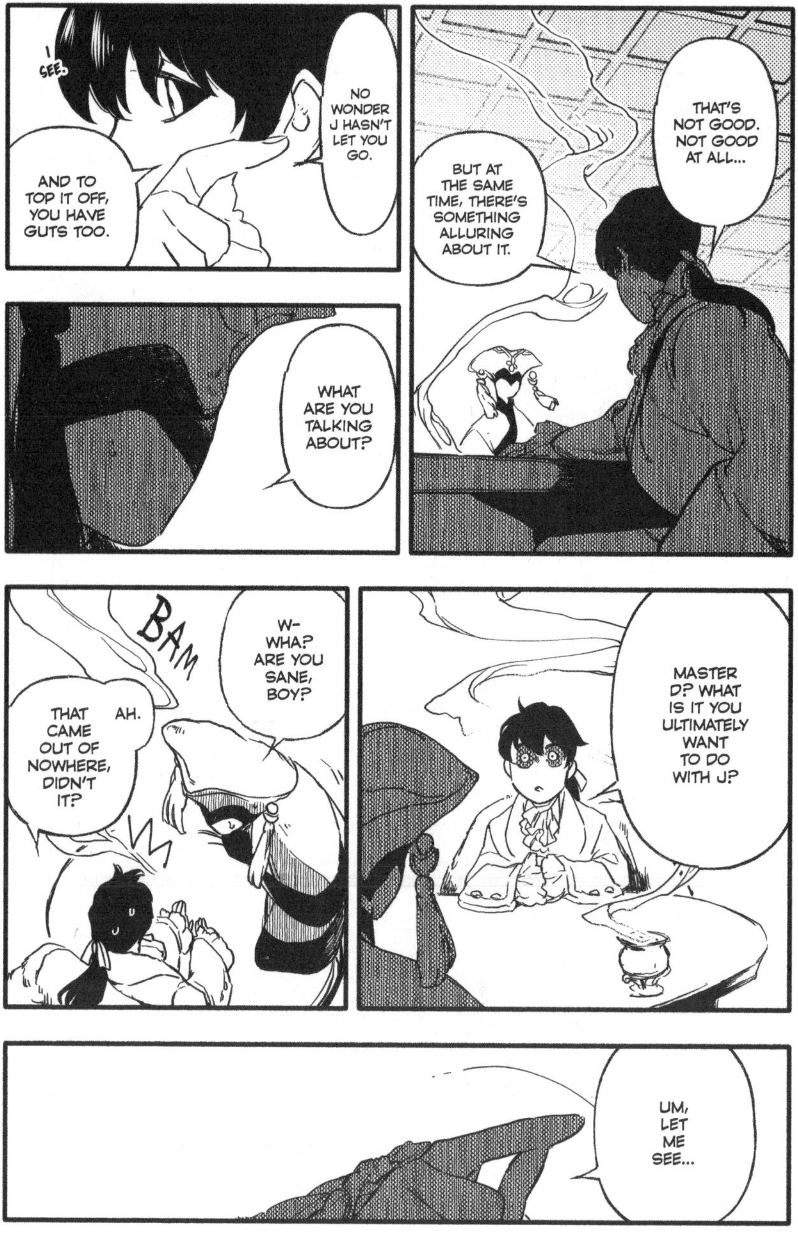
THAT'S NOT GOOD. NOT GOOD AT ALL...
BUT AT THE SAME TIME, THERE'S SOMETHING ALLURING ABOUT IT.
I SEE.
NO WONDER J HASN'T LET YOU GO.
AND TO TOP IT OFF, YOU HAVE GUTS TOO.
WHAT ARE YOU TALKING ABOUT?
MASTER D? WHAT IS IT YOU ULTIMATELY WANT TO DO WITH J?
BAM
W-WHA? ARE YOU SANE, BOY?
AH.
THAT CAME OUT OF NOWHERE, DIDN'T IT?
UM, LET ME SEE...

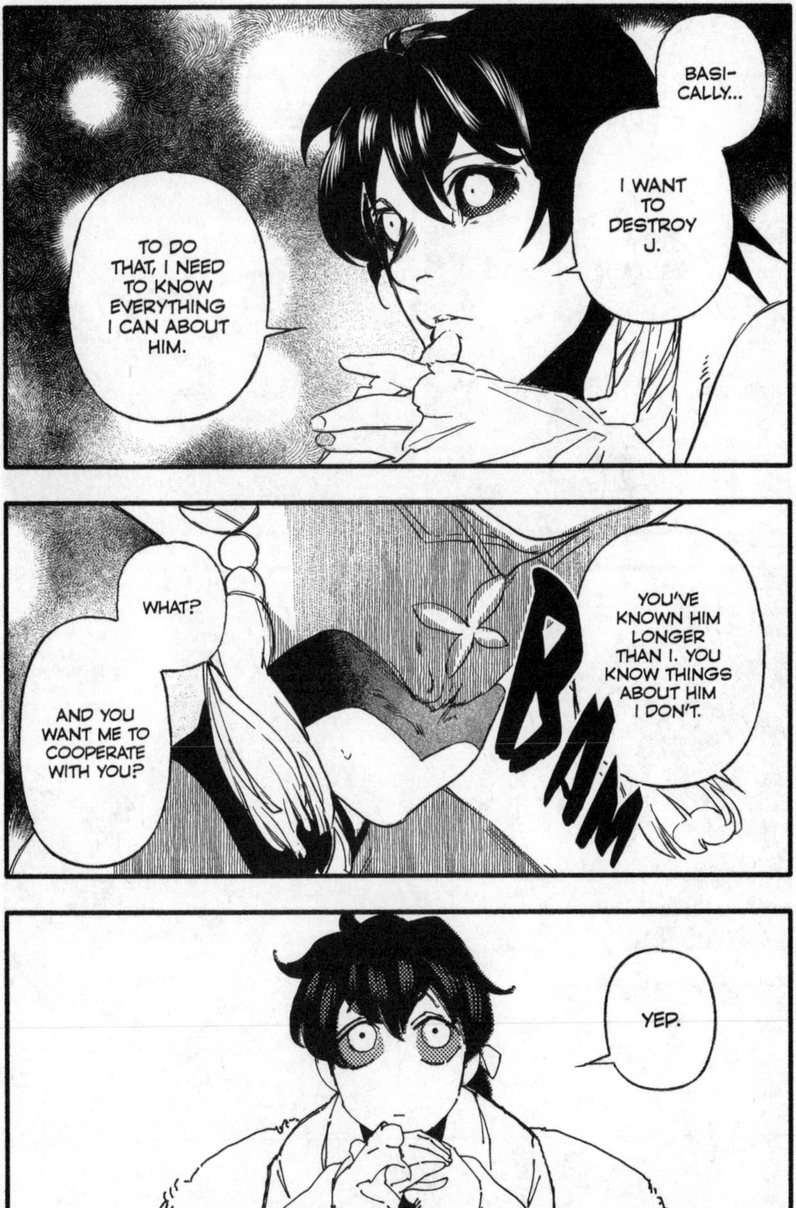
BASI-CALLY...
I WANT TO DESTROY J.
TO DO THAT, I NEED TO KNOW EVERYTHING I CAN ABOUT HIM.
YOU'VE KNOWN HIM LONGER THAN I. YOU KNOW THINGS ABOUT HIM I DON'T.
BAM
WHAT?
AND YOU WANT ME TO COOPERATE WITH YOU?
YEP.

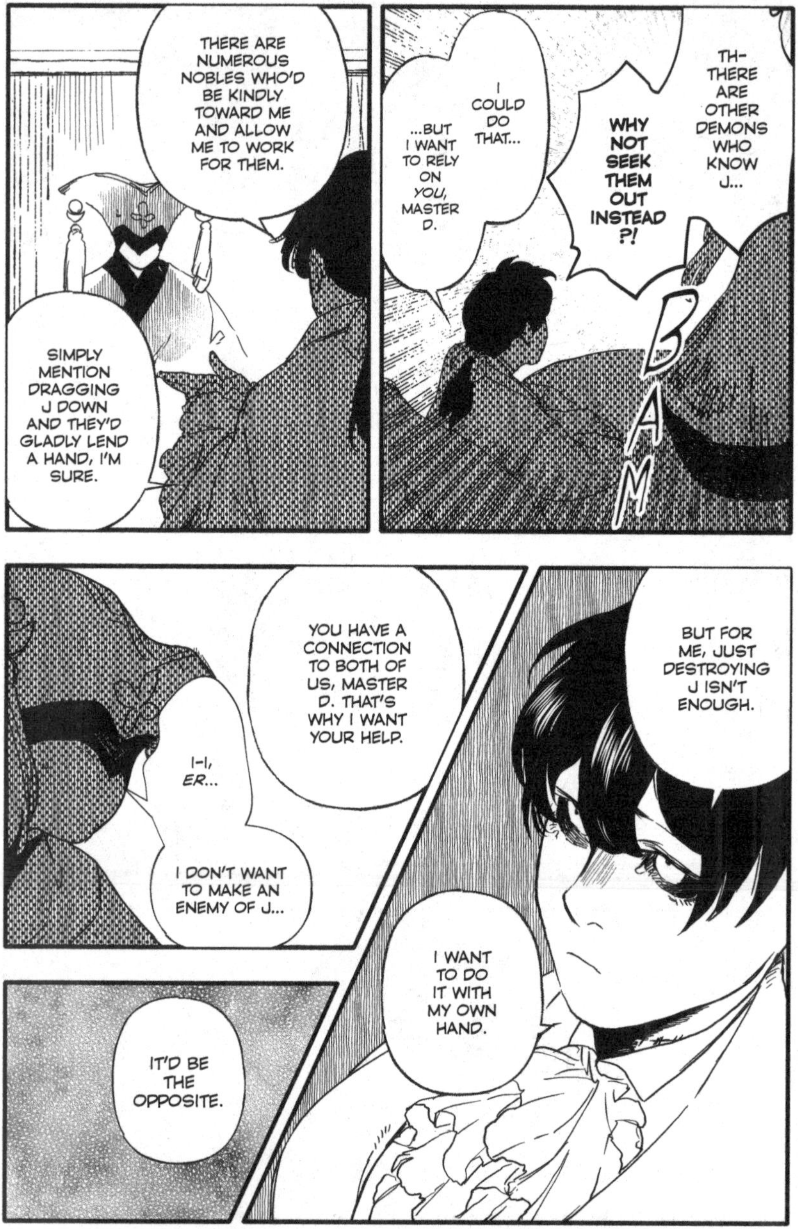
TH-THERE ARE OTHER DEMONS WHO KNOW J...
WHY NOT SEEK THEM OUT INSTEAD?!
BAM
I COULD DO THAT...
...BUT I WANT TO RELY ON *YOU*, MASTER D.
THERE ARE NUMEROUS NOBLES WHO'D BE KINDLY TOWARD ME AND ALLOW ME TO WORK FOR THEM.
SIMPLY MENTION DRAGGING J DOWN AND THEY'D GLADLY LEND A HAND, I'M SURE.
BUT FOR ME, JUST DESTROYING J ISN'T ENOUGH.
I WANT TO DO IT WITH MY OWN HAND.
YOU HAVE A CONNECTION TO BOTH OF US, MASTER D. THAT'S WHY I WANT YOUR HELP.
I-I, *ER*...
I DON'T WANT TO MAKE AN ENEMY OF J...
IT'D BE THE OPPOSITE.

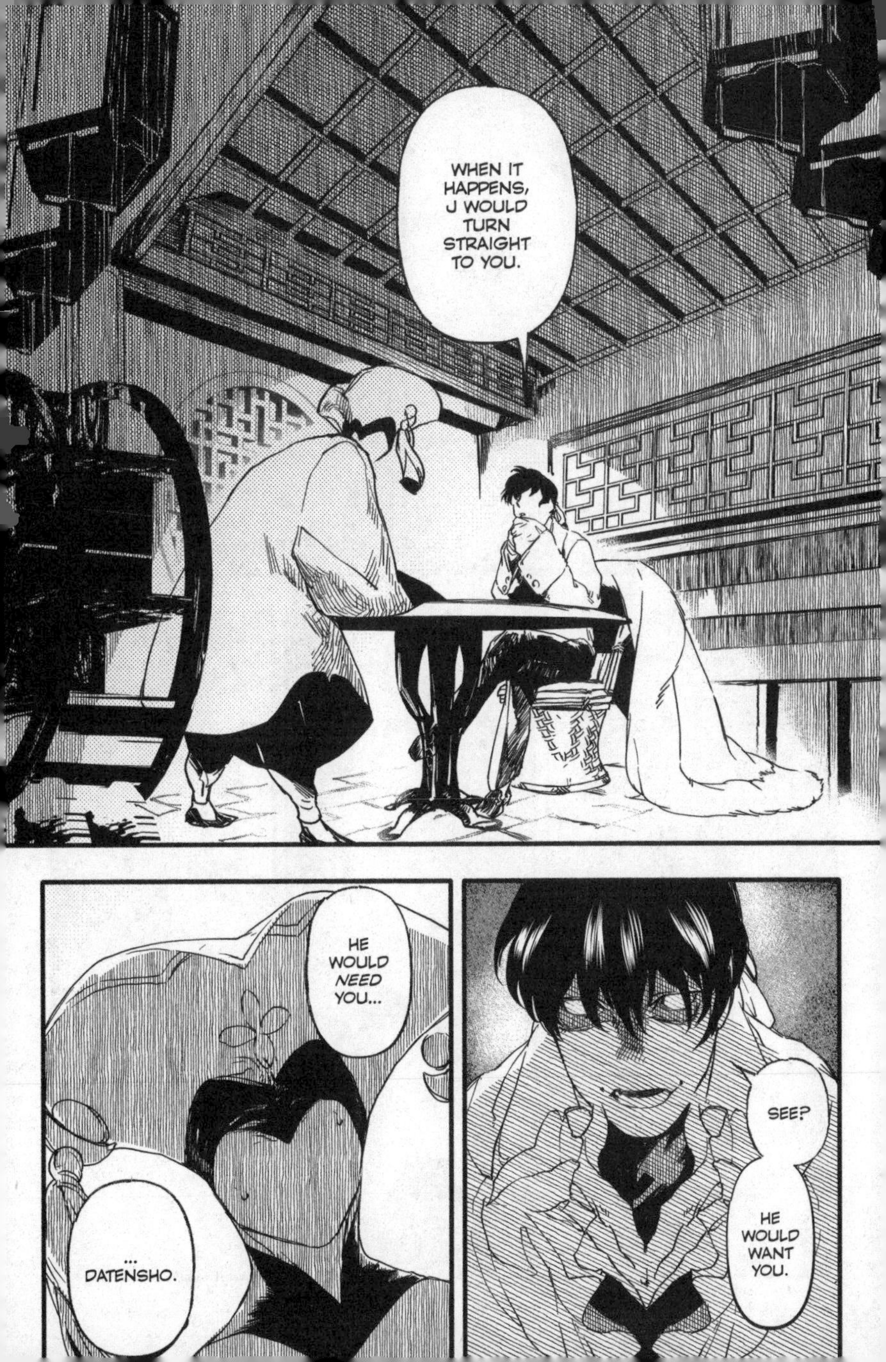
WHEN IT HAPPENS, I WOULD TURN STRAIGHT TO YOU.
SEE?
HE WOULD WANT YOU.
HE WOULD *NEED* YOU...
...DATENSHO.

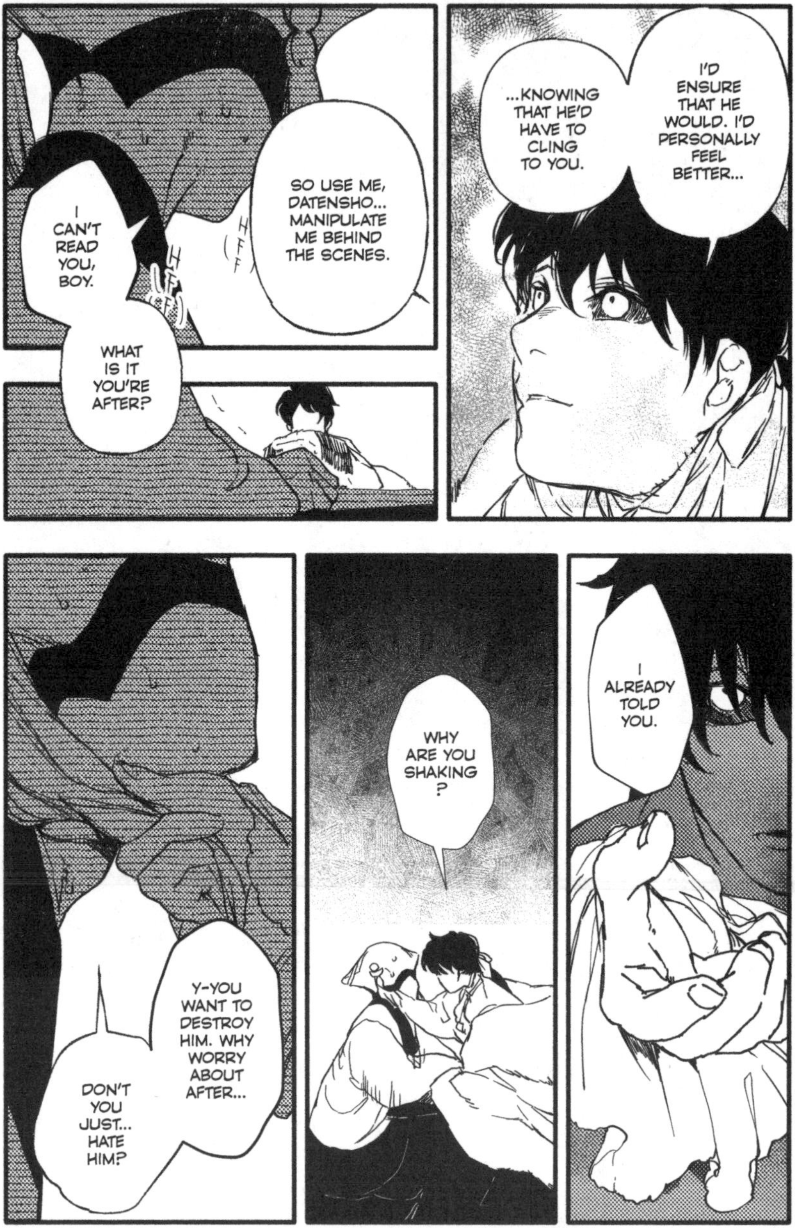
I'D ENSURE THAT HE WOULD. I'D PERSONALLY FEEL BETTER...
...KNOWING THAT HE'D HAVE TO CLING TO YOU.
SO USE ME, DATENSHO... MANIPULATE ME BEHIND THE SCENES.
HFF
HFF
I CAN'T READ YOU, BOY.
WHAT IS IT YOU'RE AFTER?
I ALREADY TOLD YOU.
WHY ARE YOU SHAKING?
Y-YOU WANT TO DESTROY HIM. WHY WORRY ABOUT AFTER...
DON'T YOU JUST... HATE HIM?

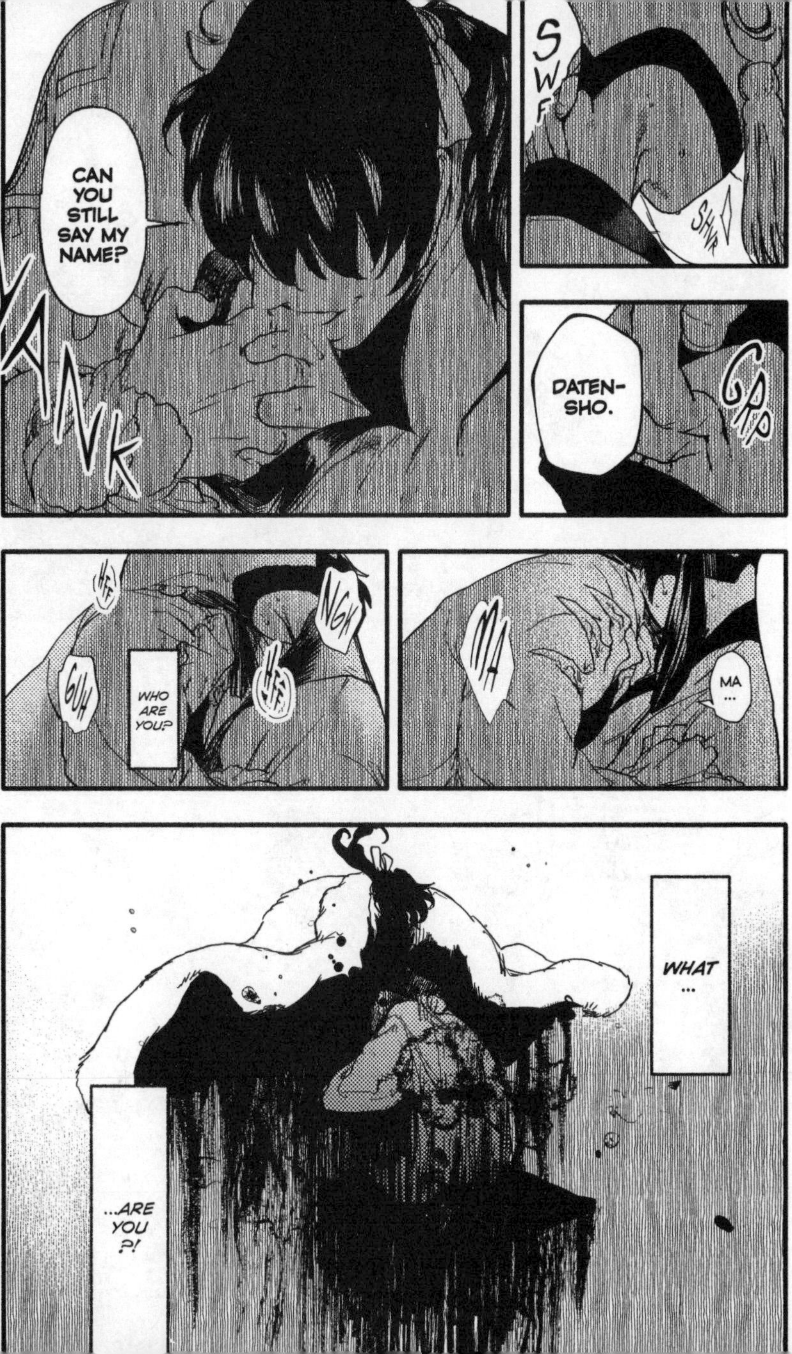
SWF
SHVR
GRP
DATEN-SHO.
CAN YOU STILL SAY MY NAME?
YANK
MA ...
MA
NGK
HFF
HFF
WHO ARE YOU?
GUH
WHAT ...
...ARE YOU ?!

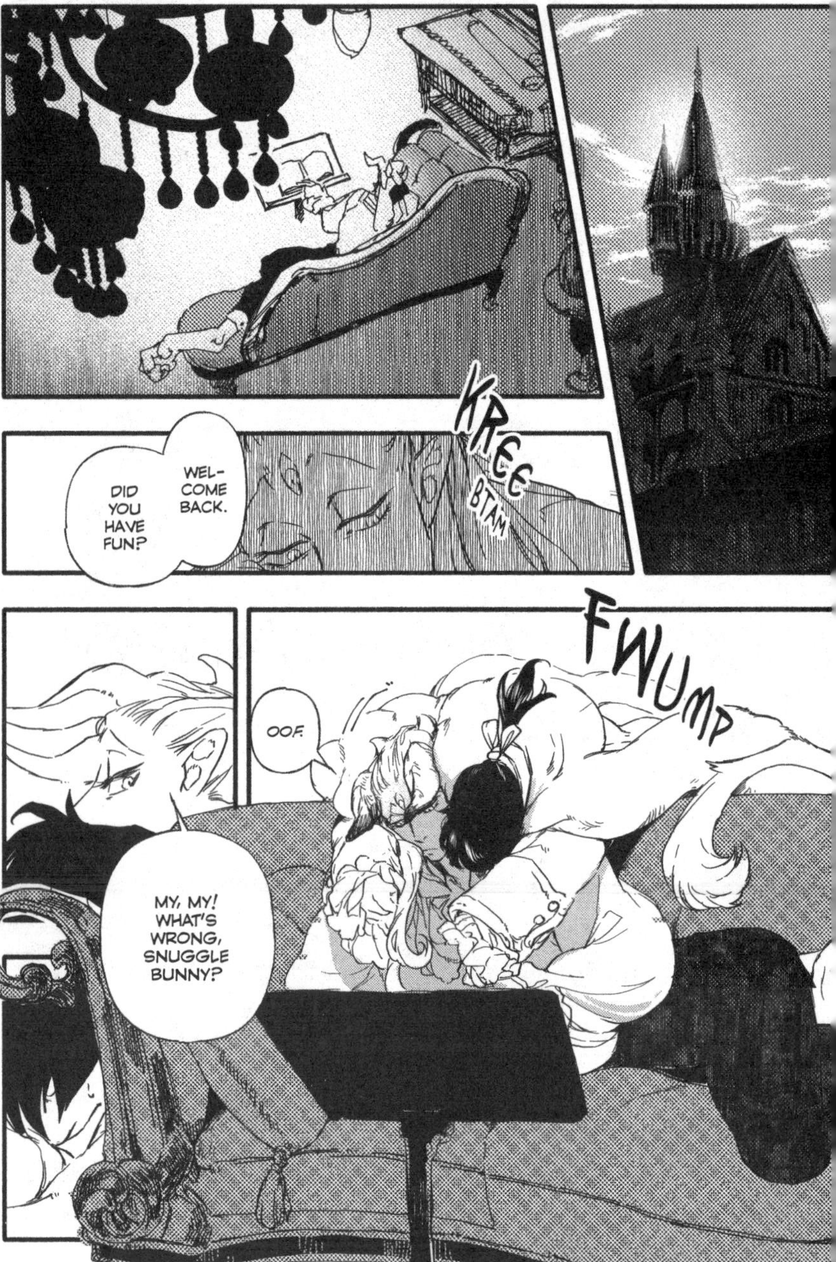
KREE
BTAM
WEL-COME BACK.
DID YOU HAVE FUN?
FWUMP
OOF.
MY, MY! WHAT'S WRONG, SNUGGLE BUNNY?

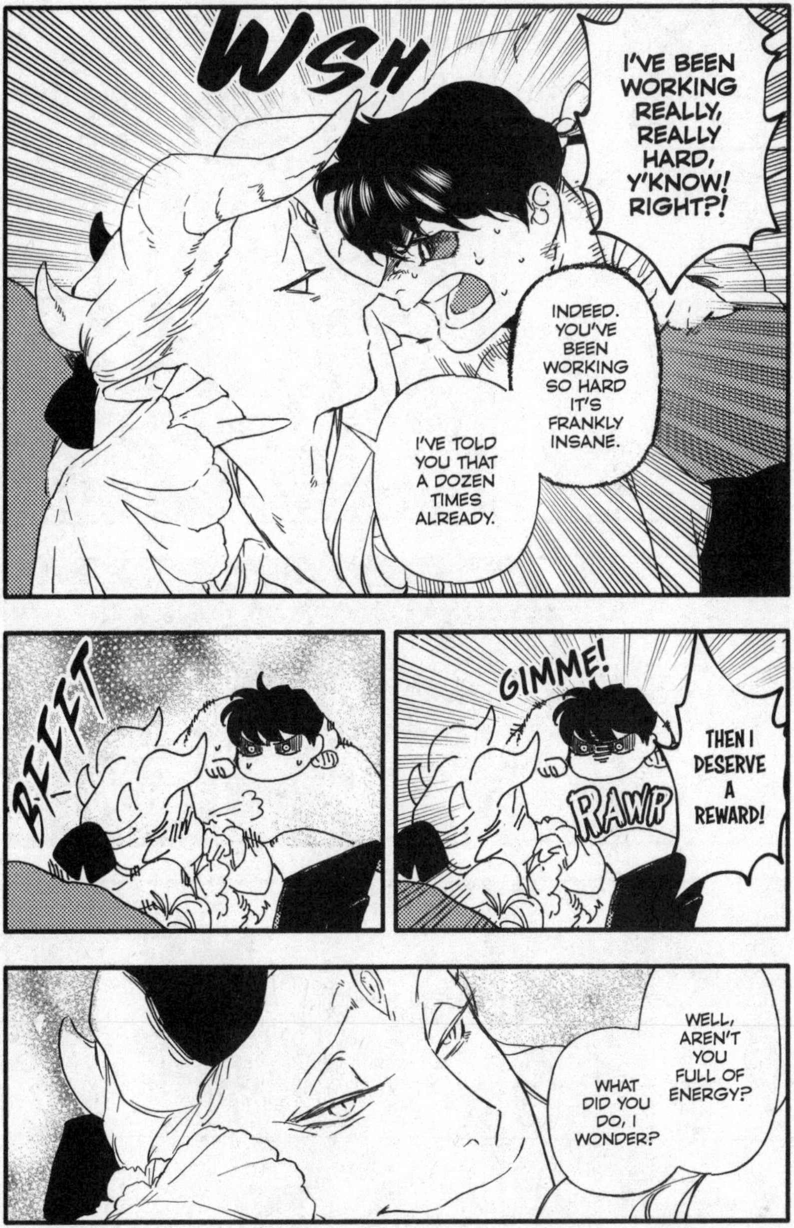
I'VE BEEN WORKING REALLY, REALLY HARD, Y'KNOW! RIGHT?!
WSH
INDEED. YOU'VE BEEN WORKING SO HARD IT'S FRANKLY INSANE.
I'VE TOLD YOU THAT A DOZEN TIMES ALREADY.
GIMME!
THEN I DESERVE A REWARD!
RAWR
BFFFT
WELL, AREN'T YOU FULL OF ENERGY?
WHAT DID YOU DO, I WONDER?

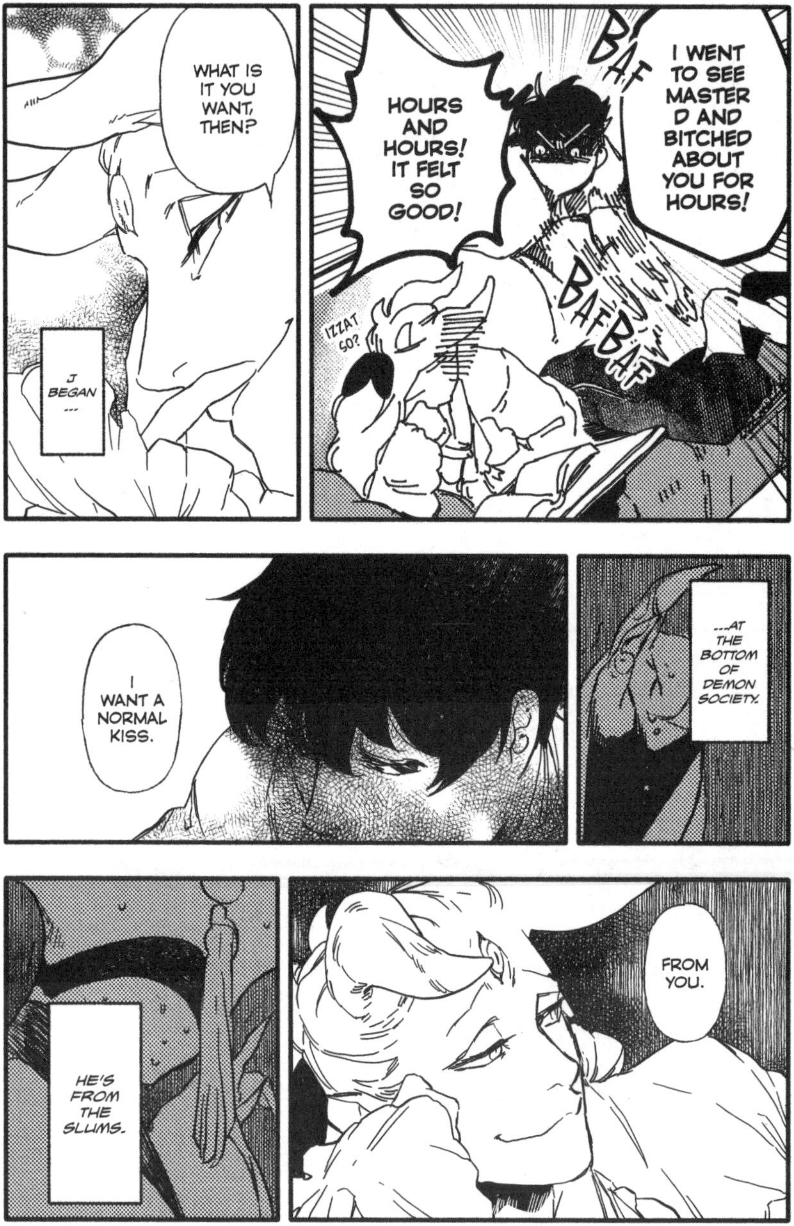
BAF
I WENT TO SEE MASTER D AND BITCHED ABOUT YOU FOR HOURS!
HOURS AND HOURS! IT FELT SO GOOD!
BAF
BAF
BAF
IZZAT SO?
WHAT IS IT YOU WANT, THEN?
J BEGAN ...
...AT THE BOTTOM OF DEMON SOCIETY.
I WANT A NORMAL KISS.
FROM YOU.
HE'S FROM THE SLUMS.

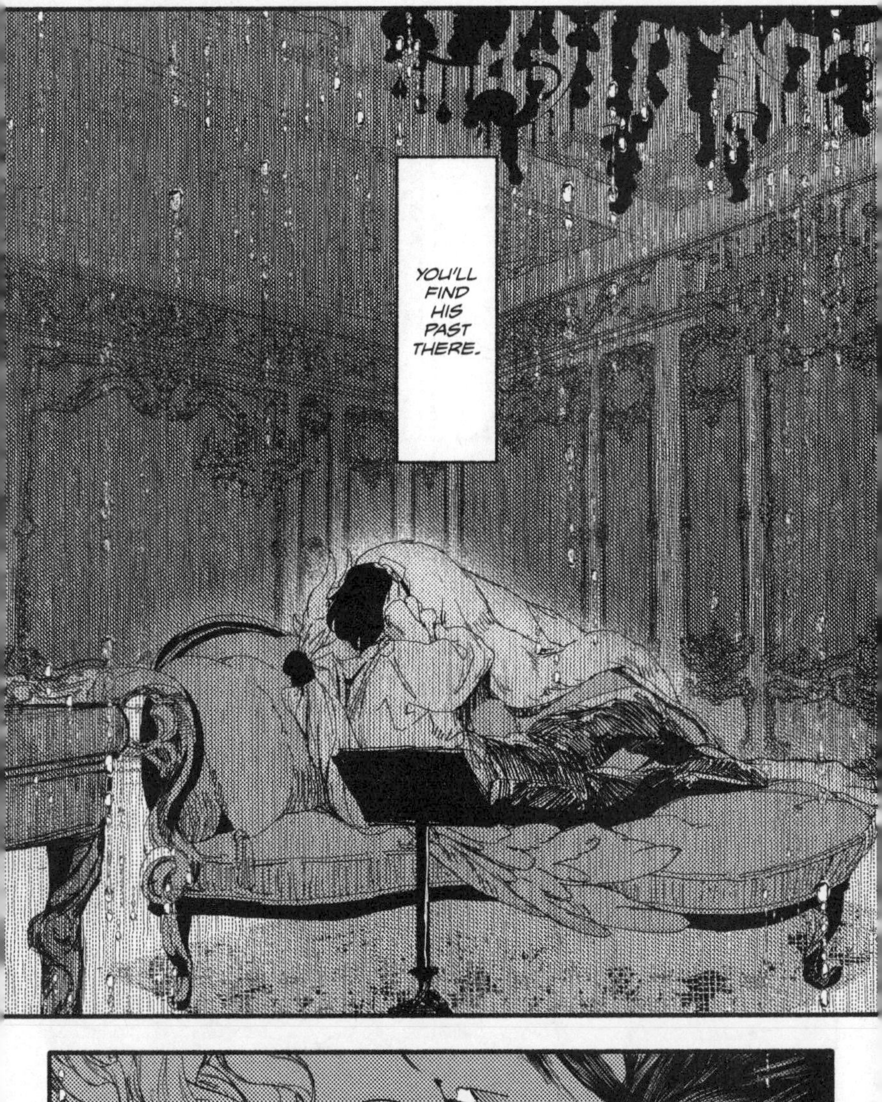
YOU'LL FIND HIS PAST THERE.

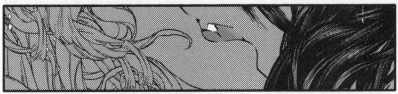

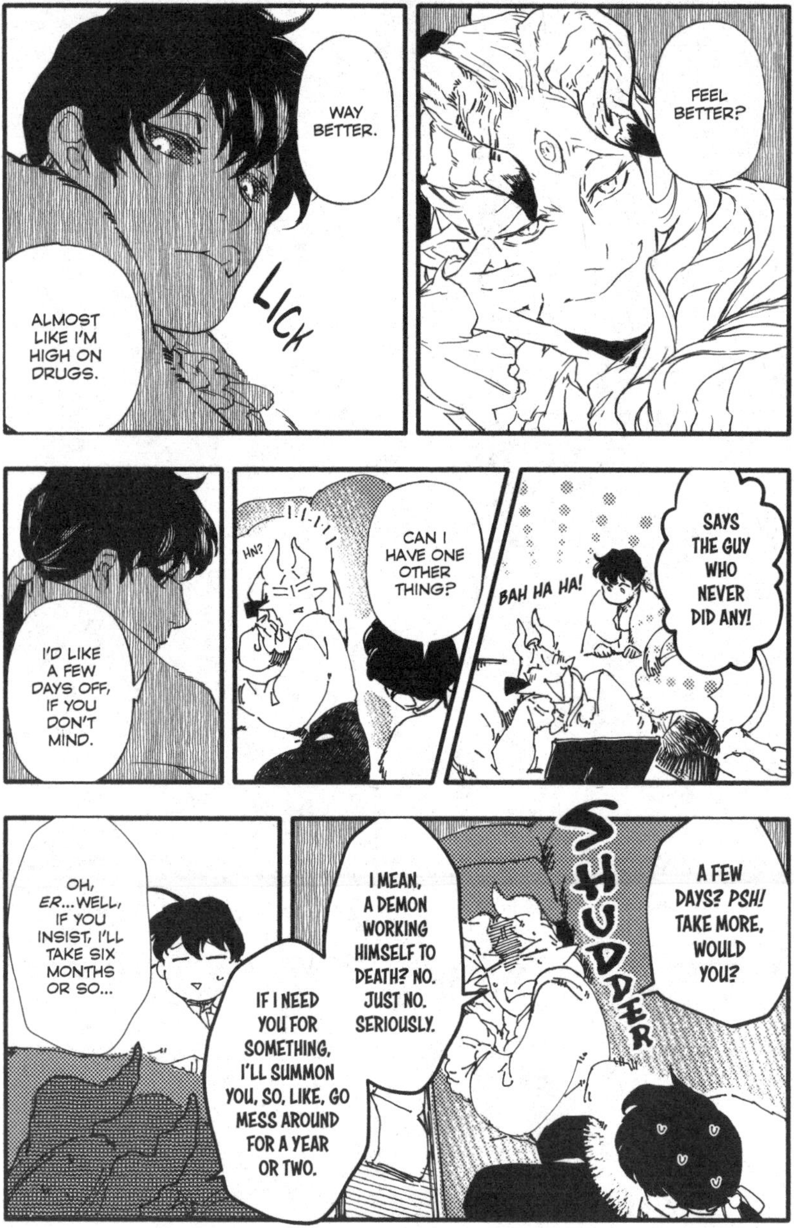
FEEL BETTER?
WAY BETTER.
LICK
ALMOST LIKE I'M HIGH ON DRUGS.
SAYS THE GUY WHO NEVER DID ANY!
BAH HA HA!
HN?
CAN I HAVE ONE OTHER THING?
I'D LIKE A FEW DAYS OFF, IF YOU DON'T MIND.
SHUDDER
A FEW DAYS? *PSH!* TAKE MORE, WOULD YOU?
I MEAN, A DEMON WORKING HIMSELF TO DEATH? NO. JUST NO. SERIOUSLY.
IF I NEED YOU FOR SOMETHING, I'LL SUMMON YOU, SO, LIKE, GO MESS AROUND FOR A YEAR OR TWO.
OH, *ER*...WELL, IF YOU INSIST, I'LL TAKE SIX MONTHS OR SO...

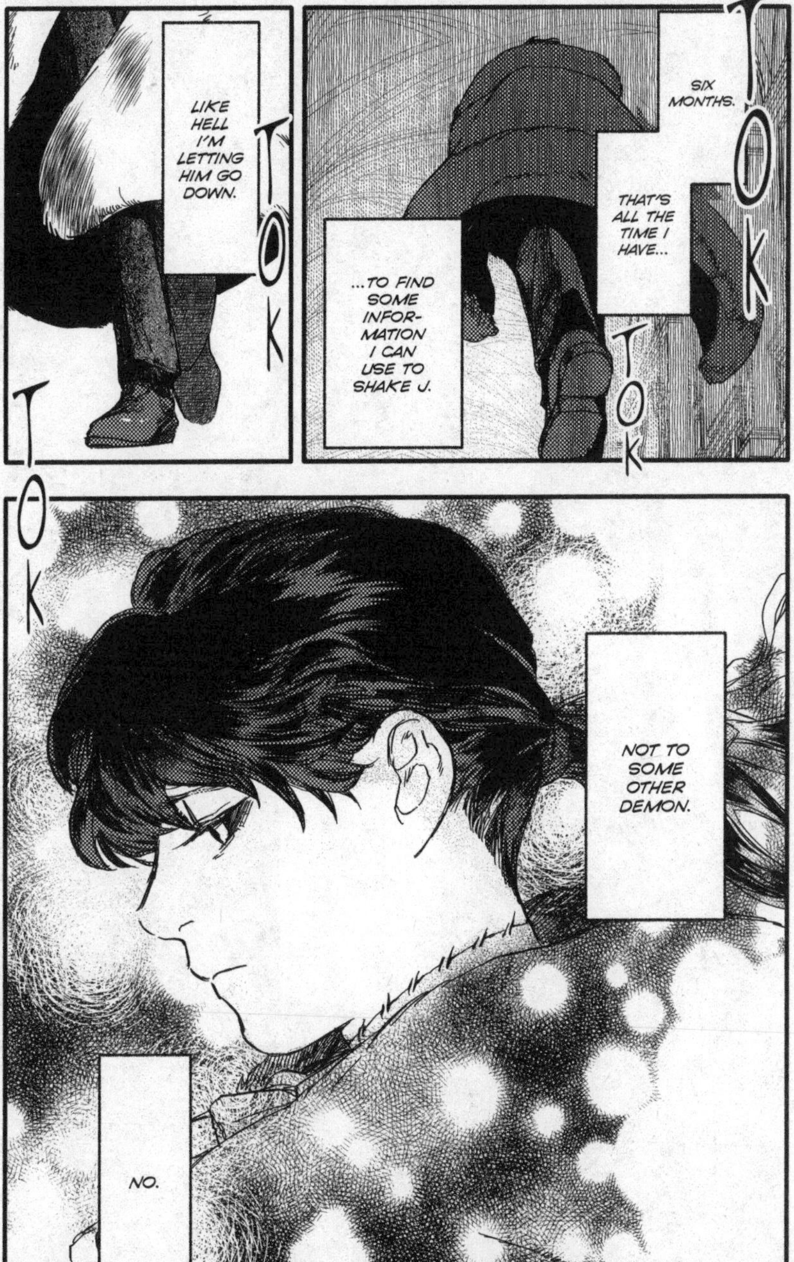
TOK
SIX MONTHS.
THAT'S ALL THE TIME I HAVE...
...TO FIND SOME INFOR-MATION I CAN USE TO SHAKE J.
TOK
LIKE HELL I'M LETTING HIM GO DOWN.
TOK
TOK
NOT TO SOME OTHER DEMON.
NO.

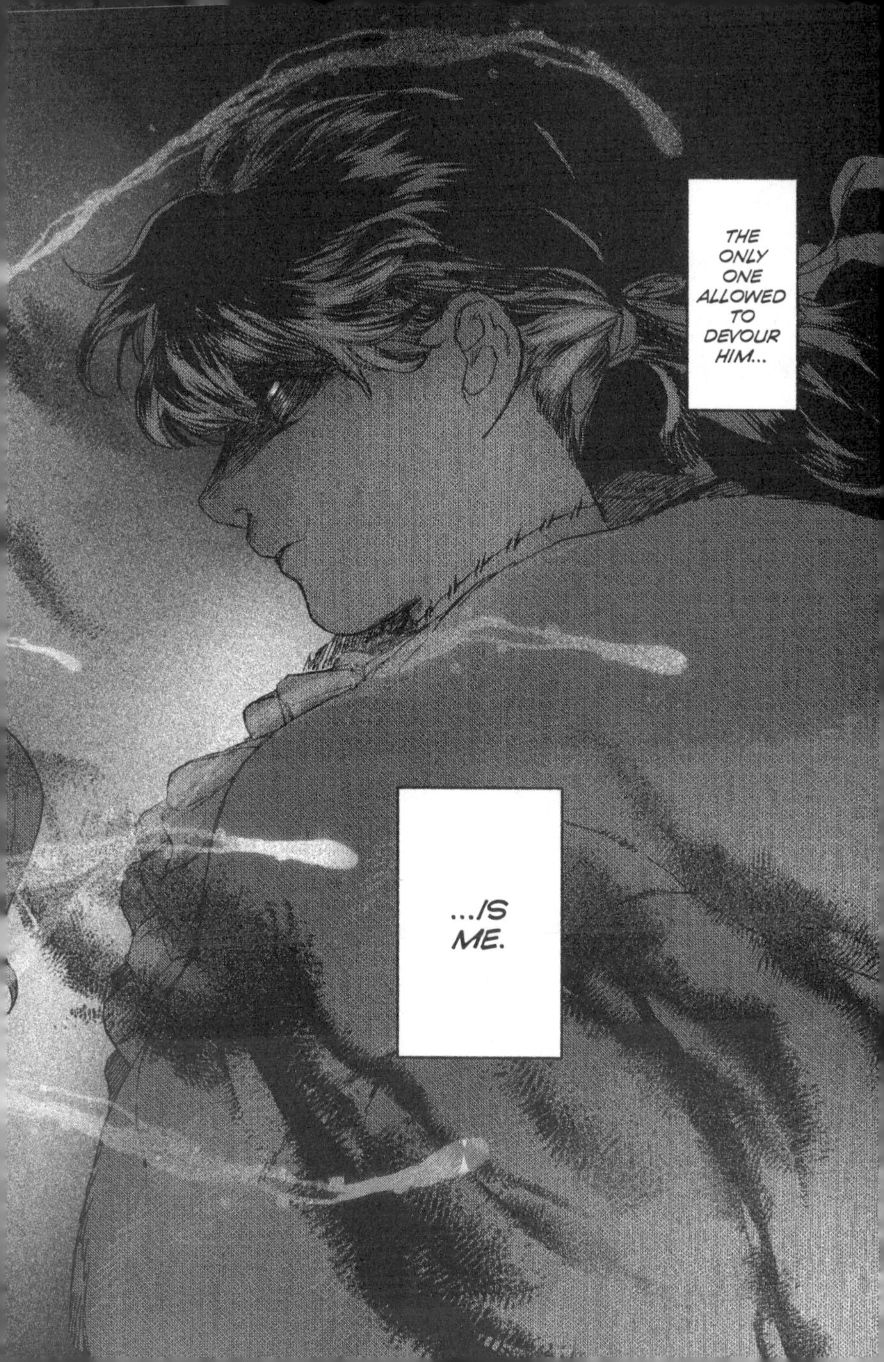
THE ONLY ONE ALLOWED TO DEVOUR HIM...
...IS ME.

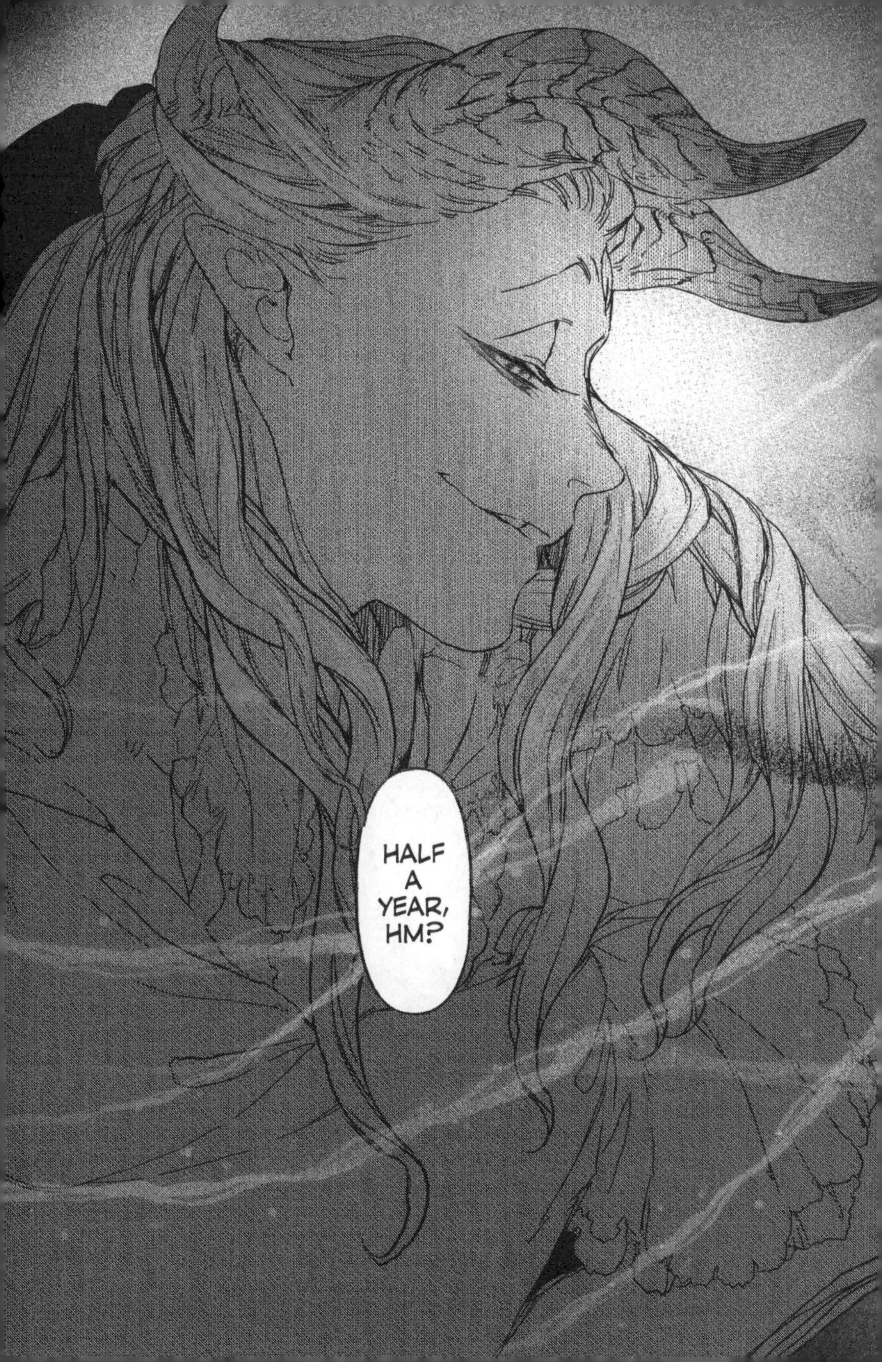
HALF A YEAR, HM?

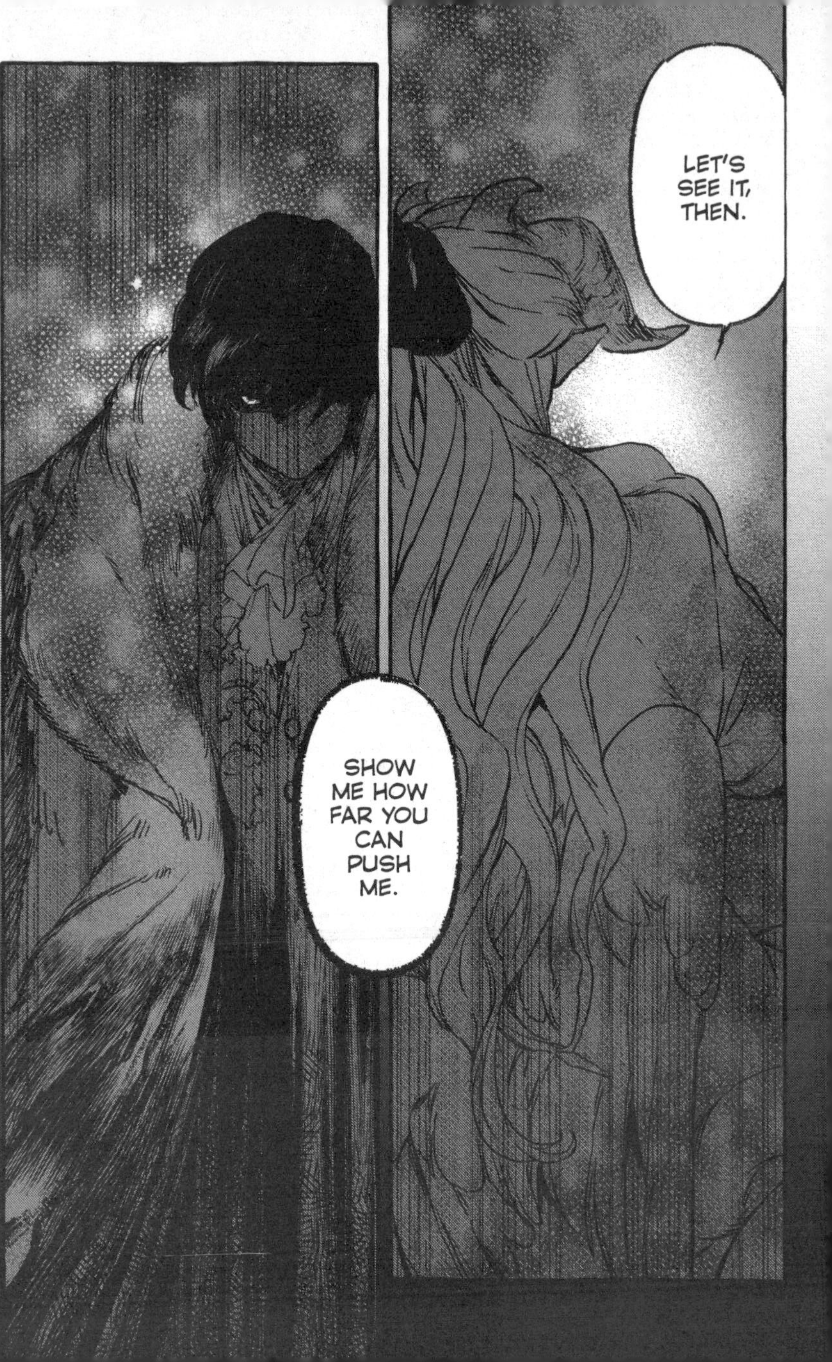
LET'S SEE IT, THEN.
SHOW ME HOW FAR YOU CAN PUSH ME.

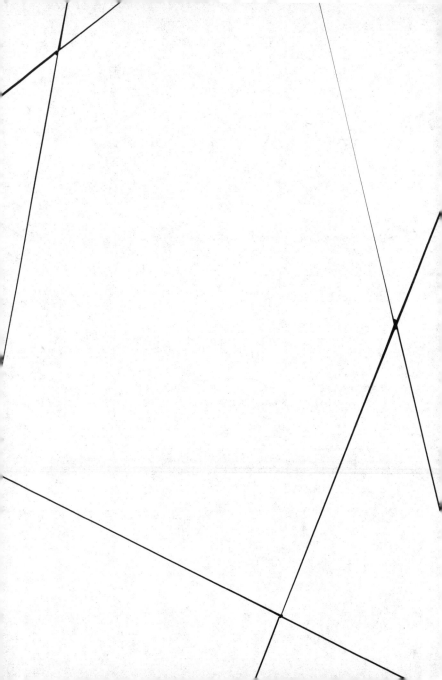

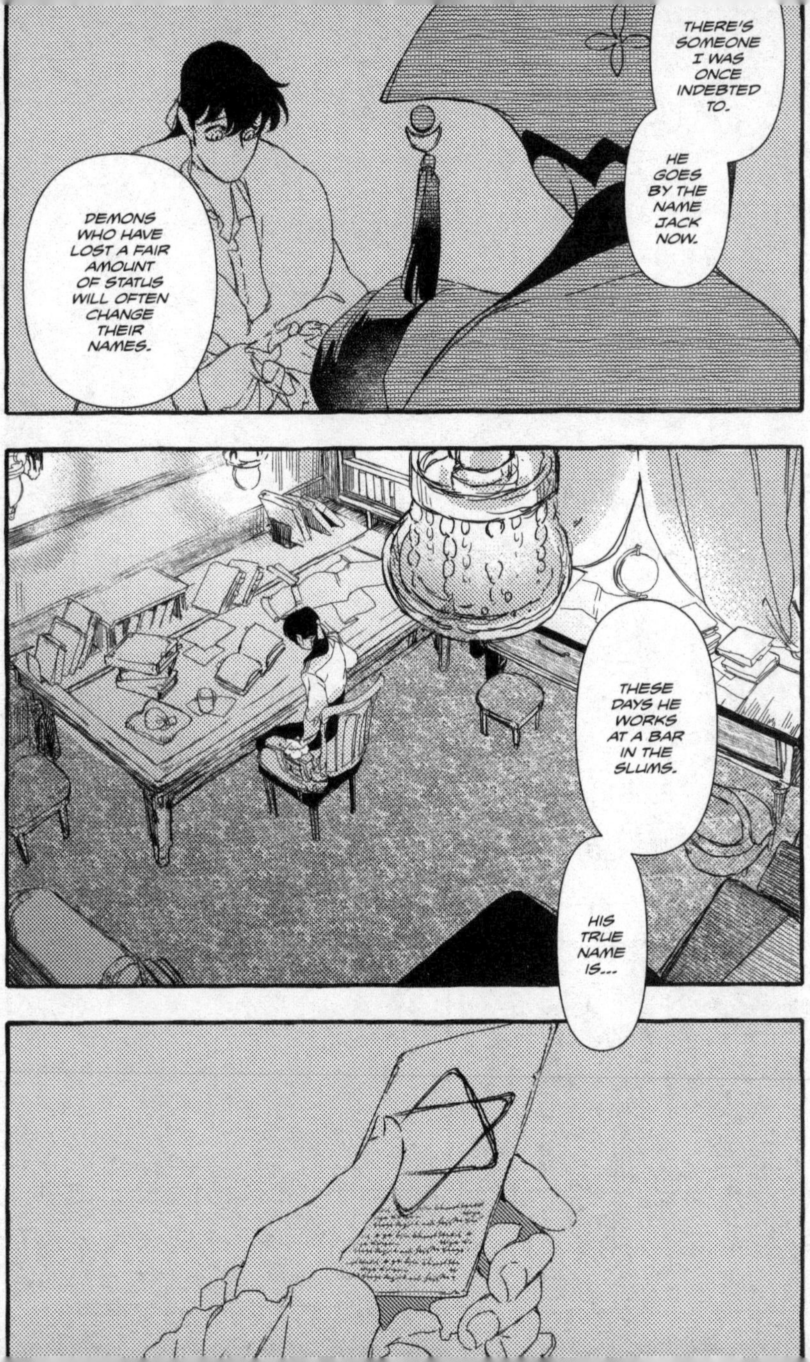
THERE'S SOMEONE I WAS ONCE INDEBTED TO.
HE GOES BY THE NAME JACK NOW.
DEMONS WHO HAVE LOST A FAIR AMOUNT OF STATUS WILL OFTEN CHANGE THEIR NAMES.
THESE DAYS HE WORKS AT A BAR IN THE SLUMS.
HIS TRUE NAME IS...

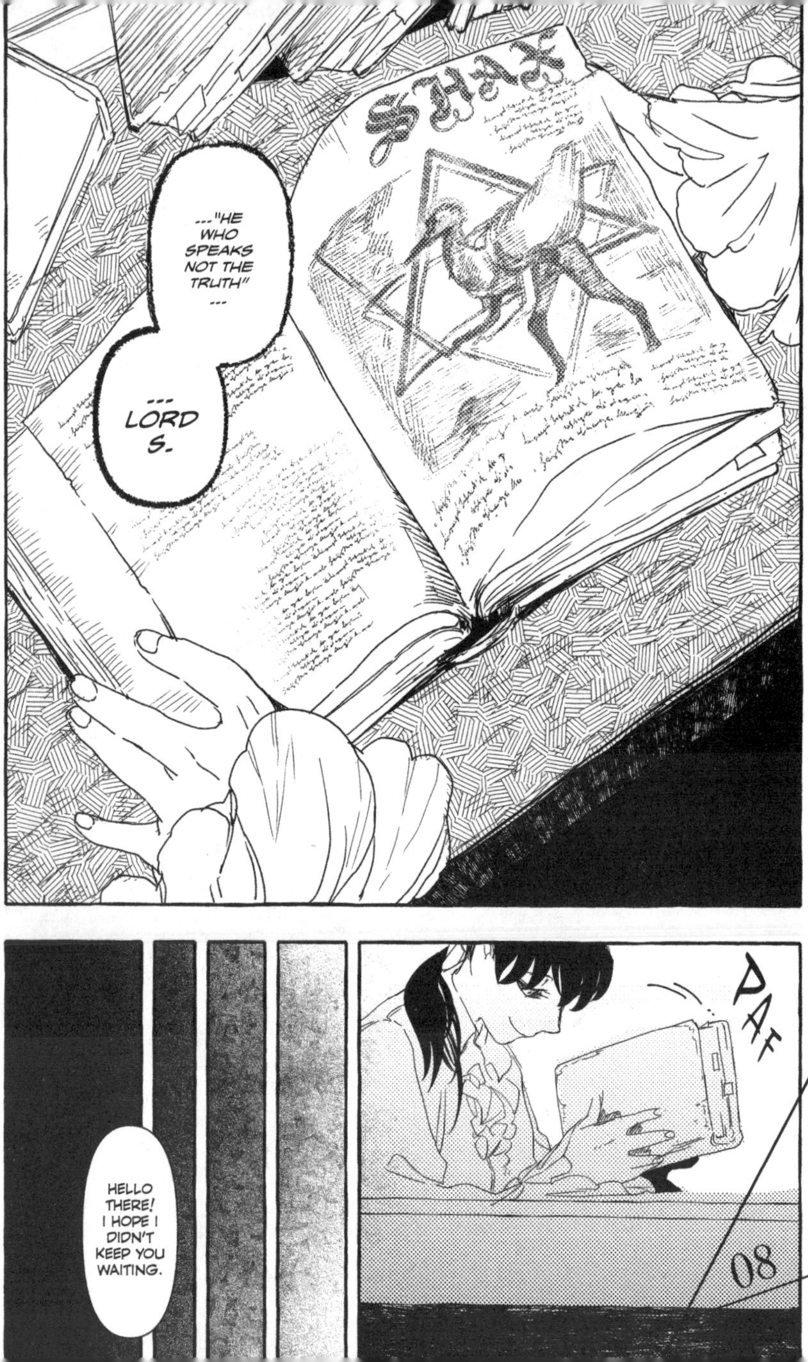
SHAX
..."HE WHO SPEAKS NOT THE TRUTH"... ...LORD S.
PAF
08
HELLO THERE! I HOPE I DIDN'T KEEP YOU WAITING.

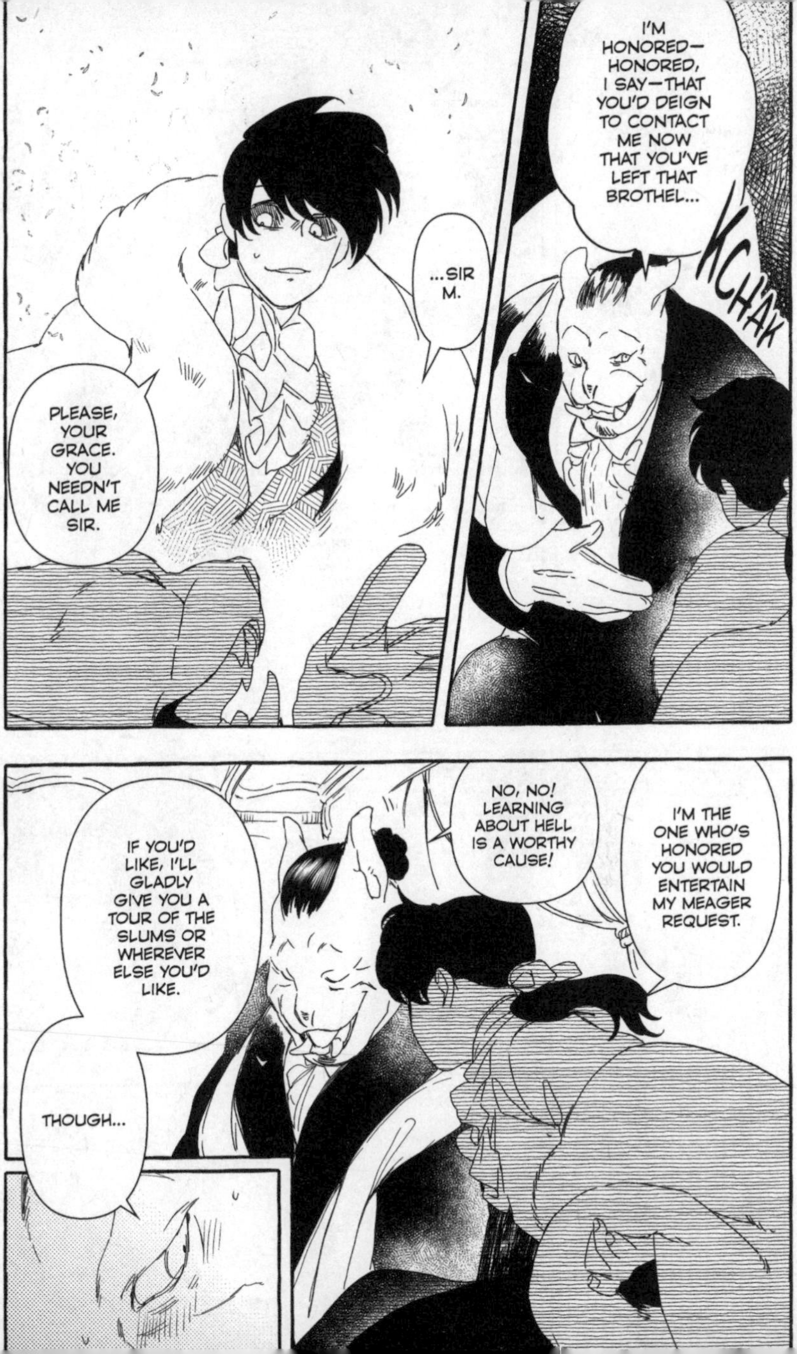
I'M HONORED— HONORED, I SAY—THAT YOU'D DEIGN TO CONTACT ME NOW THAT YOU'VE LEFT THAT BROTHEL...
KCHAK
...SIR M.
PLEASE, YOUR GRACE. YOU NEEDN'T CALL ME SIR.
I'M THE ONE WHO'S HONORED YOU WOULD ENTERTAIN MY MEAGER REQUEST.
NO, NO! LEARNING ABOUT HELL IS A WORTHY CAUSE!
IF YOU'D LIKE, I'LL GLADLY GIVE YOU A TOUR OF THE SLUMS OR WHEREVER ELSE YOU'D LIKE.
THOUGH...

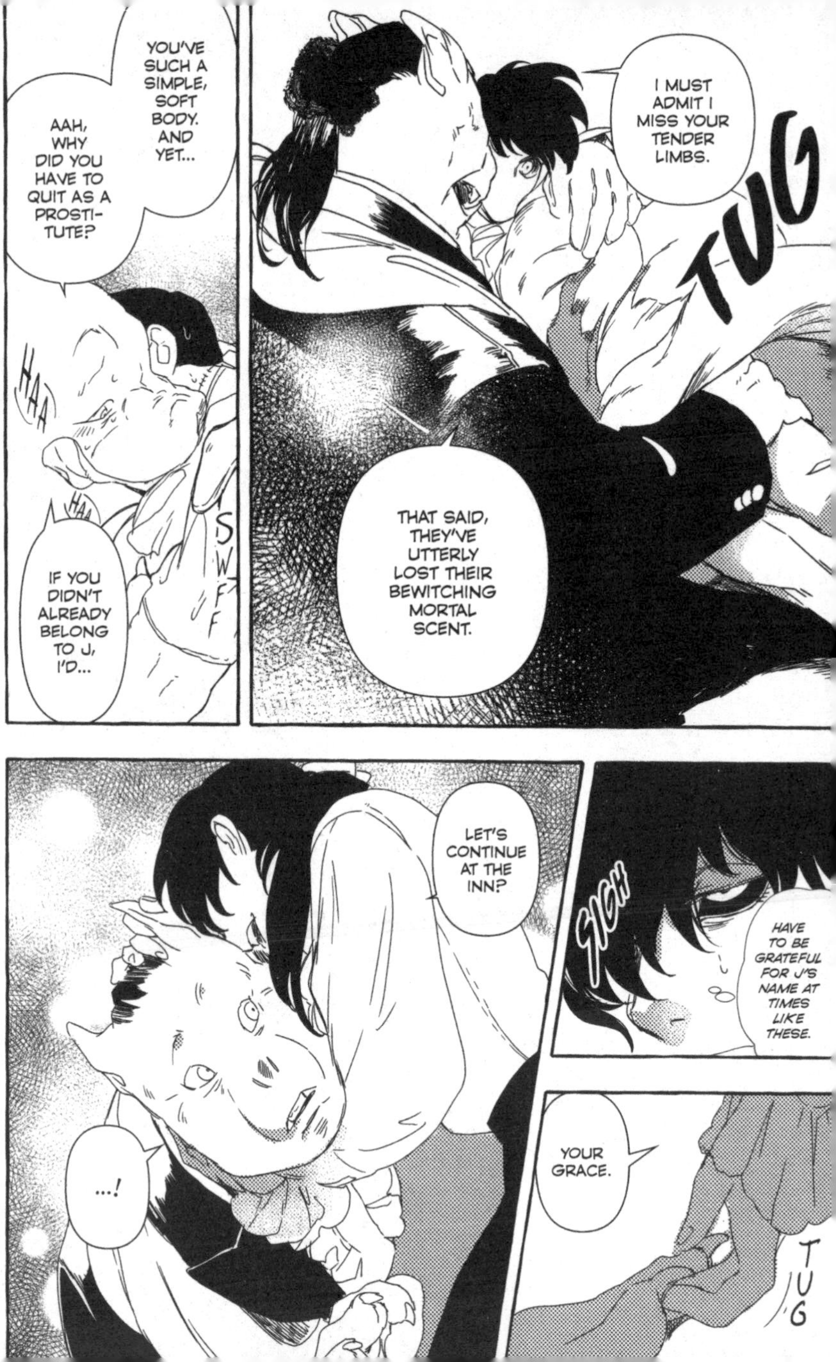
I MUST ADMIT I MISS YOUR TENDER LIMBS.
TUG
THAT SAID, THEY'VE UTTERLY LOST THEIR BEWITCHING MORTAL SCENT.
YOU'VE SUCH A SIMPLE, SOFT BODY. AND YET...
AAH, WHY DID YOU HAVE TO QUIT AS A PROSTITUTE?
HAA
HAA
SWFF
IF YOU DIDN'T ALREADY BELONG TO J, I'D...
SIGH
HAVE TO BE GRATEFUL FOR J'S NAME AT TIMES LIKE THESE.
YOUR GRACE.
TUG
LET'S CONTINUE AT THE INN?
...!

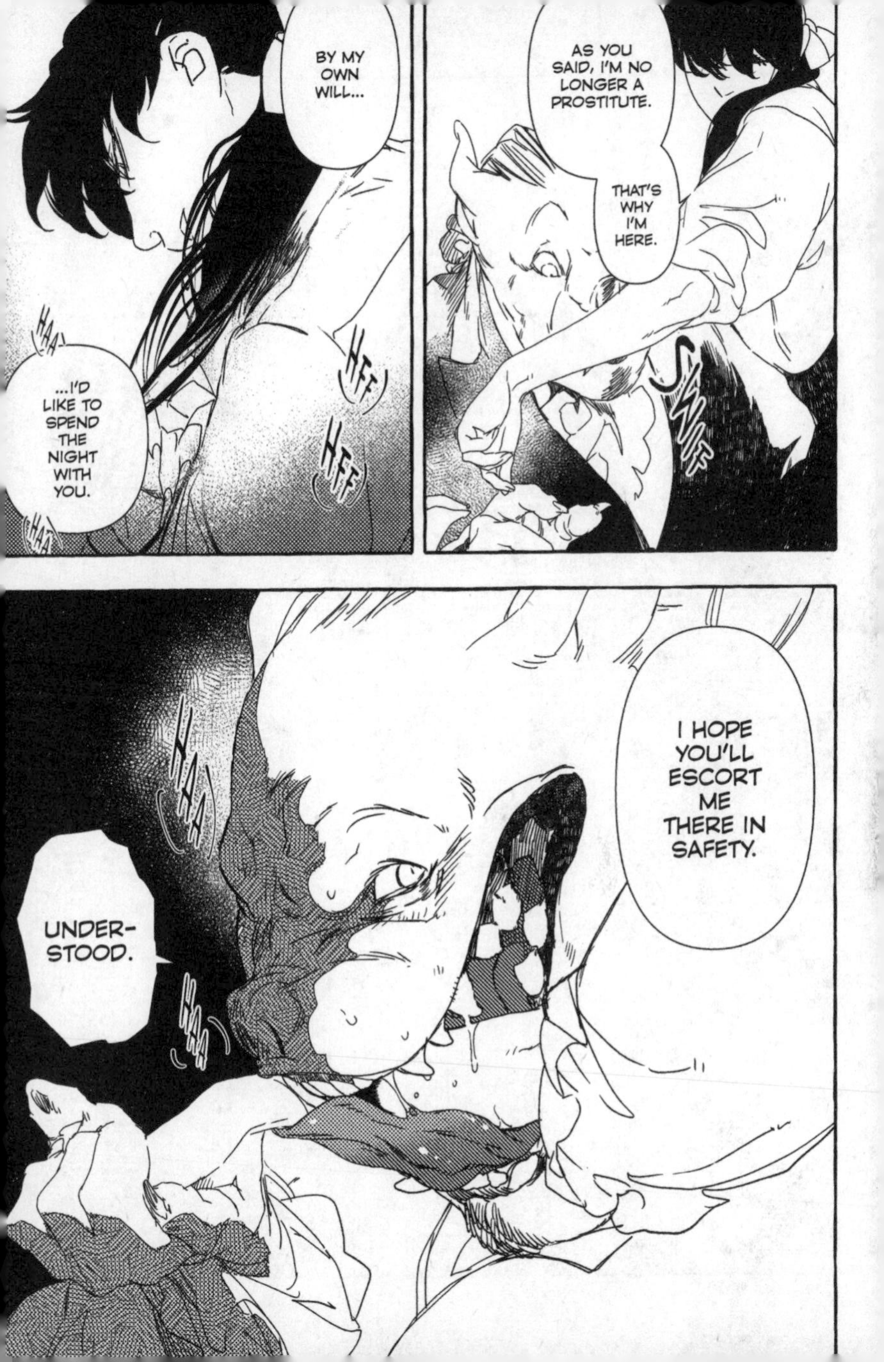
AS YOU SAID, I'M NO LONGER A PROSTITUTE.
THAT'S WHY I'M HERE.
SNIFF
BY MY OWN WILL...
HAA
HFF
HFF
...I'D LIKE TO SPEND THE NIGHT WITH YOU.
HAA
I HOPE YOU'LL ESCORT ME THERE IN SAFETY.
HAA
UNDER-STOOD.
HAA

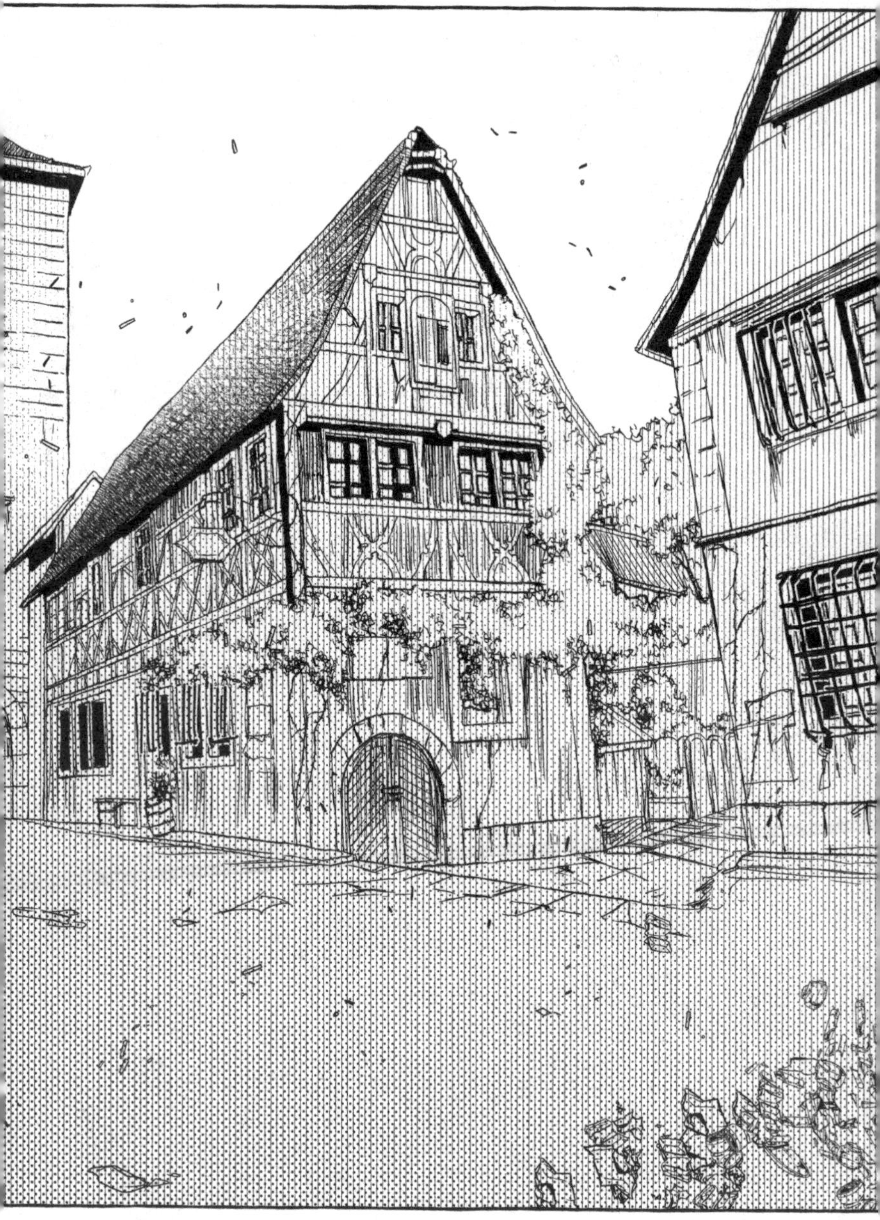

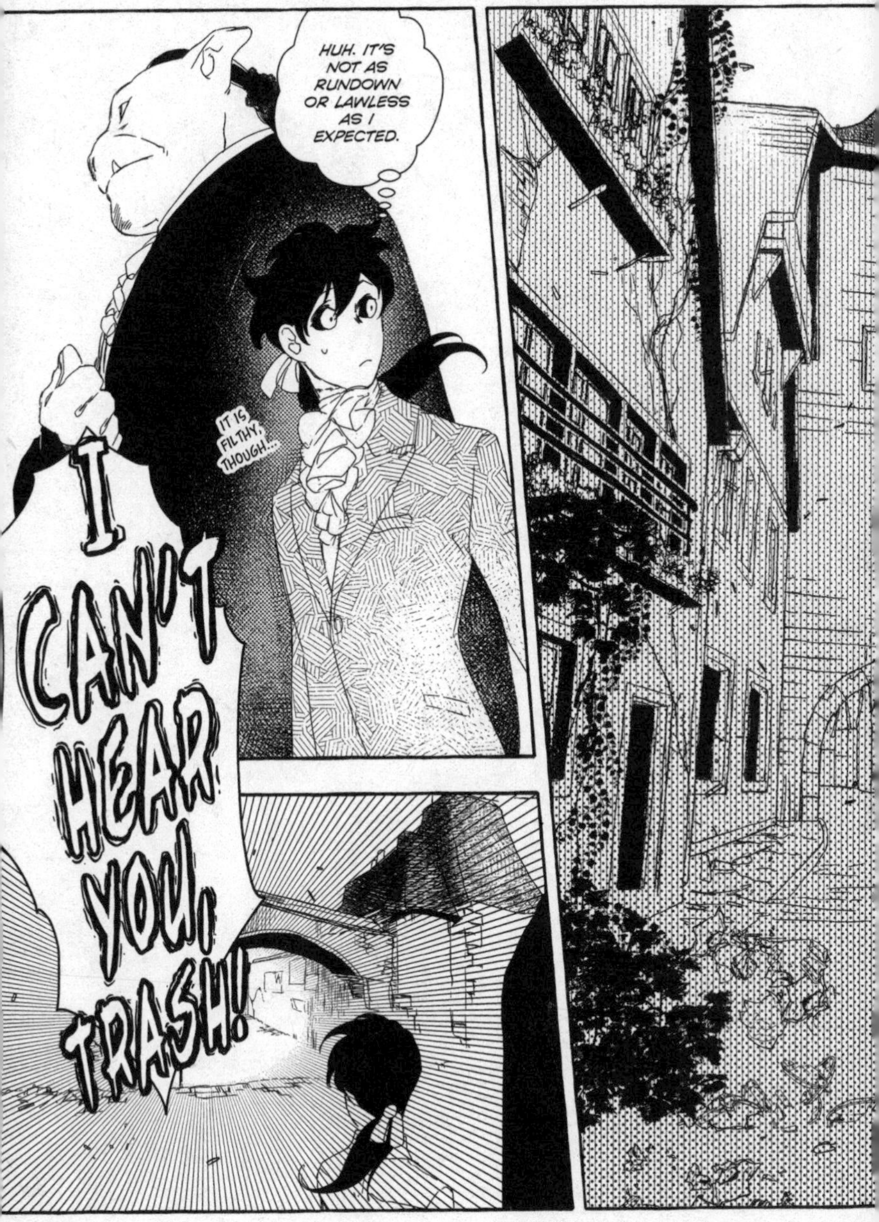
HUH. IT'S NOT AS RUNDOWN OR LAWLESS AS I EXPECTED.
IT IS FILTHY, THOUGH...
I CAN'T HEAR YOU, TRASH!

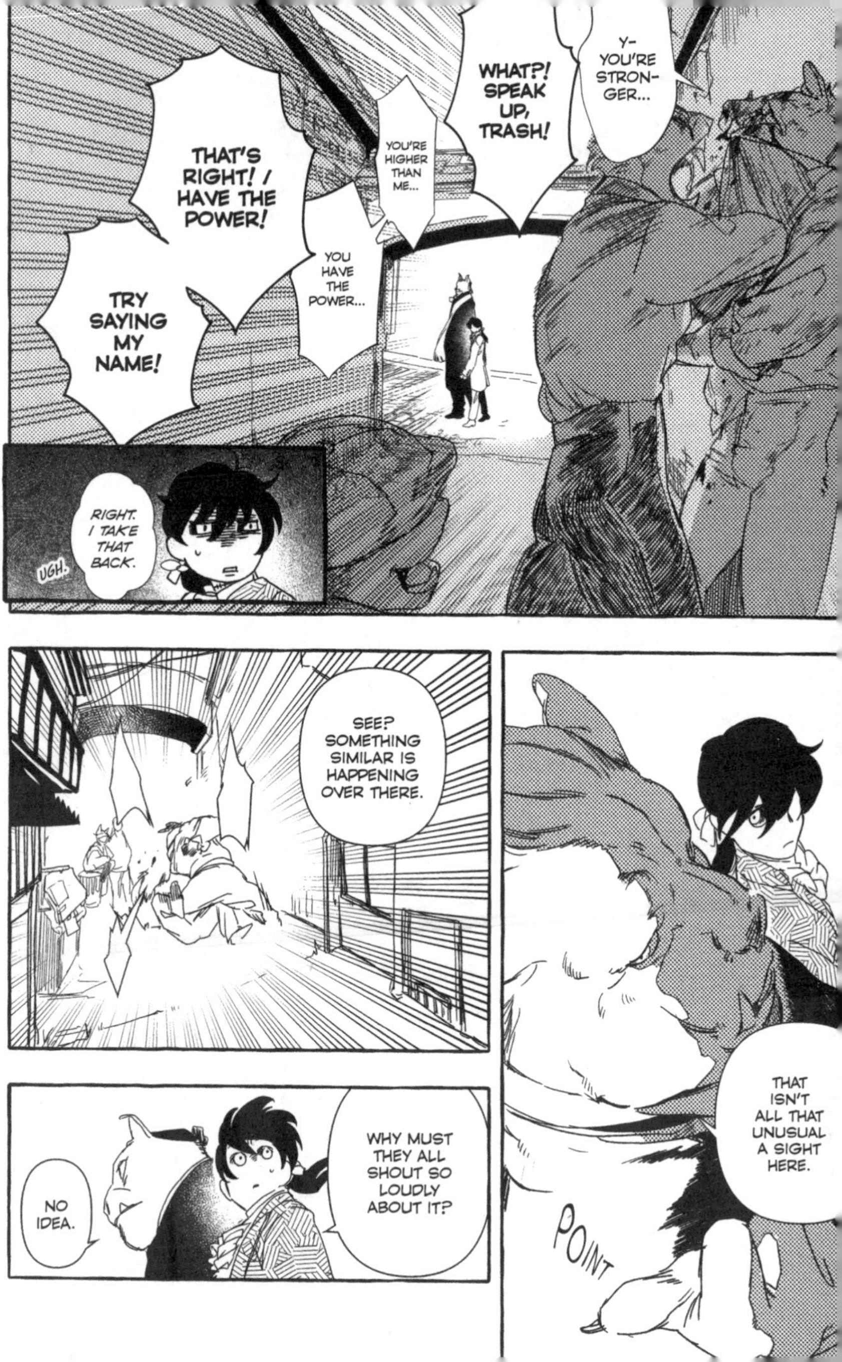
Y-YOU'RE STRONGER...
WHAT?! SPEAK UP, TRASH!
YOU'RE HIGHER THAN ME...
YOU HAVE THE POWER...
THAT'S RIGHT! I HAVE THE POWER!
TRY SAYING MY NAME!
RIGHT. I TAKE THAT BACK.
UGH.
THAT ISN'T ALL THAT UNUSUAL A SIGHT HERE.
POINT
SEE? SOMETHING SIMILAR IS HAPPENING OVER THERE.
WHY MUST THEY ALL SHOUT SO LOUDLY ABOUT IT?
NO IDEA.

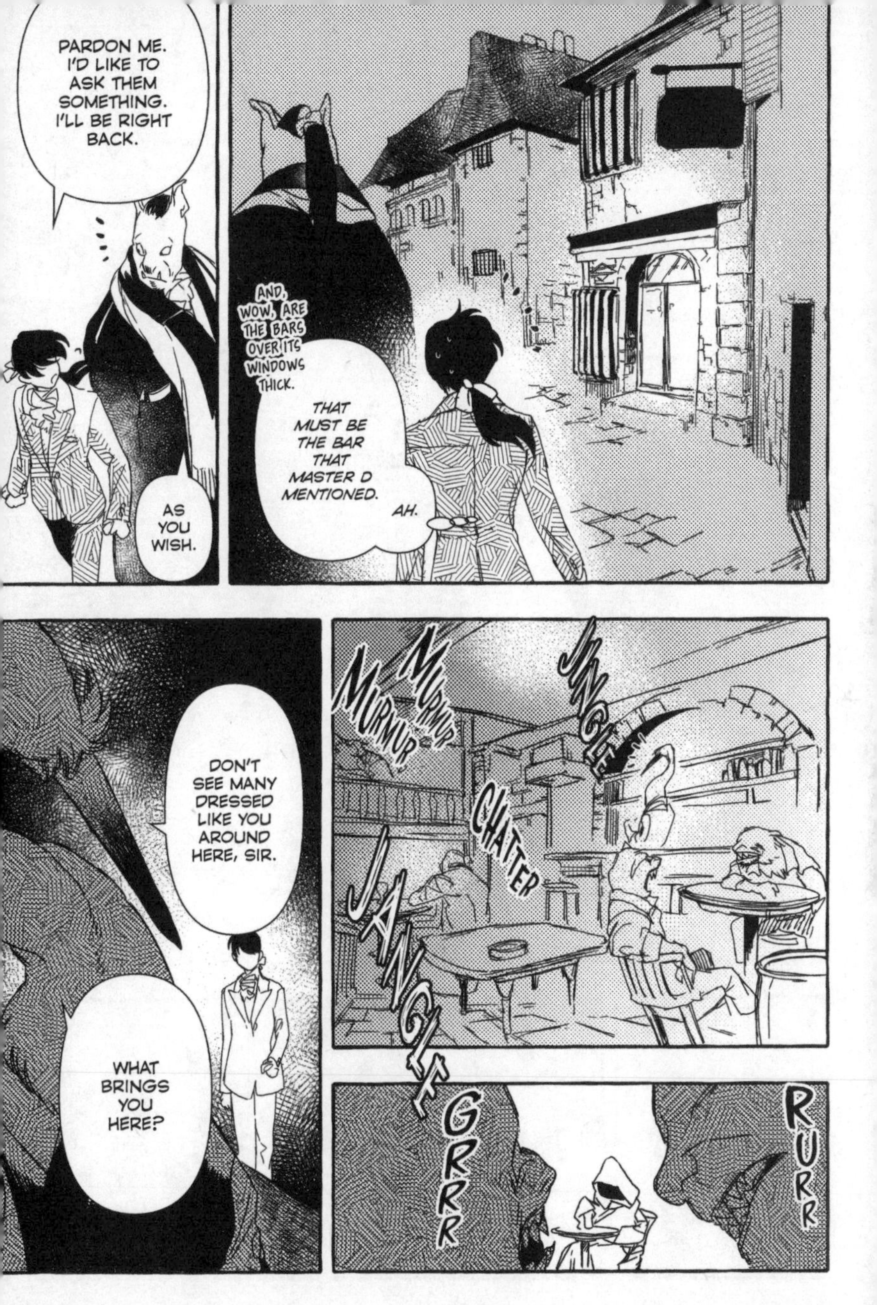
THAT MUST BE THE BAR THAT MASTER D MENTIONED.
AND, WOW, ARE THE BARS OVER ITS WINDOWS THICK.
AH.
PARDON ME. I'D LIKE TO ASK THEM SOMETHING. I'LL BE RIGHT BACK.
AS YOU WISH.
JANGLE
MURMUR MURMUR
CHATTER
JANGLE
RURR
GRRR
DON'T SEE MANY DRESSED LIKE YOU AROUND HERE, SIR.
WHAT BRINGS YOU HERE?

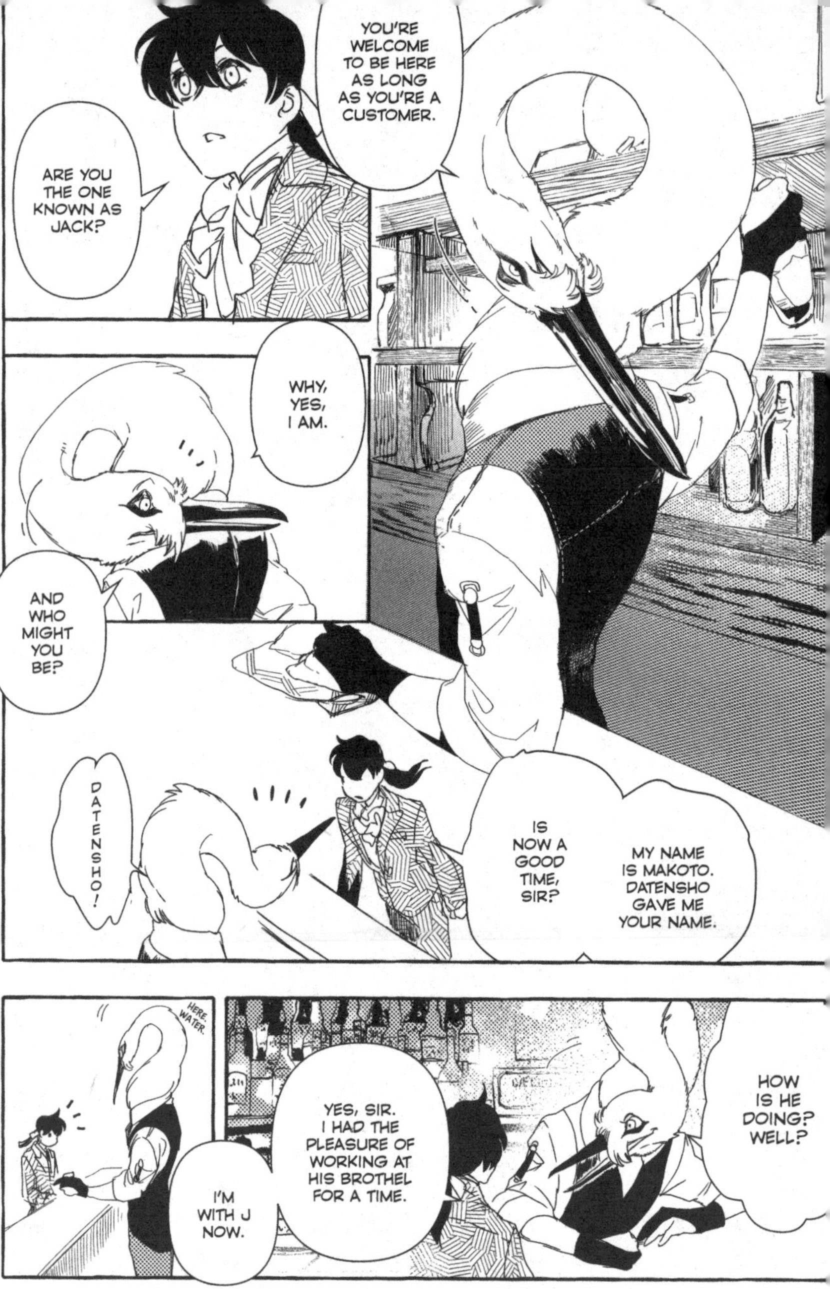
YOU'RE WELCOME TO BE HERE AS LONG AS YOU'RE A CUSTOMER.
ARE YOU THE ONE KNOWN AS JACK?
WHY, YES, I AM.
AND WHO MIGHT YOU BE?
MY NAME IS MAKOTO. DATENSHO GAVE ME YOUR NAME.
IS NOW A GOOD TIME, SIR?
DATENSHO!
HOW IS HE DOING? WELL?
YES, SIR. I HAD THE PLEASURE OF WORKING AT HIS BROTHEL FOR A TIME.
I'M WITH J NOW.
HERE. WATER.

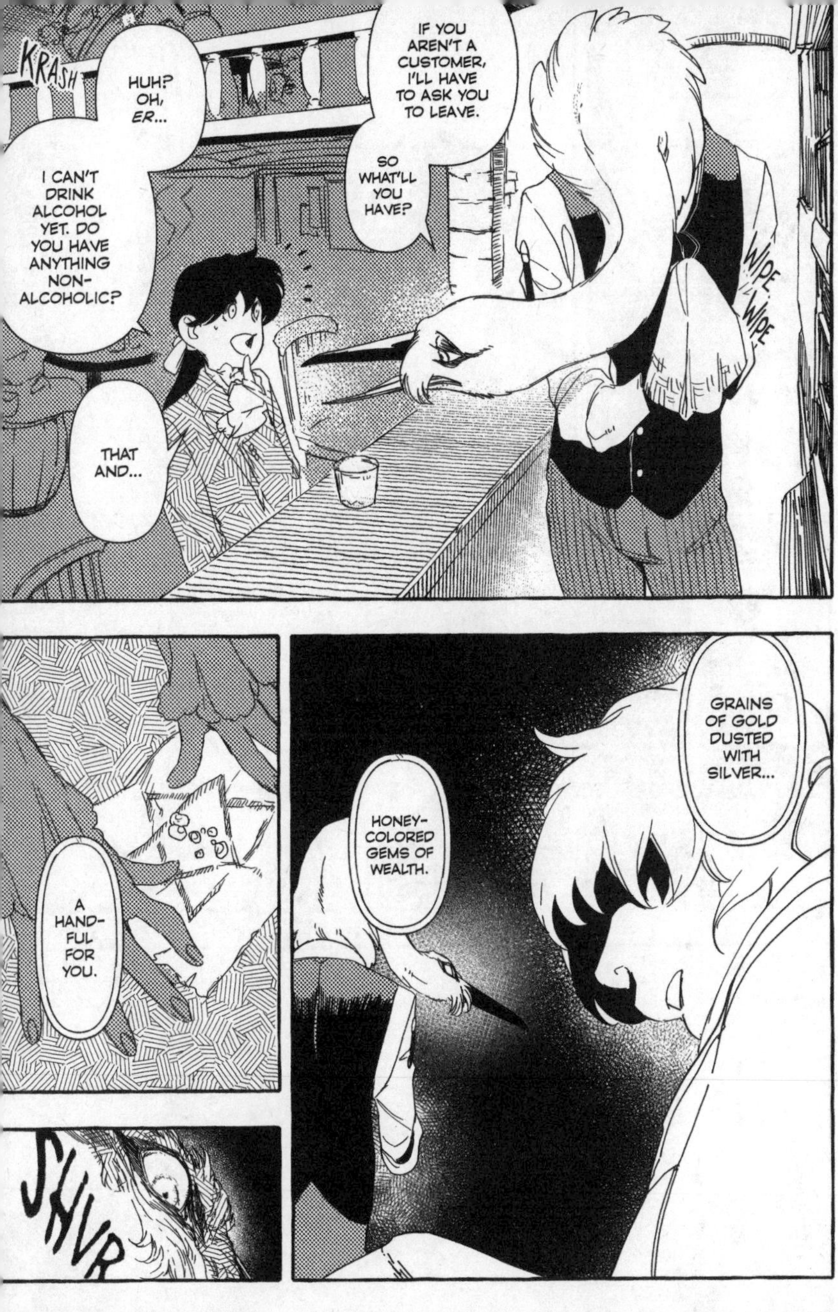
IF YOU AREN'T A CUSTOMER, I'LL HAVE TO ASK YOU TO LEAVE.
SO WHAT'LL YOU HAVE?
WIPE WIPE
KRASH
HUH? OH, ER...
I CAN'T DRINK ALCOHOL YET. DO YOU HAVE ANYTHING NON-ALCOHOLIC?
THAT AND...
GRAINS OF GOLD DUSTED WITH SILVER...
HONEY-COLORED GEMS OF WEALTH.
A HANDFUL FOR YOU.
SHIVR

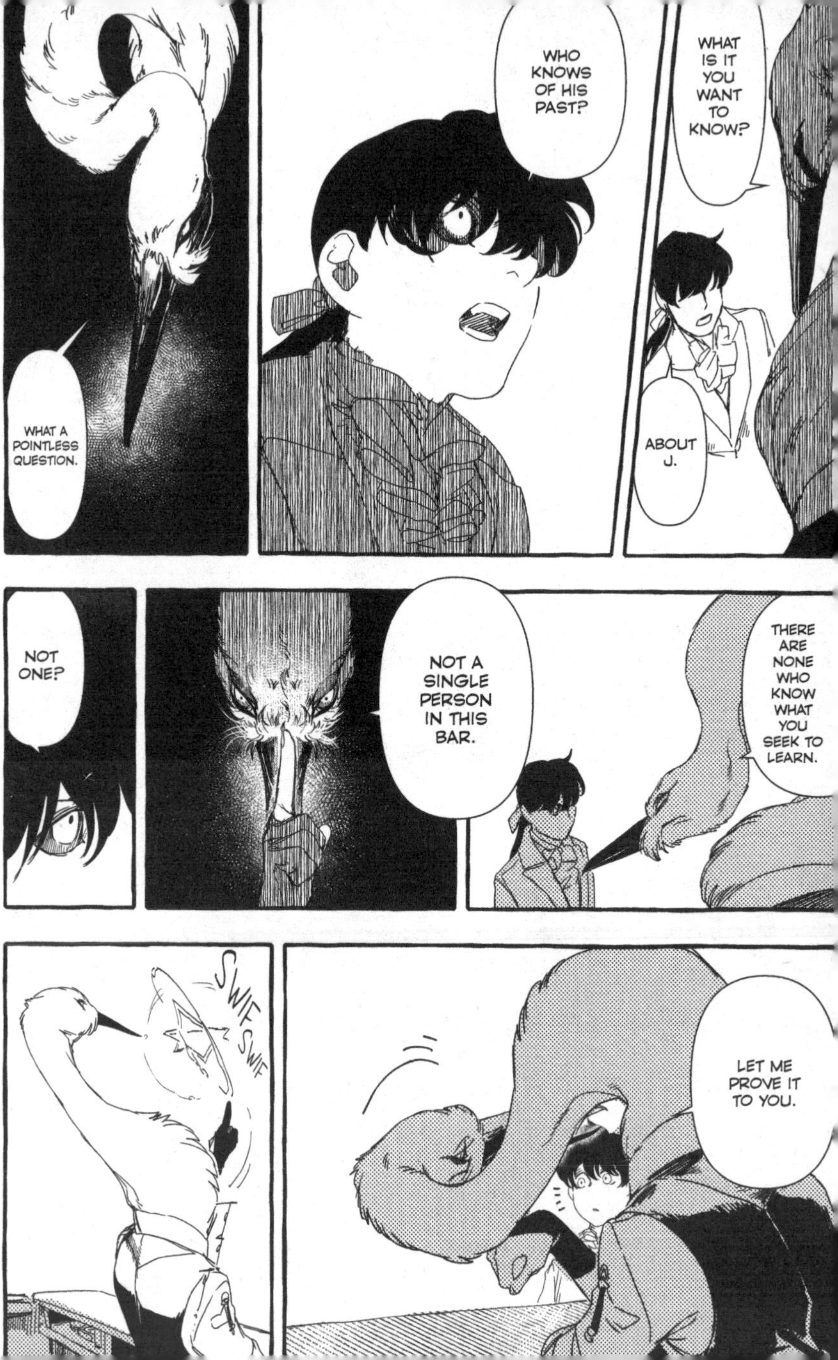
WHAT IS IT YOU WANT TO KNOW?
ABOUT J.
WHO KNOWS OF HIS PAST?
WHAT A POINTLESS QUESTION.
THERE ARE NONE WHO KNOW WHAT YOU SEEK TO LEARN.
NOT A SINGLE PERSON IN THIS BAR.
NOT ONE?
LET ME PROVE IT TO YOU.
SWIF SWIF

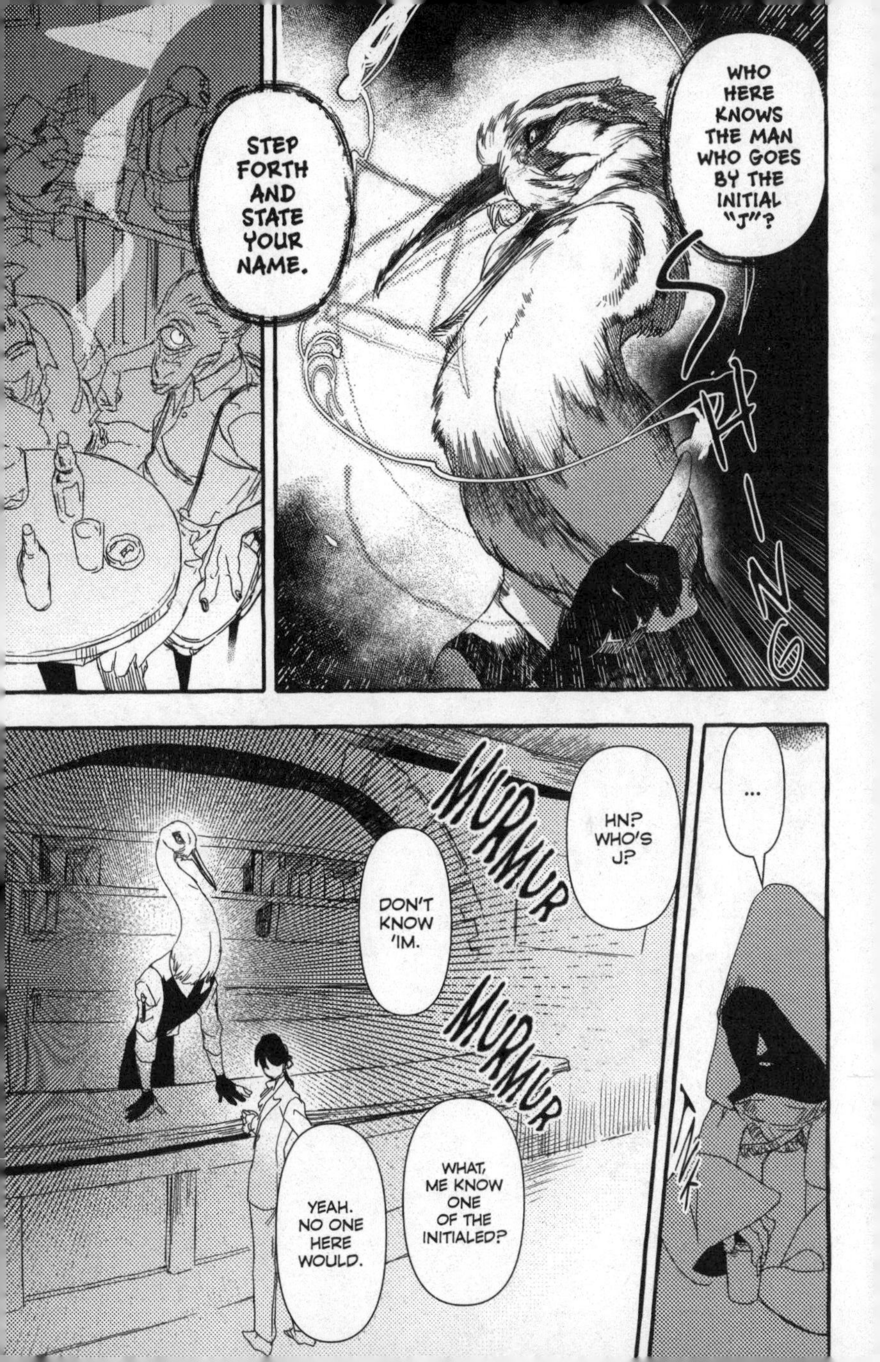
WHO HERE KNOWS THE MAN WHO GOES BY THE INITIAL "J"?
SHI—NG
STEP FORTH AND STATE YOUR NAME.
...
TINK
HN? WHO'S J?
MURMUR
DON'T KNOW 'IM.
MURMUR
WHAT, ME KNOW ONE OF THE INITIALED?
YEAH. NO ONE HERE WOULD.

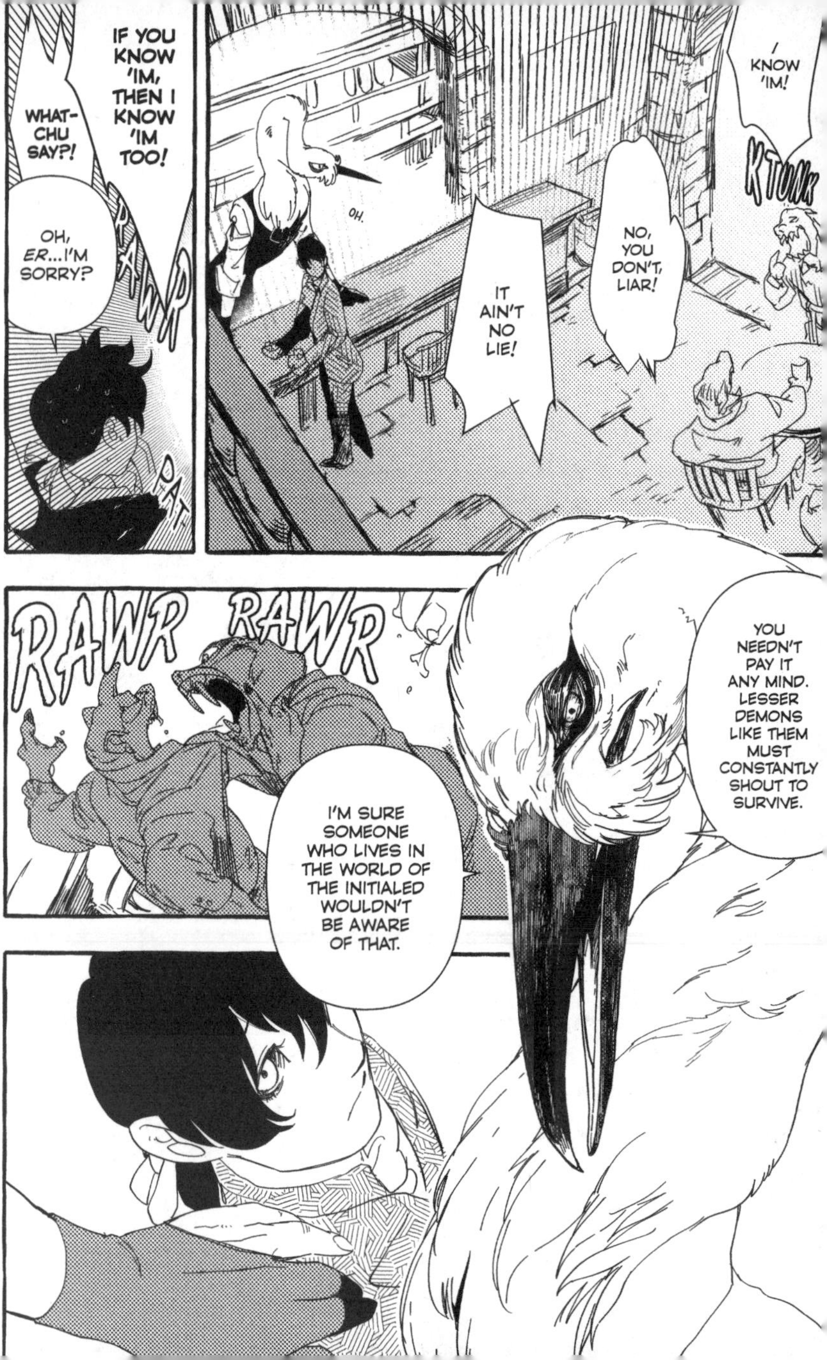
I KNOW 'IM!
KTUNK
NO, YOU DON'T, LIAR!
IT AIN'T NO LIE!
OH.
IF YOU KNOW 'IM, THEN I KNOW 'IM TOO!
WHAT-CHU SAY?!
RAWR
OH, ER...I'M SORRY?
PAT
YOU NEEDN'T PAY IT ANY MIND. LESSER DEMONS LIKE THEM MUST CONSTANTLY SHOUT TO SURVIVE.
RAWR RAWR
I'M SURE SOMEONE WHO LIVES IN THE WORLD OF THE INITIALED WOULDN'T BE AWARE OF THAT.

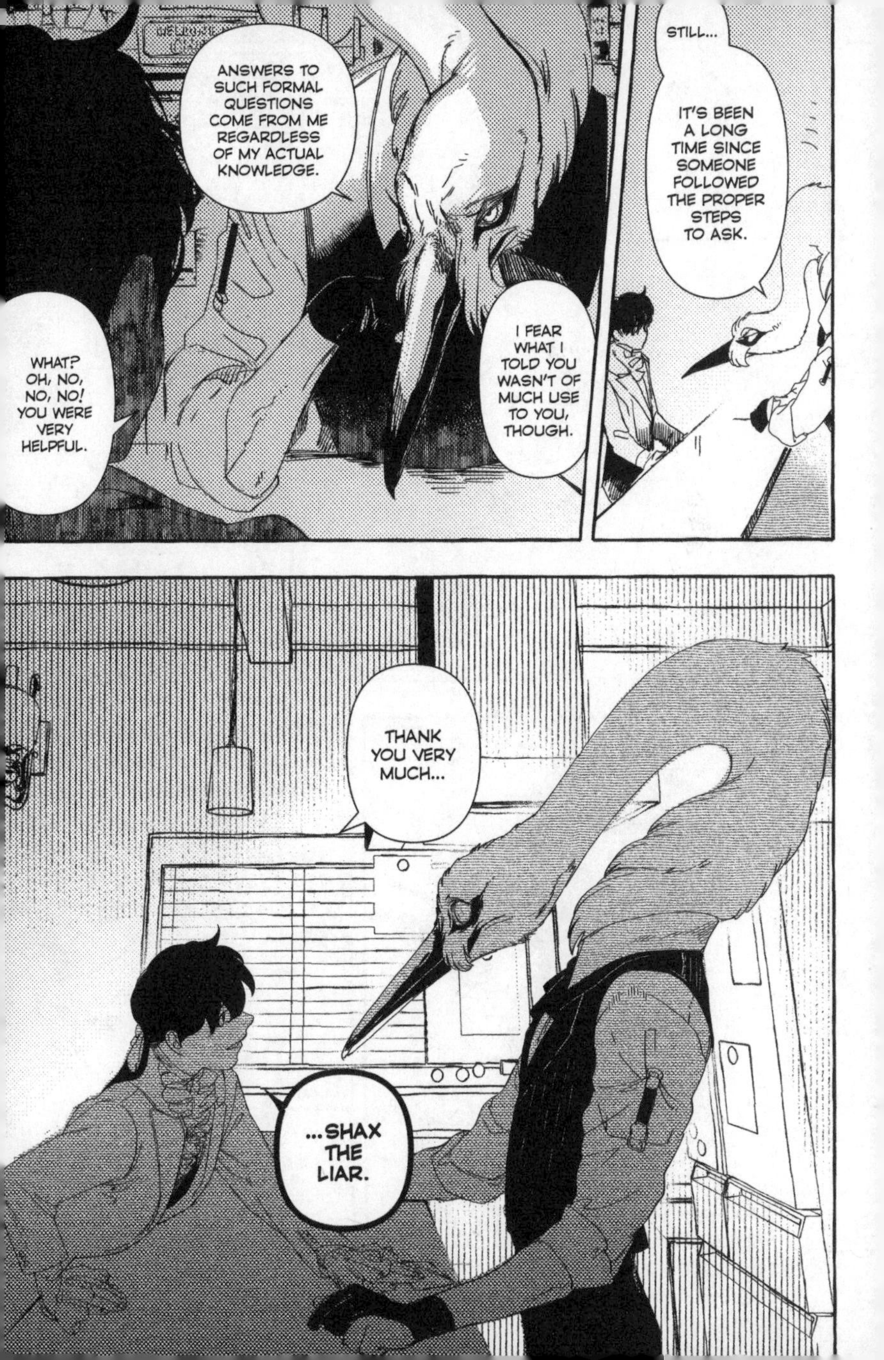
STILL...
IT'S BEEN A LONG TIME SINCE SOMEONE FOLLOWED THE PROPER STEPS TO ASK.
ANSWERS TO SUCH FORMAL QUESTIONS COME FROM ME REGARDLESS OF MY ACTUAL KNOWLEDGE.
I FEAR WHAT I TOLD YOU WASN'T OF MUCH USE TO YOU, THOUGH.
WHAT? OH, NO, NO, NO! YOU WERE VERY HELPFUL.
THANK YOU VERY MUCH...
...SHAX THE LIAR.

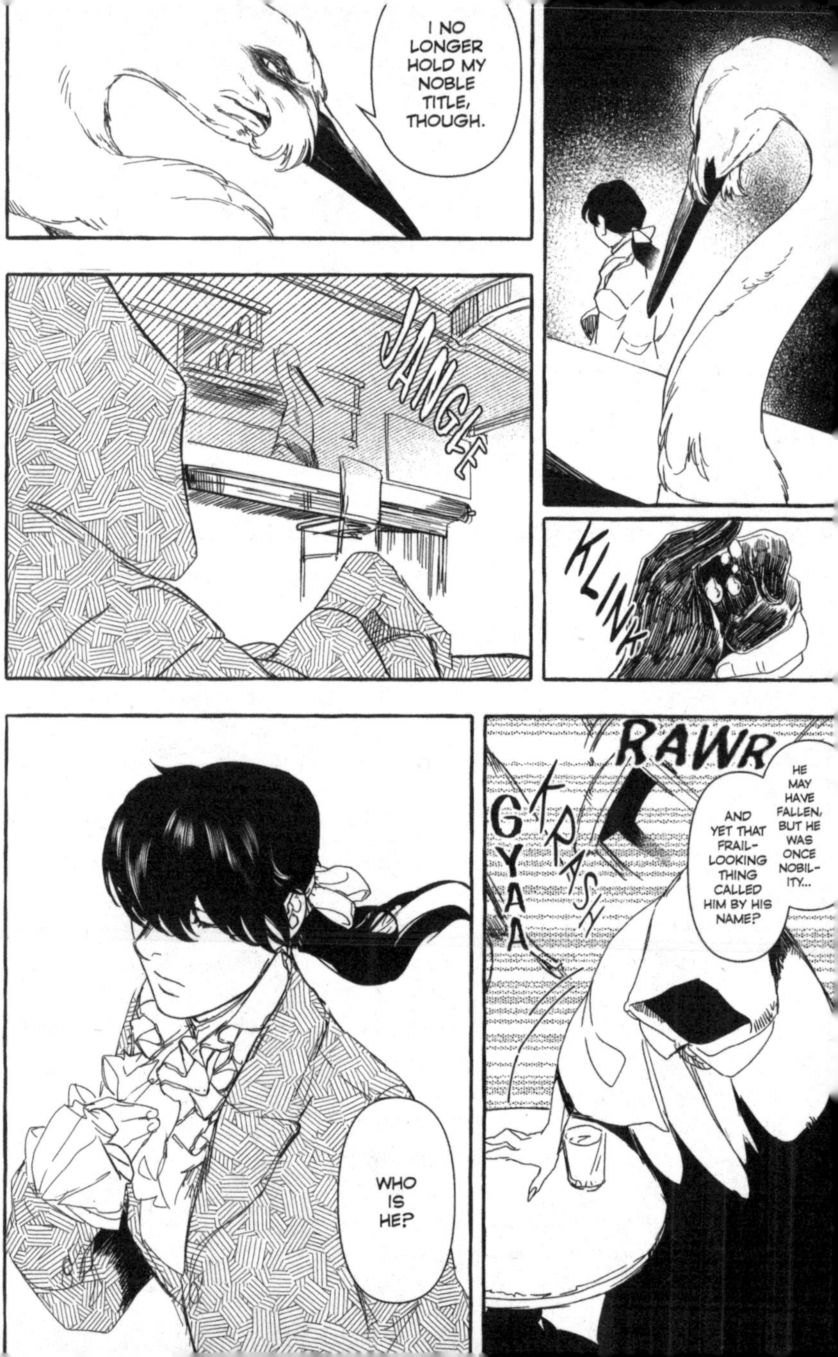
I NO LONGER HOLD MY NOBLE TITLE, THOUGH.
KLINK
JANGLE
RAWR
KRASH
GYAA
HE MAY HAVE FALLEN, BUT HE WAS ONCE NOBILITY...
AND YET THAT FRAIL-LOOKING THING CALLED HIM BY HIS NAME?
WHO IS HE?

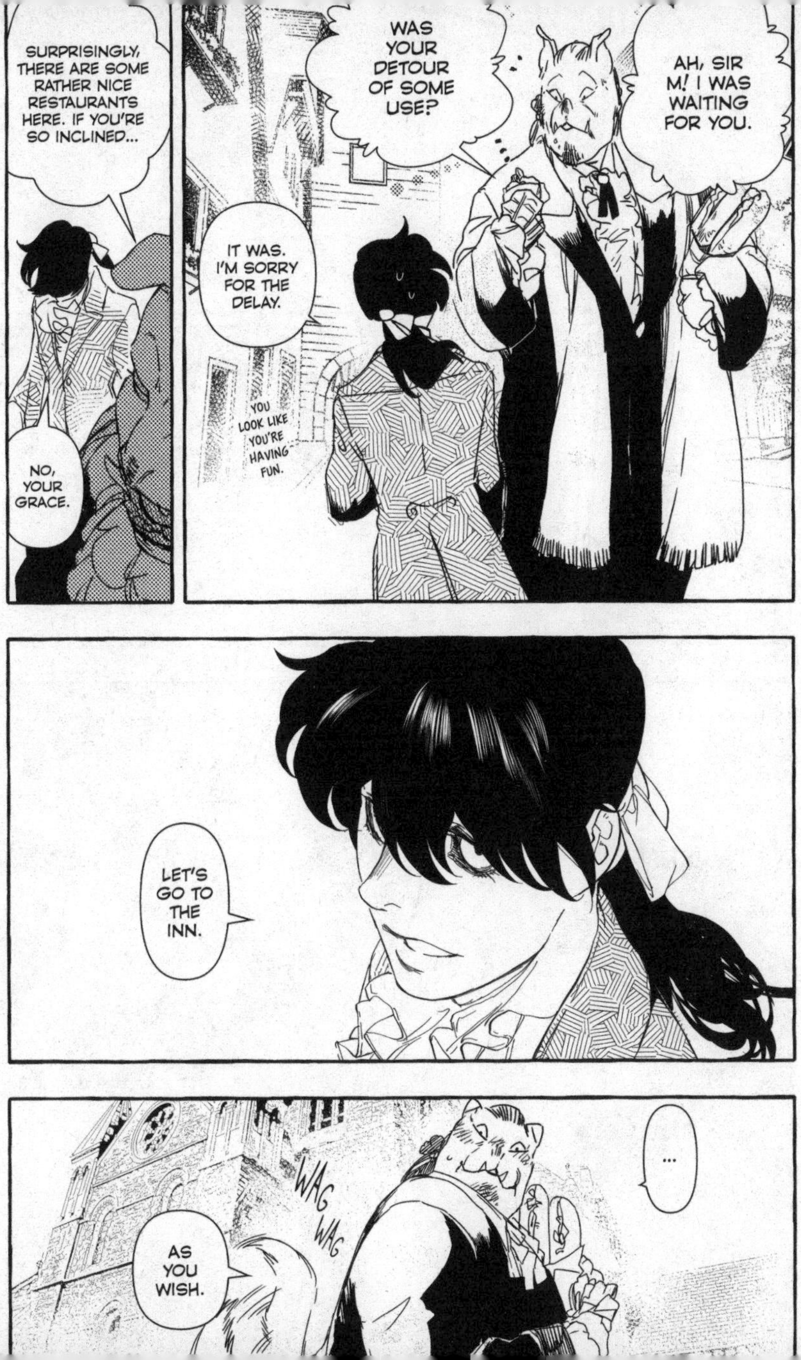
AH, SIR M! I WAS WAITING FOR YOU.
WAS YOUR DETOUR OF SOME USE?
IT WAS. I'M SORRY FOR THE DELAY.
YOU LOOK LIKE YOU'RE HAVING FUN.
SURPRISINGLY, THERE ARE SOME RATHER NICE RESTAURANTS HERE. IF YOU'RE SO INCLINED...
NO, YOUR GRACE.
LET'S GO TO THE INN.
...
WAG WAG
AS YOU WISH.

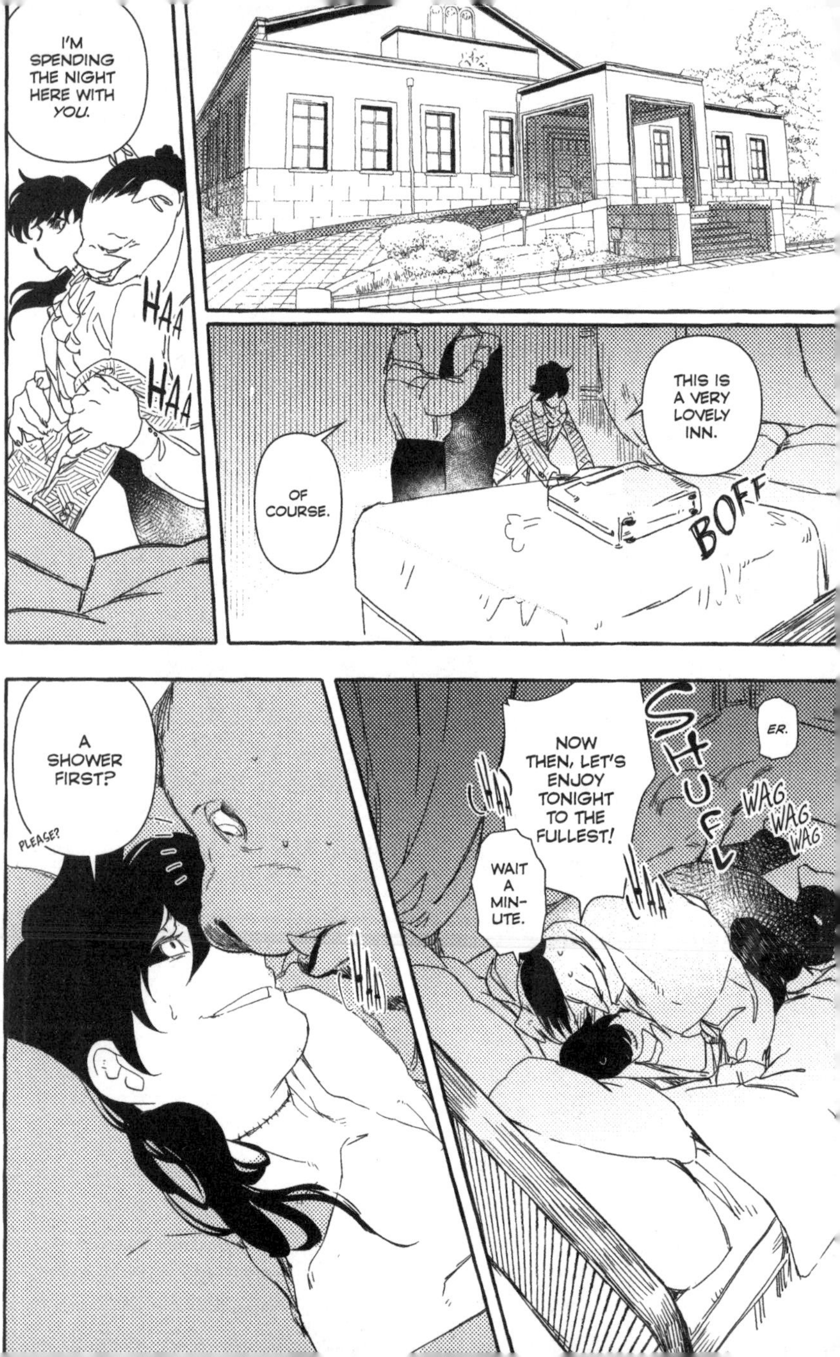
THIS IS A VERY LOVELY INN.
OF COURSE.
BOFF
I'M SPENDING THE NIGHT HERE WITH *YOU*.
HAA HAA
ER.
NOW THEN, LET'S ENJOY TONIGHT TO THE FULLEST!
SHUFFL
WAG WAG WAG
HAA
HAA
WAIT A MIN-UTE.
A SHOWER FIRST?
PLEASE?
HAA

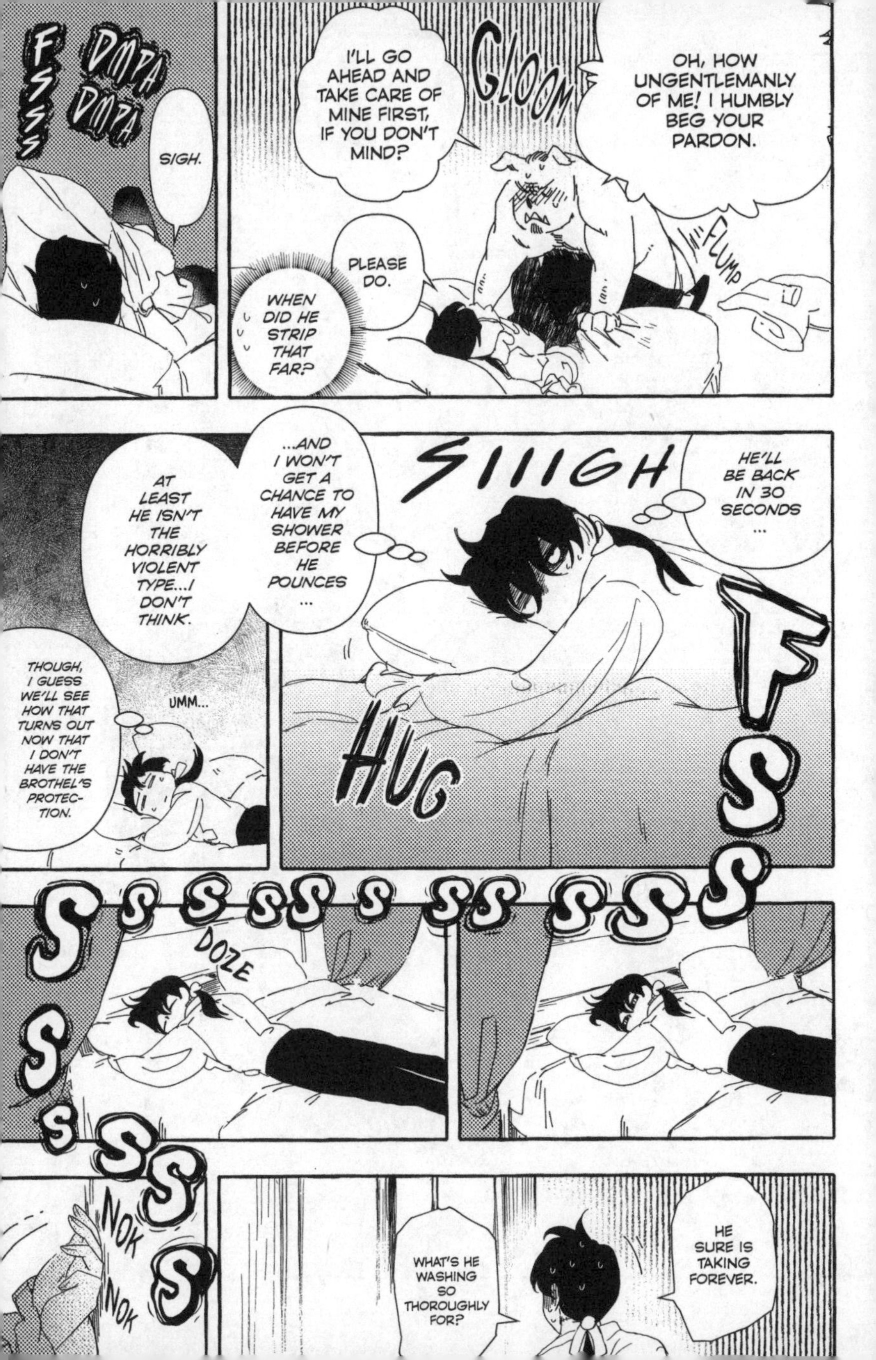
OH, HOW UNGENTLEMANLY OF ME! I HUMBLY BEG YOUR PARDON.
GLOOM
I'LL GO AHEAD AND TAKE CARE OF MINE FIRST, IF YOU DON'T MIND?
FLUMP
PLEASE DO.
WHEN DID HE STRIP THAT FAR?
FSSS
DMPA DMPA
SIGH.
HE'LL BE BACK IN 30 SECONDS ...
SIIIGH
...AND I WON'T GET A CHANCE TO HAVE MY SHOWER BEFORE HE POUNCES ...
HUG
AT LEAST HE ISN'T THE HORRIBLY VIOLENT TYPE...I DON'T THINK.
UMM...
THOUGH, I GUESS WE'LL SEE HOW THAT TURNS OUT NOW THAT I DON'T HAVE THE BROTHEL'S PROTECTION.
FSSSSSSSSSSSSSSSSSSSS
DOZE
HE SURE IS TAKING FOREVER.
WHAT'S HE WASHING SO THOROUGHLY FOR?
NOK
NOK

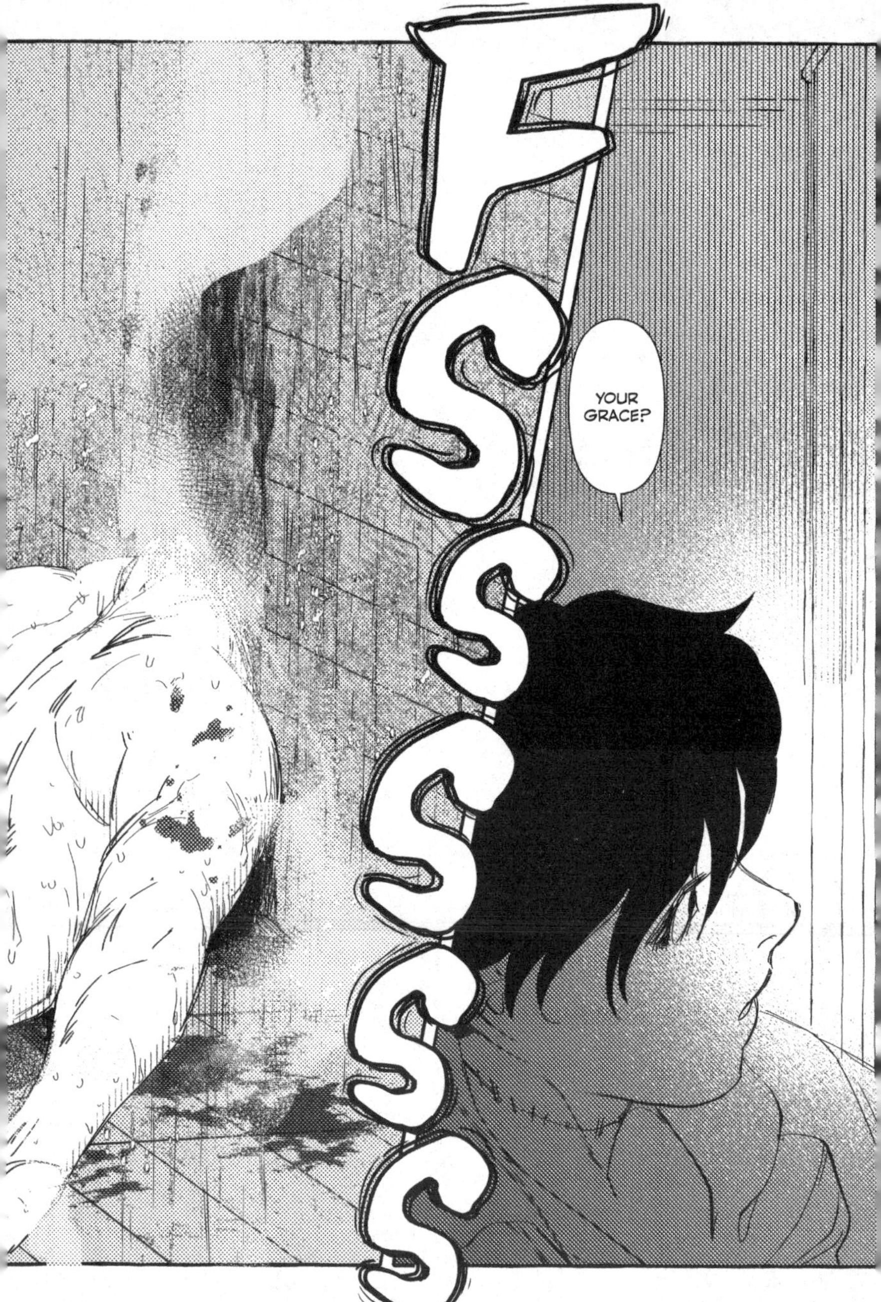
FSSSSSS
YOUR GRACE?

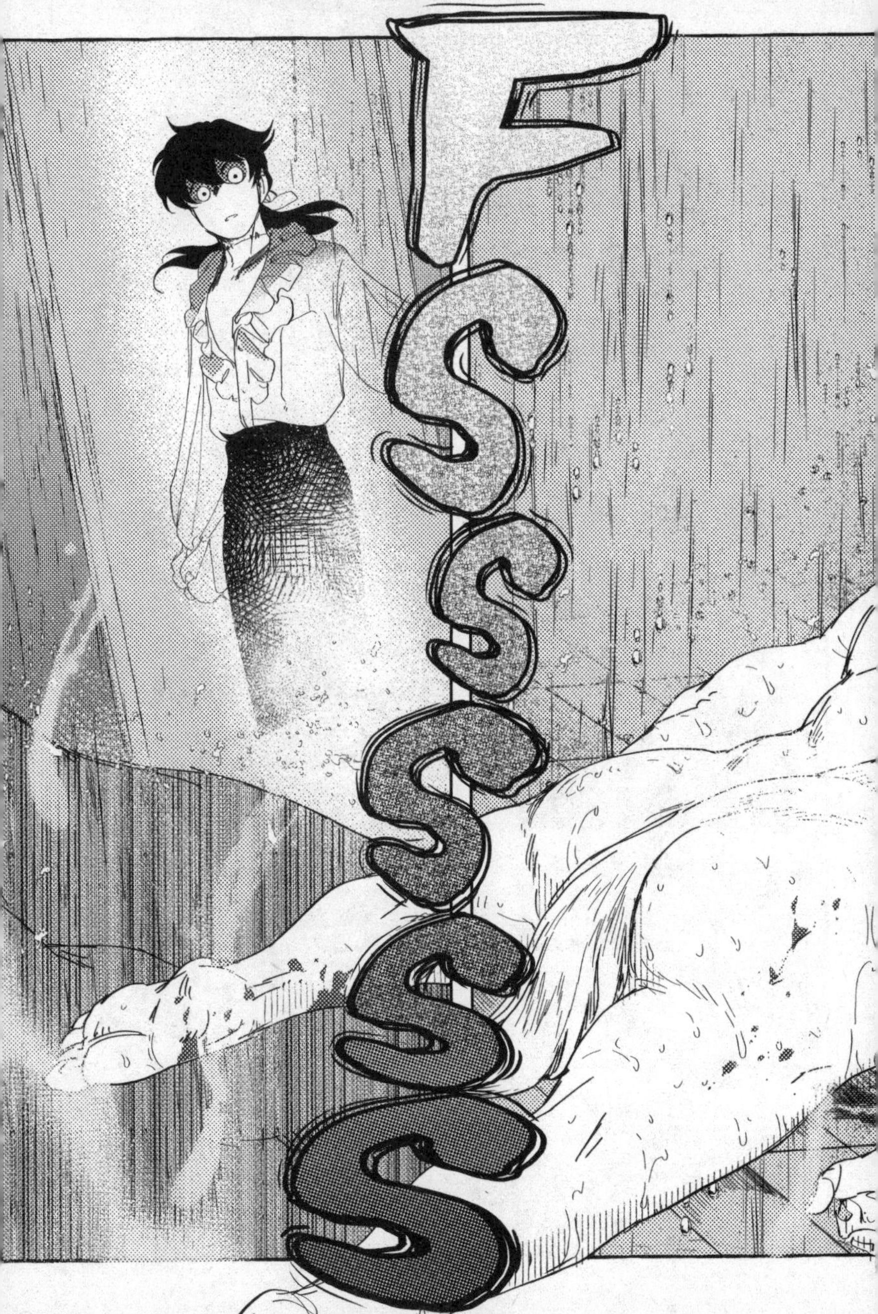
FSSSSS

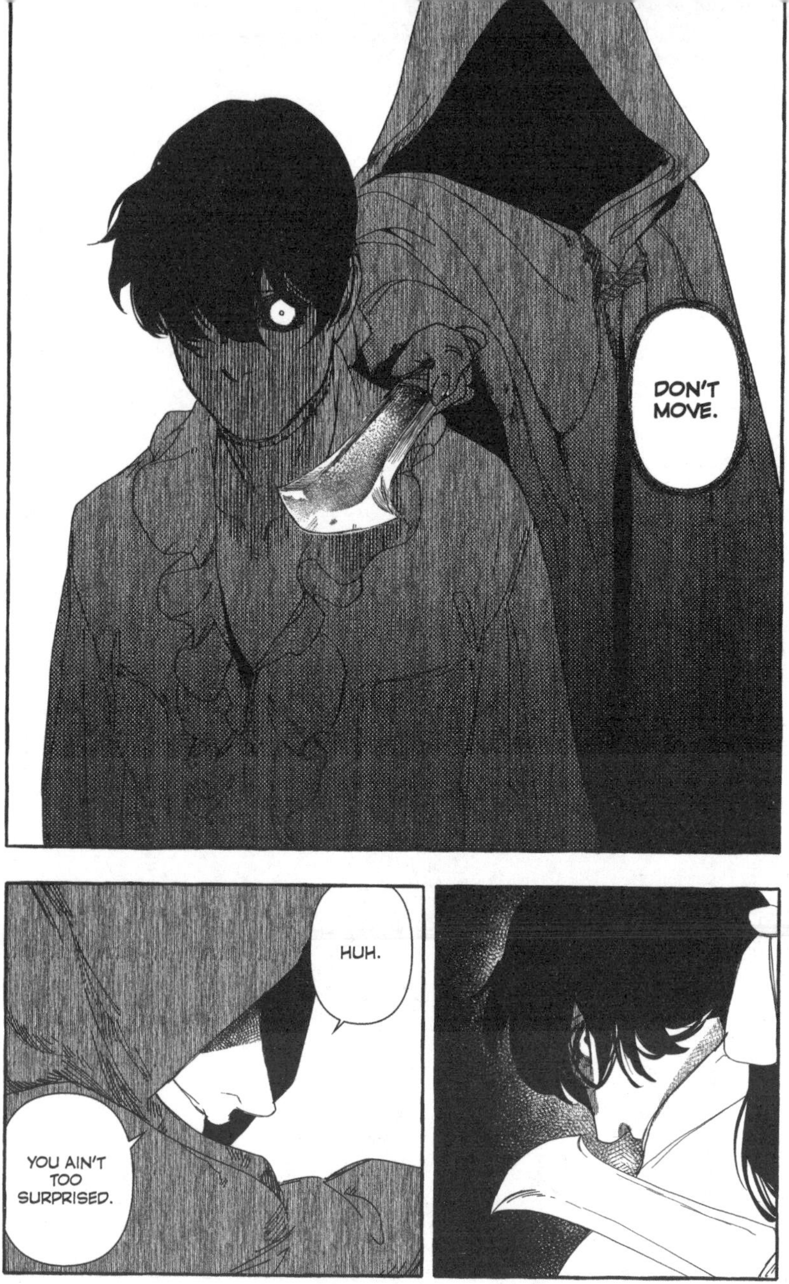
DON'T MOVE.
HUH.
YOU AIN'T TOO SURPRISED.

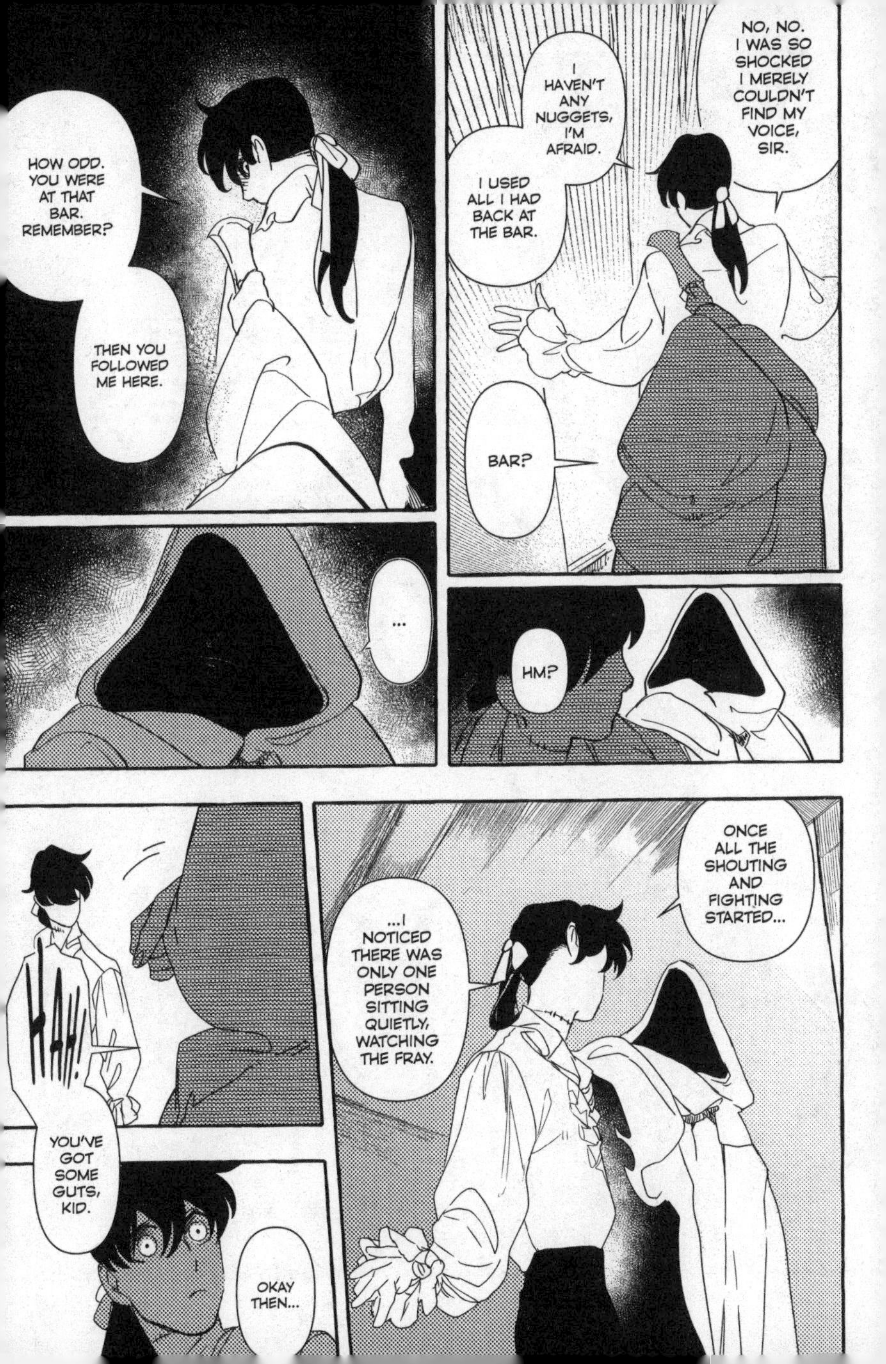
NO, NO. I WAS SO SHOCKED I MERELY COULDN'T FIND MY VOICE, SIR.
I HAVEN'T ANY NUGGETS, I'M AFRAID.
I USED ALL I HAD BACK AT THE BAR.
BAR?
HOW ODD. YOU WERE AT THAT BAR. REMEMBER?
THEN YOU FOLLOWED ME HERE.
HM?
...
ONCE ALL THE SHOUTING AND FIGHTING STARTED...
...I NOTICED THERE WAS ONLY ONE PERSON SITTING QUIETLY, WATCHING THE FRAY.
HAH!
YOU'VE GOT SOME GUTS, KID.
OKAY THEN...

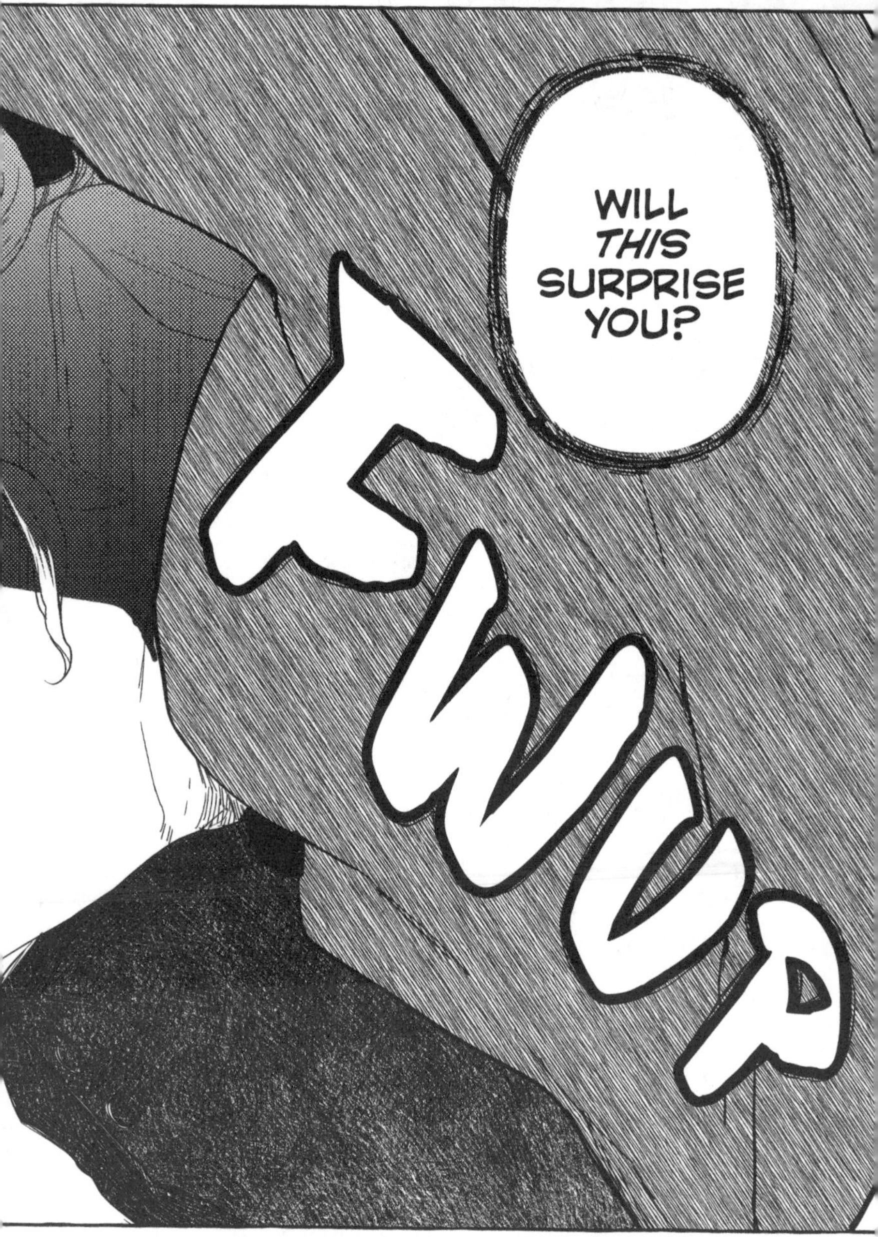
WILL *THIS* SURPRISE YOU?
FWUP

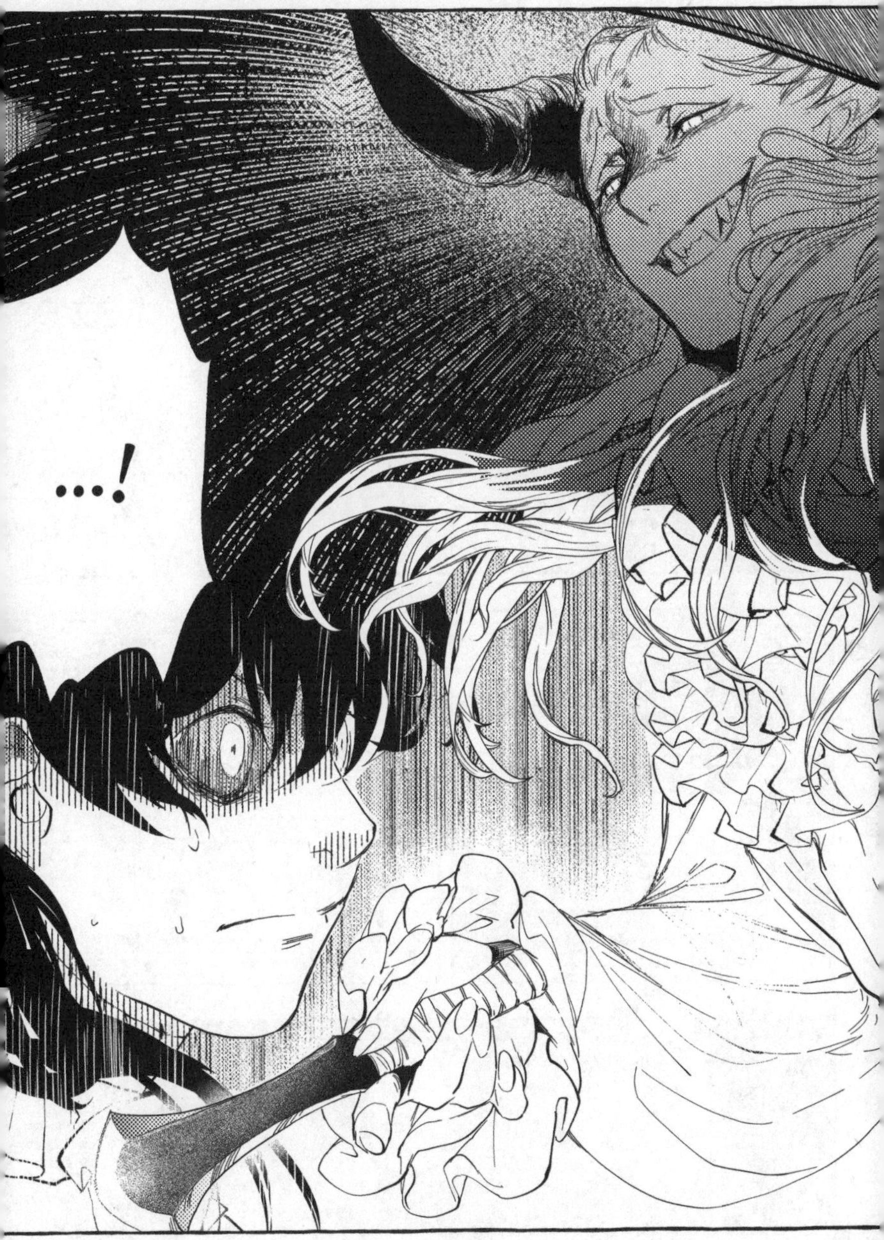
...!

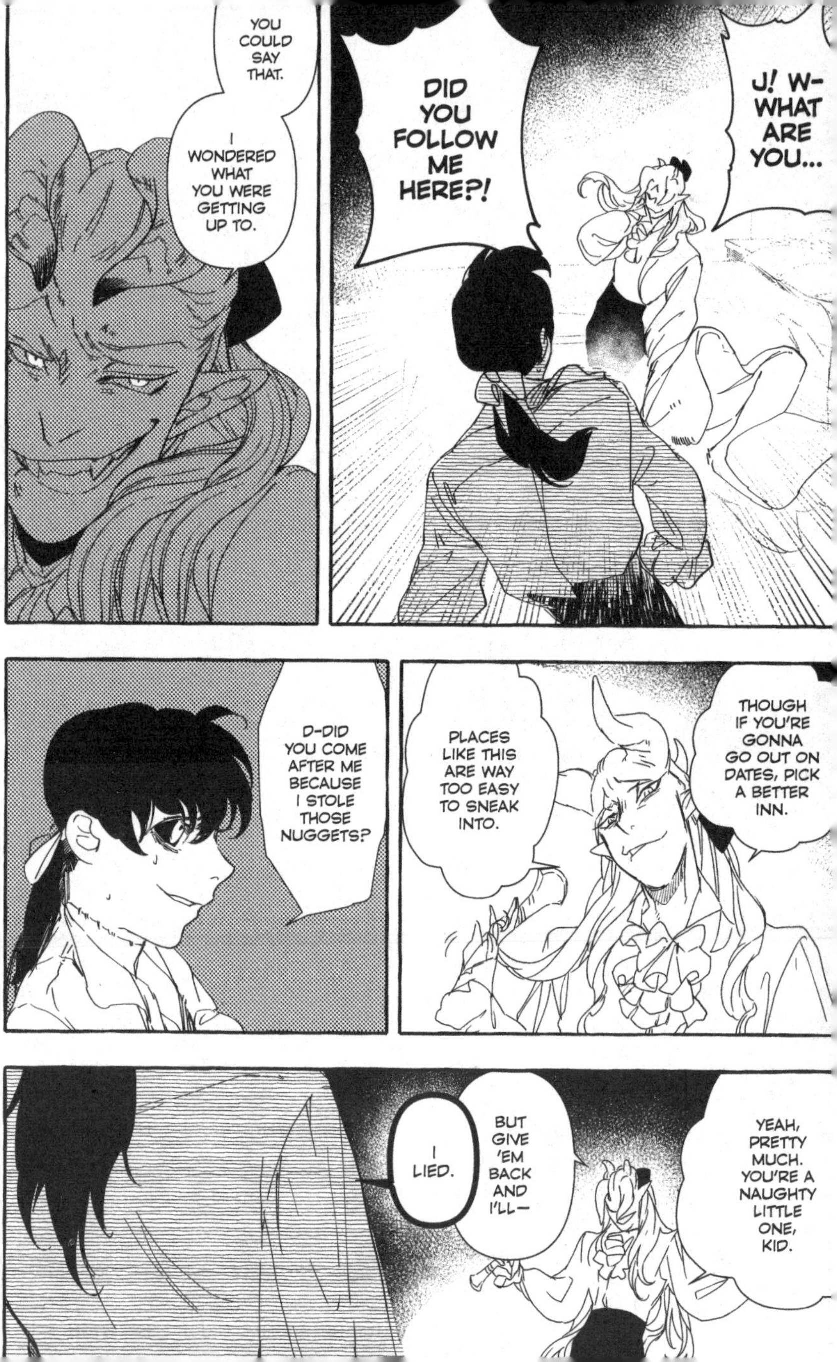
J! W-WHAT ARE YOU...
DID YOU FOLLOW ME HERE?!
YOU COULD SAY THAT.
I WONDERED WHAT YOU WERE GETTING UP TO.
THOUGH IF YOU'RE GONNA GO OUT ON DATES, PICK A BETTER INN.
PLACES LIKE THIS ARE WAY TOO EASY TO SNEAK INTO.
D-DID YOU COME AFTER ME BECAUSE I STOLE THOSE NUGGETS?
YEAH, PRETTY MUCH. YOU'RE A NAUGHTY LITTLE ONE, KID.
BUT GIVE 'EM BACK AND I'LL—
I LIED.

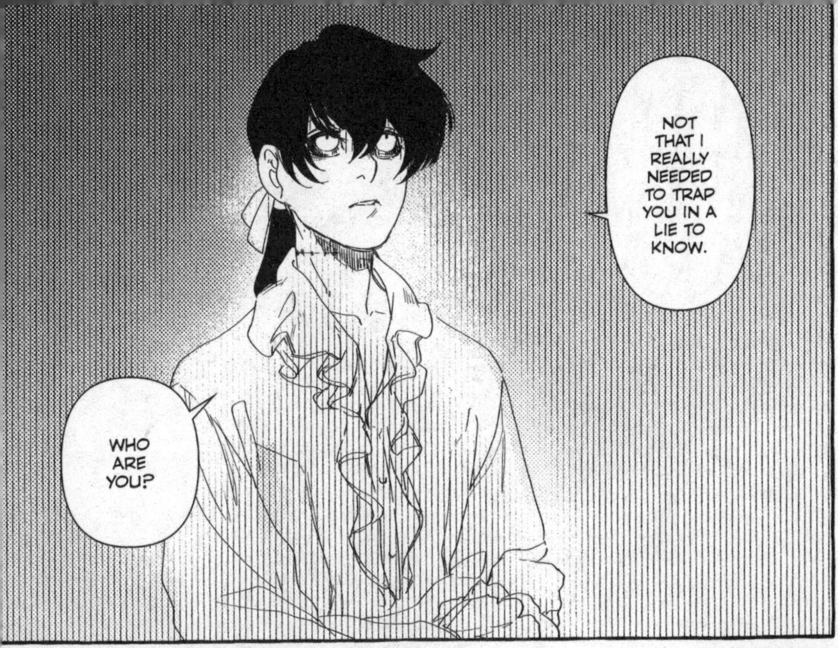
NOT THAT I REALLY NEEDED TO TRAP YOU IN A LIE TO KNOW.
WHO ARE YOU?
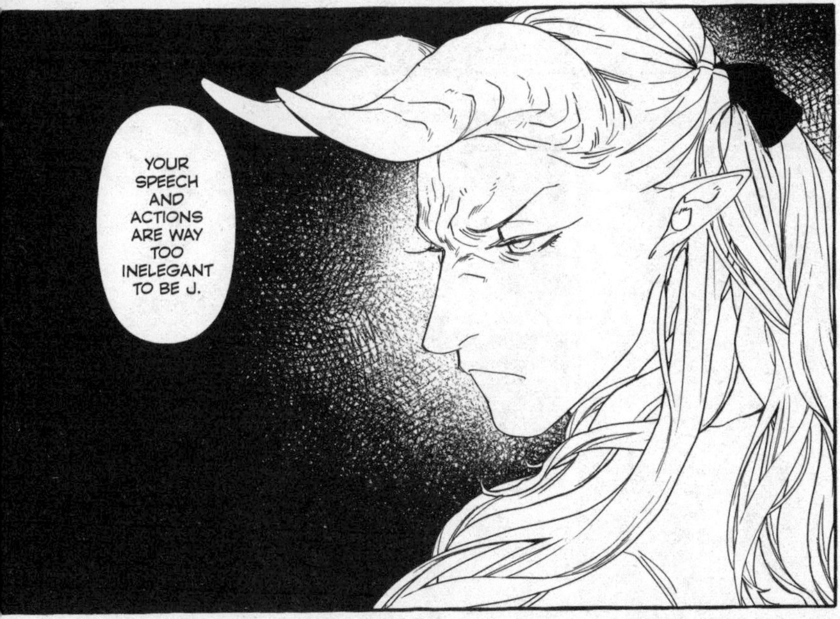
YOUR SPEECH AND ACTIONS ARE WAY TOO INELEGANT TO BE J.

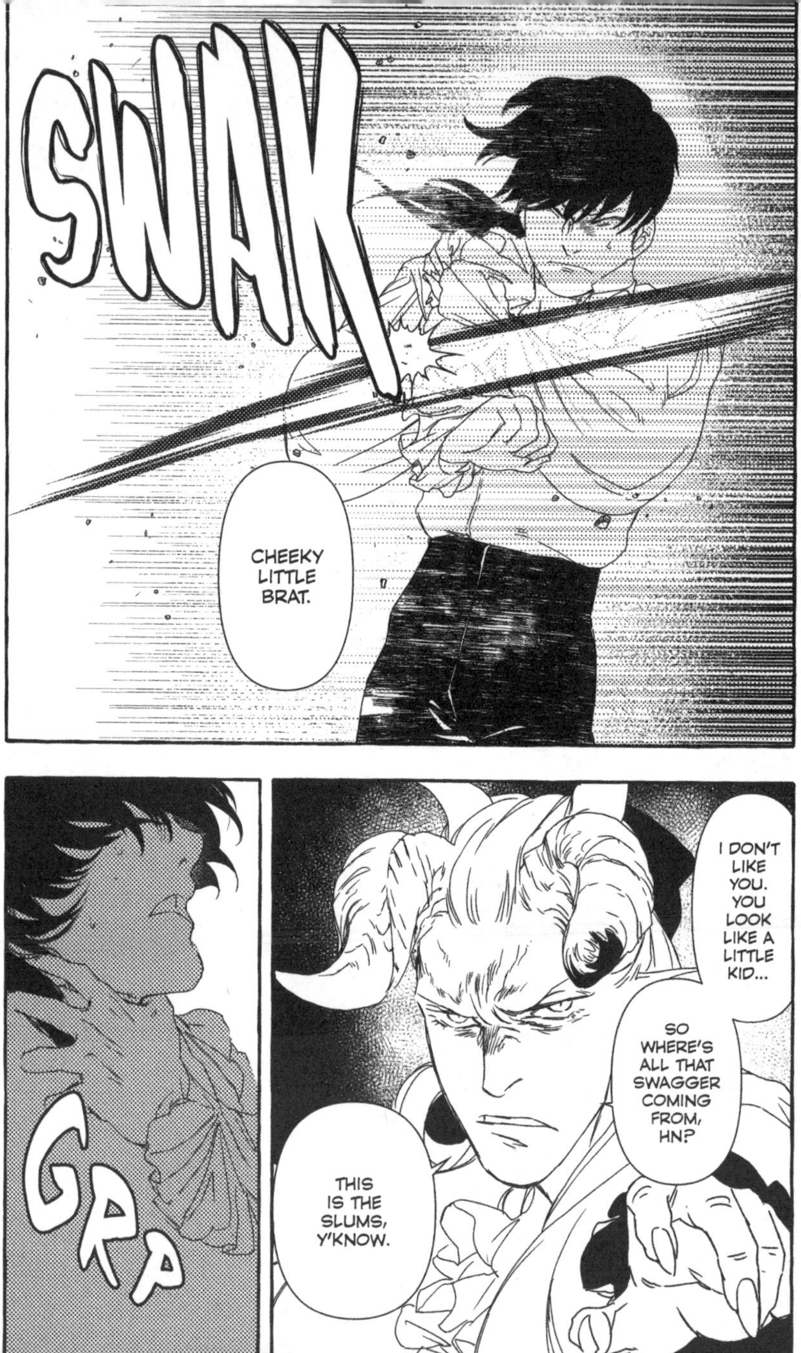
SWAK
CHEEKY LITTLE BRAT.
I DON'T LIKE YOU. YOU LOOK LIKE A LITTLE KID...
SO WHERE'S ALL THAT SWAGGER COMING FROM, HN?
THIS IS THE SLUMS, Y'KNOW.
GRP

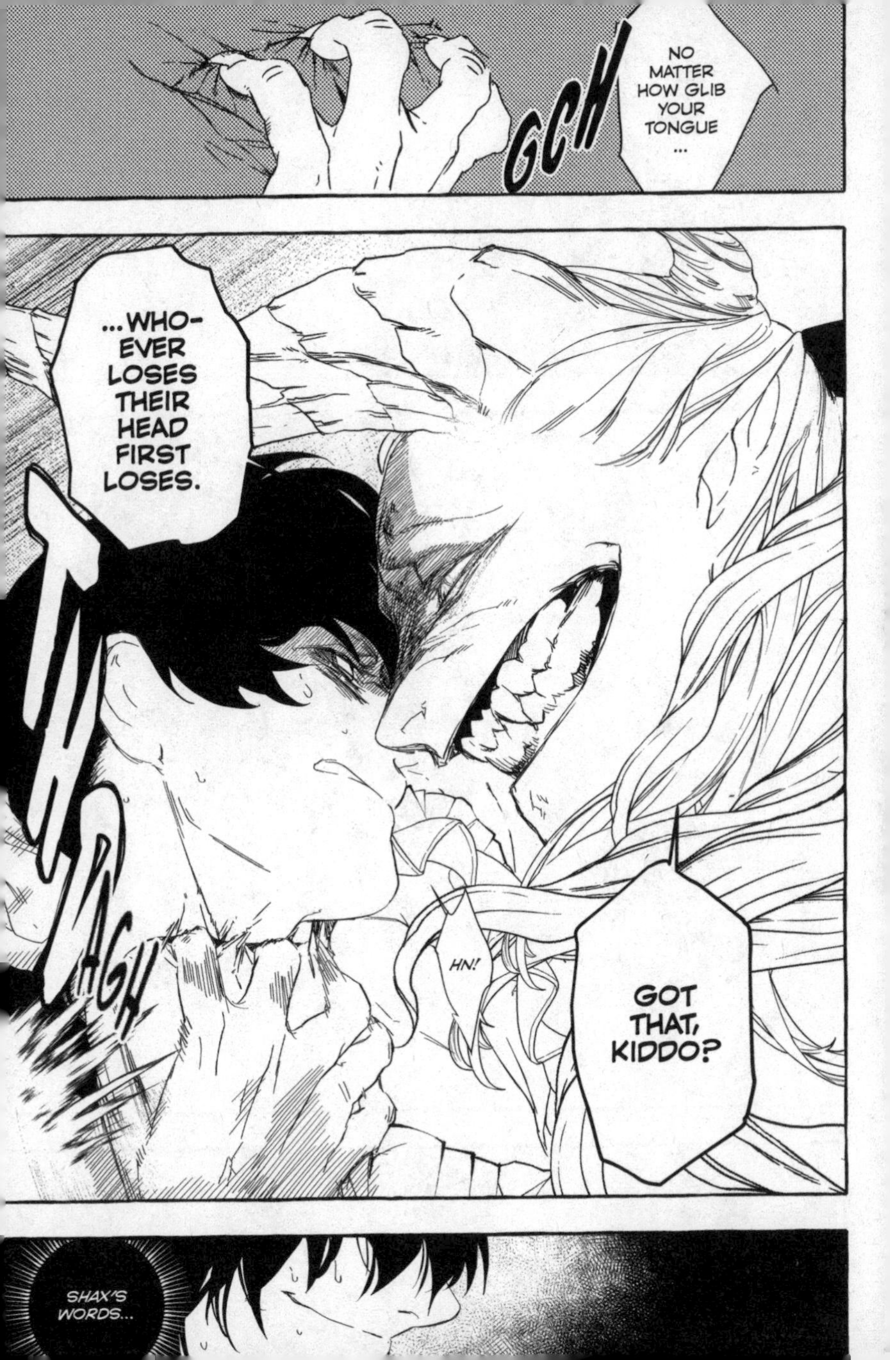
NO MATTER HOW GLIB YOUR TONGUE ...
GCH
...WHO-EVER LOSES THEIR HEAD FIRST LOSES.
HN!
GOT THAT, KIDDO?
THAGH
SHAX'S WORDS...

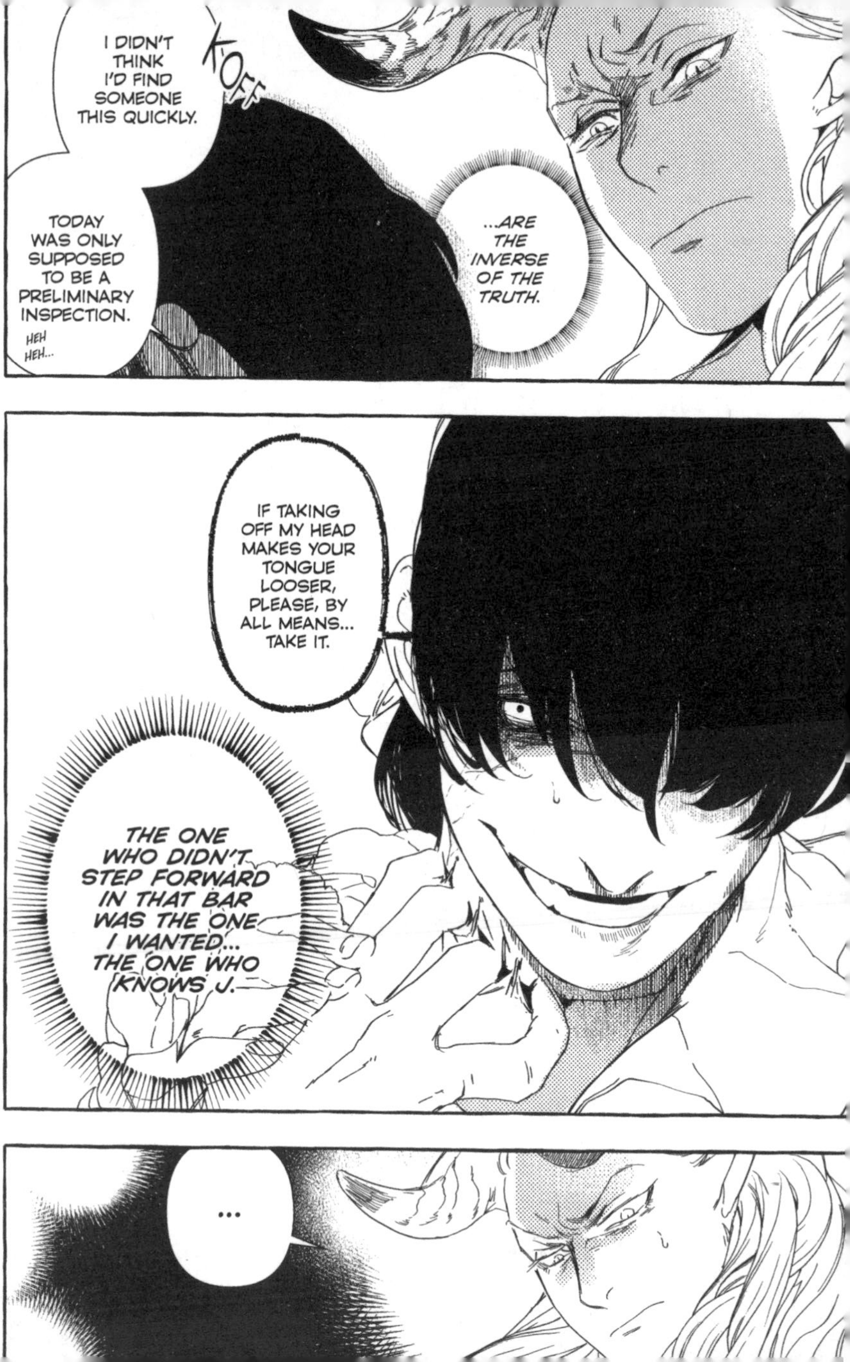
...ARE THE INVERSE OF THE TRUTH.
K-OFF
I DIDN'T THINK I'D FIND SOMEONE THIS QUICKLY.
TODAY WAS ONLY SUPPOSED TO BE A PRELIMINARY INSPECTION.
HEH HEH...
IF TAKING OFF MY HEAD MAKES YOUR TONGUE LOOSER, PLEASE, BY ALL MEANS... TAKE IT.
THE ONE WHO DIDN'T STEP FORWARD IN THAT BAR WAS THE ONE I WANTED... THE ONE WHO KNOWS J.
...

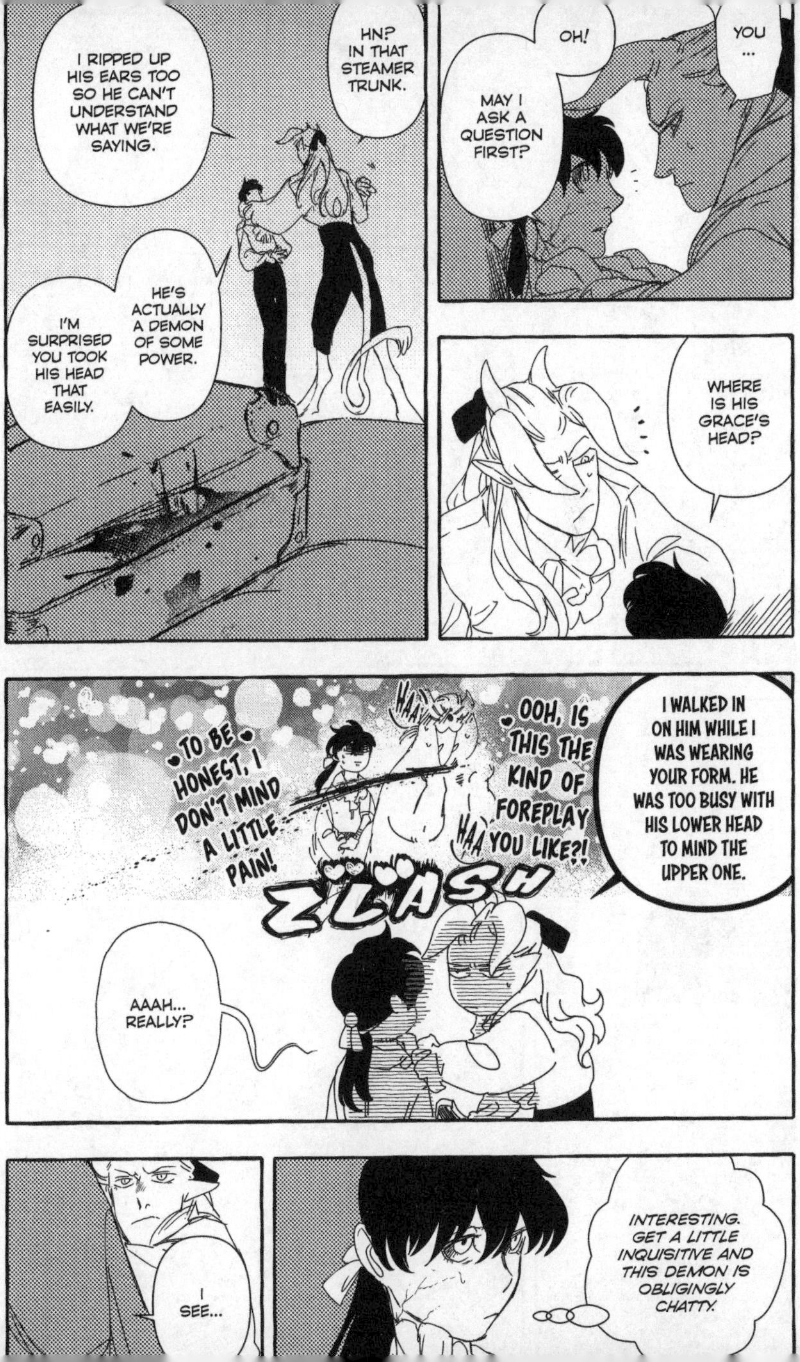
YOU ...
OH!
MAY I ASK A QUESTION FIRST?
WHERE IS HIS GRACE'S HEAD?
HN? IN THAT STEAMER TRUNK.
I RIPPED UP HIS EARS TOO SO HE CAN'T UNDERSTAND WHAT WE'RE SAYING.
HE'S ACTUALLY A DEMON OF SOME POWER.
I'M SURPRISED YOU TOOK HIS HEAD THAT EASILY.
I WALKED IN ON HIM WHILE I WAS WEARING YOUR FORM. HE WAS TOO BUSY WITH HIS LOWER HEAD TO MIND THE UPPER ONE.
HAA
OOH, IS THIS THE KIND OF FOREPLAY YOU LIKE?!
HAA
TO BE HONEST, I DON'T MIND A LITTLE PAIN!
ZLASH
AAAH... REALLY?
INTERESTING. GET A LITTLE INQUISITIVE AND THIS DEMON IS OBLIGINGLY CHATTY.
I SEE...

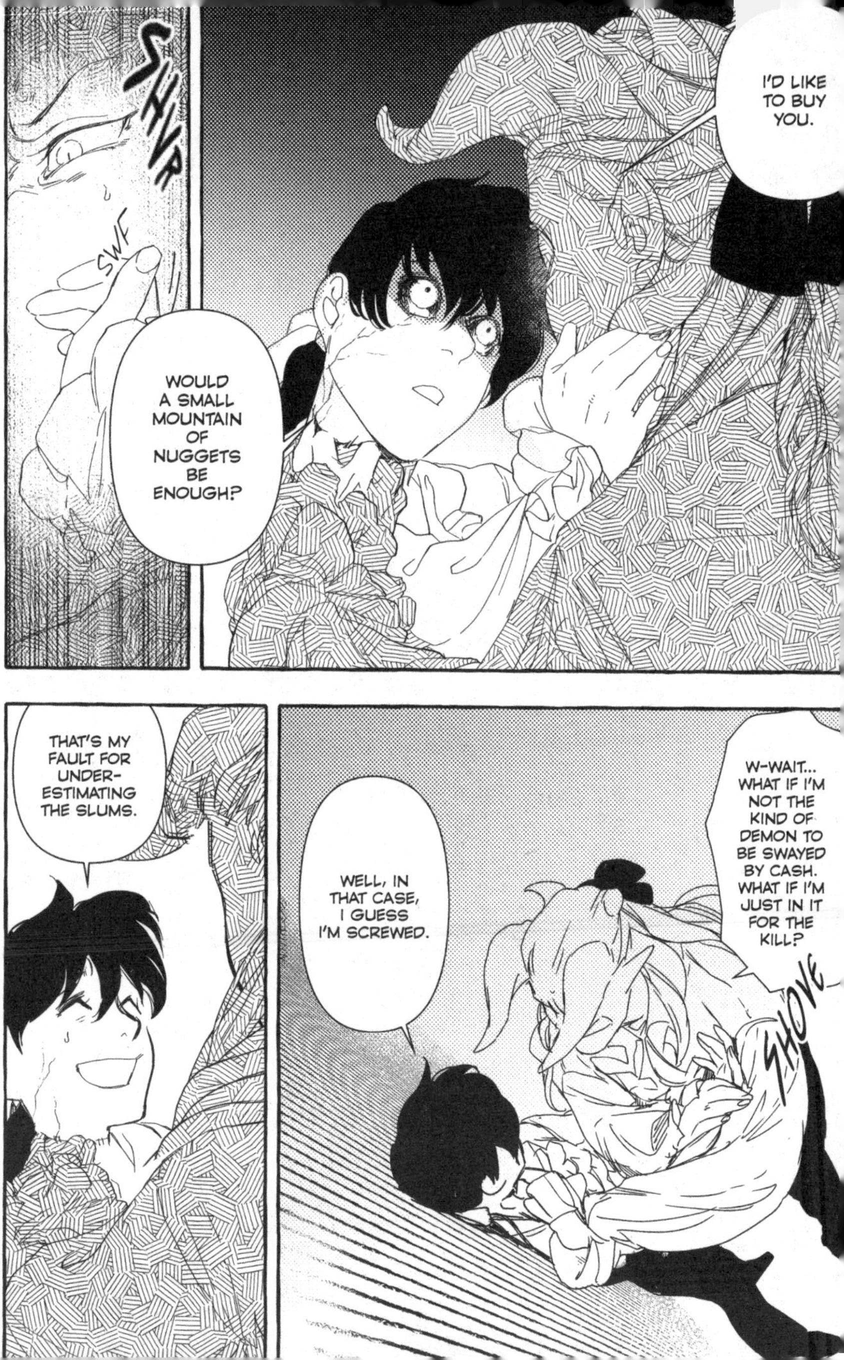
I'D LIKE TO BUY YOU.
WOULD A SMALL MOUNTAIN OF NUGGETS BE ENOUGH?
SHVR
SWF
W-WAIT... WHAT IF I'M NOT THE KIND OF DEMON TO BE SWAYED BY CASH. WHAT IF I'M JUST IN IT FOR THE KILL?
WELL, IN THAT CASE, I GUESS I'M SCREWED.
SHOVE
THAT'S MY FAULT FOR UNDER-ESTIMATING THE SLUMS.

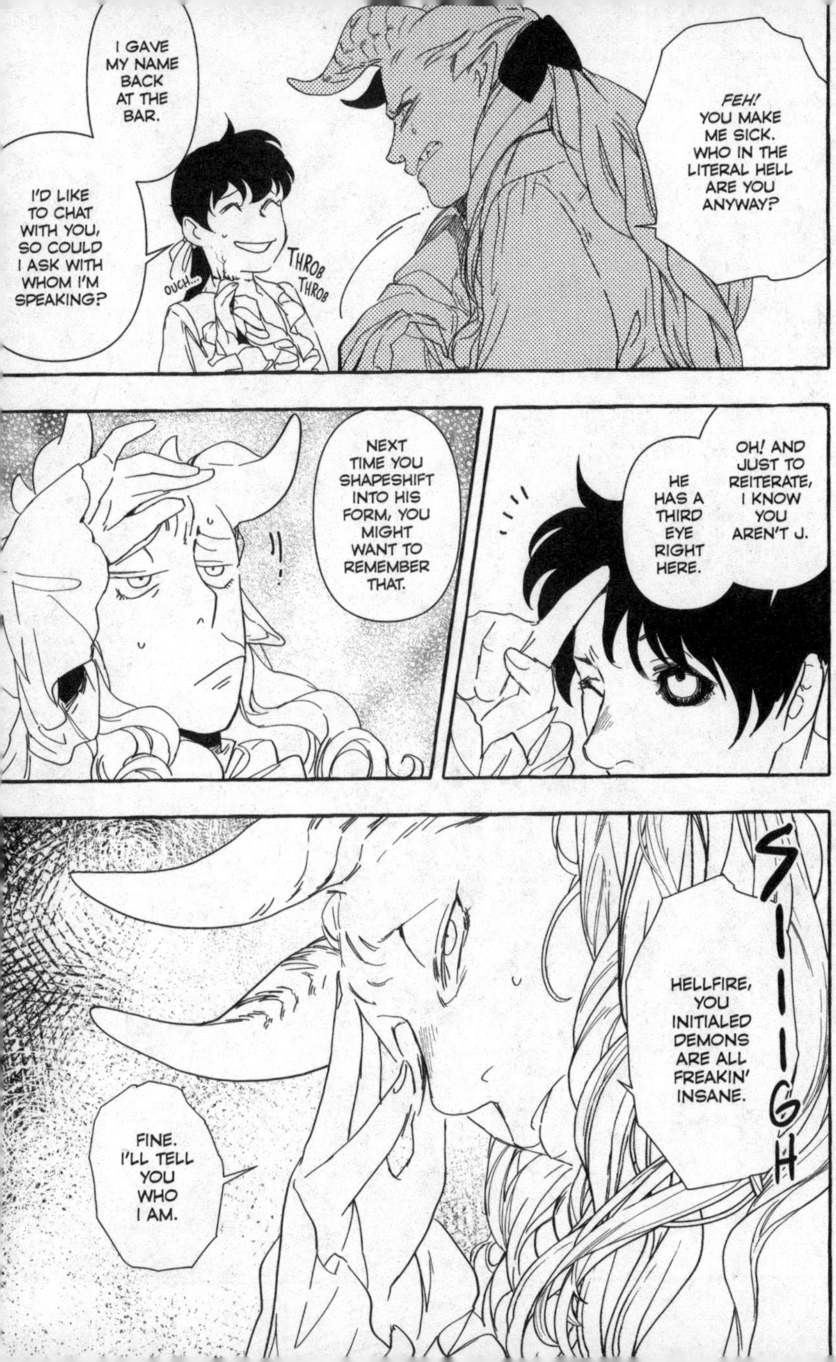
FEH! YOU MAKE ME SICK. WHO IN THE LITERAL HELL ARE YOU ANYWAY?
I GAVE MY NAME BACK AT THE BAR.
I'D LIKE TO CHAT WITH YOU, SO COULD I ASK WITH WHOM I'M SPEAKING?
THROB THROB
OUCH...
OH! AND JUST TO REITERATE, I KNOW YOU AREN'T J.
HE HAS A THIRD EYE RIGHT HERE.
NEXT TIME YOU SHAPESHIFT INTO HIS FORM, YOU MIGHT WANT TO REMEMBER THAT.
SIIIGH
HELLFIRE, YOU INITIALED DEMONS ARE ALL FREAKIN' INSANE.
FINE. I'LL TELL YOU WHO I AM.

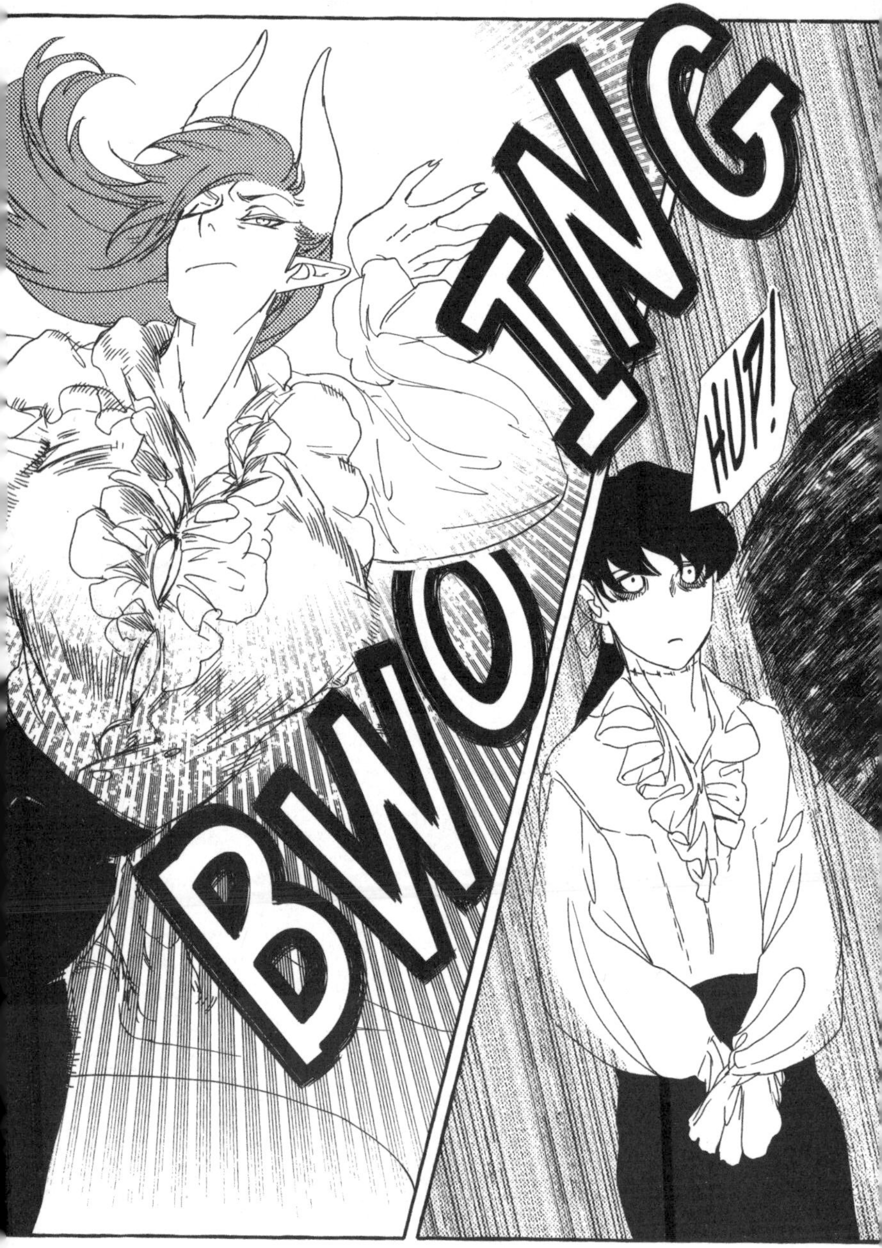
HUP!
BWOING

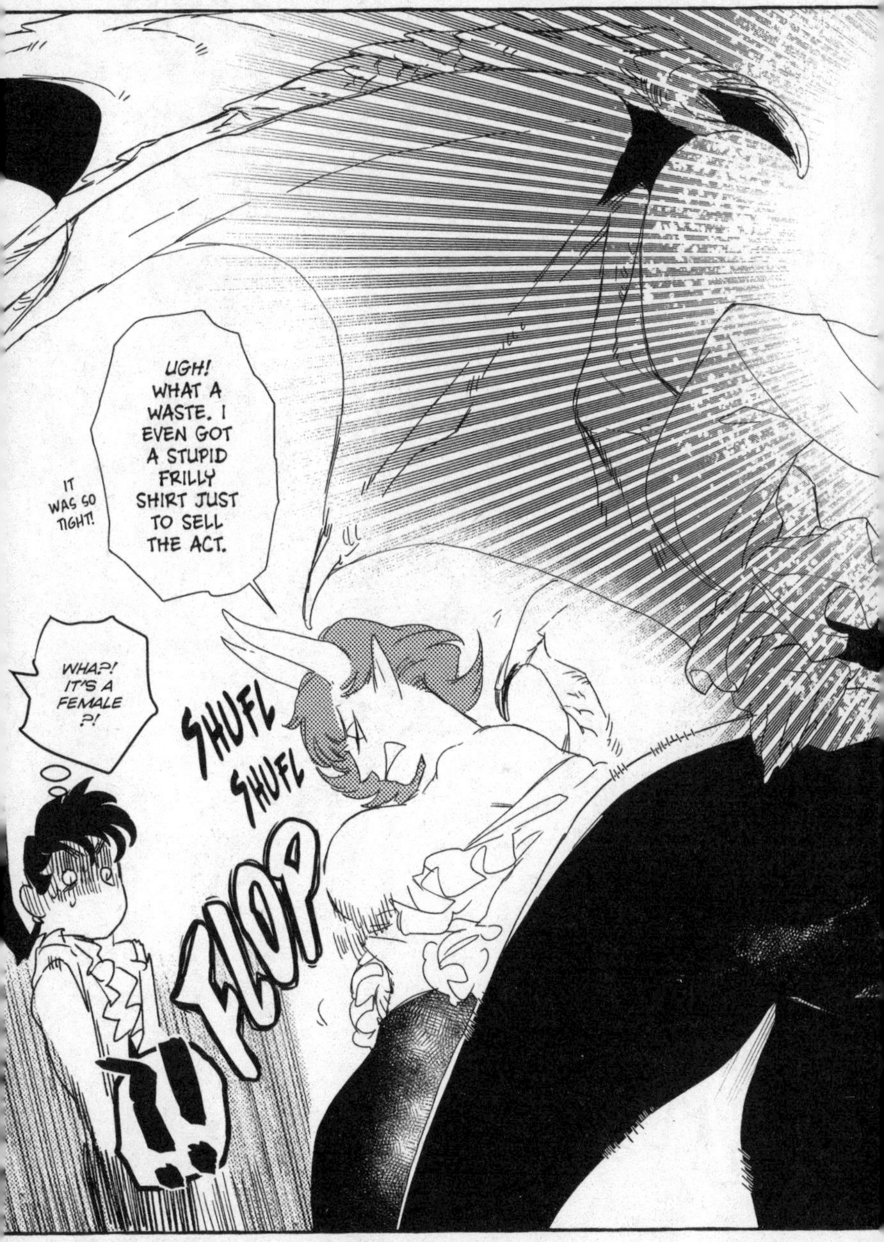
UGH! WHAT A WASTE. I EVEN GOT A STUPID FRILLY SHIRT JUST TO SELL THE ACT.
IT WAS SO TIGHT!
SHUFL SHUFL
WHA?! IT'S A FEMALE ?!
FLOP
?!!

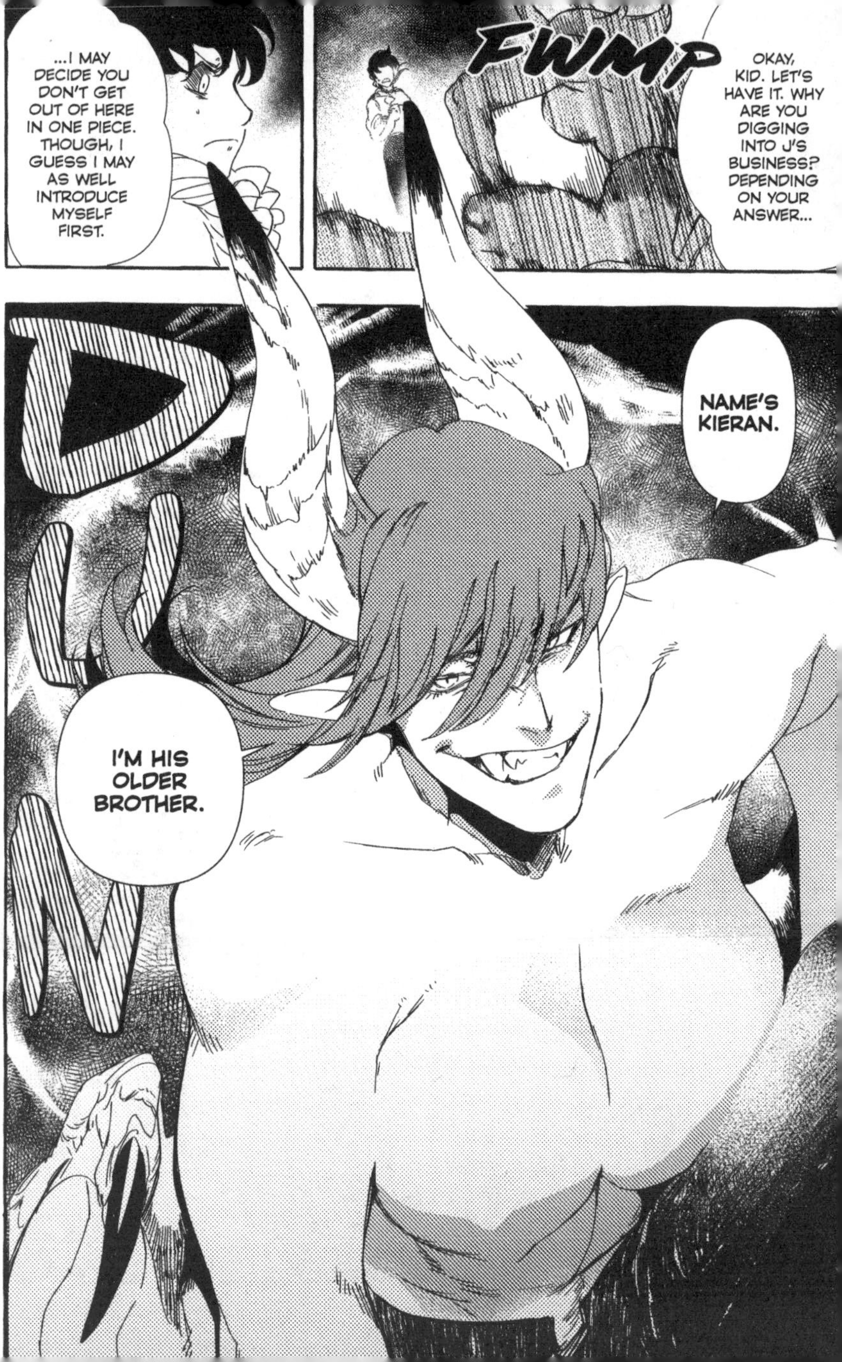
OKAY, KID. LET'S HAVE IT. WHY ARE YOU DIGGING INTO J'S BUSINESS? DEPENDING ON YOUR ANSWER...
FWMP
...I MAY DECIDE YOU DON'T GET OUT OF HERE IN ONE PIECE. THOUGH, I GUESS I MAY AS WELL INTRODUCE MYSELF FIRST.
NAME'S KIERAN.
DUN
I'M HIS OLDER BROTHER.

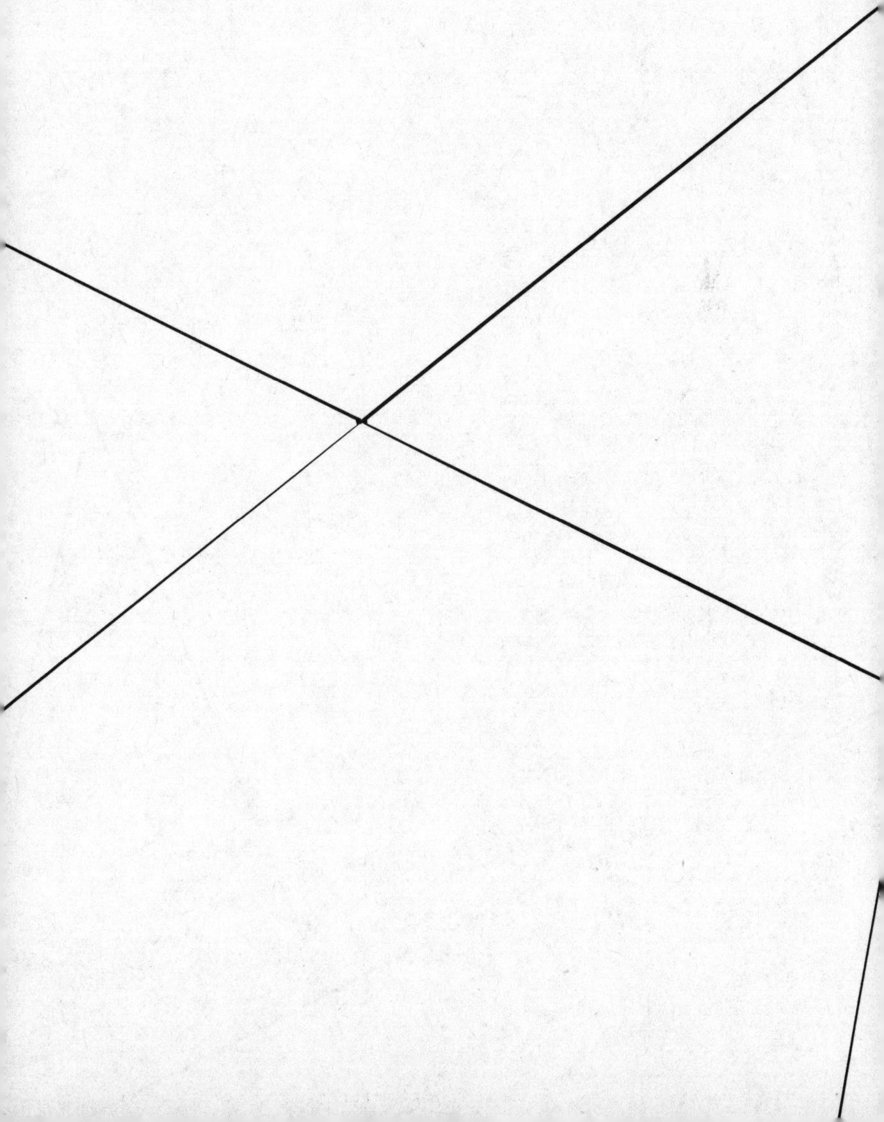

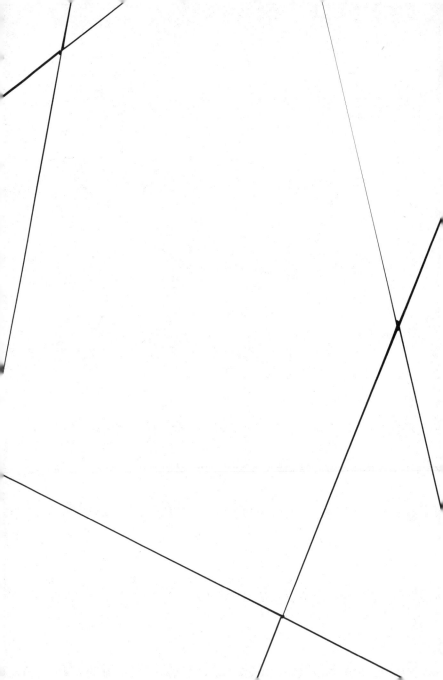

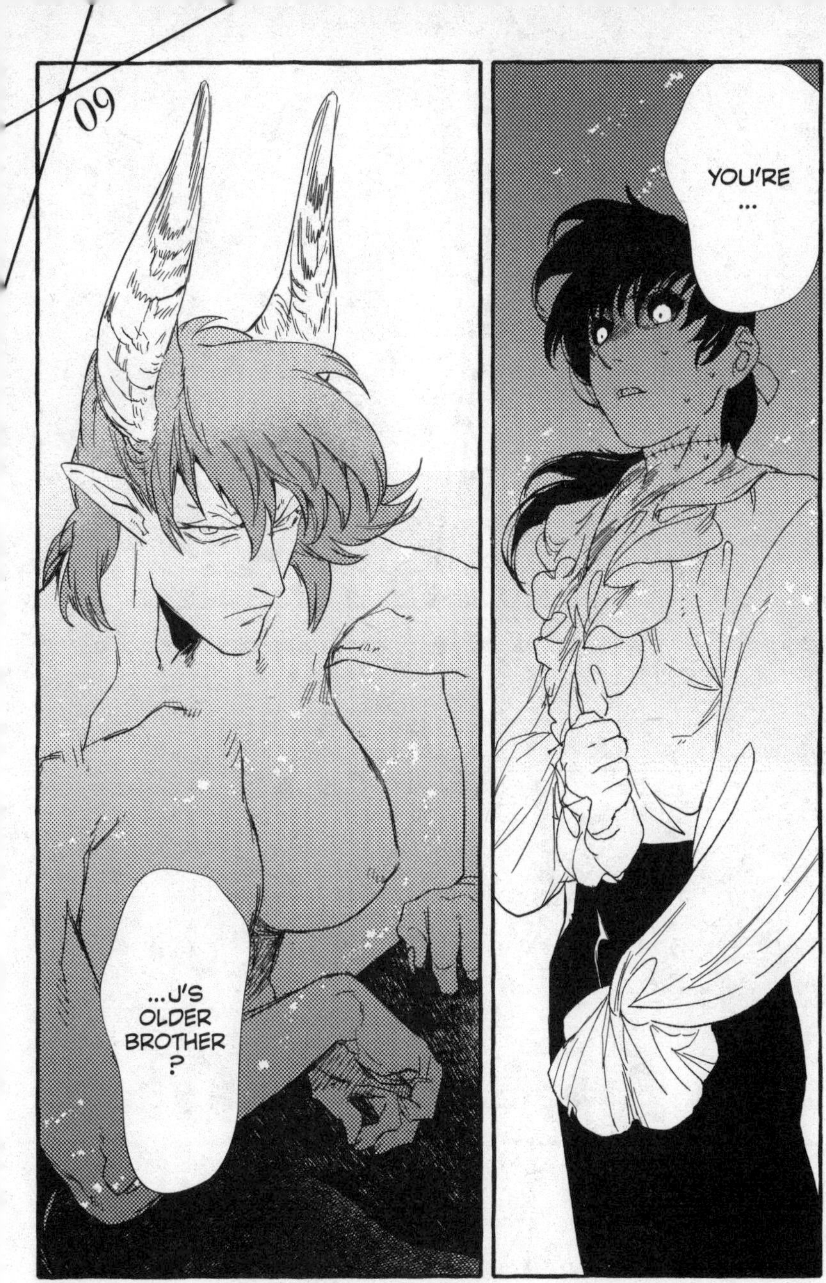
YOU'RE ...
...J'S OLDER BROTHER ?
09

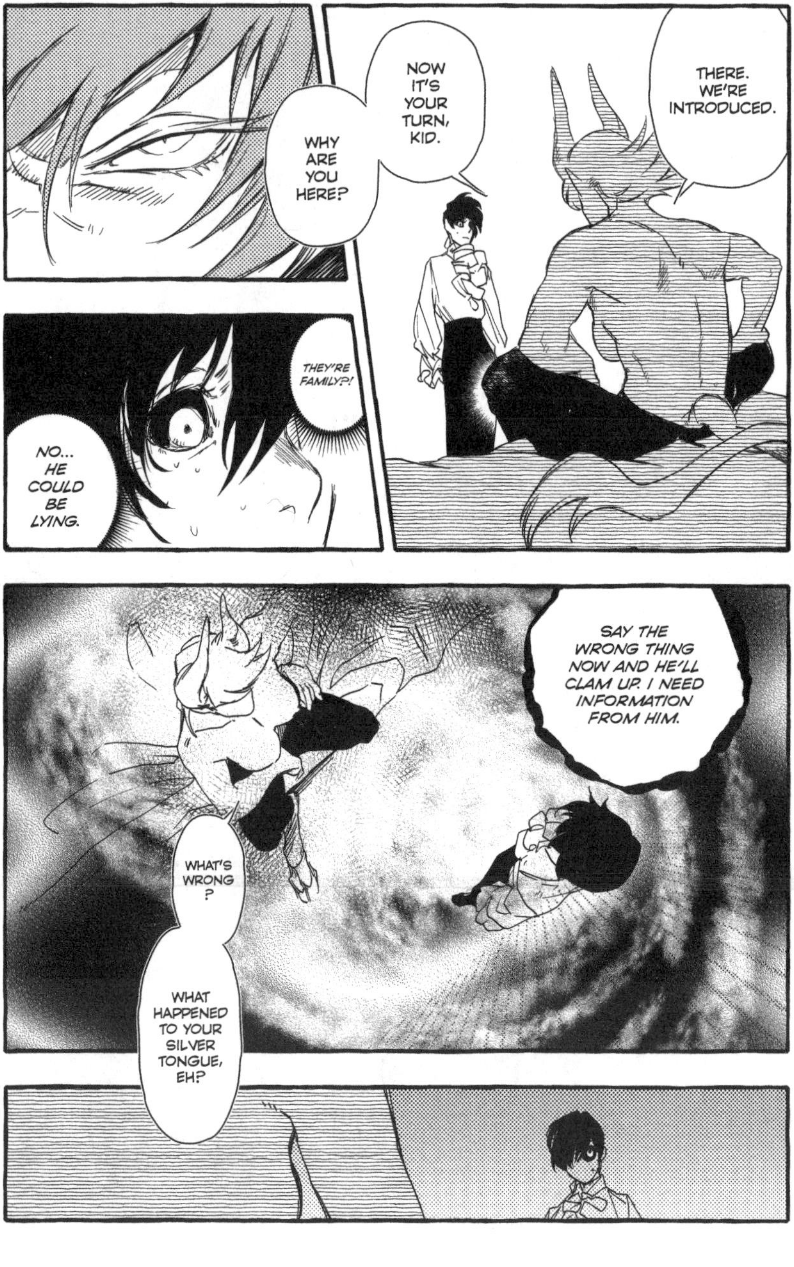
THERE. WE'RE INTRODUCED.
NOW IT'S YOUR TURN, KID.
WHY ARE YOU HERE?
THEY'RE FAMILY?!
NO... HE COULD BE LYING.
SAY THE WRONG THING NOW AND HE'LL CLAM UP. I NEED INFORMATION FROM HIM.
WHAT'S WRONG?
WHAT HAPPENED TO YOUR SILVER TONGUE, EH?

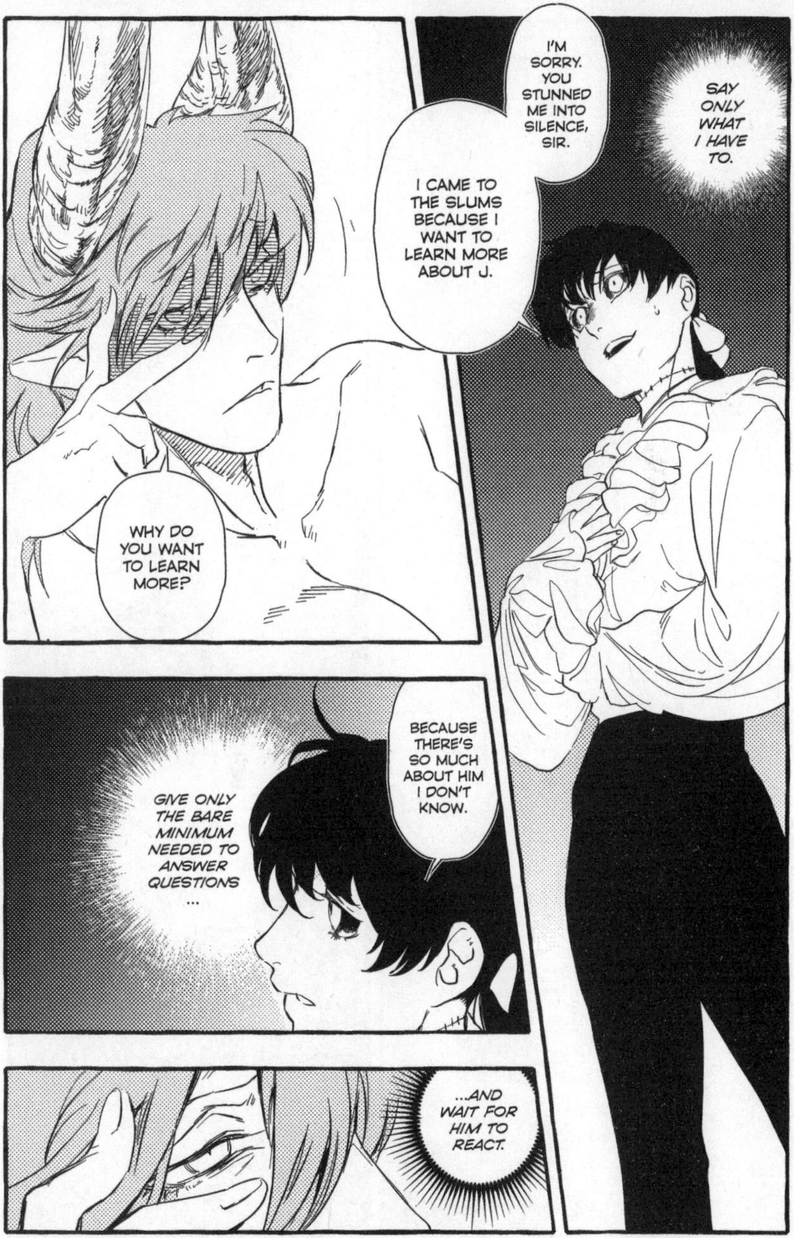
I'M SORRY. YOU STUNNED ME INTO SILENCE, SIR.
I CAME TO THE SLUMS BECAUSE I WANT TO LEARN MORE ABOUT J.
SAY ONLY WHAT I HAVE TO.
WHY DO YOU WANT TO LEARN MORE?
BECAUSE THERE'S SO MUCH ABOUT HIM I DON'T KNOW.
GIVE ONLY THE BARE MINIMUM NEEDED TO ANSWER QUESTIONS ...
...AND WAIT FOR HIM TO REACT.

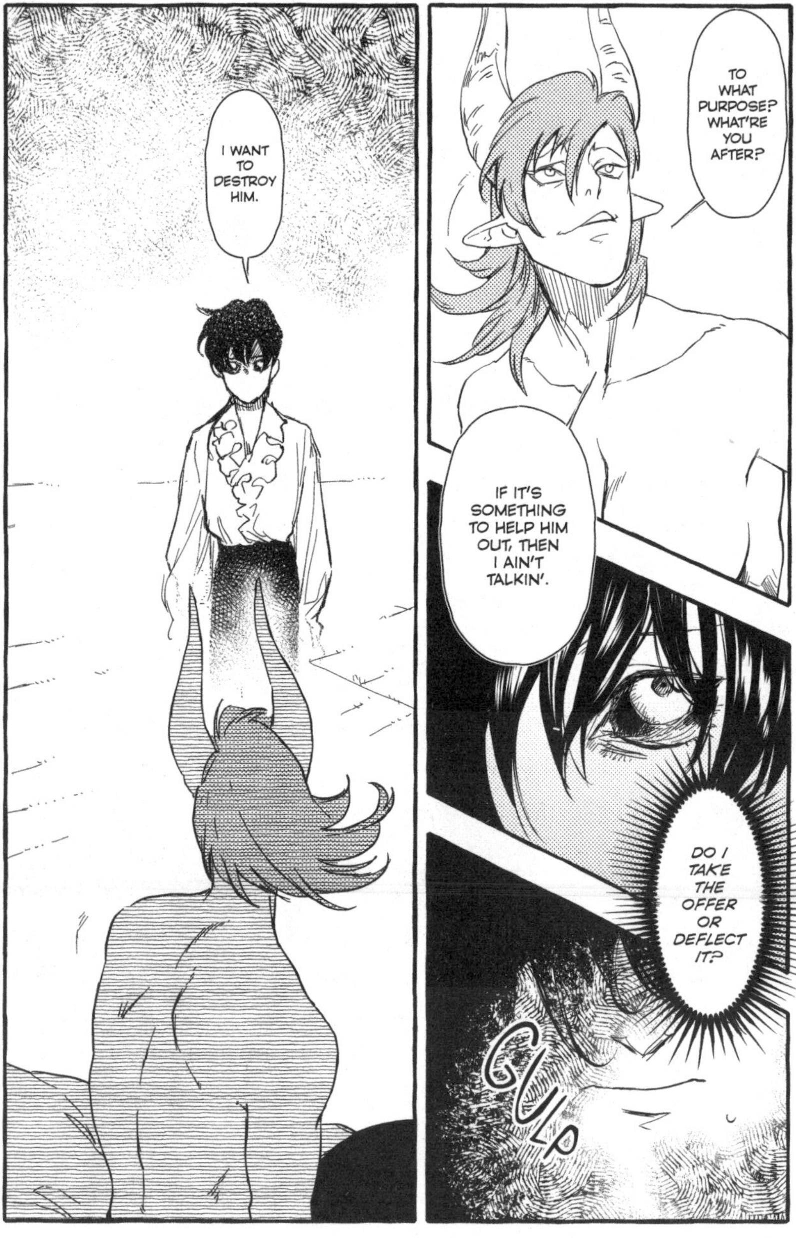
TO WHAT PURPOSE? WHAT'RE YOU AFTER?
IF IT'S SOMETHING TO HELP HIM OUT, THEN I AIN'T TALKIN'.
DO I TAKE THE OFFER OR DEFLECT IT?
GULP
I WANT TO DESTROY HIM.

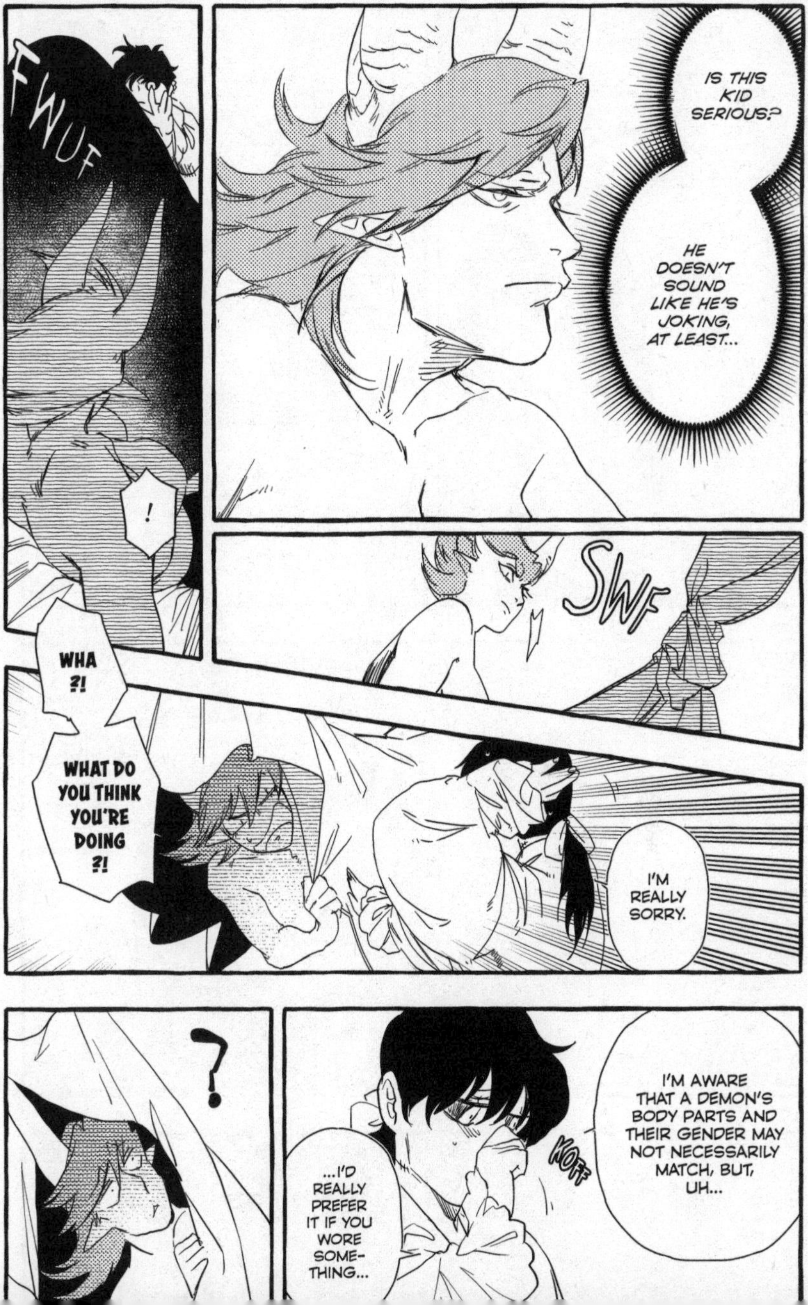
IS THIS KID SERIOUS?
HE DOESN'T SOUND LIKE HE'S JOKING, AT LEAST...
SWF
FWUF
!
I'M REALLY SORRY.
WHA ?!
WHAT DO YOU THINK YOU'RE DOING ?!
I'M AWARE THAT A DEMON'S BODY PARTS AND THEIR GENDER MAY NOT NECESSARILY MATCH, BUT, UH...
KOFF
...I'D REALLY PREFER IT IF YOU WORE SOME-THING...
?

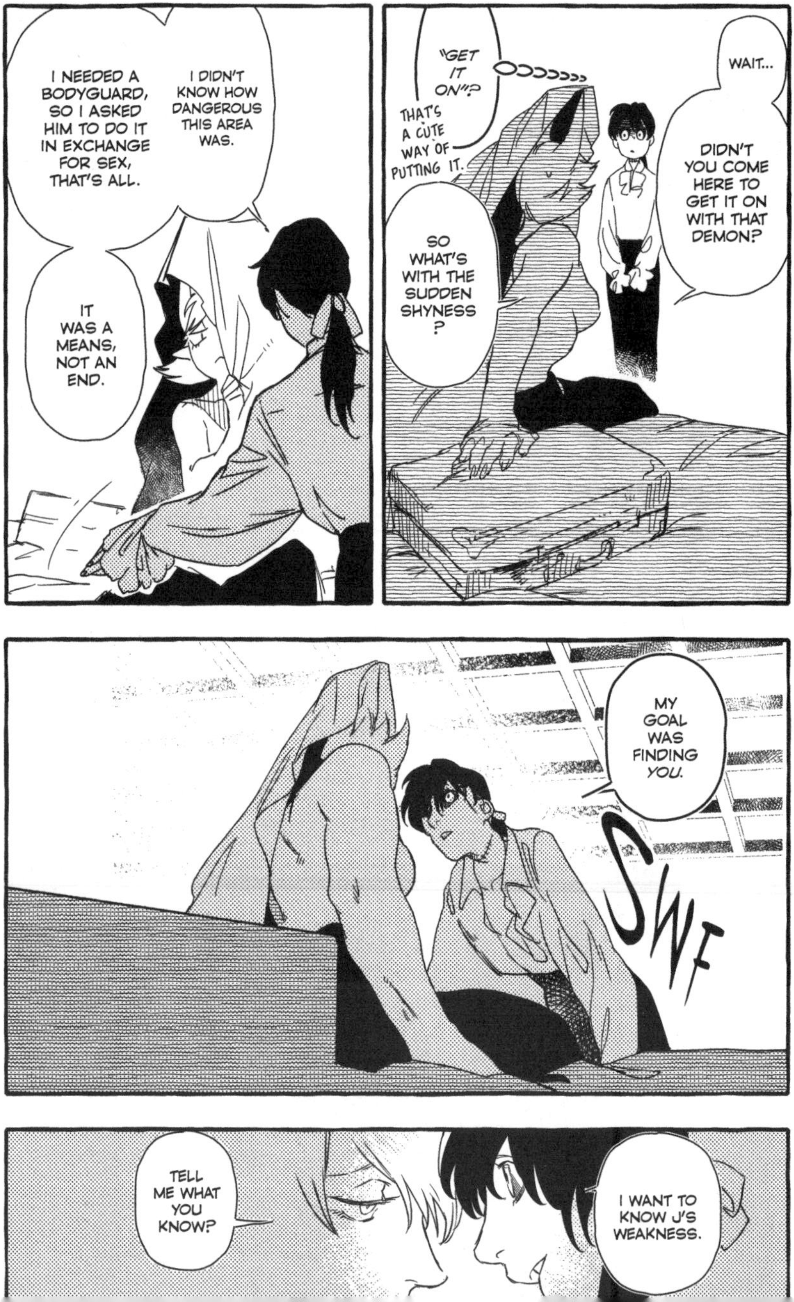
WAIT...
DIDN'T YOU COME HERE TO GET IT ON WITH THAT DEMON?
"GET IT ON"?
THAT'S A CUTE WAY OF PUTTING IT.
SO WHAT'S WITH THE SUDDEN SHYNESS?
I DIDN'T KNOW HOW DANGEROUS THIS AREA WAS.
I NEEDED A BODYGUARD, SO I ASKED HIM TO DO IT IN EXCHANGE FOR SEX, THAT'S ALL.
IT WAS A MEANS, NOT AN END.
MY GOAL WAS FINDING YOU.
SWF
I WANT TO KNOW J'S WEAKNESS.
TELL ME WHAT YOU KNOW?

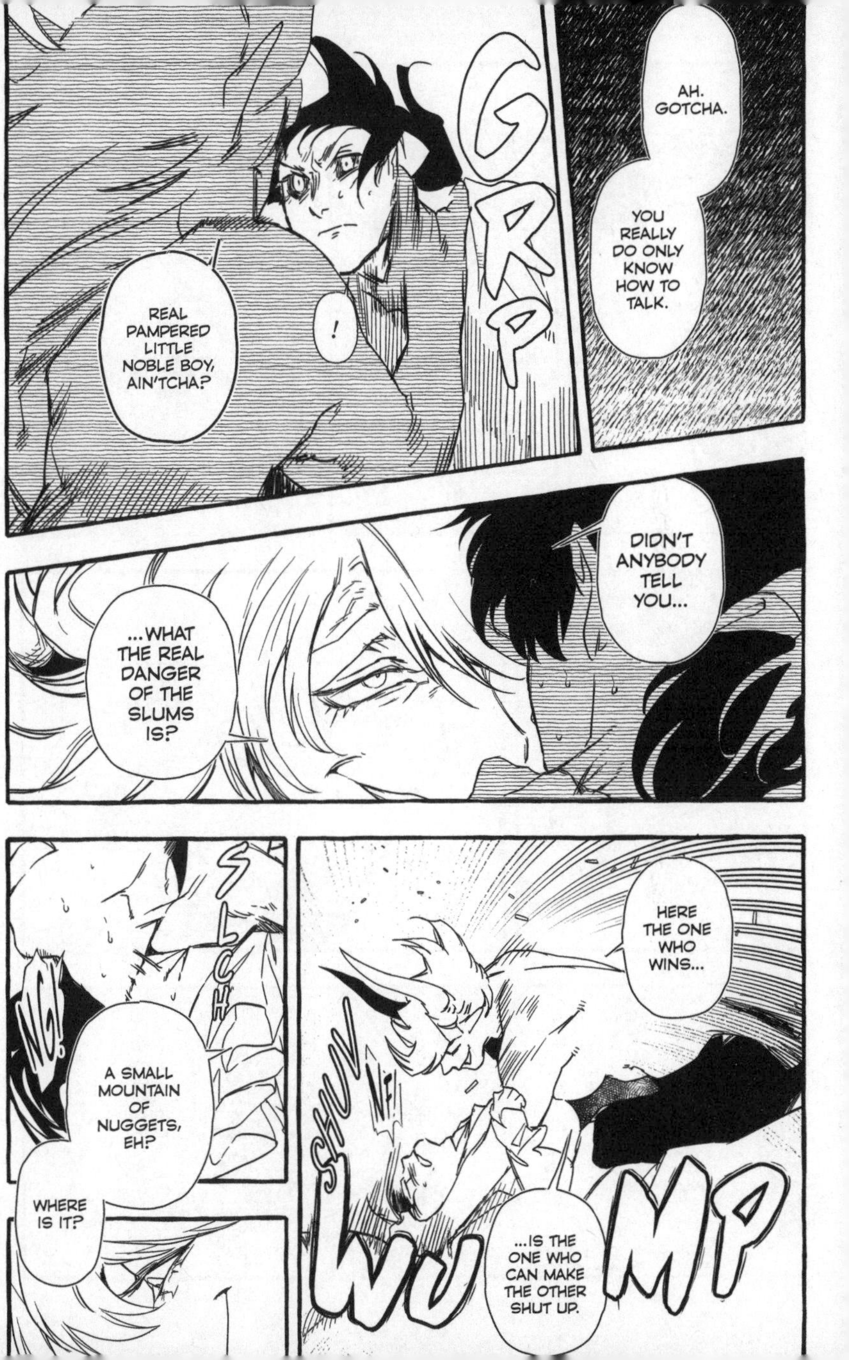
AH. GOTCHA.
YOU REALLY DO ONLY KNOW HOW TO TALK.
GRP
!
REAL PAMPERED LITTLE NOBLE BOY, AIN'TCHA?
DIDN'T ANYBODY TELL YOU...
...WHAT THE REAL DANGER OF THE SLUMS IS?
HERE THE ONE WHO WINS...
SHUN
NF!
WUMP
...IS THE ONE WHO CAN MAKE THE OTHER SHUT UP.
SLCH
NG!
A SMALL MOUNTAIN OF NUGGETS, EH?
WHERE IS IT?

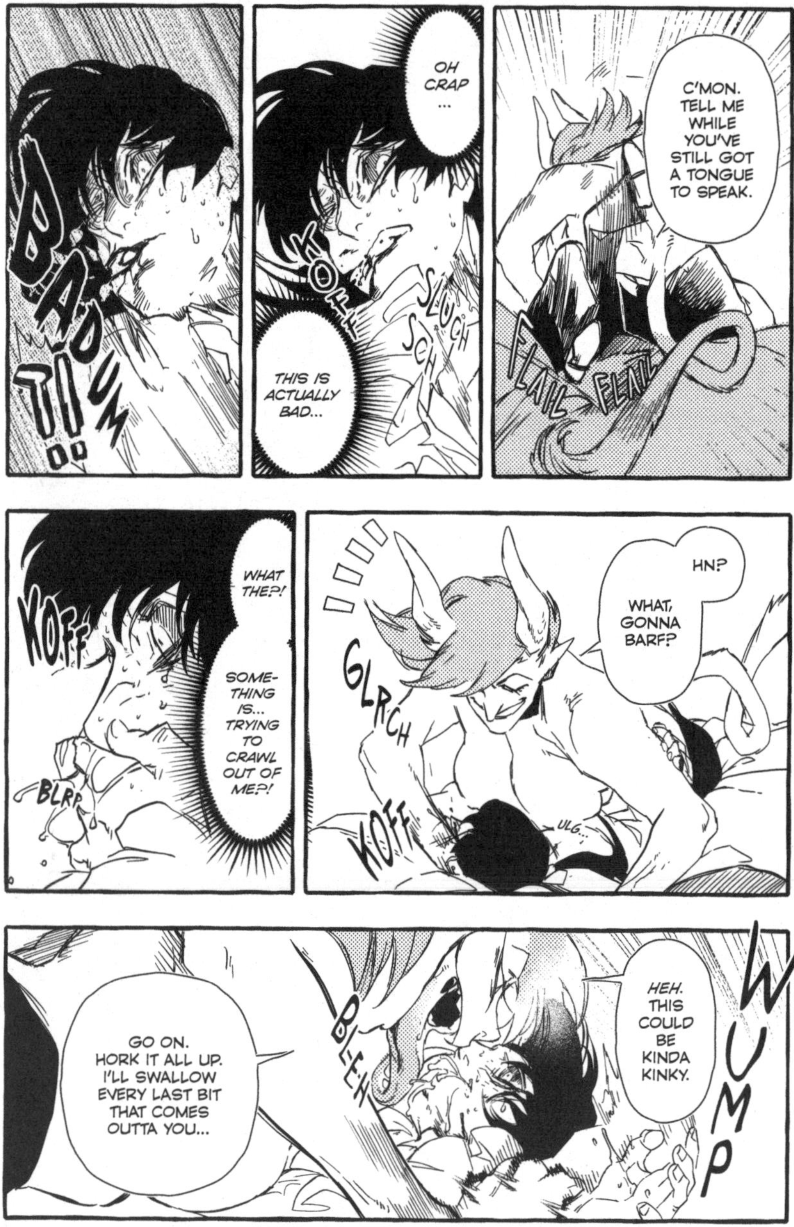
C'MON. TELL ME WHILE YOU'VE STILL GOT A TONGUE TO SPEAK.
FLAIL FLAIL
OH CRAP...
KOFF
SLUCH SCH
THIS IS ACTUALLY BAD...
BADUM
T!!
HN?
WHAT, GONNA BARF?
GLRCH
ULG...
KOFF
WHAT THE?!
SOME-THING IS... TRYING TO CRAWL OUT OF ME?!
KOFF
BLRP
WUMP
HEH. THIS COULD BE KINDA KINKY.
BLECH
GO ON. HORK IT ALL UP. I'LL SWALLOW EVERY LAST BIT THAT COMES OUTTA YOU...

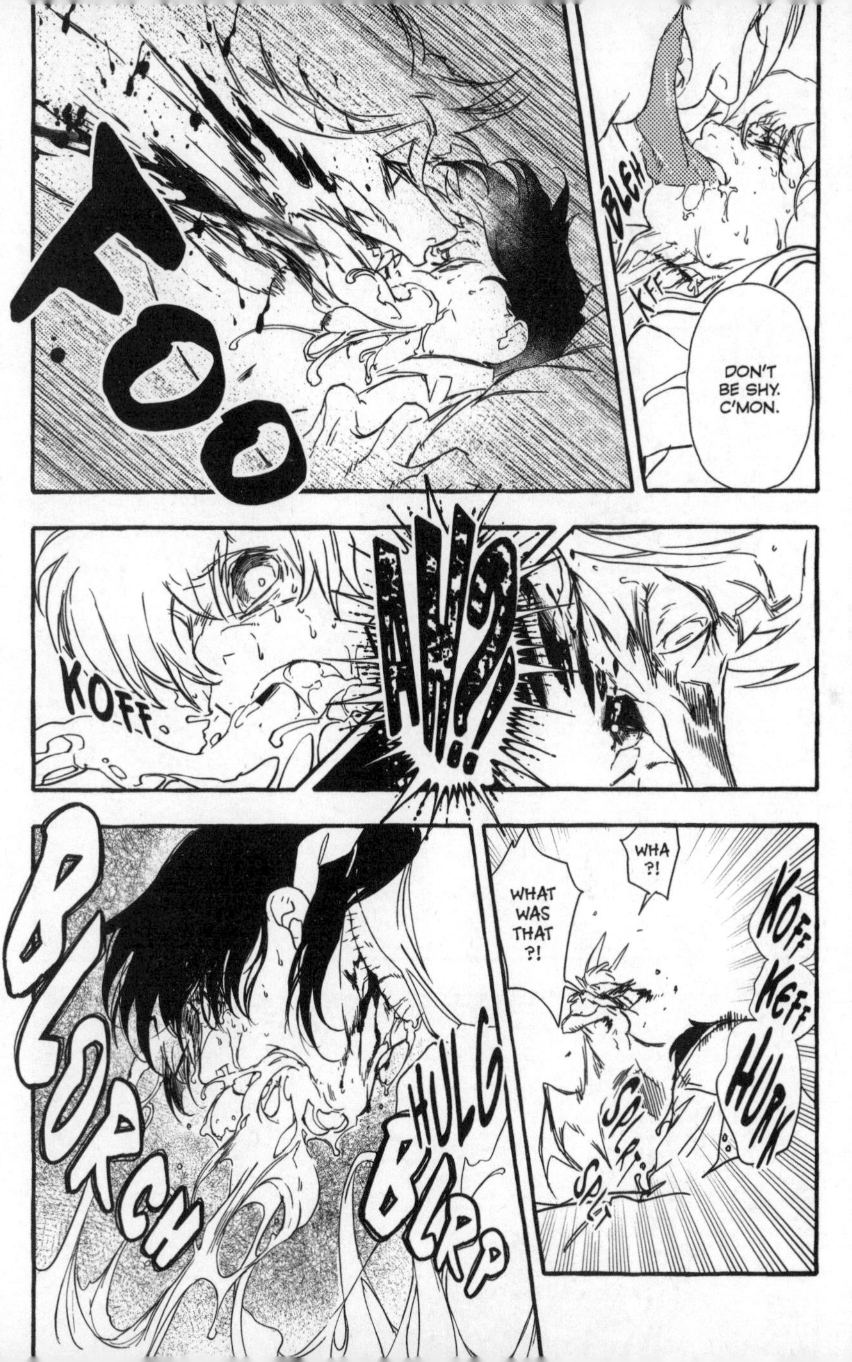
BLEH
KFF
DON'T BE SHY. C'MON.
TOO
AH?!
KOFF
WHA ?!
WHAT WAS THAT ?!
KOFF
KEFF
HURK
SPLK
SPLT
HULG
BLRP
BLORCH

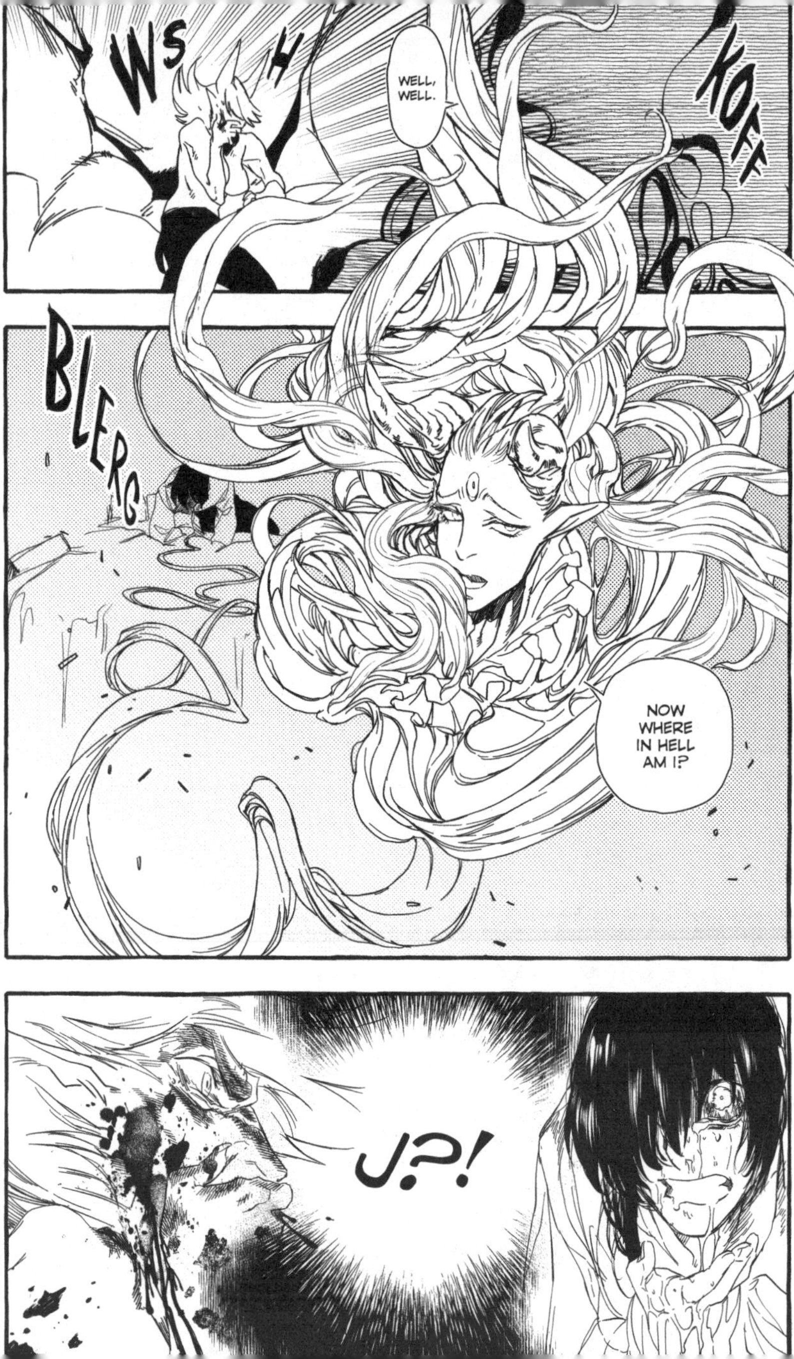
KOFF
WELL, WELL.
WSH
NOW WHERE IN HELL AM I?
BLERG
J?!

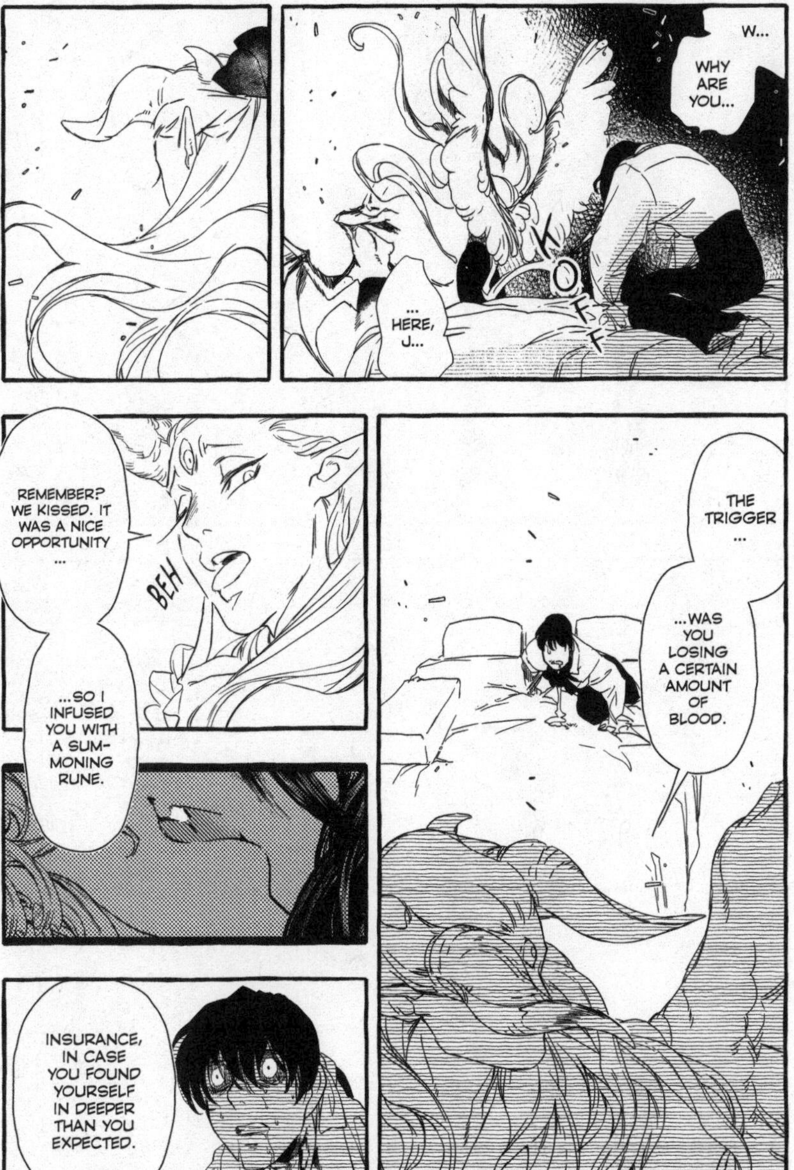
W...
WHY ARE YOU...
KOFF
... HERE, J...
THE TRIGGER ...
...WAS YOU LOSING A CERTAIN AMOUNT OF BLOOD.
REMEMBER? WE KISSED. IT WAS A NICE OPPORTUNITY ...
BEH
...SO I INFUSED YOU WITH A SUM-MONING RUNE.
INSURANCE, IN CASE YOU FOUND YOURSELF IN DEEPER THAN YOU EXPECTED.

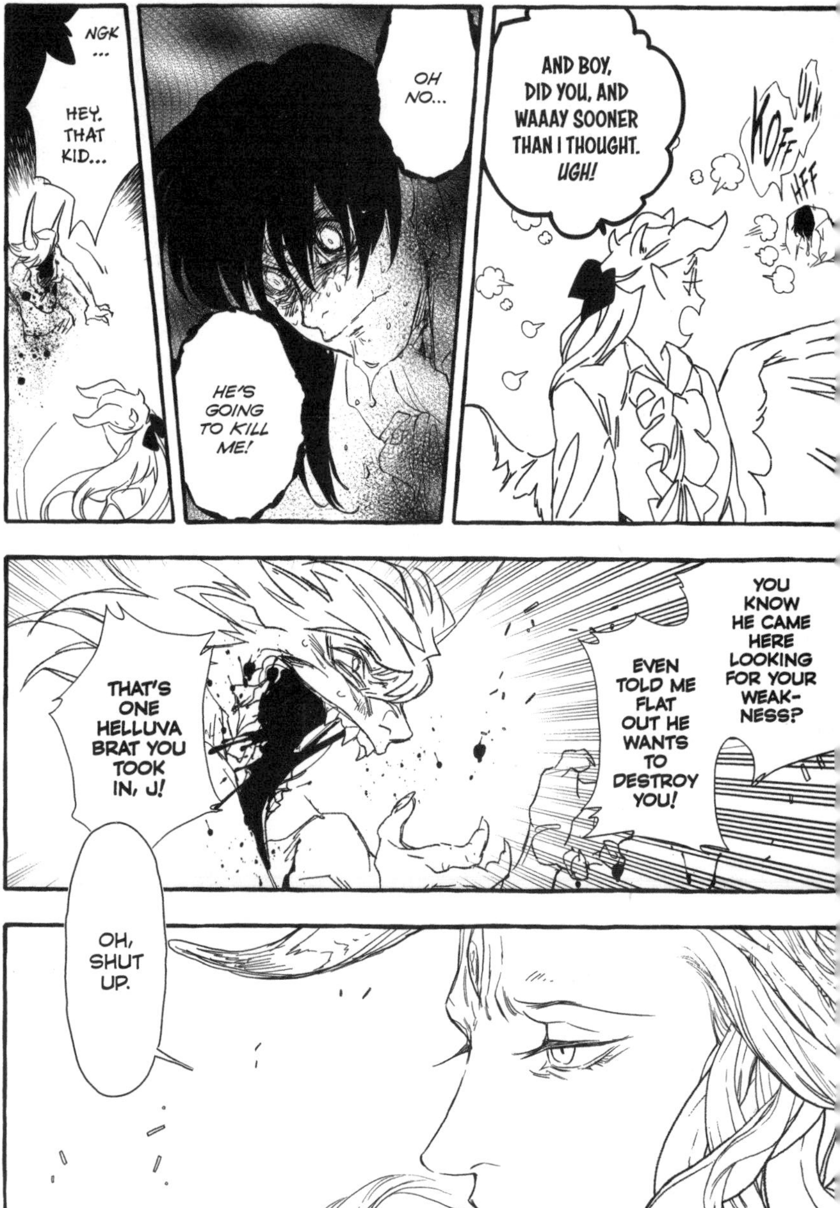
AND BOY, DID YOU, AND WAAAY SOONER THAN I THOUGHT. *UGH!*
KOFF
ULK
HFF
OH NO...
HE'S GOING TO KILL ME!
NGK ...
HEY. THAT KID...
YOU KNOW HE CAME HERE LOOKING FOR YOUR WEAK-NESS?
EVEN TOLD ME FLAT OUT HE WANTS TO DESTROY YOU!
THAT'S ONE HELLUVA BRAT YOU TOOK IN, J!
OH, SHUT UP.

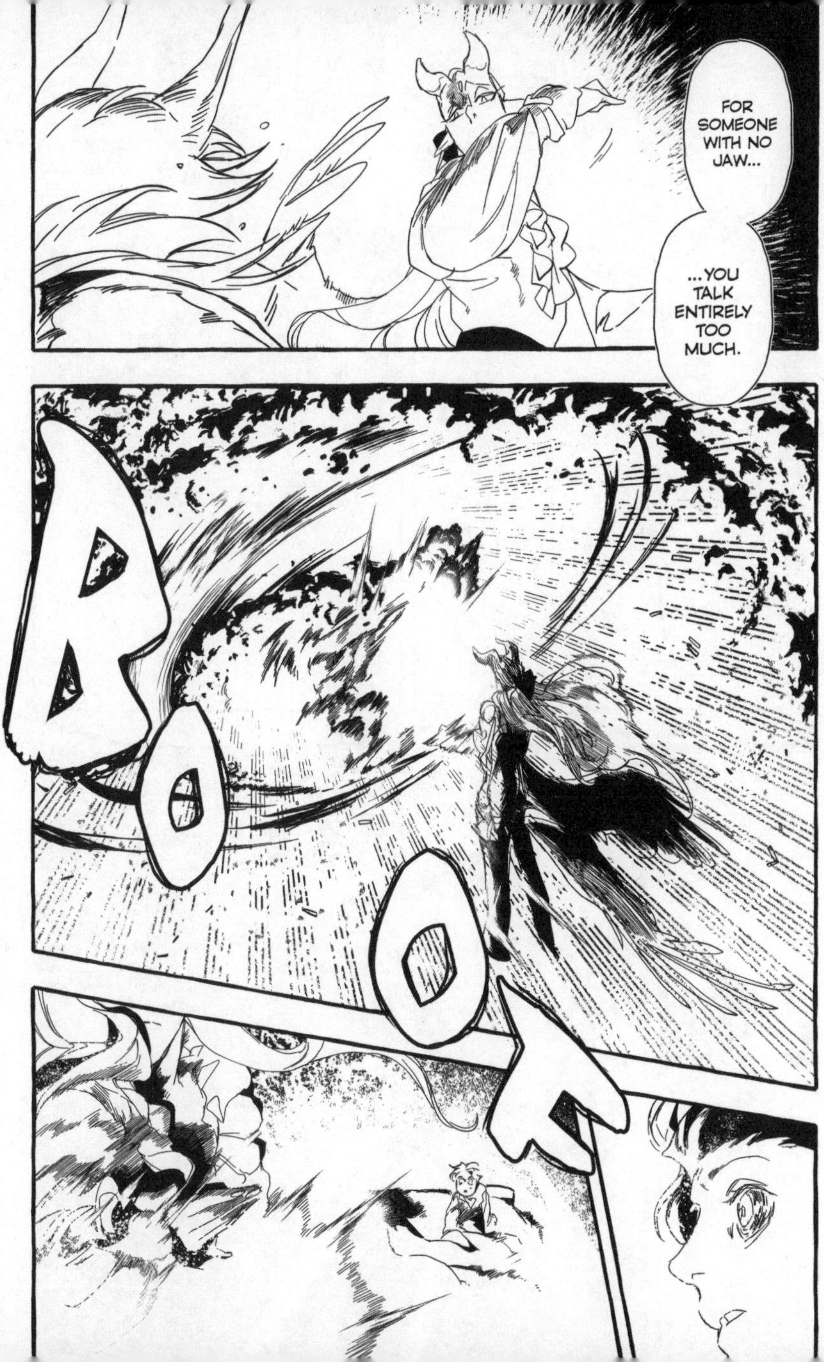
FOR SOMEONE WITH NO JAW...
...YOU TALK ENTIRELY TOO MUCH.

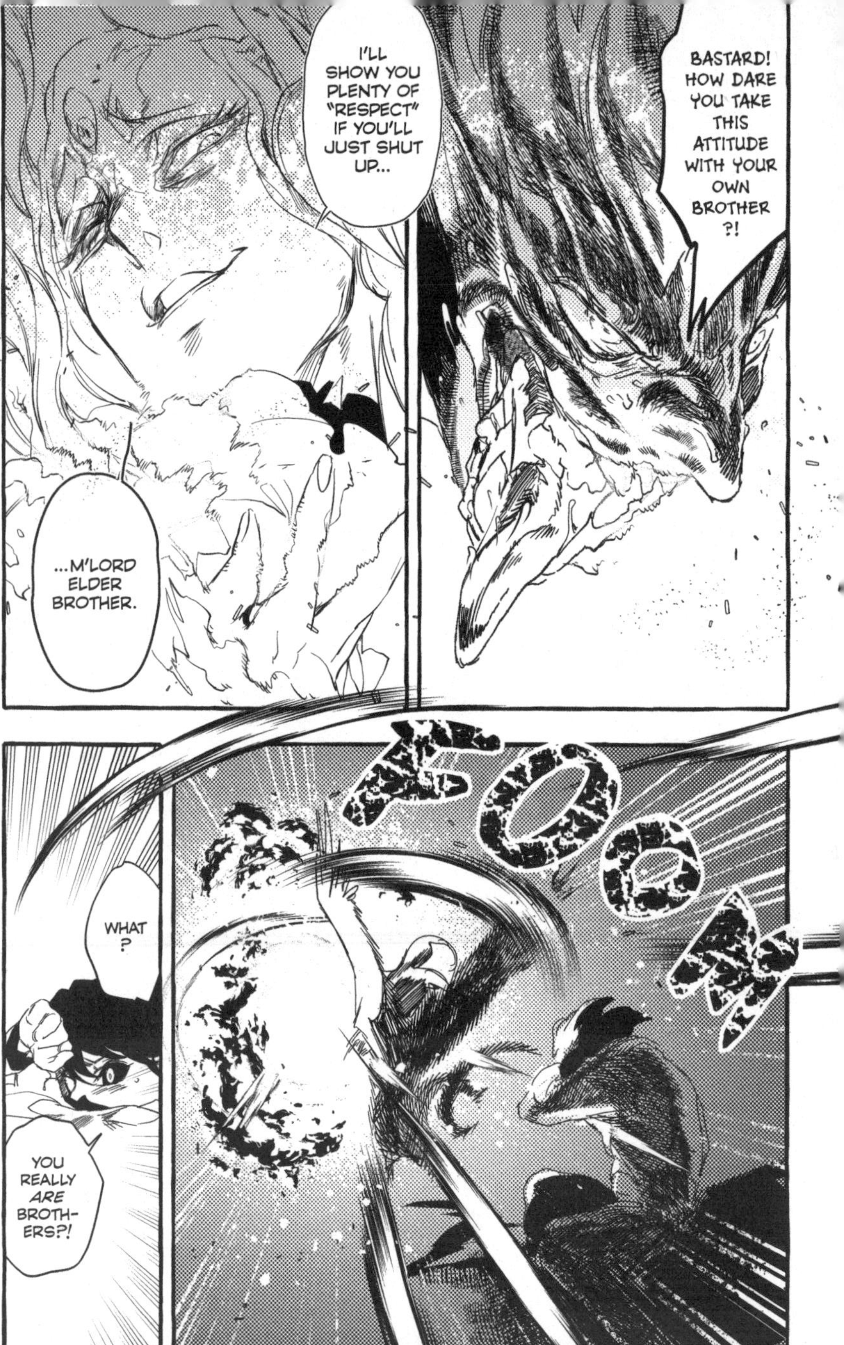
BASTARD! HOW DARE YOU TAKE THIS ATTITUDE WITH YOUR OWN BROTHER?!
I'LL SHOW YOU PLENTY OF "RESPECT" IF YOU'LL JUST SHUT UP...
...M'LORD ELDER BROTHER.
FOOM
WHAT?
YOU REALLY *ARE* BROTHERS?!

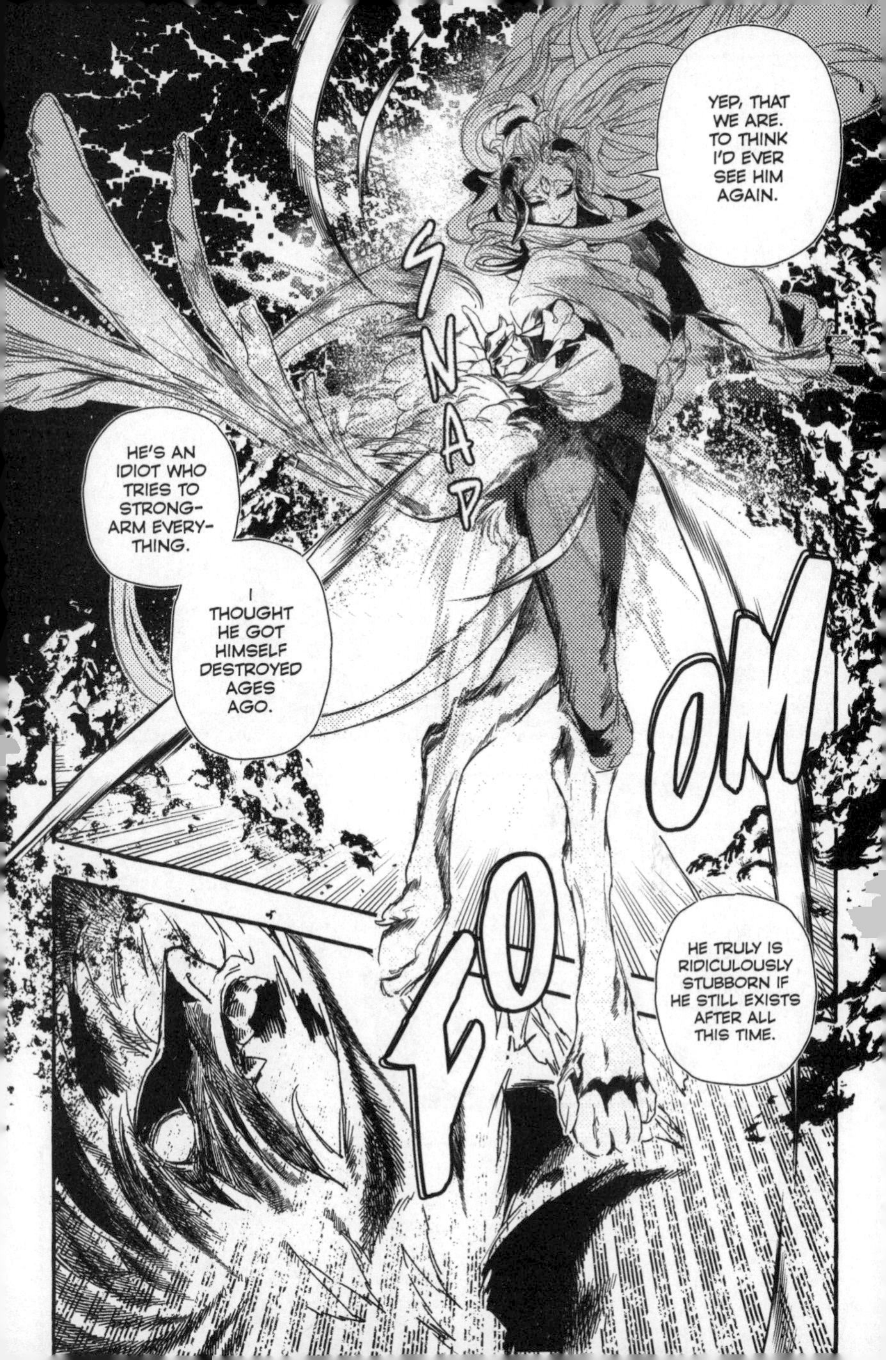
YEP, THAT WE ARE. TO THINK I'D EVER SEE HIM AGAIN.
SNAP
HE'S AN IDIOT WHO TRIES TO STRONG-ARM EVERY-THING.
I THOUGHT HE GOT HIMSELF DESTROYED AGES AGO.
FOOM
HE TRULY IS RIDICULOUSLY STUBBORN IF HE STILL EXISTS AFTER ALL THIS TIME.

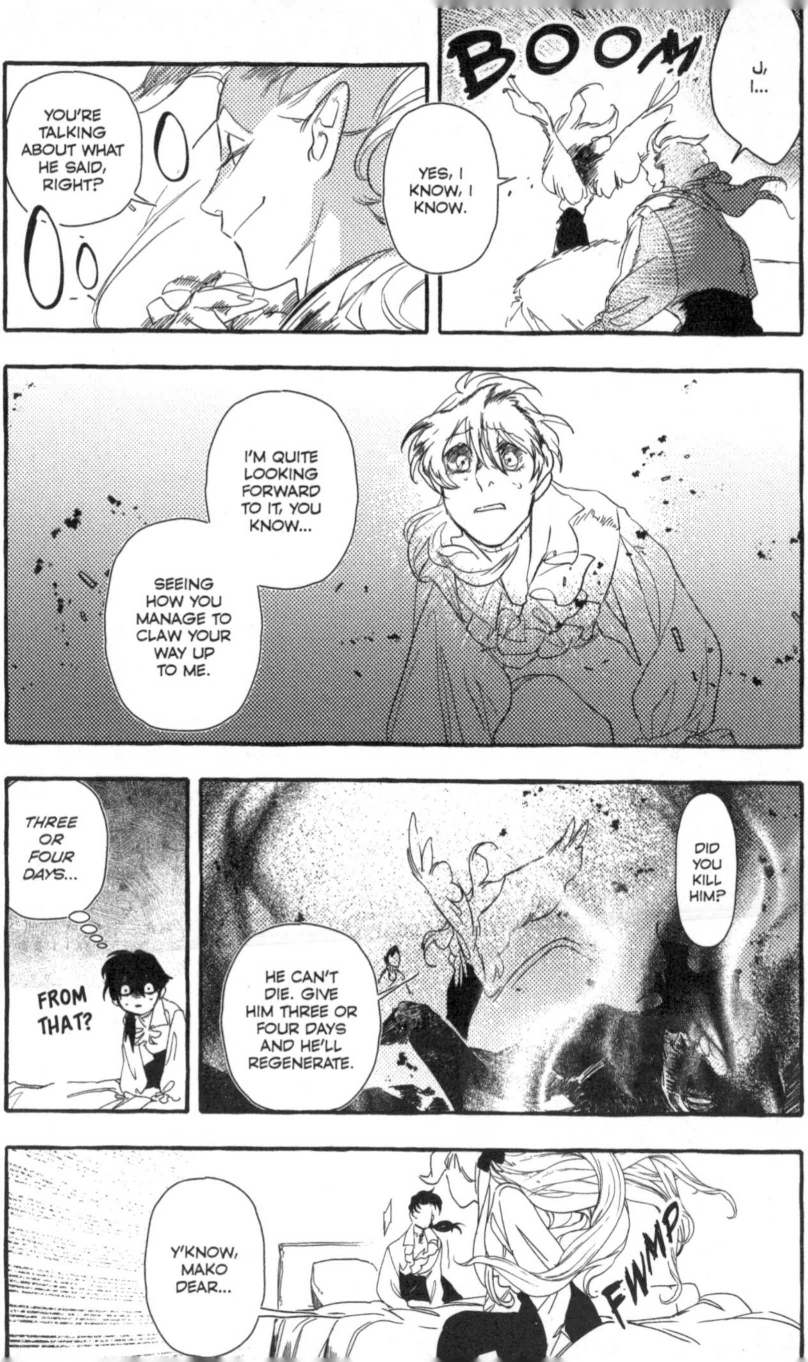
BOOM
J, I...
YOU'RE TALKING ABOUT WHAT HE SAID, RIGHT?
YES, I KNOW, I KNOW.
I'M QUITE LOOKING FORWARD TO IT, YOU KNOW...
SEEING HOW YOU MANAGE TO CLAW YOUR WAY UP TO ME.
DID YOU KILL HIM?
HE CAN'T DIE. GIVE HIM THREE OR FOUR DAYS AND HE'LL REGENERATE.
THREE OR FOUR DAYS...
FROM THAT?
FWMP
Y'KNOW, MAKO DEAR...

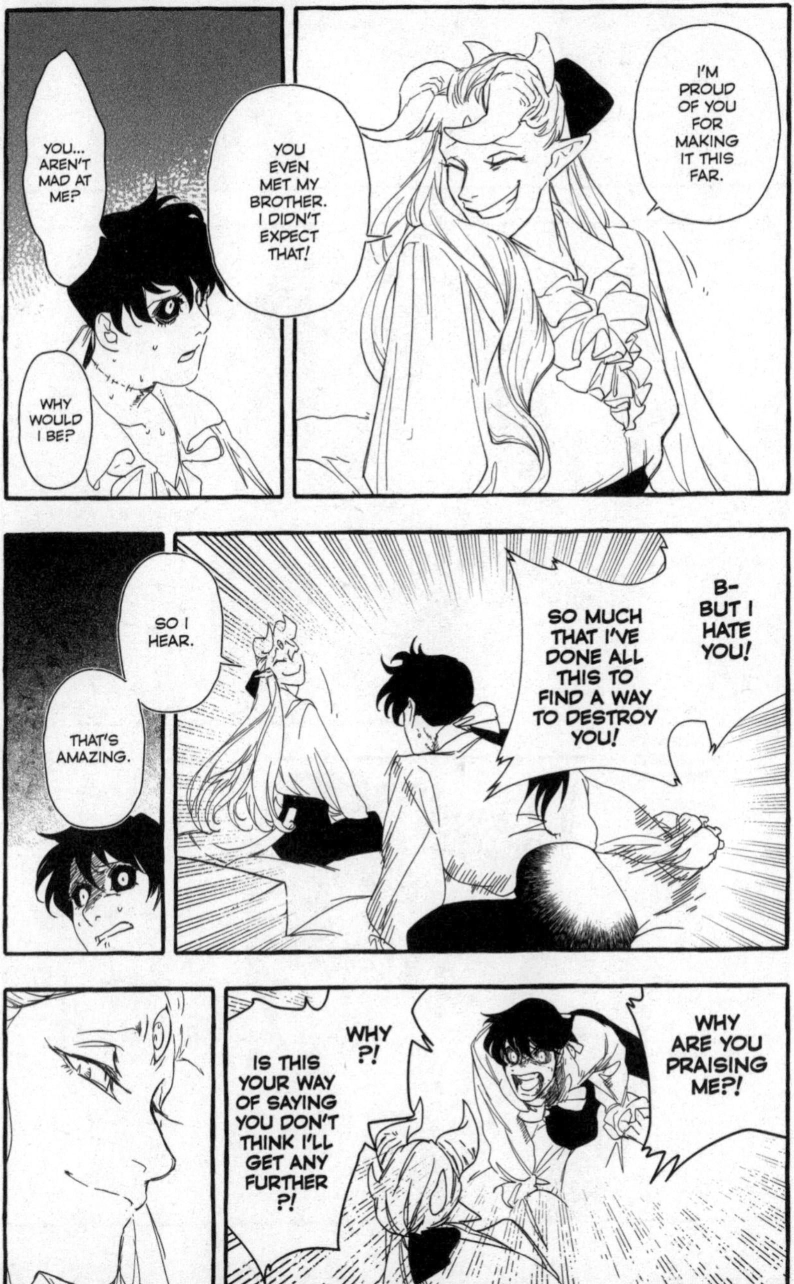
I'M PROUD OF YOU FOR MAKING IT THIS FAR.
YOU EVEN MET MY BROTHER. I DIDN'T EXPECT THAT!
YOU... AREN'T MAD AT ME?
WHY WOULD I BE?
B- BUT I HATE YOU!
SO MUCH THAT I'VE DONE ALL THIS TO FIND A WAY TO DESTROY YOU!
SO I HEAR.
THAT'S AMAZING.
WHY ARE YOU PRAISING ME?!
WHY?!
IS THIS YOUR WAY OF SAYING YOU DON'T THINK I'LL GET ANY FURTHER?!

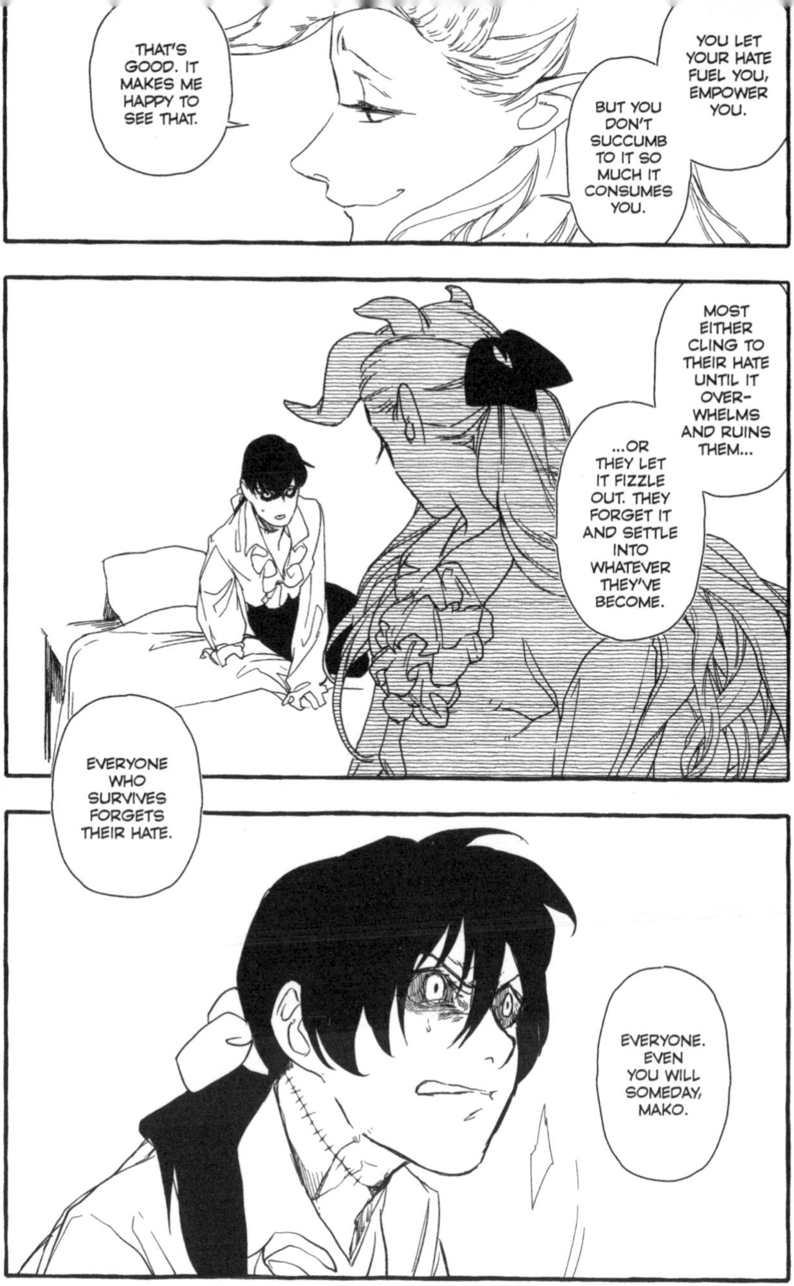
YOU LET YOUR HATE FUEL YOU, EMPOWER YOU.
BUT YOU DON'T SUCCUMB TO IT SO MUCH IT CONSUMES YOU.
THAT'S GOOD. IT MAKES ME HAPPY TO SEE THAT.
MOST EITHER CLING TO THEIR HATE UNTIL IT OVER-WHELMS AND RUINS THEM...
...OR THEY LET IT FIZZLE OUT. THEY FORGET IT AND SETTLE INTO WHATEVER THEY'VE BECOME.
EVERYONE WHO SURVIVES FORGETS THEIR HATE.
EVERYONE. EVEN YOU WILL SOMEDAY, MAKO.

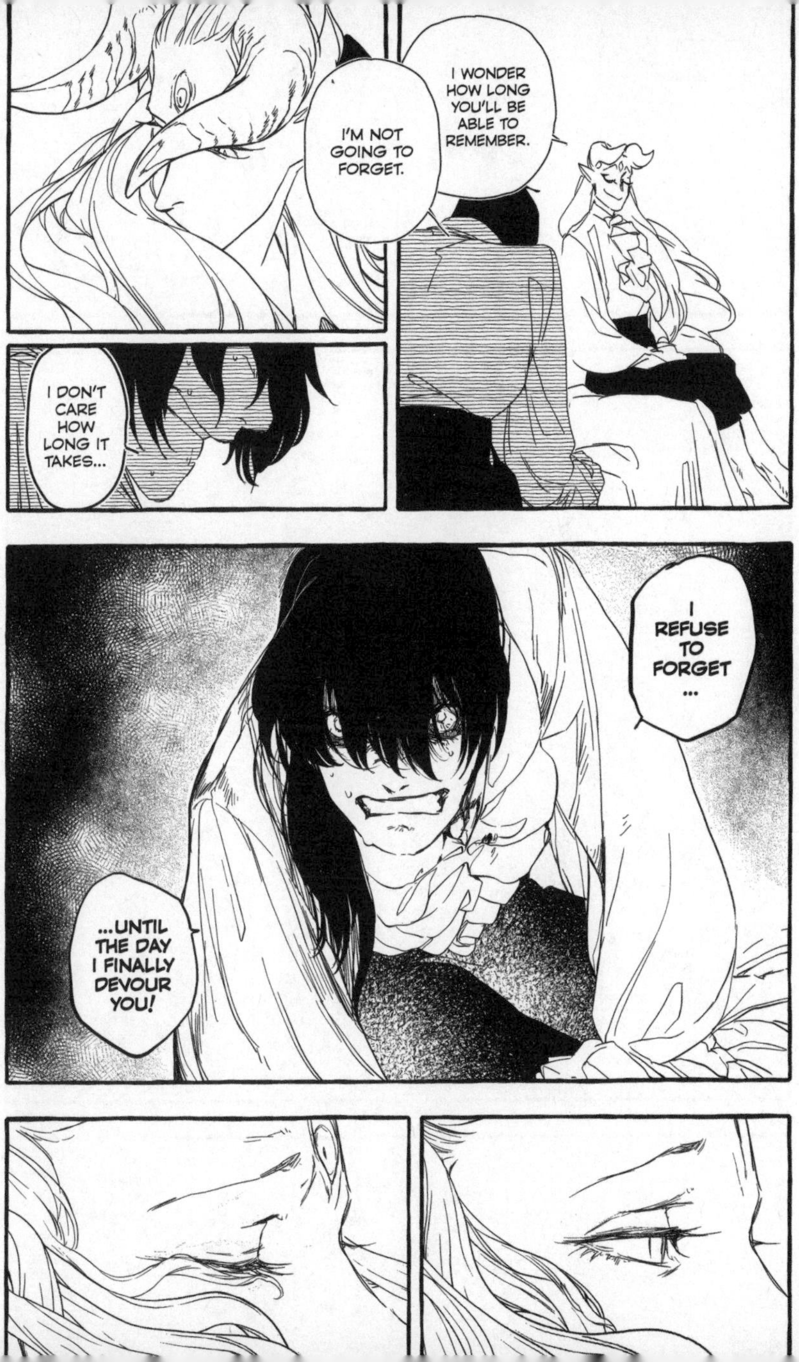
I WONDER HOW LONG YOU'LL BE ABLE TO REMEMBER.
I'M NOT GOING TO FORGET.
I DON'T CARE HOW LONG IT TAKES...
I REFUSE TO FORGET ...
...UNTIL THE DAY I FINALLY DEVOUR YOU!

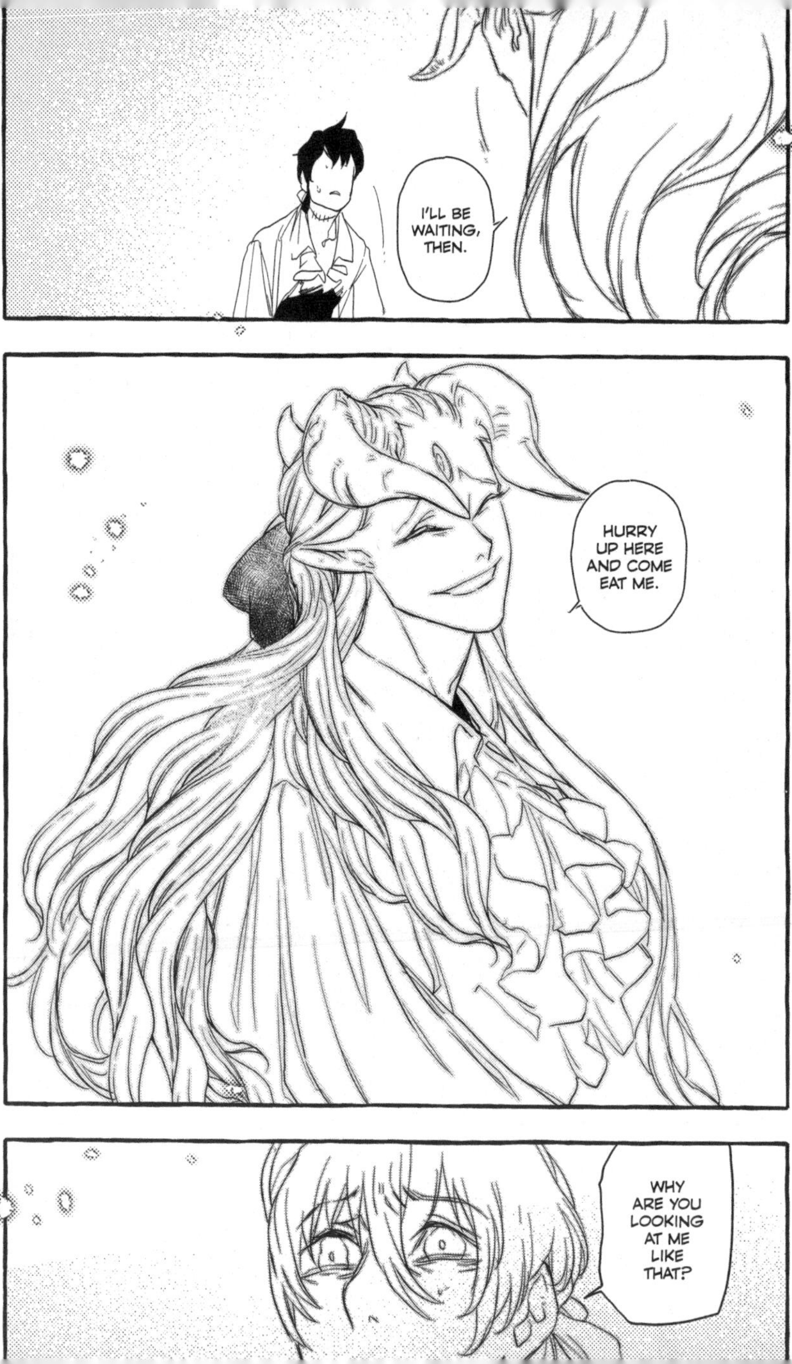
I'LL BE WAITING, THEN.
HURRY UP HERE AND COME EAT ME.
WHY ARE YOU LOOKING AT ME LIKE THAT?

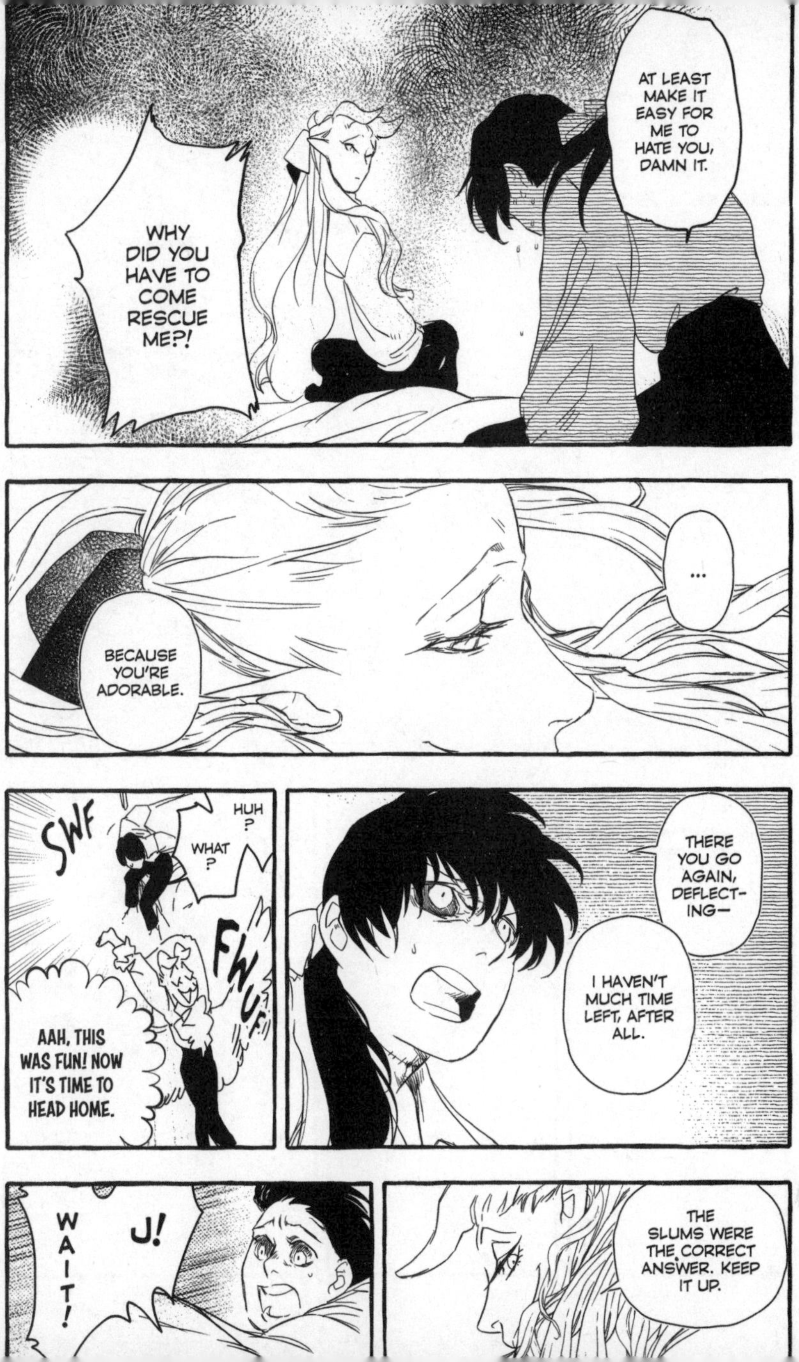
AT LEAST MAKE IT EASY FOR ME TO HATE YOU, DAMN IT.
WHY DID YOU HAVE TO COME RESCUE ME?!
...
BECAUSE YOU'RE ADORABLE.
THERE YOU GO AGAIN, DEFLECTING—
I HAVEN'T MUCH TIME LEFT, AFTER ALL.
HUH?
WHAT?
SWF
FWUF
AAH, THIS WAS FUN! NOW IT'S TIME TO HEAD HOME.
THE SLUMS WERE THE CORRECT ANSWER. KEEP IT UP.
J!
WAIT!

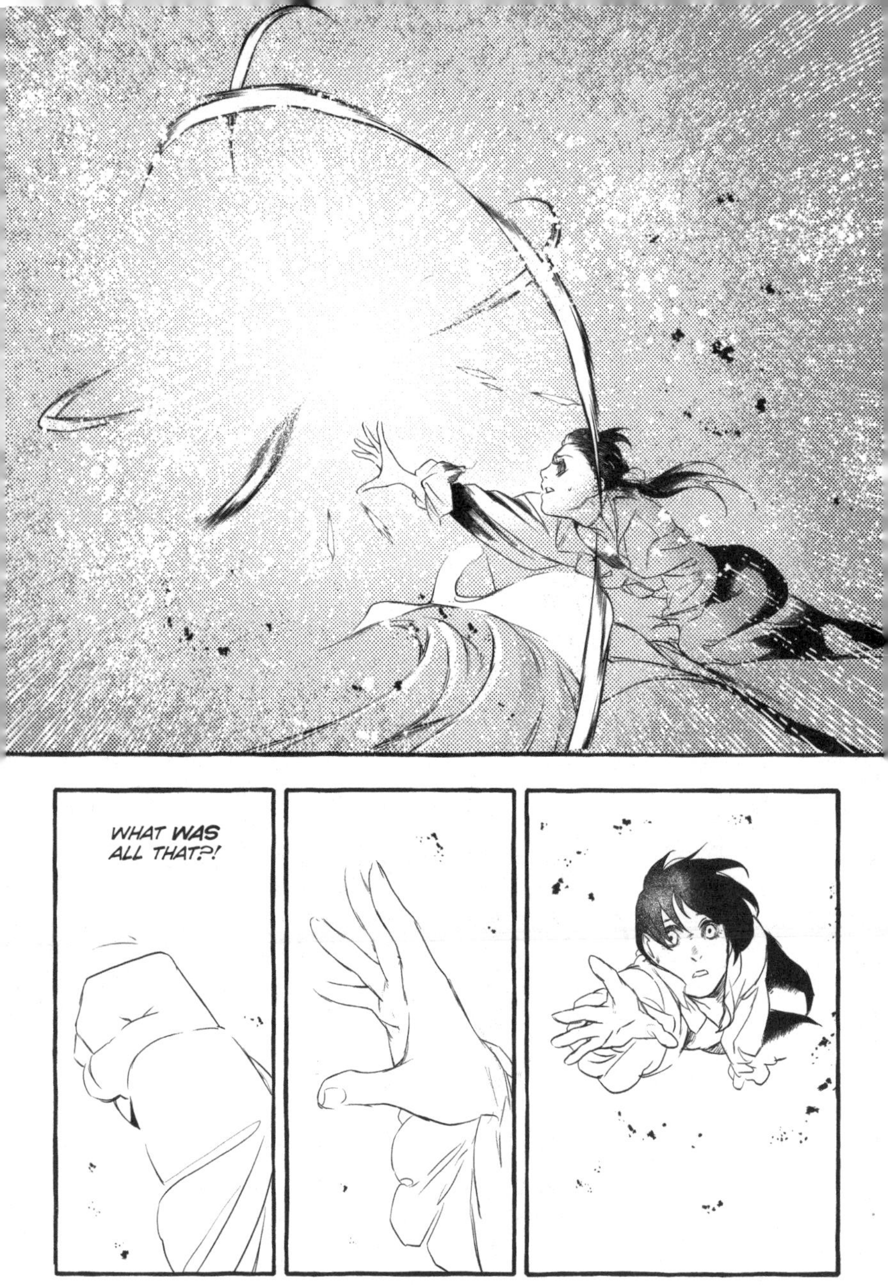
WHAT WAS ALL THAT?!

...!

THROB

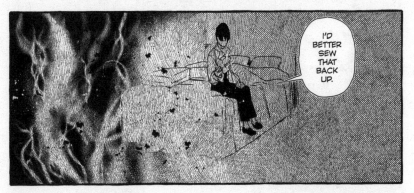

I'D BETTER SEW THAT BACK UP.

KCHAK

WILL I BE ABLE TO PATCH HIM UP WITH WHAT I HAVE?

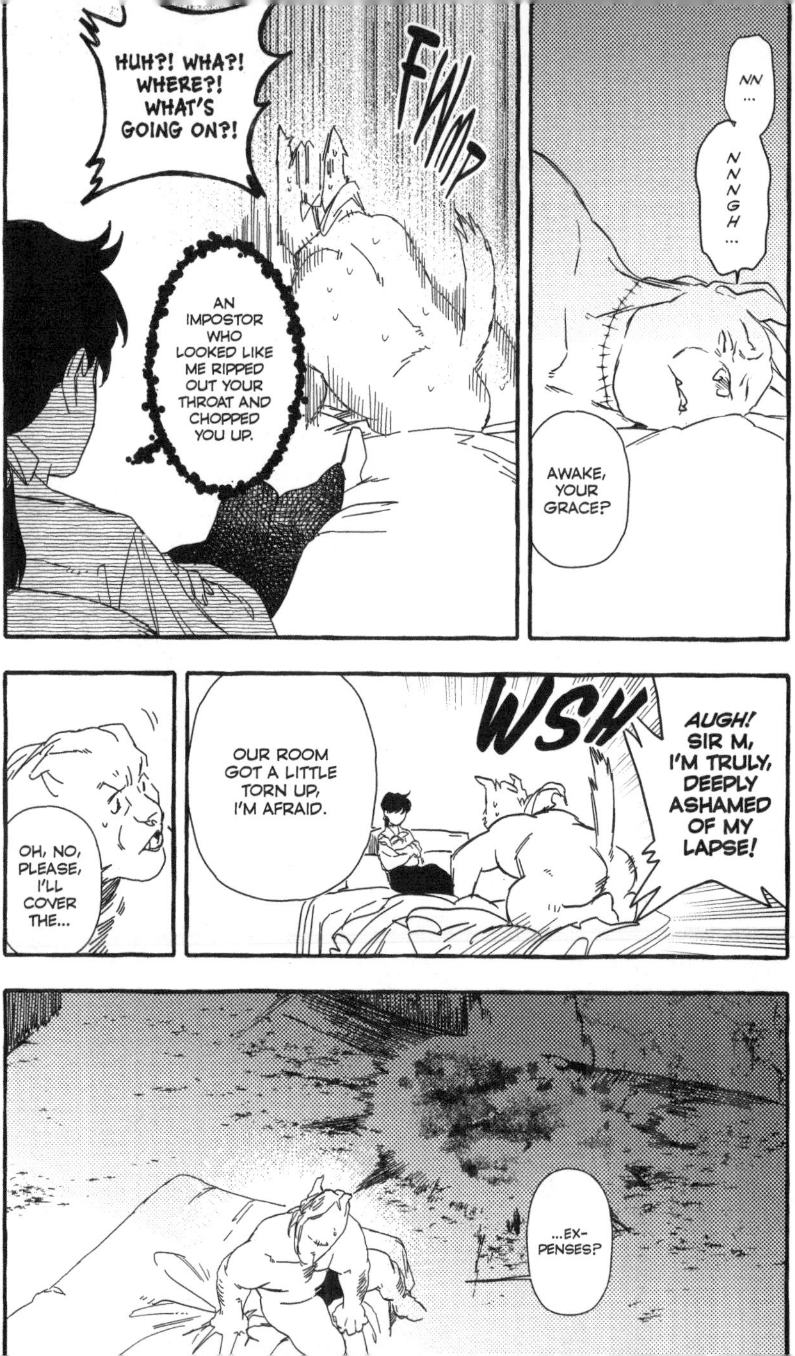
NN...
NNNGH...
AWAKE, YOUR GRACE?
FWMP
HUH?! WHA?! WHERE?! WHAT'S GOING ON?!
AN IMPOSTOR WHO LOOKED LIKE ME RIPPED OUT YOUR THROAT AND CHOPPED YOU UP.
AUGH! SIR M, I'M TRULY, DEEPLY ASHAMED OF MY LAPSE!
WSH
OUR ROOM GOT A LITTLE TORN UP, I'M AFRAID.
OH, NO, PLEASE, I'LL COVER THE...
...EX-PENSES?

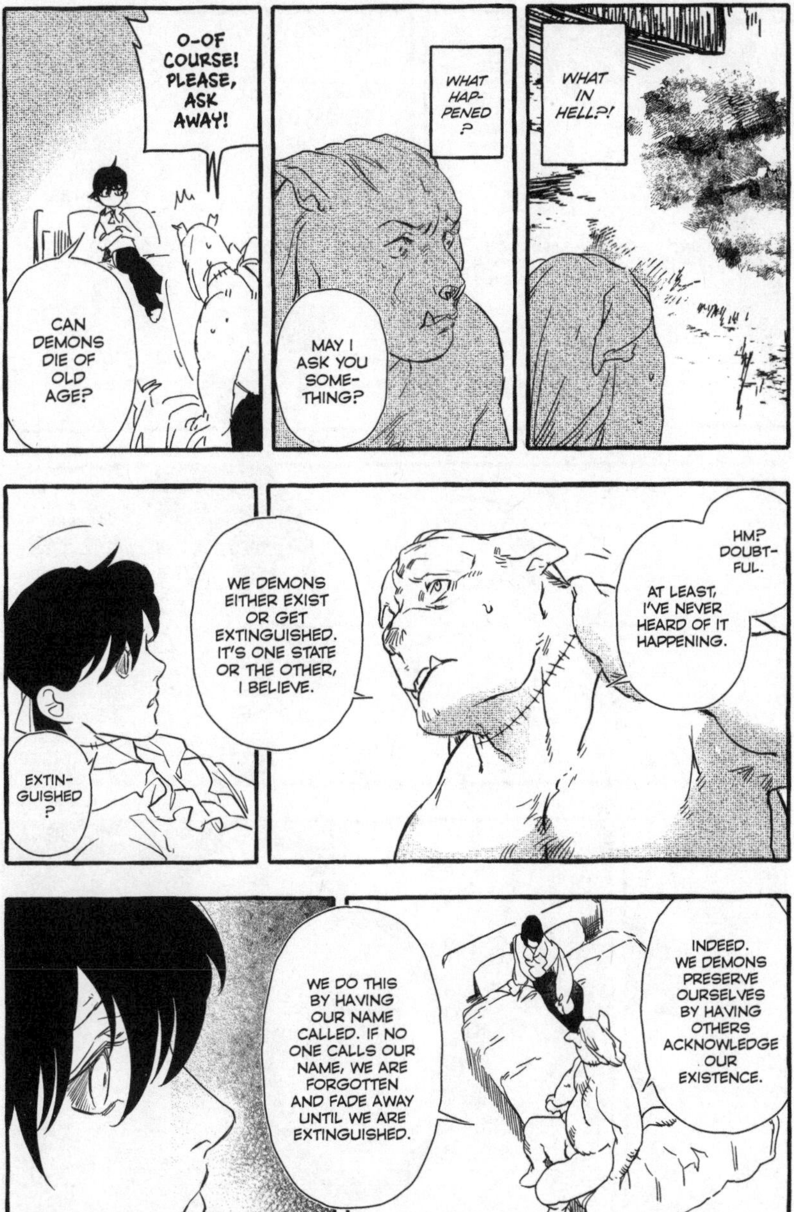
WHAT IN HELL?!
WHAT HAPPENED?
MAY I ASK YOU SOMETHING?
O-OF COURSE! PLEASE, ASK AWAY!
CAN DEMONS DIE OF OLD AGE?
HM? DOUBTFUL.
AT LEAST, I'VE NEVER HEARD OF IT HAPPENING.
WE DEMONS EITHER EXIST OR GET EXTINGUISHED. IT'S ONE STATE OR THE OTHER, I BELIEVE.
EXTINGUISHED?
INDEED. WE DEMONS PRESERVE OURSELVES BY HAVING OTHERS ACKNOWLEDGE OUR EXISTENCE.
WE DO THIS BY HAVING OUR NAME CALLED. IF NO ONE CALLS OUR NAME, WE ARE FORGOTTEN AND FADE AWAY UNTIL WE ARE EXTINGUISHED.

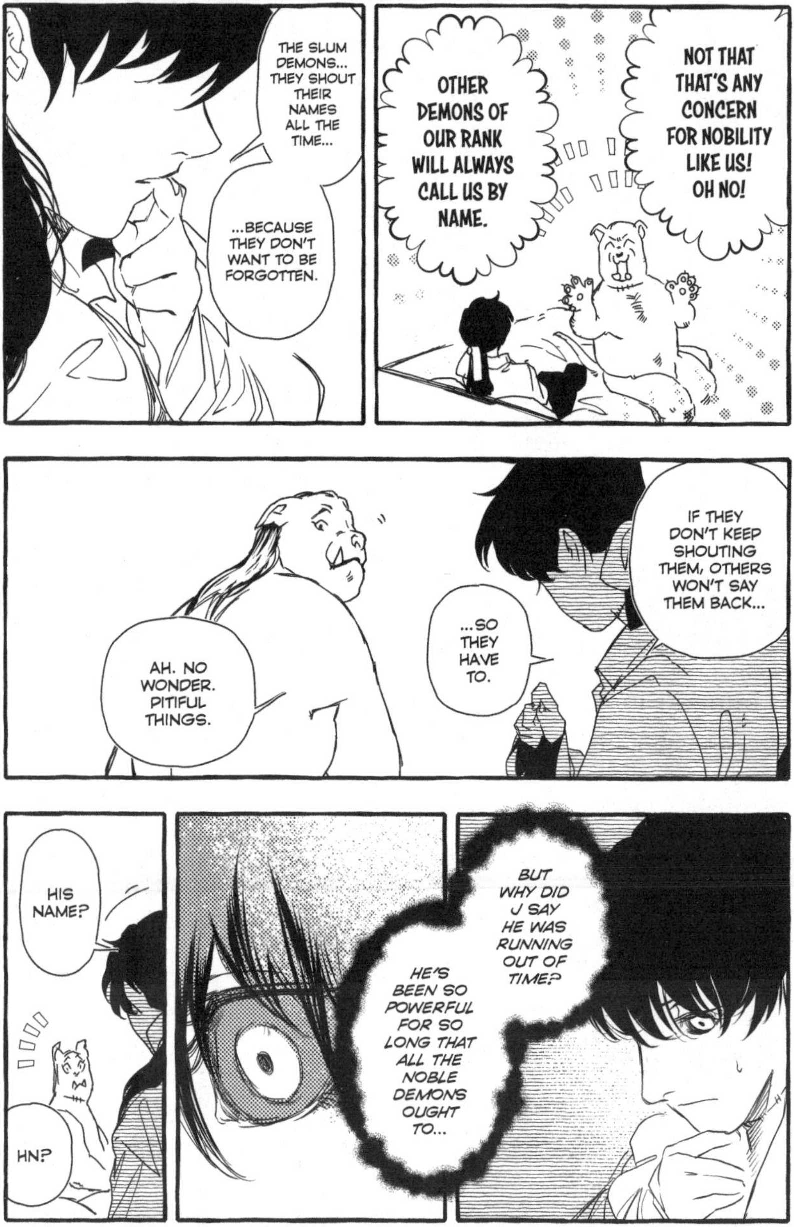
OTHER DEMONS OF OUR RANK WILL ALWAYS CALL US BY NAME.
NOT THAT THAT'S ANY CONCERN FOR NOBILITY LIKE US! OH NO!
THE SLUM DEMONS... THEY SHOUT THEIR NAMES ALL THE TIME...
...BECAUSE THEY DON'T WANT TO BE FORGOTTEN.
IF THEY DON'T KEEP SHOUTING THEM, OTHERS WON'T SAY THEM BACK...
...SO THEY HAVE TO.
AH. NO WONDER. PITIFUL THINGS.
BUT WHY DID I SAY HE WAS RUNNING OUT OF TIME?
HE'S BEEN SO POWERFUL FOR SO LONG THAT ALL THE NOBLE DEMONS OUGHT TO...
HIS NAME?
HN?

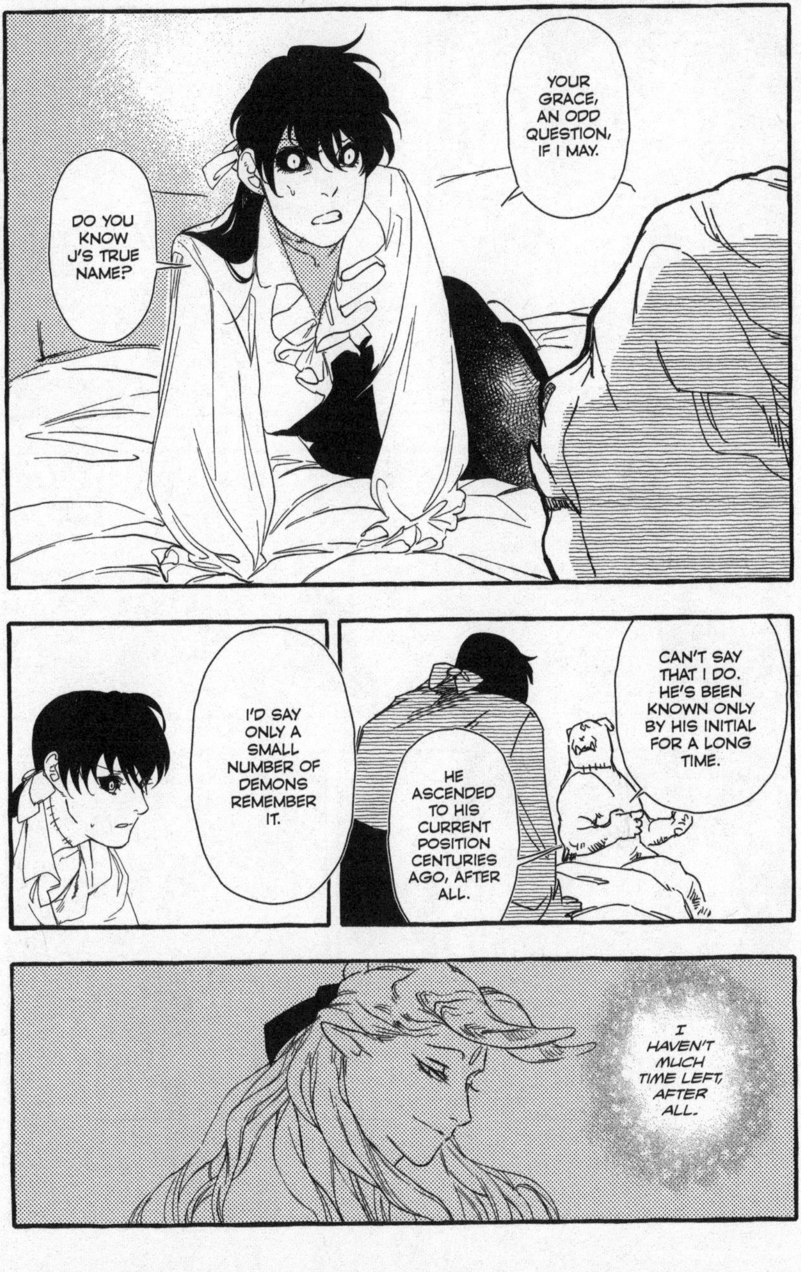
YOUR GRACE, AN ODD QUESTION, IF I MAY.
DO YOU KNOW J'S TRUE NAME?
CAN'T SAY THAT I DO. HE'S BEEN KNOWN ONLY BY HIS INITIAL FOR A LONG TIME.
HE ASCENDED TO HIS CURRENT POSITION CENTURIES AGO, AFTER ALL.
I'D SAY ONLY A SMALL NUMBER OF DEMONS REMEMBER IT.
I HAVEN'T MUCH TIME LEFT, AFTER ALL.

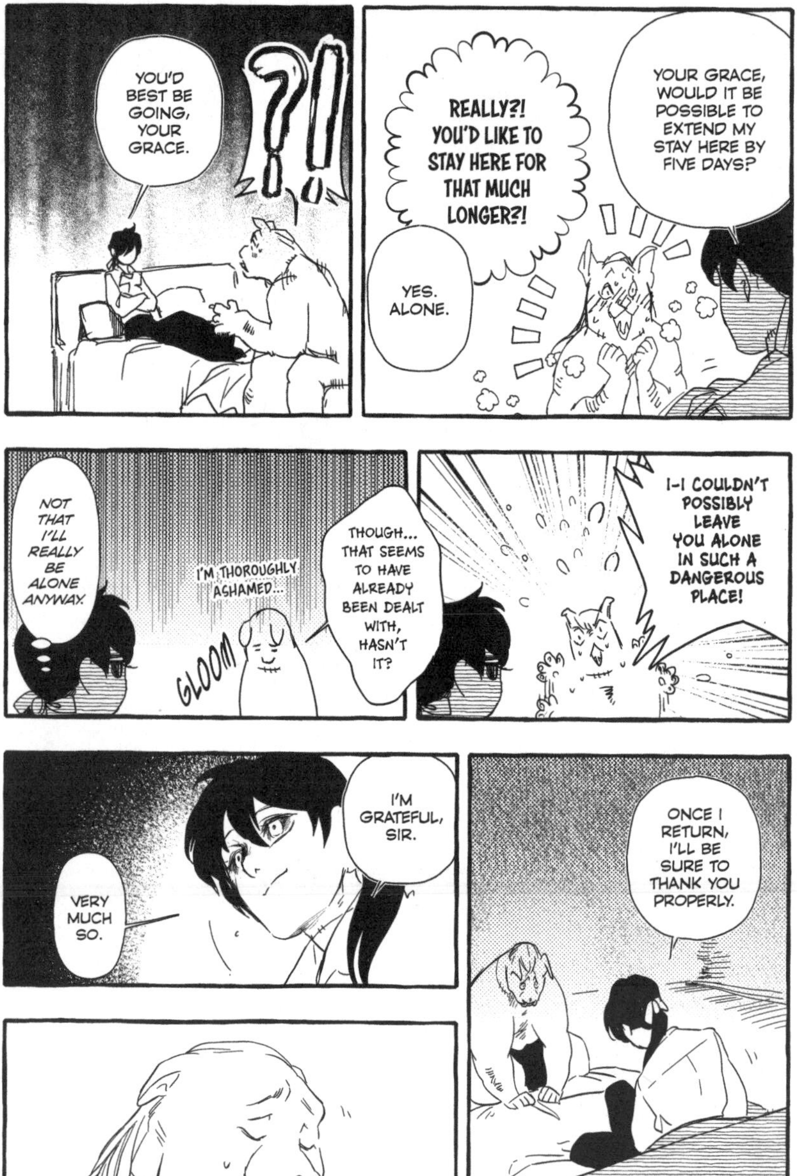
YOUR GRACE, WOULD IT BE POSSIBLE TO EXTEND MY STAY HERE BY FIVE DAYS?
REALLY?! YOU'D LIKE TO STAY HERE FOR THAT MUCH LONGER?!
YES. ALONE.
?!
YOU'D BEST BE GOING, YOUR GRACE.
I-I COULDN'T POSSIBLY LEAVE YOU ALONE IN SUCH A DANGEROUS PLACE!
THOUGH... THAT SEEMS TO HAVE ALREADY BEEN DEALT WITH, HASN'T IT?
I'M THOROUGHLY ASHAMED...
GLOOM
NOT THAT I'LL REALLY BE ALONE ANYWAY.
ONCE I RETURN, I'LL BE SURE TO THANK YOU PROPERLY.
I'M GRATEFUL, SIR.
VERY MUCH SO.

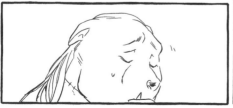

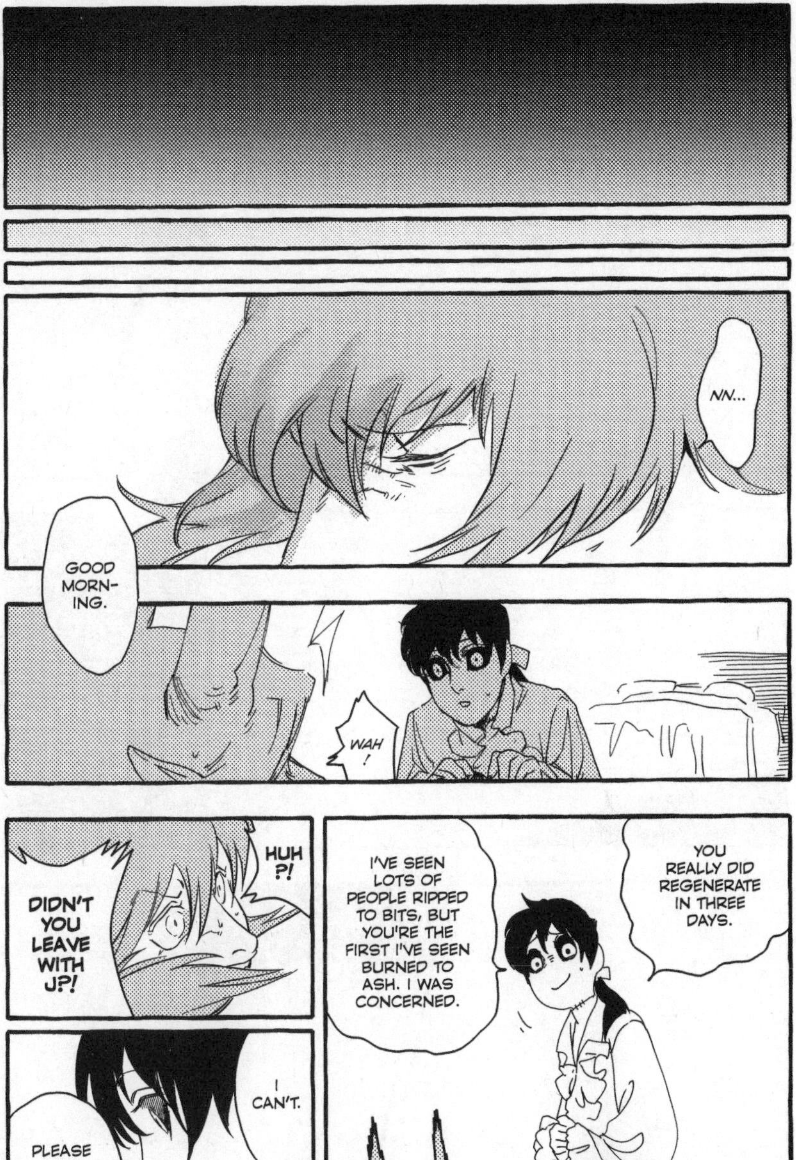
NN...
GOOD MORNING.
WAH!
YOU REALLY DID REGENERATE IN THREE DAYS.
I'VE SEEN LOTS OF PEOPLE RIPPED TO BITS, BUT YOU'RE THE FIRST I'VE SEEN BURNED TO ASH. I WAS CONCERNED.
HUH?!
DIDN'T YOU LEAVE WITH J?!
I CAN'T.
PLEASE HELP ME.

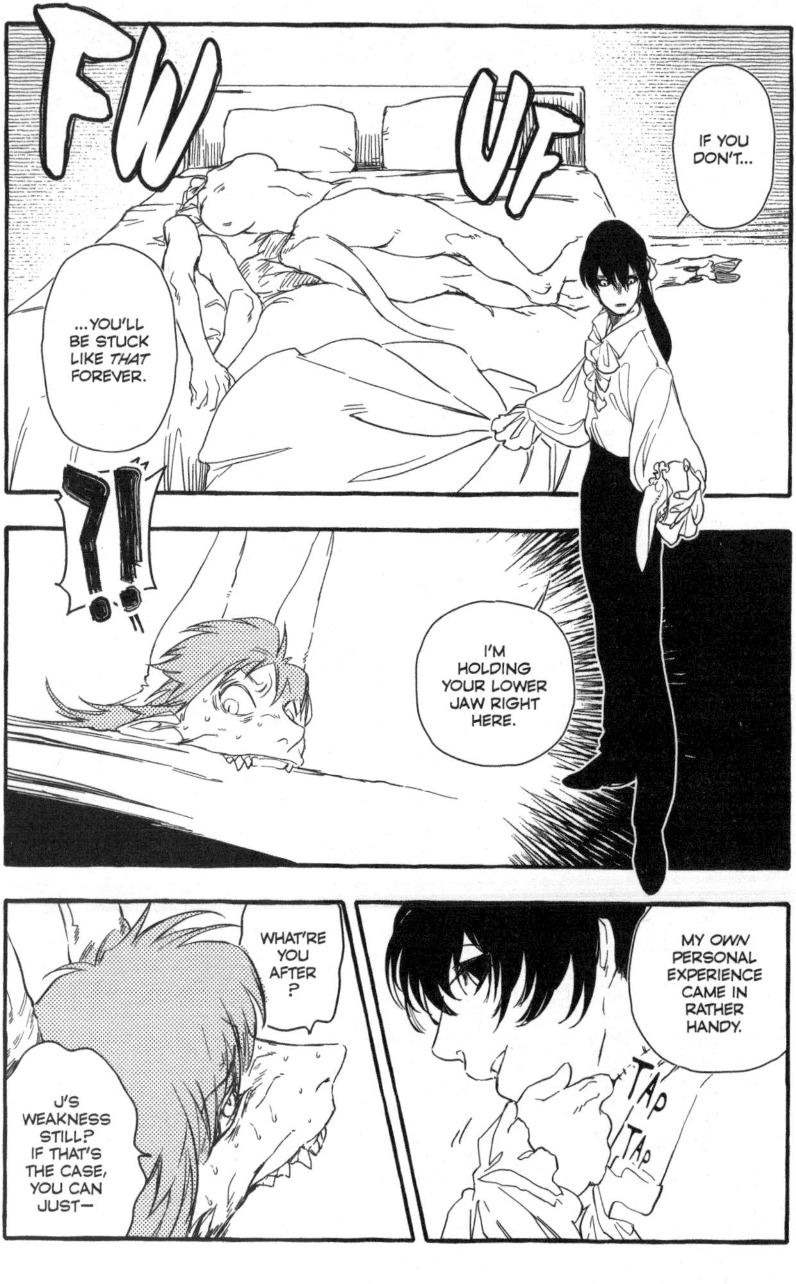
FWUF
IF YOU DON'T...
...YOU'LL BE STUCK LIKE *THAT* FOREVER.
?!
I'M HOLDING YOUR LOWER JAW RIGHT HERE.
MY *OWN* PERSONAL EXPERIENCE CAME IN RATHER HANDY.
TAP TAP
WHAT'RE YOU AFTER?
J'S WEAKNESS STILL? IF THAT'S THE CASE, YOU CAN JUST—

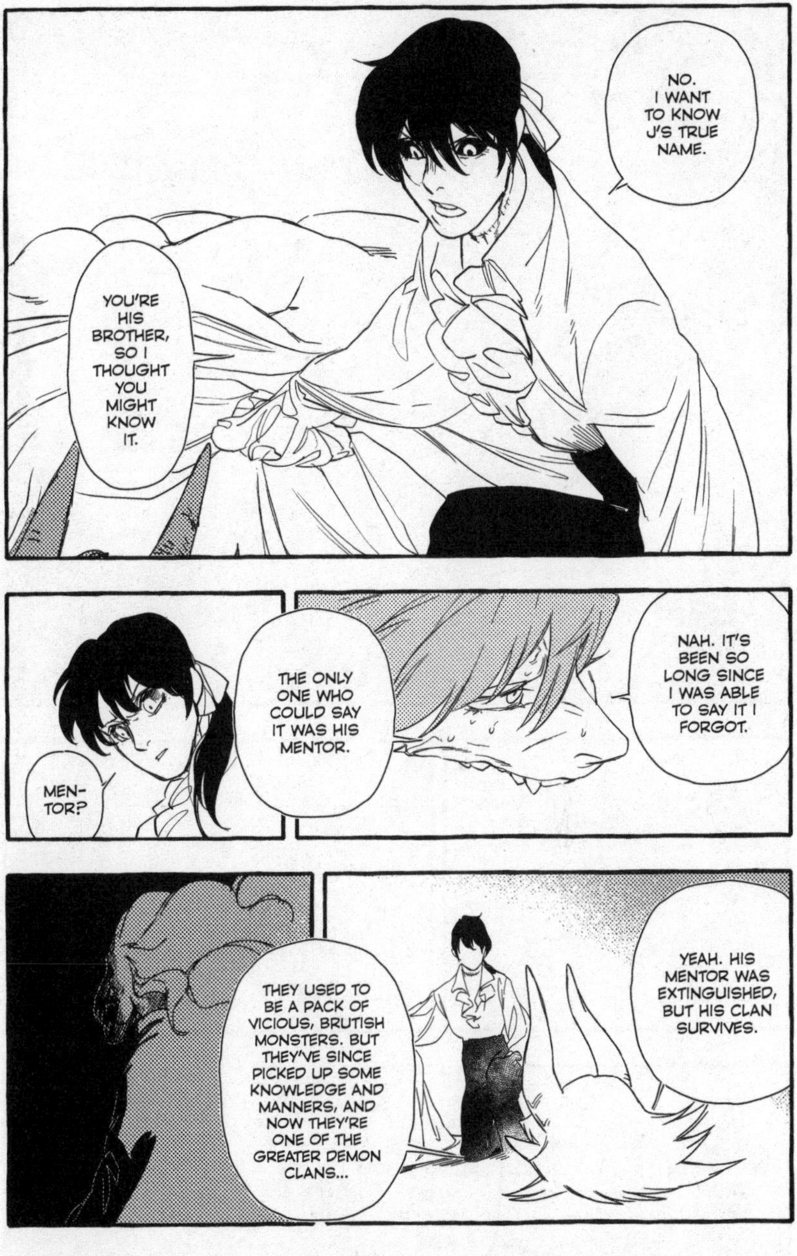
NO. I WANT TO KNOW J'S TRUE NAME.
YOU'RE HIS BROTHER, SO I THOUGHT YOU MIGHT KNOW IT.
NAH. IT'S BEEN SO LONG SINCE I WAS ABLE TO SAY IT I FORGOT.
THE ONLY ONE WHO COULD SAY IT WAS HIS MENTOR.
MEN-TOR?
YEAH. HIS MENTOR WAS EXTINGUISHED, BUT HIS CLAN SURVIVES.
THEY USED TO BE A PACK OF VICIOUS, BRUTISH MONSTERS. BUT THEY'VE SINCE PICKED UP SOME KNOWLEDGE AND MANNERS, AND NOW THEY'RE ONE OF THE GREATER DEMON CLANS...

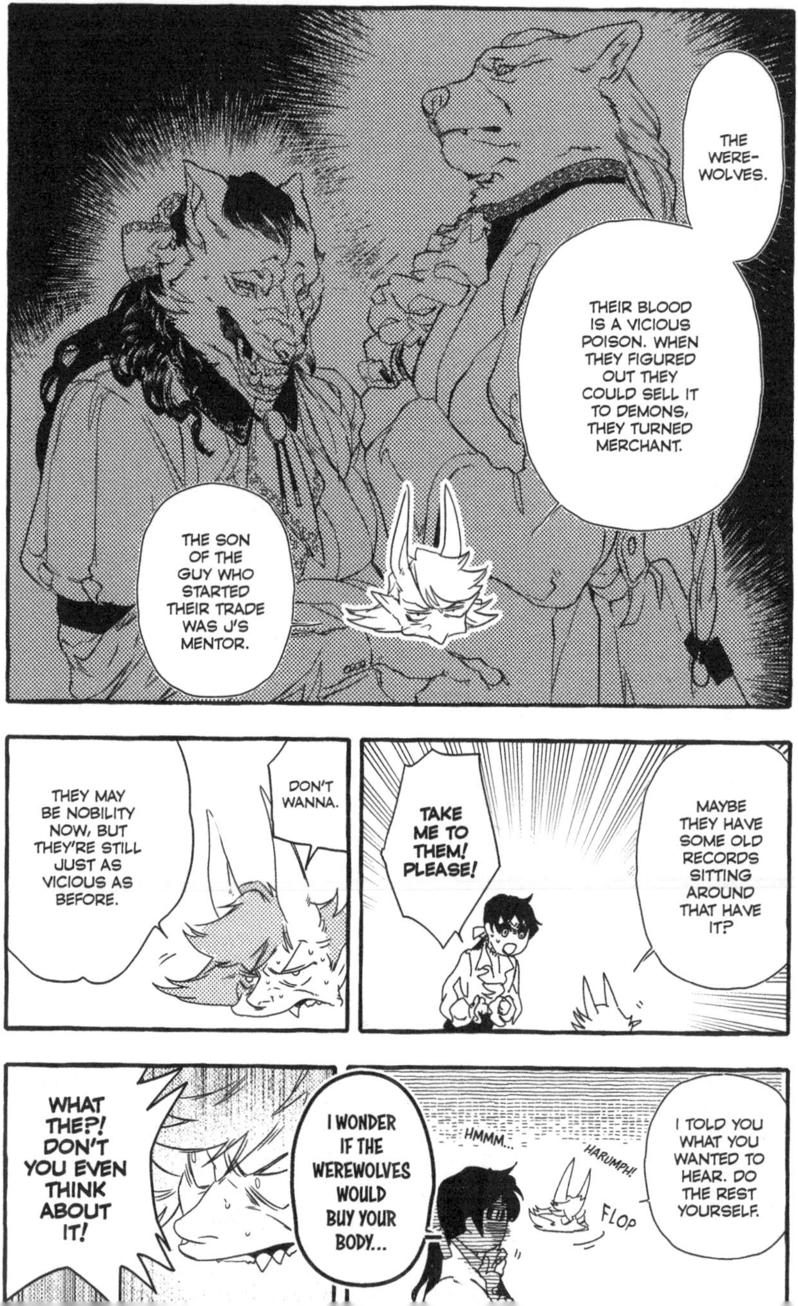
THE WERE-WOLVES.
THEIR BLOOD IS A VICIOUS POISON. WHEN THEY FIGURED OUT THEY COULD SELL IT TO DEMONS, THEY TURNED MERCHANT.
THE SON OF THE GUY WHO STARTED THEIR TRADE WAS J'S MENTOR.
MAYBE THEY HAVE SOME OLD RECORDS SITTING AROUND THAT HAVE IT?
TAKE ME TO THEM! PLEASE!
DON'T WANNA.
THEY MAY BE NOBILITY NOW, BUT THEY'RE STILL JUST AS VICIOUS AS BEFORE.
I TOLD YOU WHAT YOU WANTED TO HEAR. DO THE REST YOURSELF.
HARUMPH!
FLOP
HMMM...
I WONDER IF THE WEREWOLVES WOULD BUY YOUR BODY...
WHAT THE?! DON'T YOU EVEN THINK ABOUT IT!

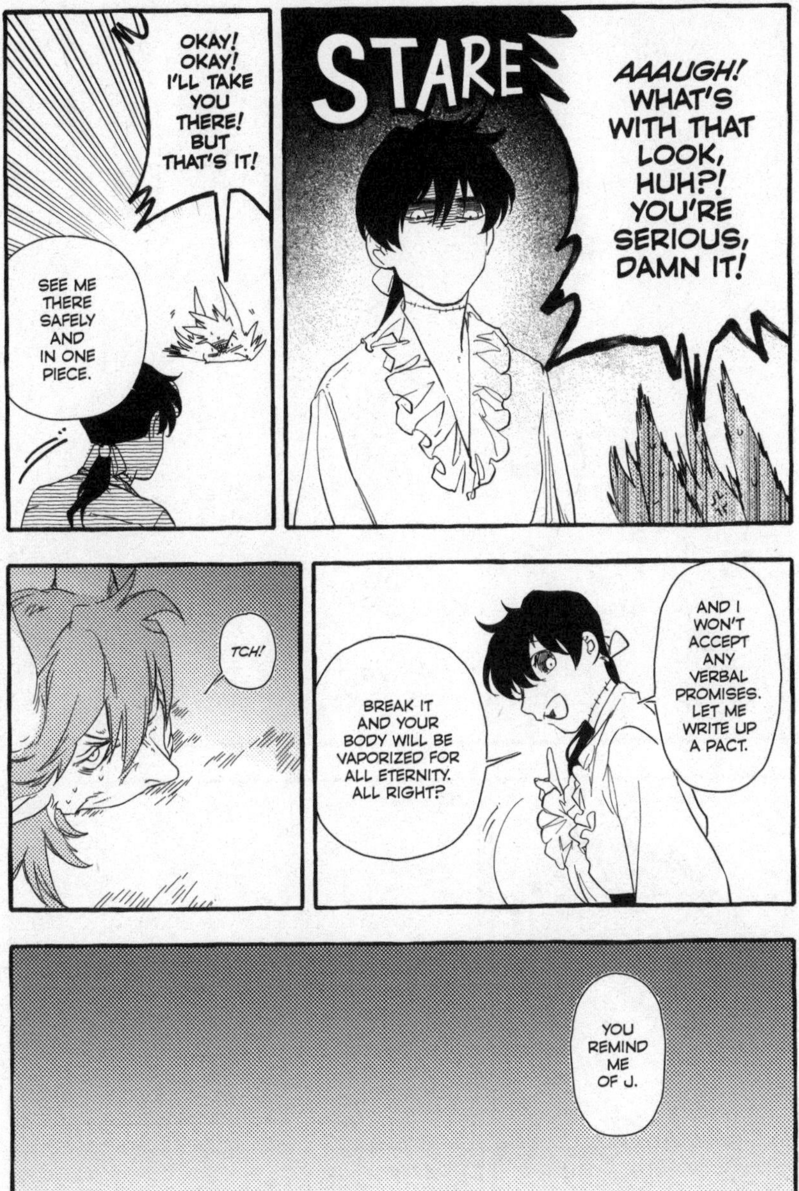
STARE
AAAUGH! WHAT'S WITH THAT LOOK, HUH?! YOU'RE SERIOUS, DAMN IT!
OKAY! OKAY! I'LL TAKE YOU THERE! BUT THAT'S IT!
SEE ME THERE SAFELY AND IN ONE PIECE.
AND I WON'T ACCEPT ANY VERBAL PROMISES. LET ME WRITE UP A PACT.
BREAK IT AND YOUR BODY WILL BE VAPORIZED FOR ALL ETERNITY. ALL RIGHT?
TCH!
YOU REMIND ME OF J.

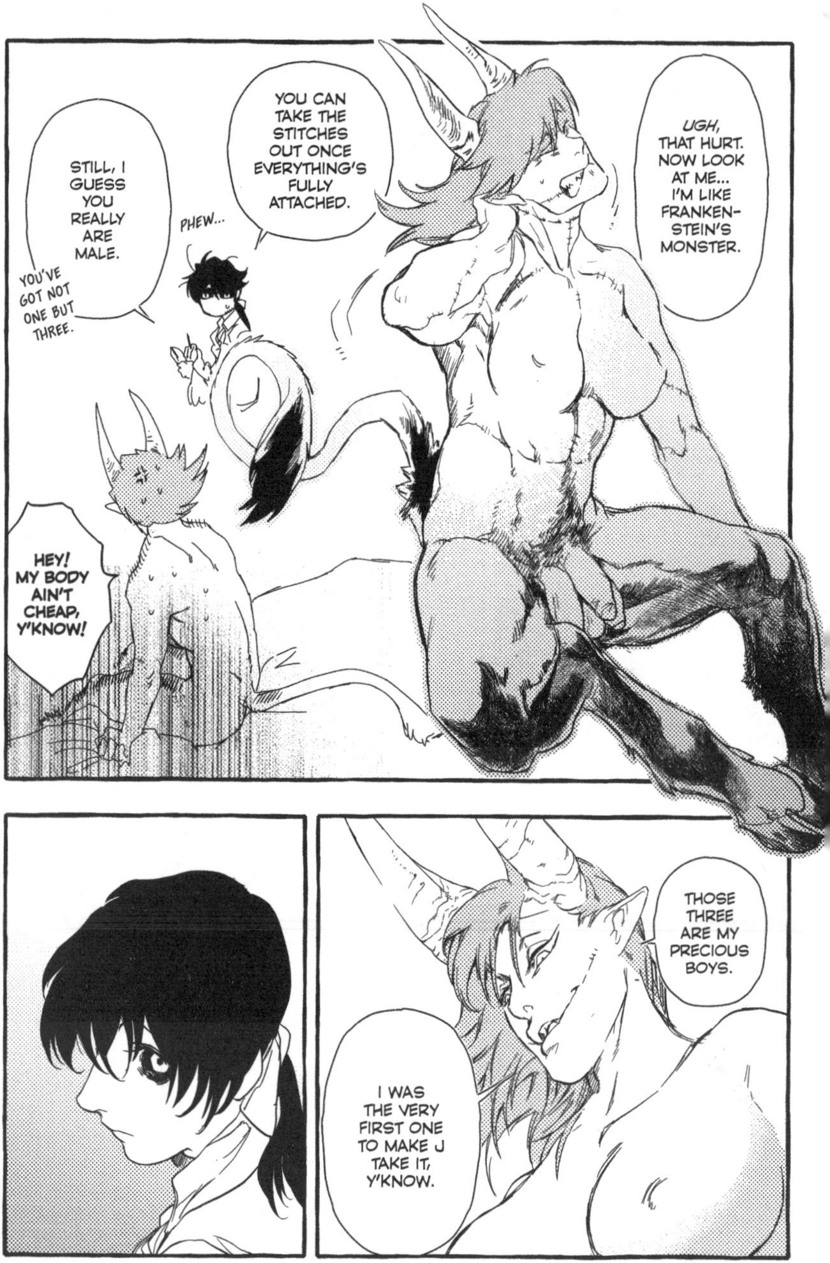
UGH, THAT HURT. NOW LOOK AT ME... I'M LIKE FRANKEN-STEIN'S MONSTER.
YOU CAN TAKE THE STITCHES OUT ONCE EVERYTHING'S FULLY ATTACHED.
PHEW...
STILL, I GUESS YOU REALLY ARE MALE.
YOU'VE GOT NOT ONE BUT THREE.
HEY! MY BODY AIN'T CHEAP, Y'KNOW!
THOSE THREE ARE MY PRECIOUS BOYS.
I WAS THE VERY FIRST ONE TO MAKE J TAKE IT, Y'KNOW.

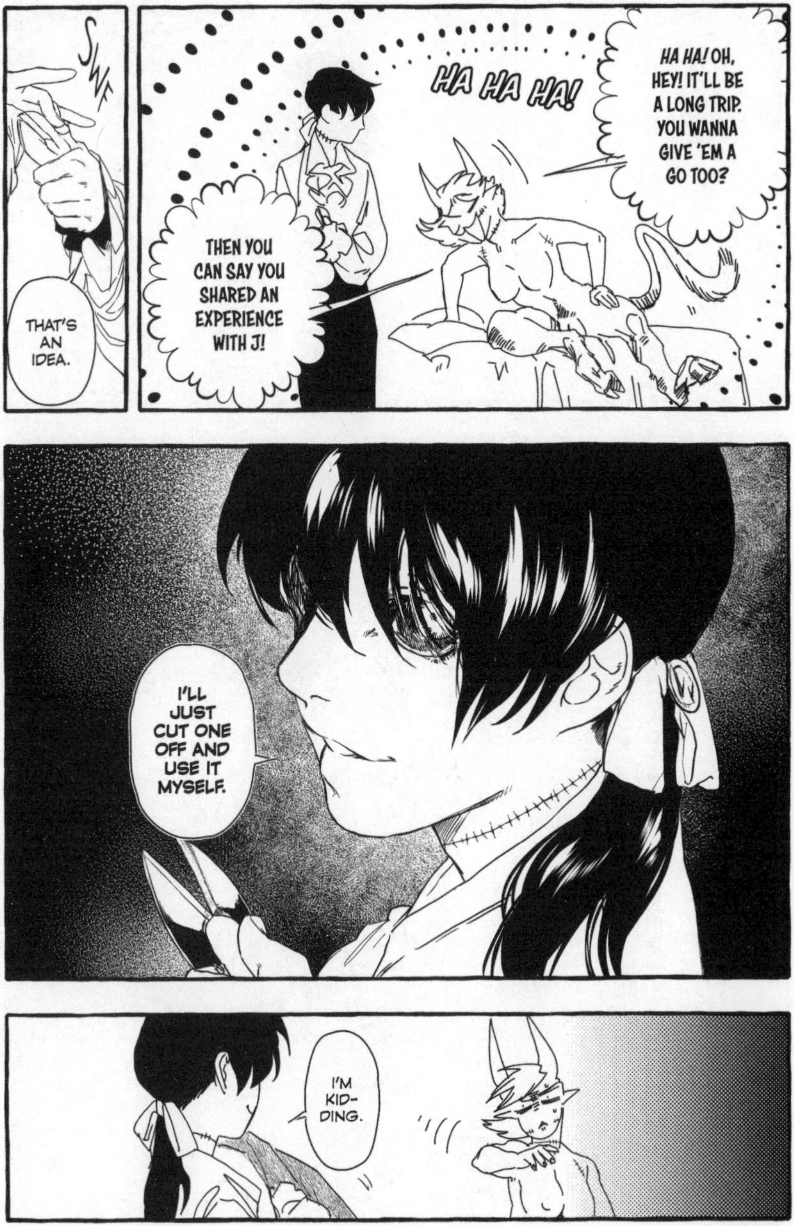
HA HA! OH, HEY! IT'LL BE A LONG TRIP. YOU WANNA GIVE 'EM A GO TOO?
HA HA HA!
THEN YOU CAN SAY YOU SHARED AN EXPERIENCE WITH J!
SWF
THAT'S AN IDEA.
I'LL JUST CUT ONE OFF AND USE IT MYSELF.
I'M KID-DING.

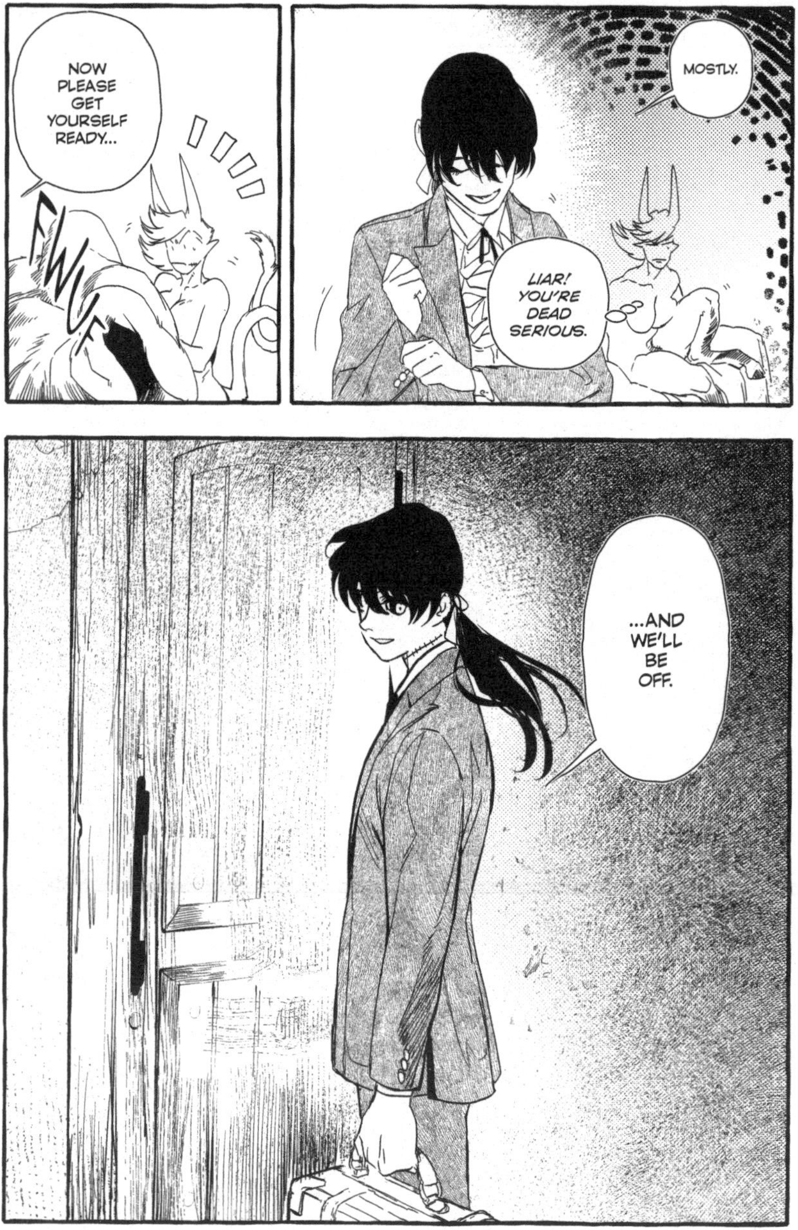
MOSTLY.
LIAR! YOU'RE DEAD SERIOUS.
NOW PLEASE GET YOURSELF READY...
FWUF
...AND WE'LL BE OFF.

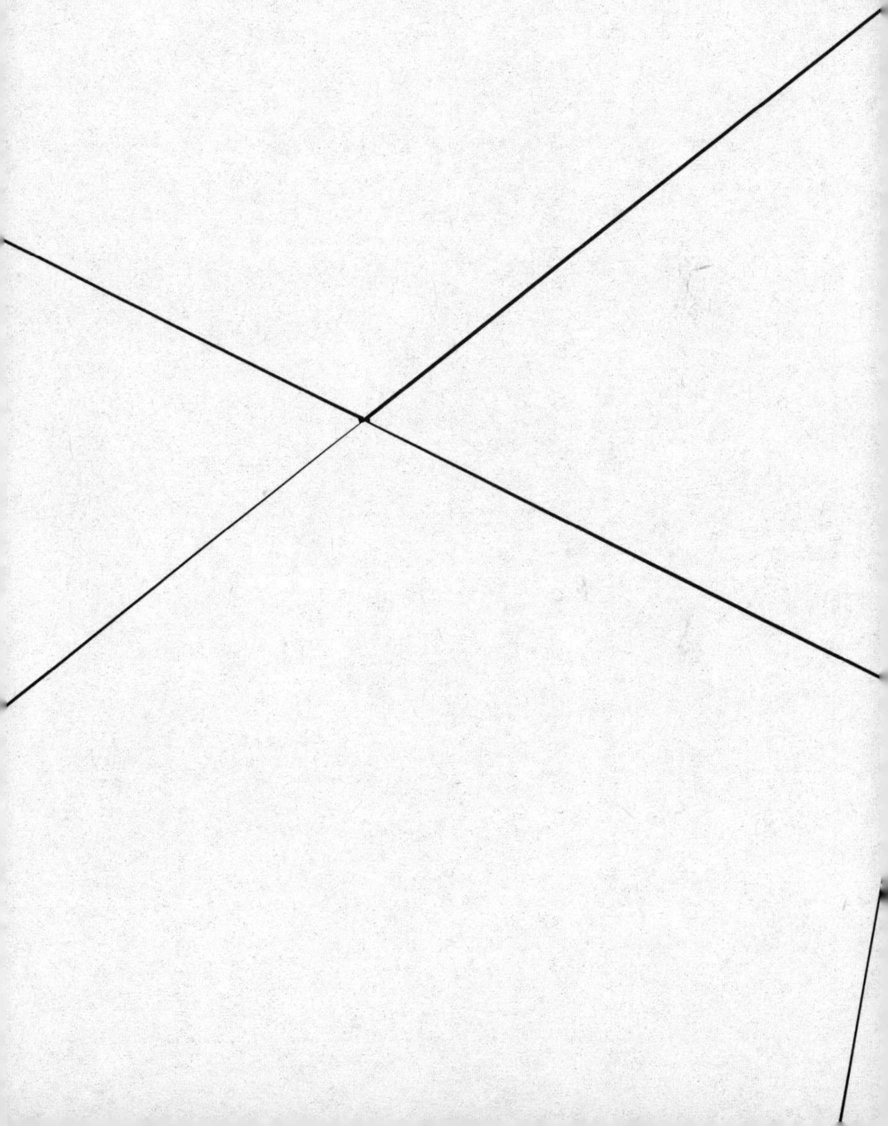

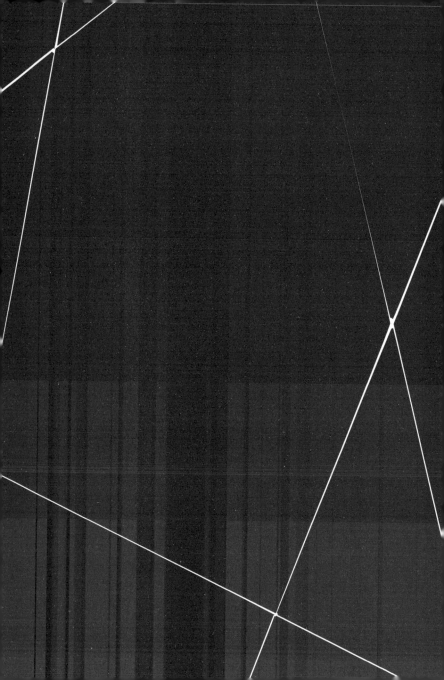

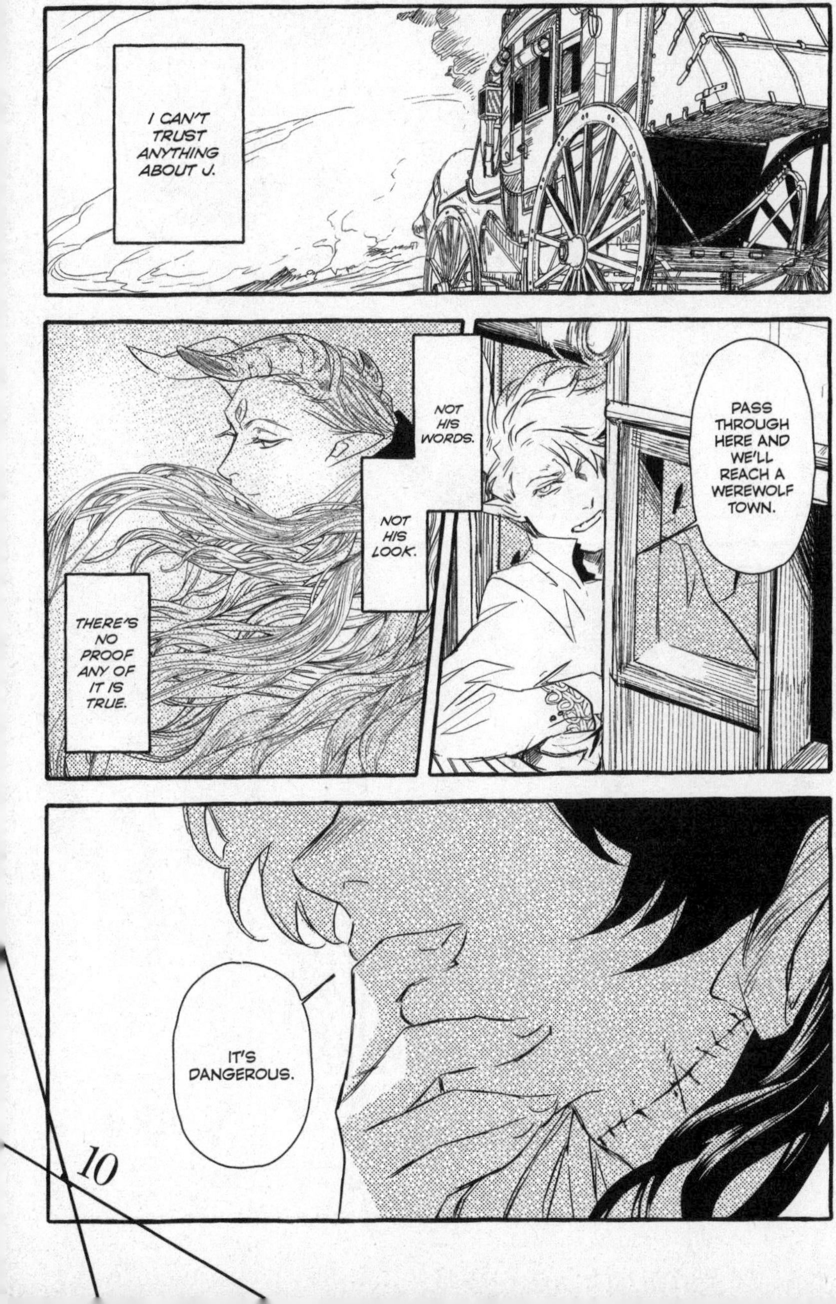
I CAN'T TRUST ANYTHING ABOUT J.
PASS THROUGH HERE AND WE'LL REACH A WEREWOLF TOWN.
NOT HIS WORDS.
NOT HIS LOOK.
THERE'S NO PROOF ANY OF IT IS TRUE.
IT'S DANGEROUS.
10

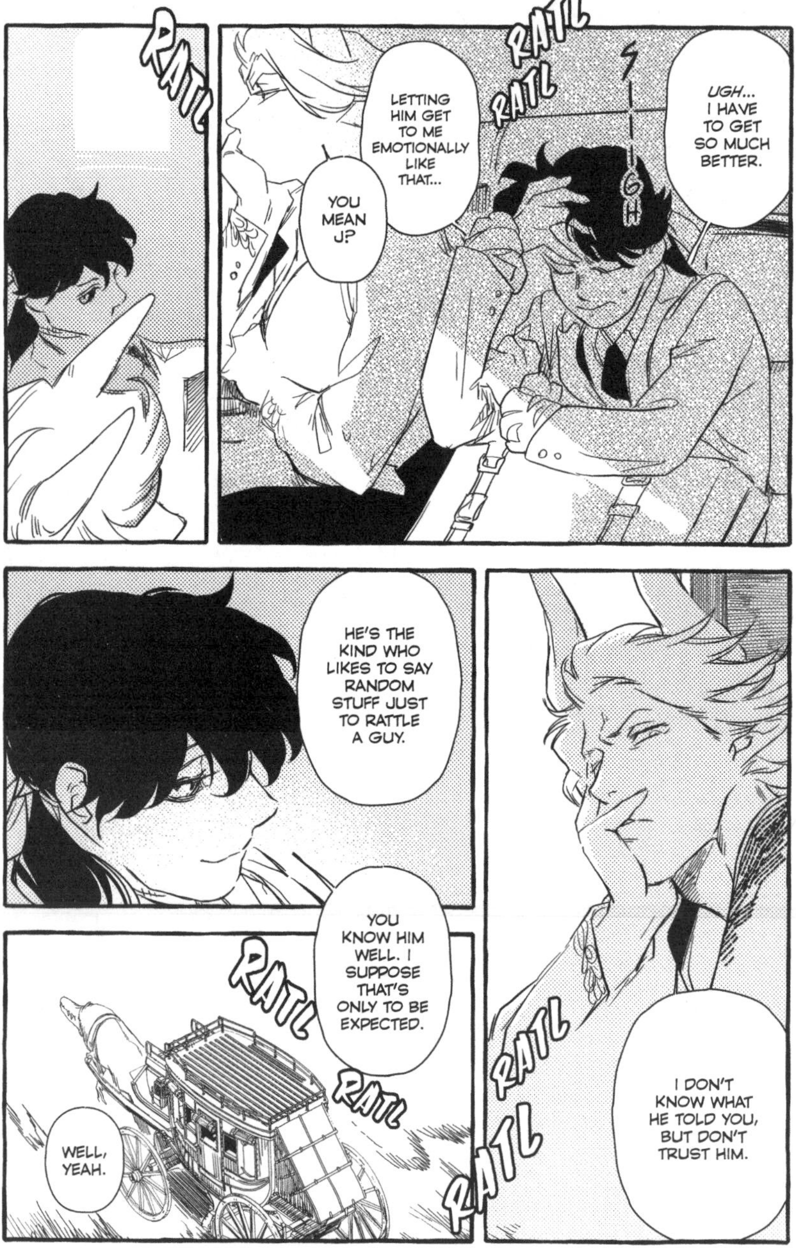
SIIGH
UGH... I HAVE TO GET SO MUCH BETTER.
RATL RATL
LETTING HIM GET TO ME EMOTIONALLY LIKE THAT...
YOU MEAN J?
RATL
I DON'T KNOW WHAT HE TOLD YOU, BUT DON'T TRUST HIM.
RATL RATL
HE'S THE KIND WHO LIKES TO SAY RANDOM STUFF JUST TO RATTLE A GUY.
YOU KNOW HIM WELL. I SUPPOSE THAT'S ONLY TO BE EXPECTED.
RATL RATL
WELL, YEAH.

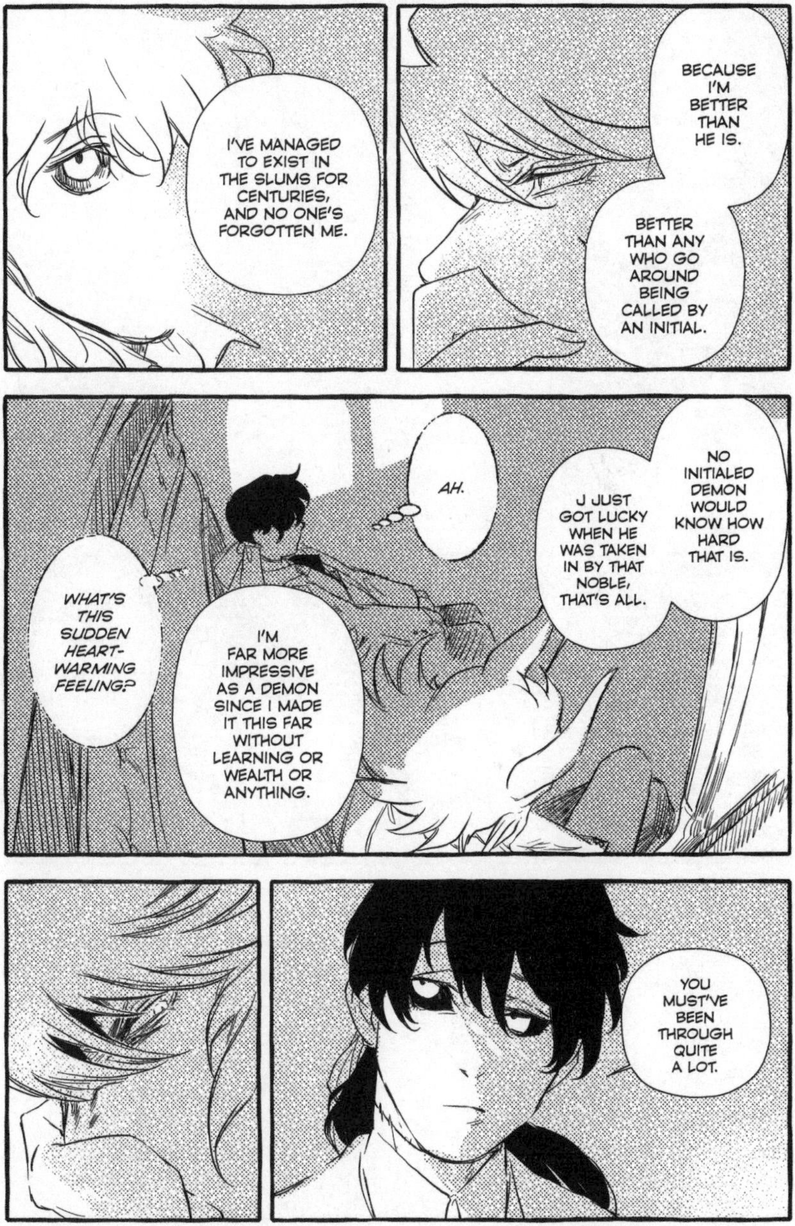
BECAUSE I'M BETTER THAN HE IS.
BETTER THAN ANY WHO GO AROUND BEING CALLED BY AN INITIAL.
I'VE MANAGED TO EXIST IN THE SLUMS FOR CENTURIES, AND NO ONE'S FORGOTTEN ME.
NO INITIALED DEMON WOULD KNOW HOW HARD THAT IS.
J JUST GOT LUCKY WHEN HE WAS TAKEN IN BY THAT NOBLE, THAT'S ALL.
AH.
I'M FAR MORE IMPRESSIVE AS A DEMON SINCE I MADE IT THIS FAR WITHOUT LEARNING OR WEALTH OR ANYTHING.
WHAT'S THIS SUDDEN HEART-WARMING FEELING?
YOU MUST'VE BEEN THROUGH QUITE A LOT.

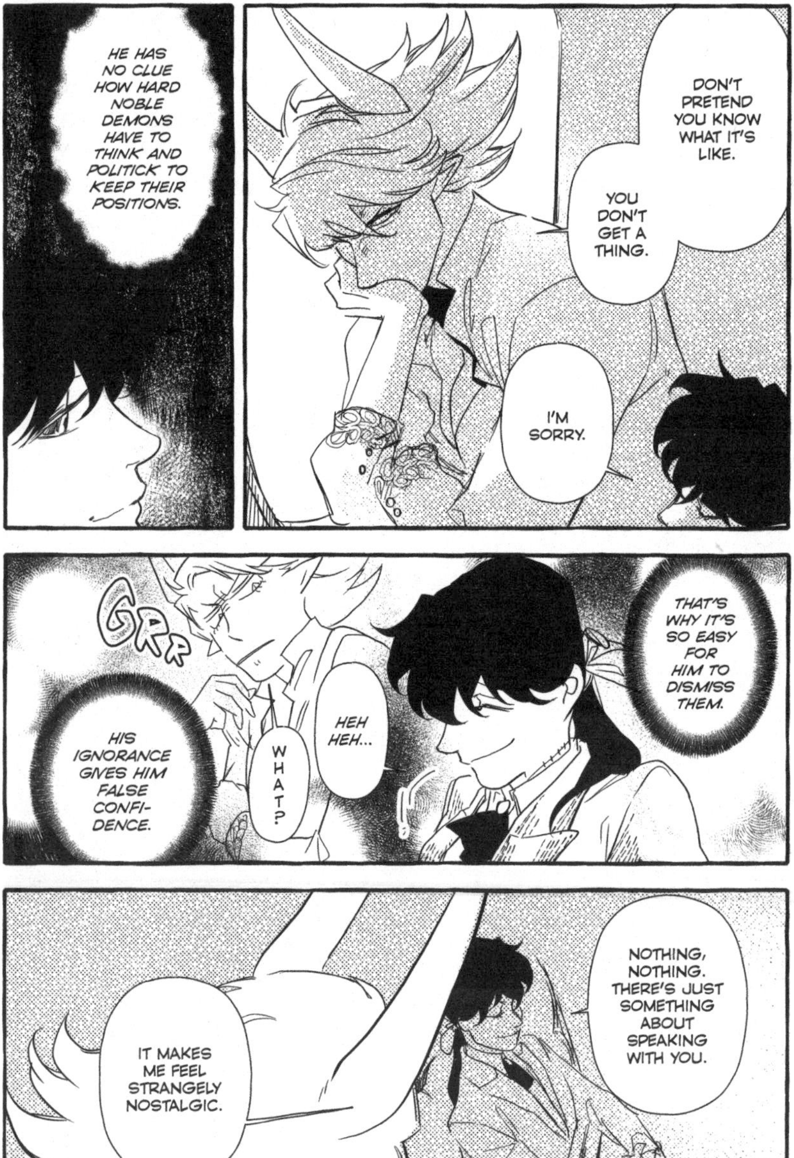
DON'T PRETEND YOU KNOW WHAT IT'S LIKE.
YOU DON'T GET A THING.
I'M SORRY.
HE HAS NO CLUE HOW HARD NOBLE DEMONS HAVE TO THINK AND POLITICK TO KEEP THEIR POSITIONS.
THAT'S WHY IT'S SO EASY FOR HIM TO DISMISS THEM.
HEH HEH...
WHAT?
GRR
HIS IGNORANCE GIVES HIM FALSE CONFI-DENCE.
NOTHING, NOTHING. THERE'S JUST SOMETHING ABOUT SPEAKING WITH YOU.
IT MAKES ME FEEL STRANGELY NOSTALGIC.

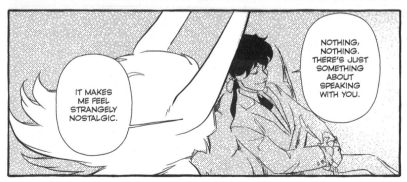

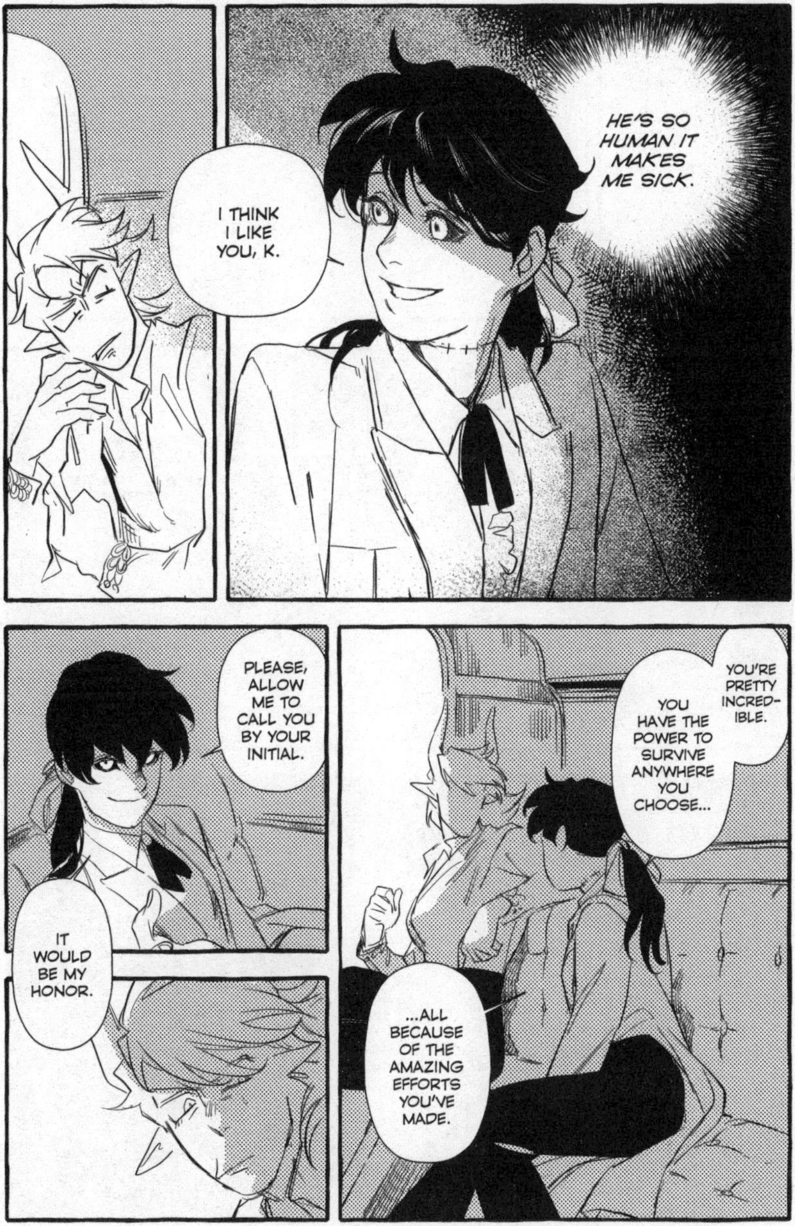
HE'S SO HUMAN IT MAKES ME SICK.
I THINK I LIKE YOU, K.
YOU'RE PRETTY INCREDIBLE.
YOU HAVE THE POWER TO SURVIVE ANYWHERE YOU CHOOSE...
...ALL BECAUSE OF THE AMAZING EFFORTS YOU'VE MADE.
PLEASE, ALLOW ME TO CALL YOU BY YOUR INITIAL.
IT WOULD BE MY HONOR.

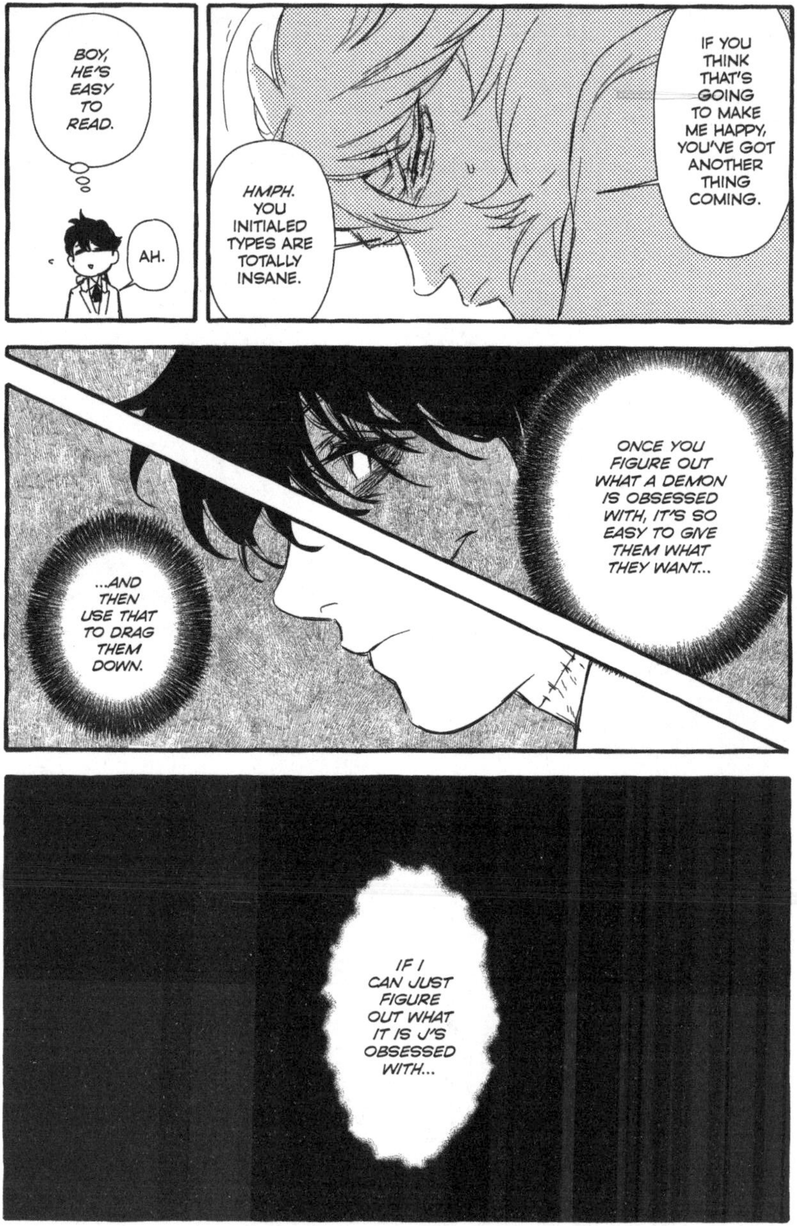
IF YOU THINK THAT'S GOING TO MAKE ME HAPPY, YOU'VE GOT ANOTHER THING COMING.
HMPH. YOU INITIALED TYPES ARE TOTALLY INSANE.
BOY, HE'S EASY TO READ.
AH.
ONCE YOU FIGURE OUT WHAT A DEMON IS OBSESSED WITH, IT'S SO EASY TO GIVE THEM WHAT THEY WANT...
...AND THEN USE THAT TO DRAG THEM DOWN.
IF I CAN JUST FIGURE OUT WHAT IT IS J'S OBSESSED WITH...

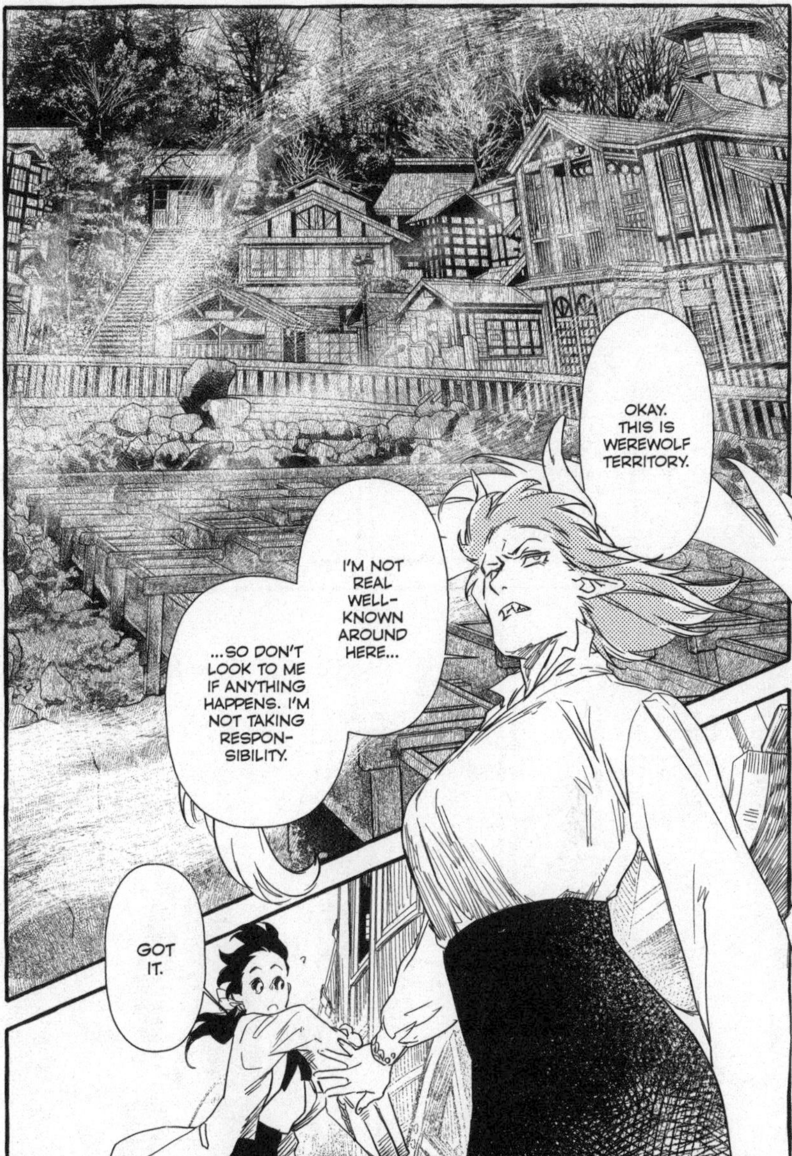
OKAY. THIS IS WEREWOLF TERRITORY.
I'M NOT REAL WELL-KNOWN AROUND HERE...
...SO DON'T LOOK TO ME IF ANYTHING HAPPENS. I'M NOT TAKING RESPON-SIBILITY.
GOT IT.

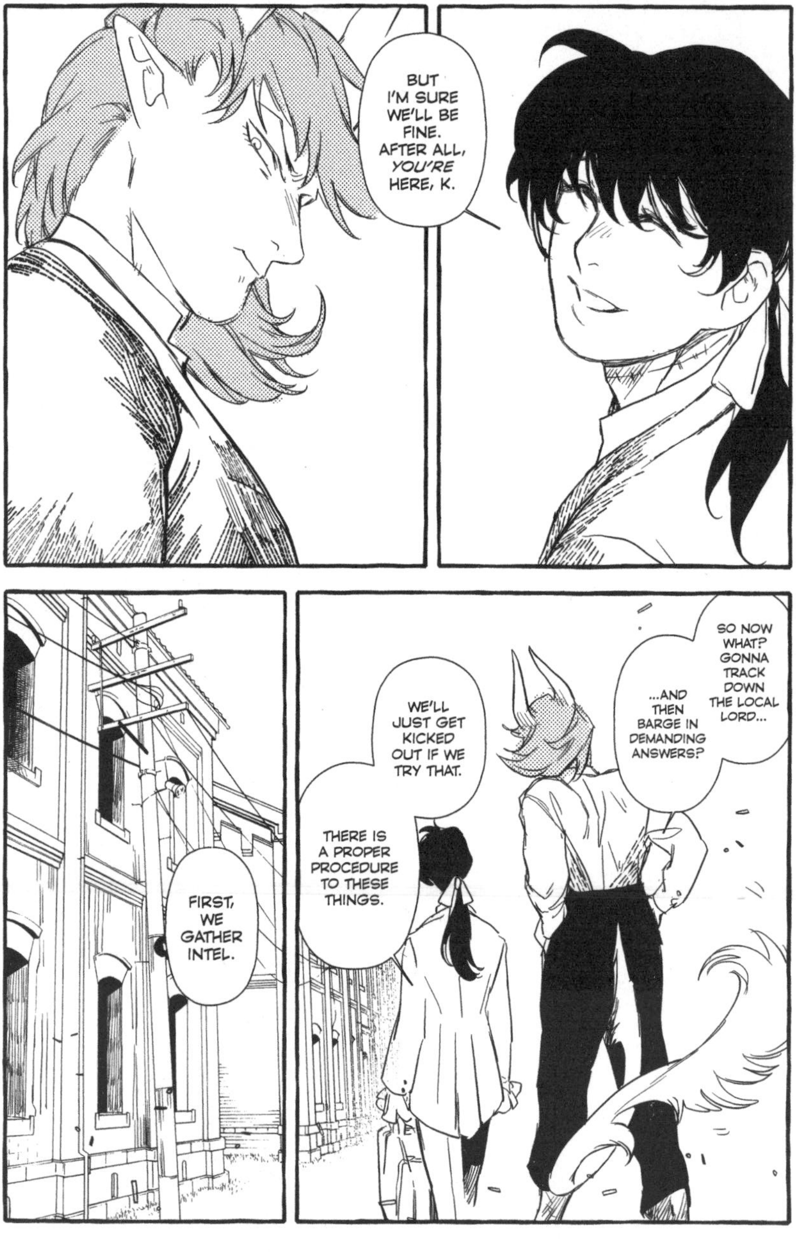
BUT I'M SURE WE'LL BE FINE. AFTER ALL, *YOU'RE* HERE, K.
SO NOW WHAT? GONNA TRACK DOWN THE LOCAL LORD...
...AND THEN BARGE IN DEMANDING ANSWERS?
WE'LL JUST GET KICKED OUT IF WE TRY THAT.
THERE IS A PROPER PROCEDURE TO THESE THINGS.
FIRST, WE GATHER INTEL.

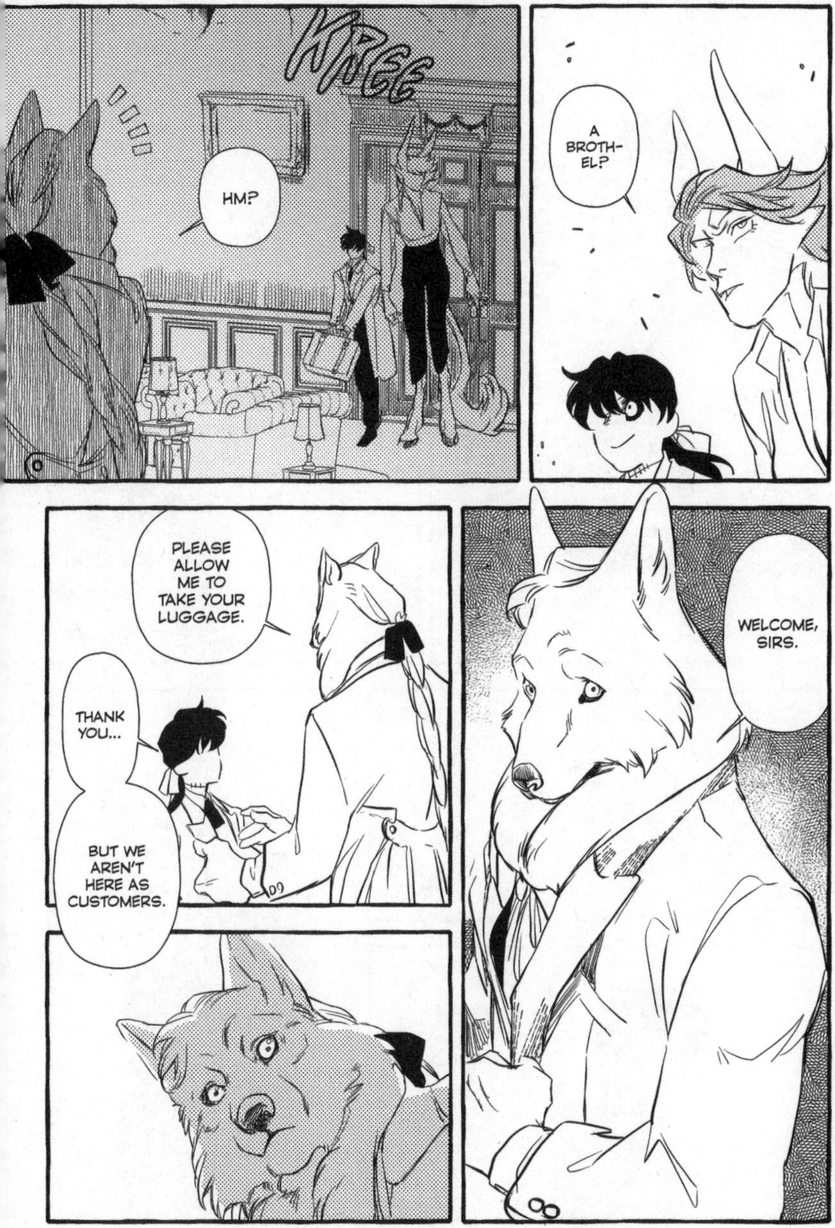
A BROTH-EL?
HM?
WELCOME, SIRS.
PLEASE ALLOW ME TO TAKE YOUR LUGGAGE.
THANK YOU...
BUT WE AREN'T HERE AS CUSTOMERS.

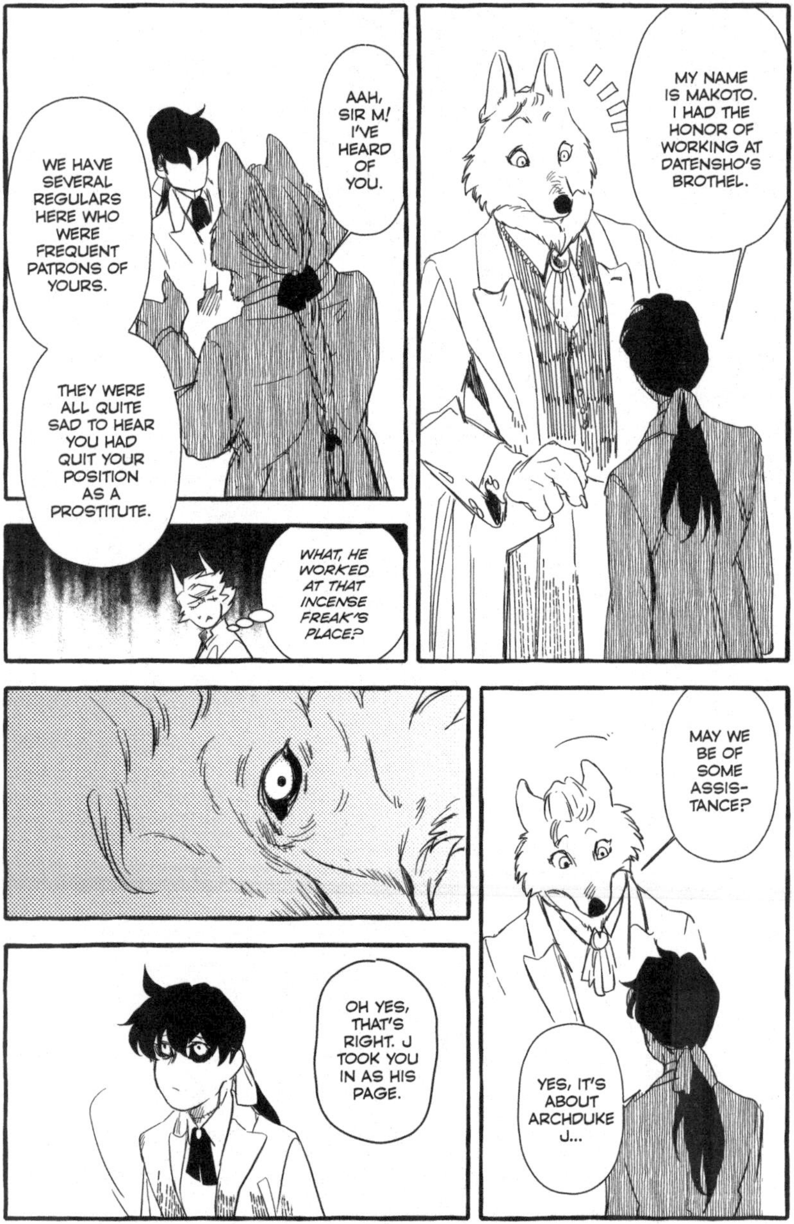
MY NAME IS MAKOTO. I HAD THE HONOR OF WORKING AT DATENSHO'S BROTHEL.
AAH, SIR M! I'VE HEARD OF YOU.
WE HAVE SEVERAL REGULARS HERE WHO WERE FREQUENT PATRONS OF YOURS.
THEY WERE ALL QUITE SAD TO HEAR YOU HAD QUIT YOUR POSITION AS A PROSTITUTE.
WHAT, HE WORKED AT THAT INCENSE FREAK'S PLACE?
MAY WE BE OF SOME ASSIS-TANCE?
YES, IT'S ABOUT ARCHDUKE J...
OH YES, THAT'S RIGHT. J TOOK YOU IN AS HIS PAGE.

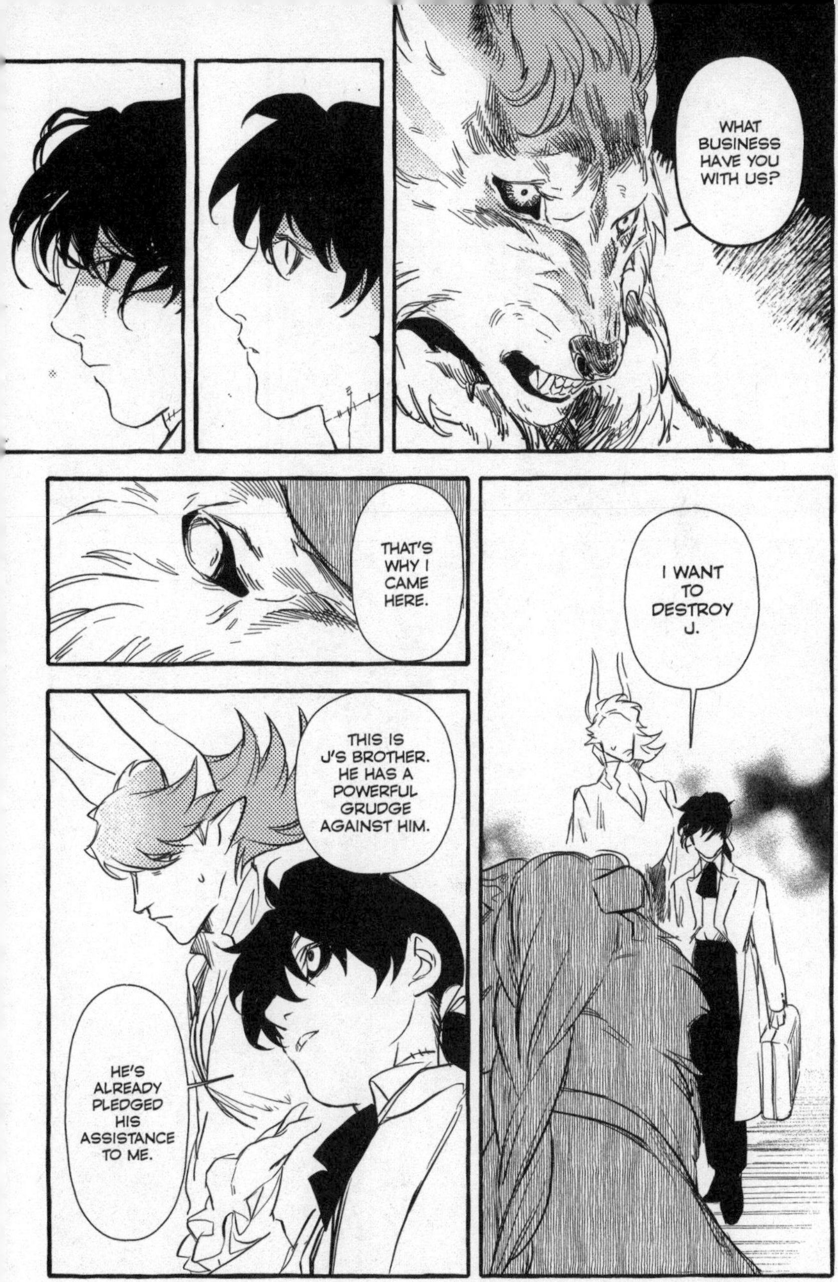
WHAT BUSINESS HAVE YOU WITH US?
I WANT TO DESTROY J.
THAT'S WHY I CAME HERE.
THIS IS J'S BROTHER. HE HAS A POWERFUL GRUDGE AGAINST HIM.
HE'S ALREADY PLEDGED HIS ASSISTANCE TO ME.

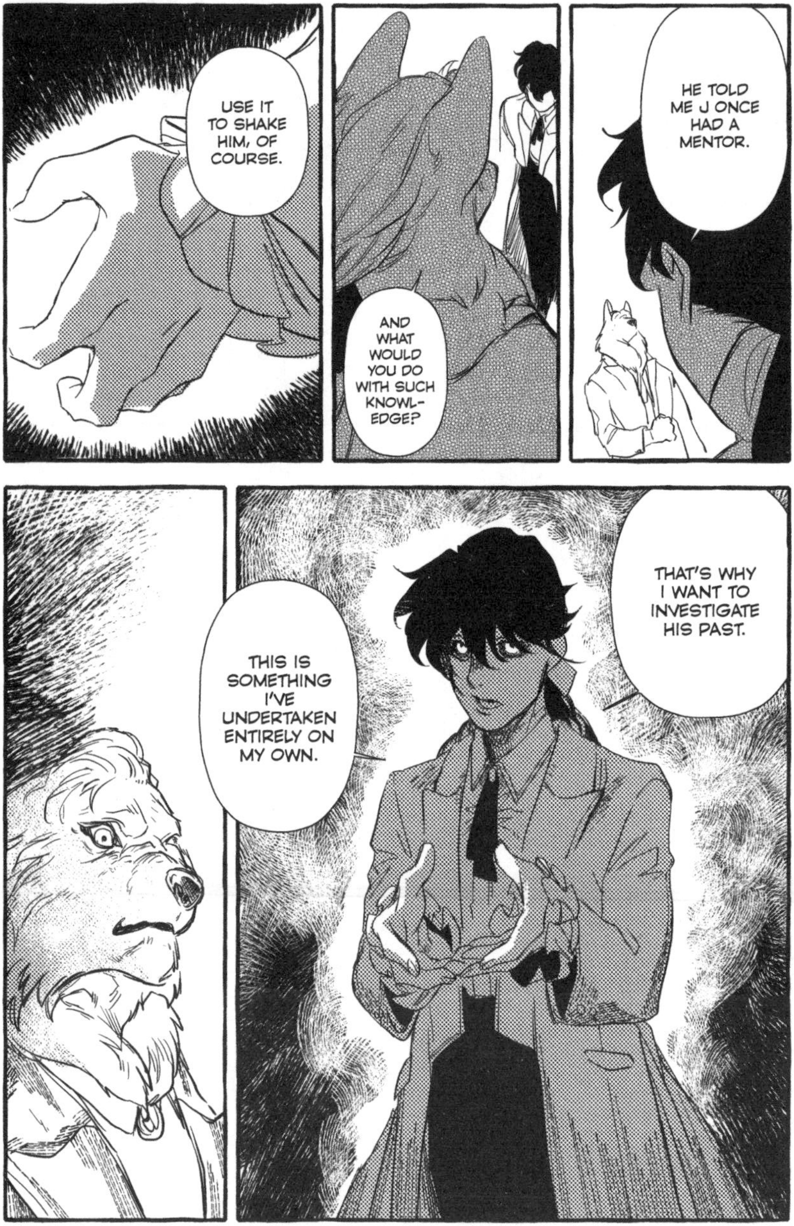
HE TOLD ME J ONCE HAD A MENTOR.
AND WHAT WOULD YOU DO WITH SUCH KNOWL-EDGE?
USE IT TO SHAKE HIM, OF COURSE.
THAT'S WHY I WANT TO INVESTIGATE HIS PAST.
THIS IS SOMETHING I'VE UNDERTAKEN ENTIRELY ON MY OWN.

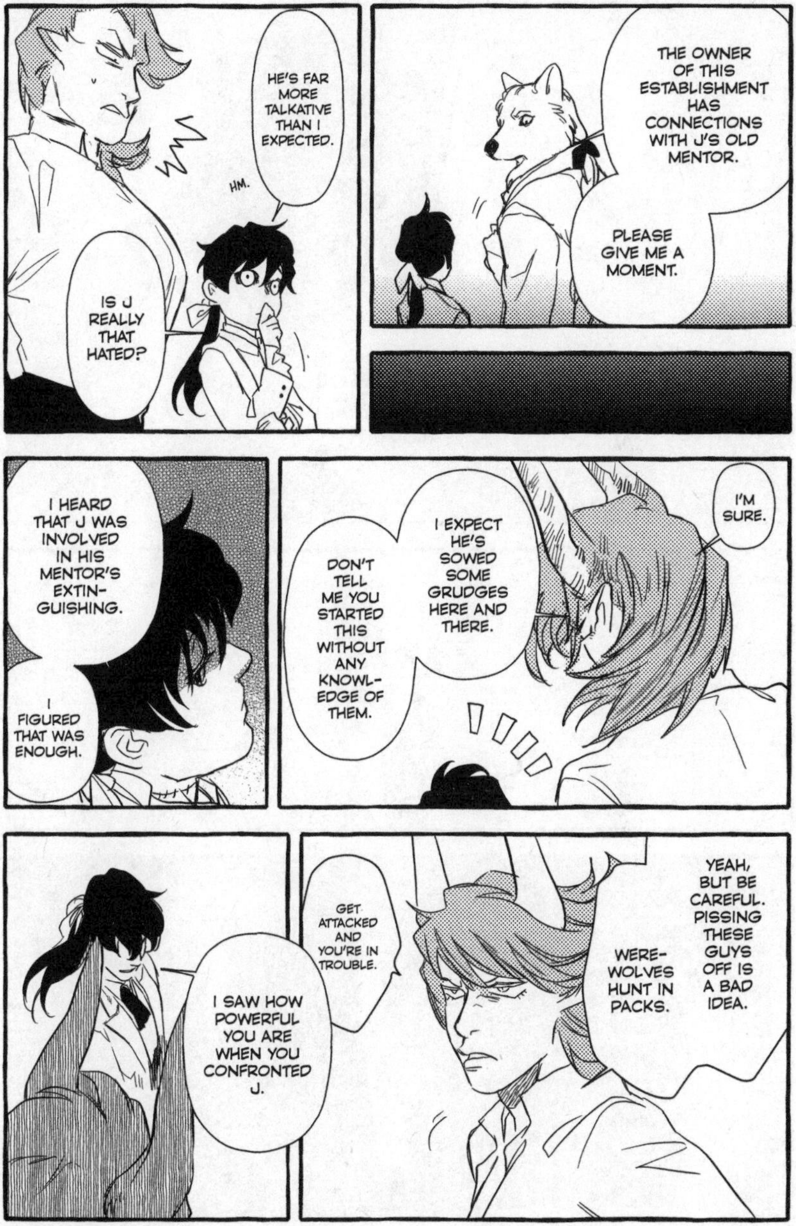
THE OWNER OF THIS ESTABLISHMENT HAS CONNECTIONS WITH J'S OLD MENTOR.
PLEASE GIVE ME A MOMENT.
HE'S FAR MORE TALKATIVE THAN I EXPECTED.
HM.
IS J REALLY THAT HATED?
I'M SURE.
I EXPECT HE'S SOWED SOME GRUDGES HERE AND THERE.
DON'T TELL ME YOU STARTED THIS WITHOUT ANY KNOWLEDGE OF THEM.
!!!!
I HEARD THAT J WAS INVOLVED IN HIS MENTOR'S EXTINGUISHING.
I FIGURED THAT WAS ENOUGH.
YEAH, BUT BE CAREFUL. PISSING THESE GUYS OFF IS A BAD IDEA.
WEREWOLVES HUNT IN PACKS.
GET ATTACKED AND YOU'RE IN TROUBLE.
I SAW HOW POWERFUL YOU ARE WHEN YOU CONFRONTED J.

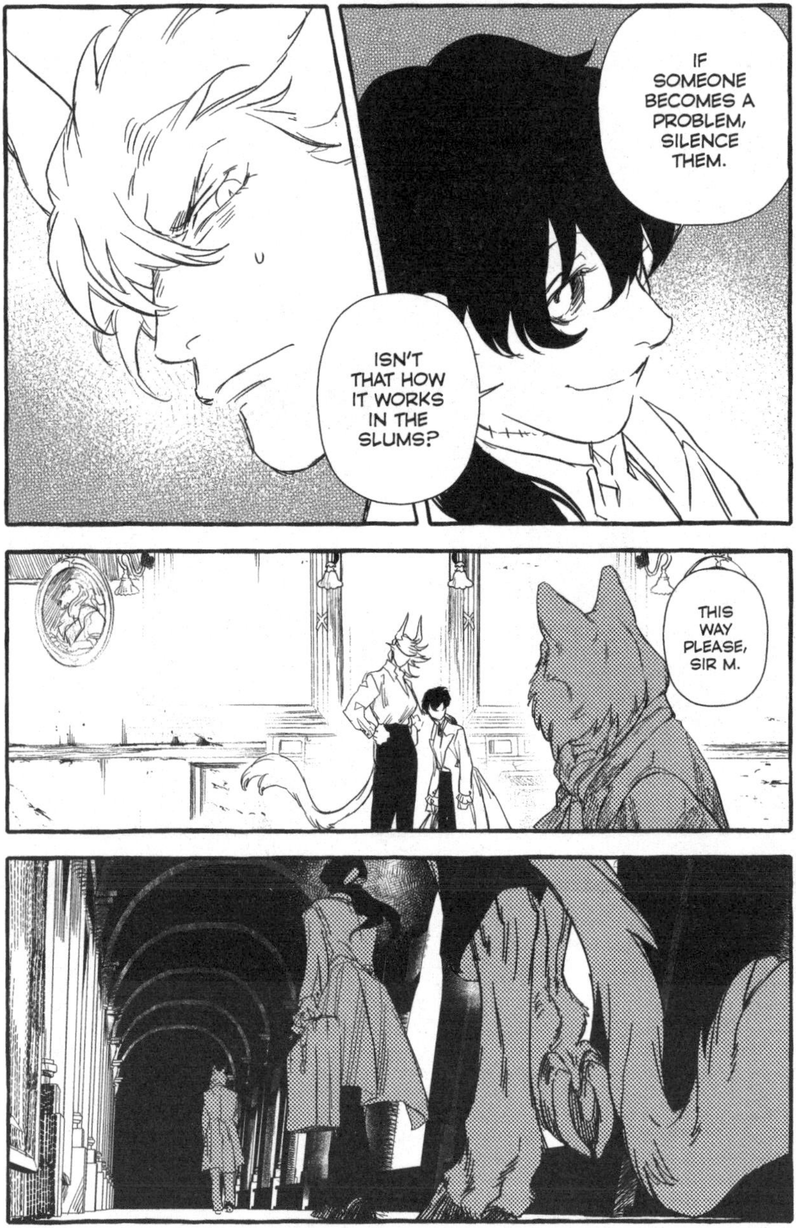
IF SOMEONE BECOMES A PROBLEM, SILENCE THEM.
ISN'T THAT HOW IT WORKS IN THE SLUMS?
THIS WAY PLEASE, SIR M.

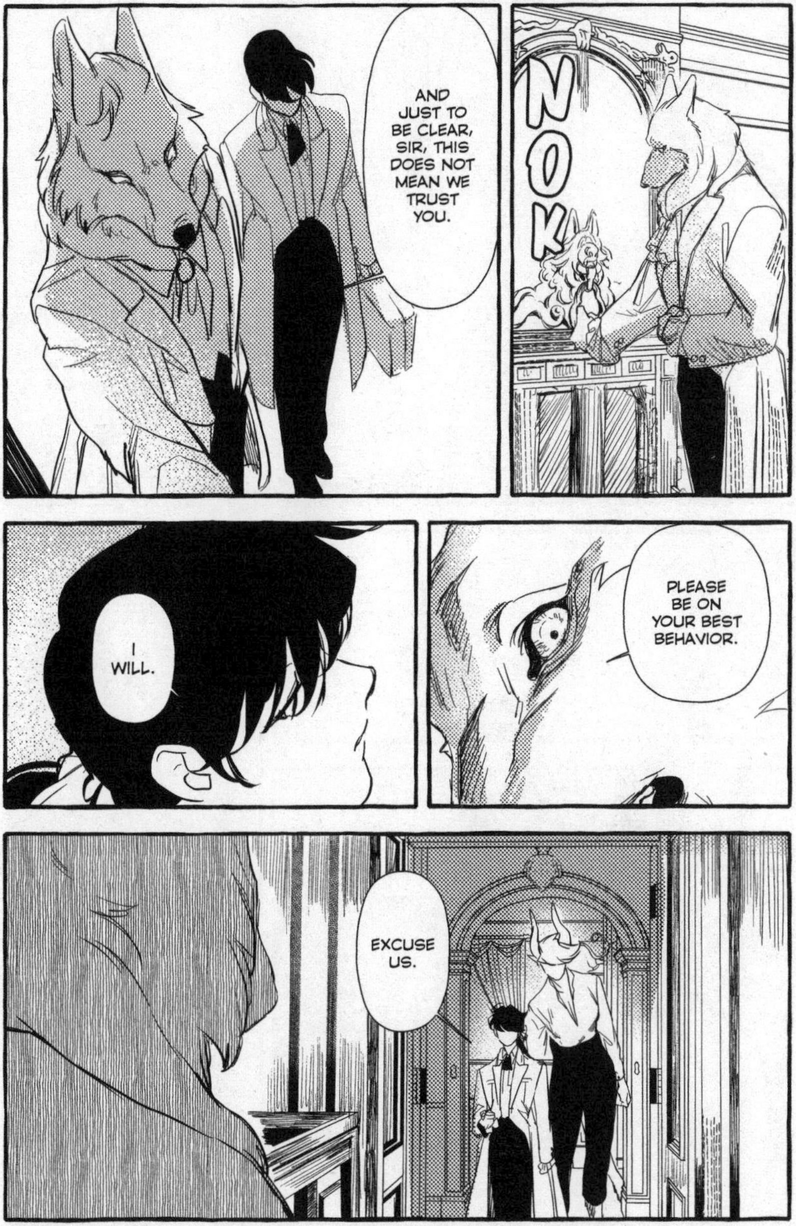
NOK
AND JUST TO BE CLEAR, SIR, THIS DOES NOT MEAN WE TRUST YOU.
PLEASE BE ON YOUR BEST BEHAVIOR.
I WILL.
EXCUSE US.

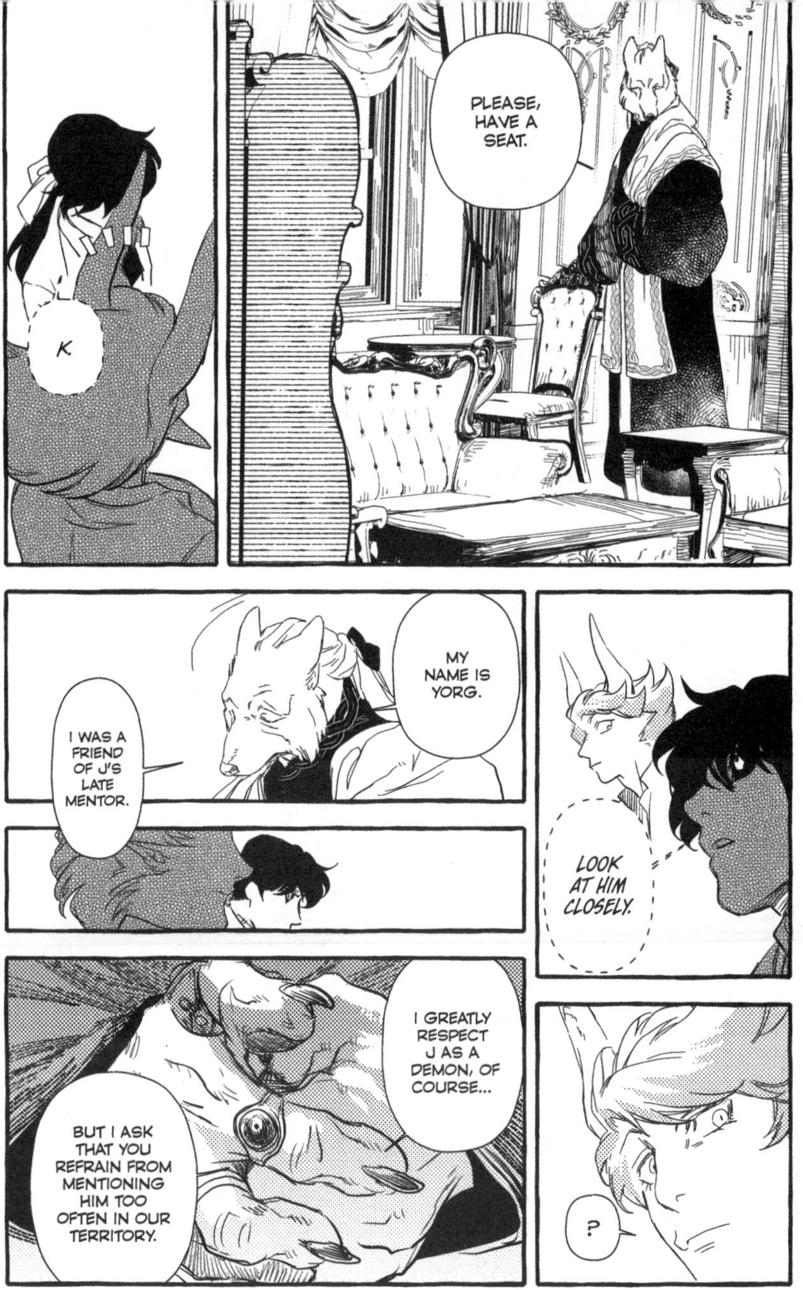
PLEASE, HAVE A SEAT.
K.
MY NAME IS YORG.
I WAS A FRIEND OF J'S LATE MENTOR.
LOOK AT HIM CLOSELY.
?
I GREATLY RESPECT J AS A DEMON, OF COURSE...
BUT I ASK THAT YOU REFRAIN FROM MENTIONING HIM TOO OFTEN IN OUR TERRITORY.

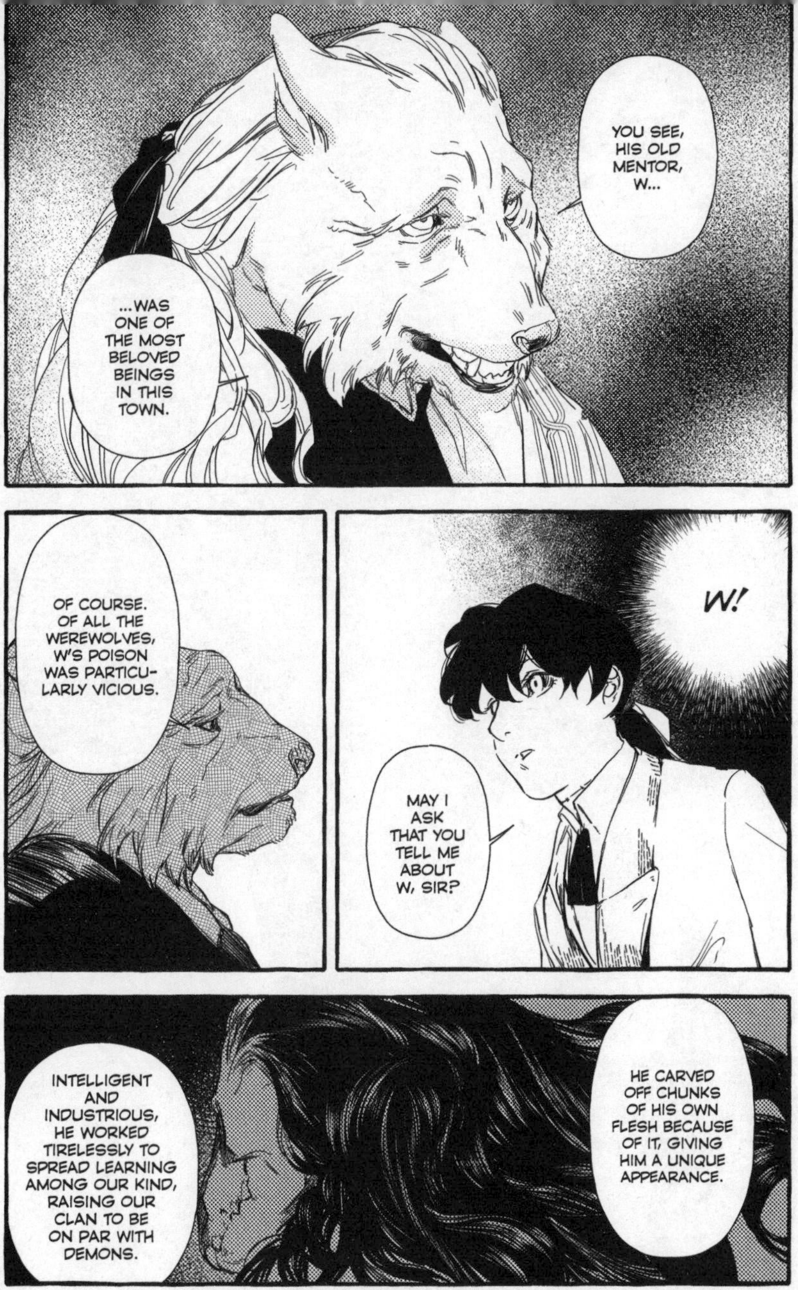
YOU SEE, HIS OLD MENTOR, W...
...WAS ONE OF THE MOST BELOVED BEINGS IN THIS TOWN.
W!
MAY I ASK THAT YOU TELL ME ABOUT W, SIR?
OF COURSE. OF ALL THE WEREWOLVES, W'S POISON WAS PARTICU-LARLY VICIOUS.
HE CARVED OFF CHUNKS OF HIS OWN FLESH BECAUSE OF IT, GIVING HIM A UNIQUE APPEARANCE.
INTELLIGENT AND INDUSTRIOUS, HE WORKED TIRELESSLY TO SPREAD LEARNING AMONG OUR KIND, RAISING OUR CLAN TO BE ON PAR WITH DEMONS.

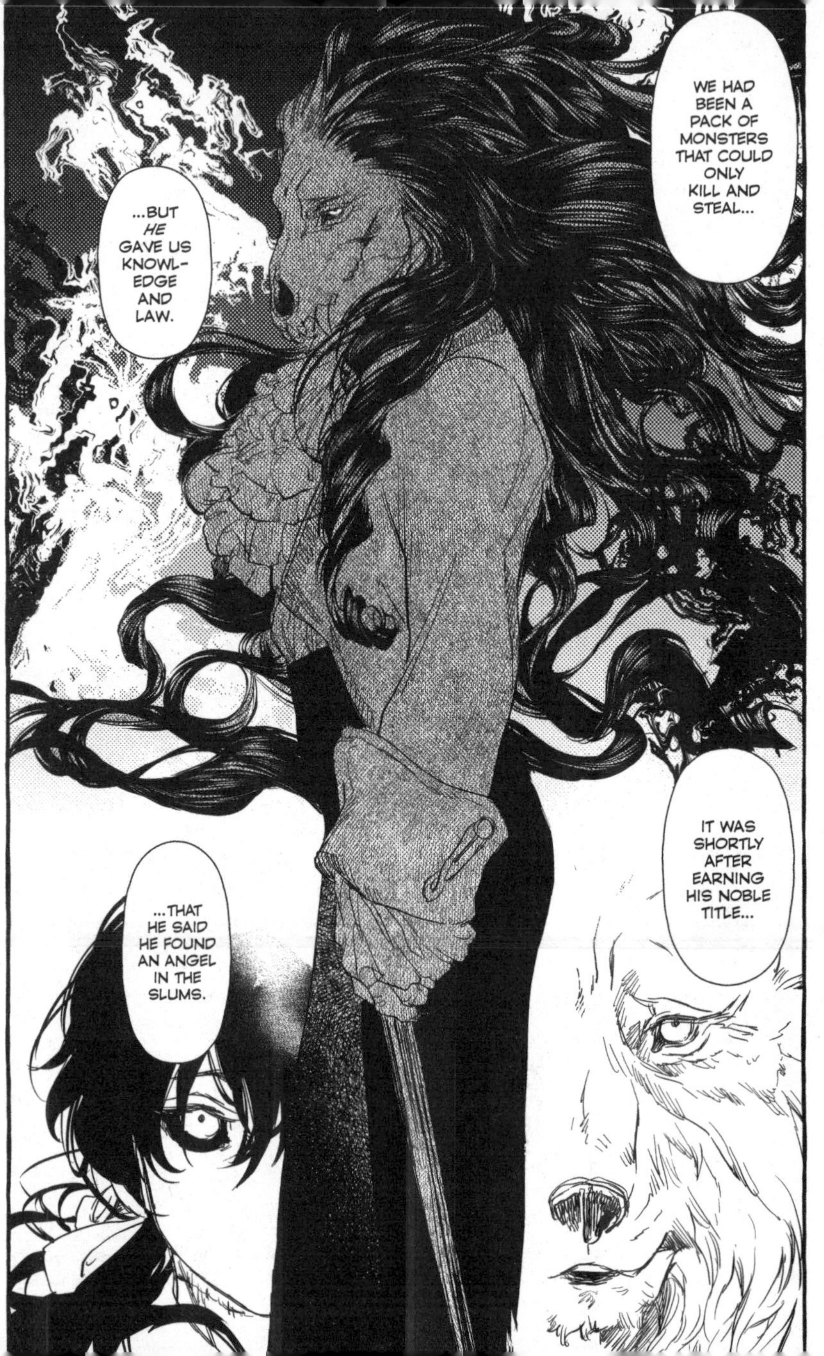
WE HAD BEEN A PACK OF MONSTERS THAT COULD ONLY KILL AND STEAL...
...BUT *HE* GAVE US KNOWL-EDGE AND LAW.
IT WAS SHORTLY AFTER EARNING HIS NOBLE TITLE...
...THAT HE SAID HE FOUND AN ANGEL IN THE SLUMS.

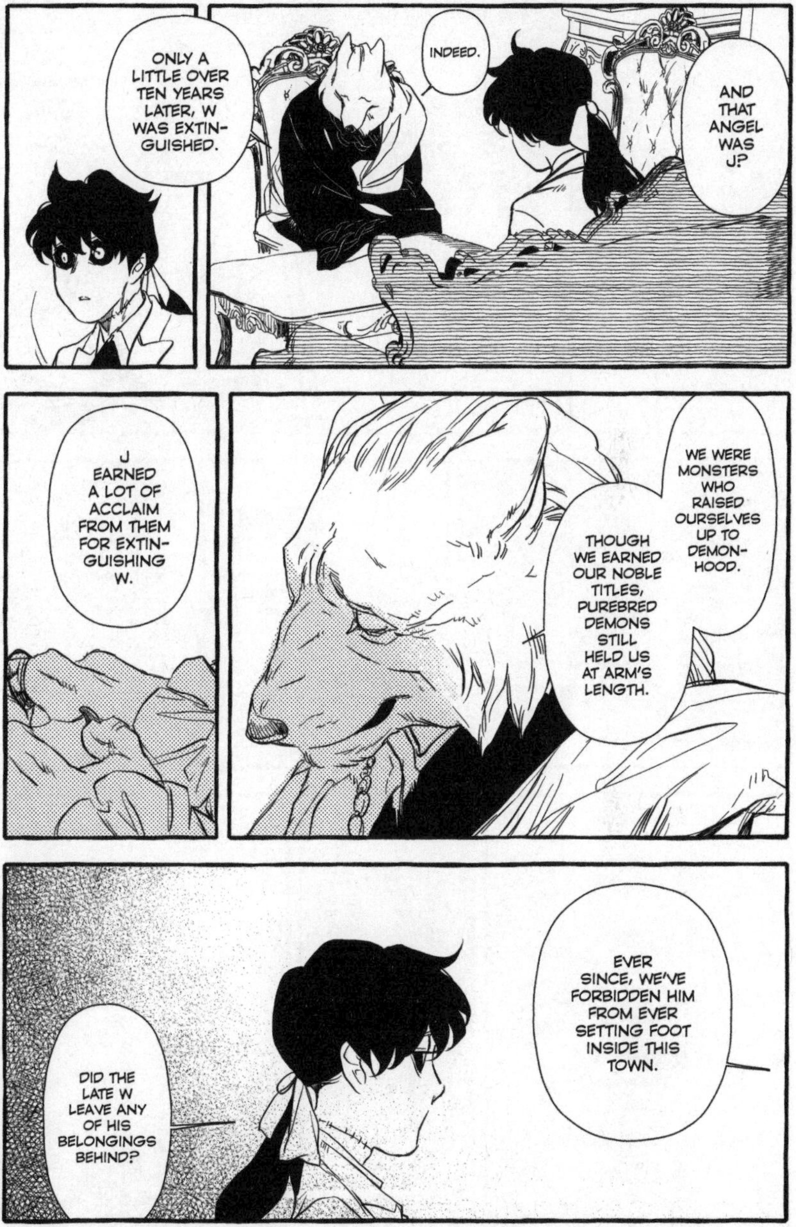
AND THAT ANGEL WAS J?
INDEED.
ONLY A LITTLE OVER TEN YEARS LATER, W WAS EXTINGUISHED.
WE WERE MONSTERS WHO RAISED OURSELVES UP TO DEMONHOOD.
THOUGH WE EARNED OUR NOBLE TITLES, PUREBRED DEMONS STILL HELD US AT ARM'S LENGTH.
J EARNED A LOT OF ACCLAIM FROM THEM FOR EXTINGUISHING W.
EVER SINCE, WE'VE FORBIDDEN HIM FROM EVER SETTING FOOT INSIDE THIS TOWN.
DID THE LATE W LEAVE ANY OF HIS BELONGINGS BEHIND?

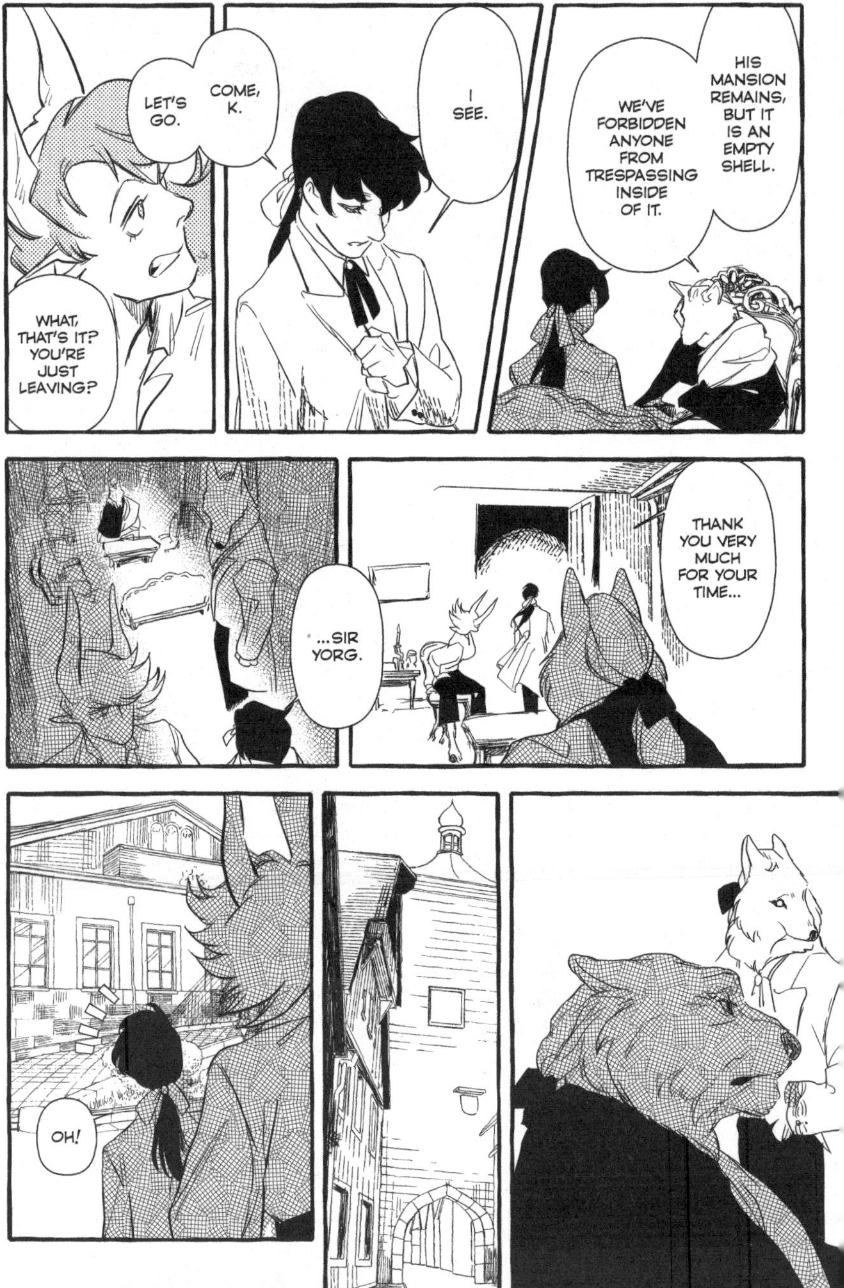
HIS MANSION REMAINS, BUT IT IS AN EMPTY SHELL.
WE'VE FORBIDDEN ANYONE FROM TRESPASSING INSIDE OF IT.
I SEE.
COME, K.
LET'S GO.
WHAT, THAT'S IT? YOU'RE JUST LEAVING?
THANK YOU VERY MUCH FOR YOUR TIME...
...SIR YORG.
OH!

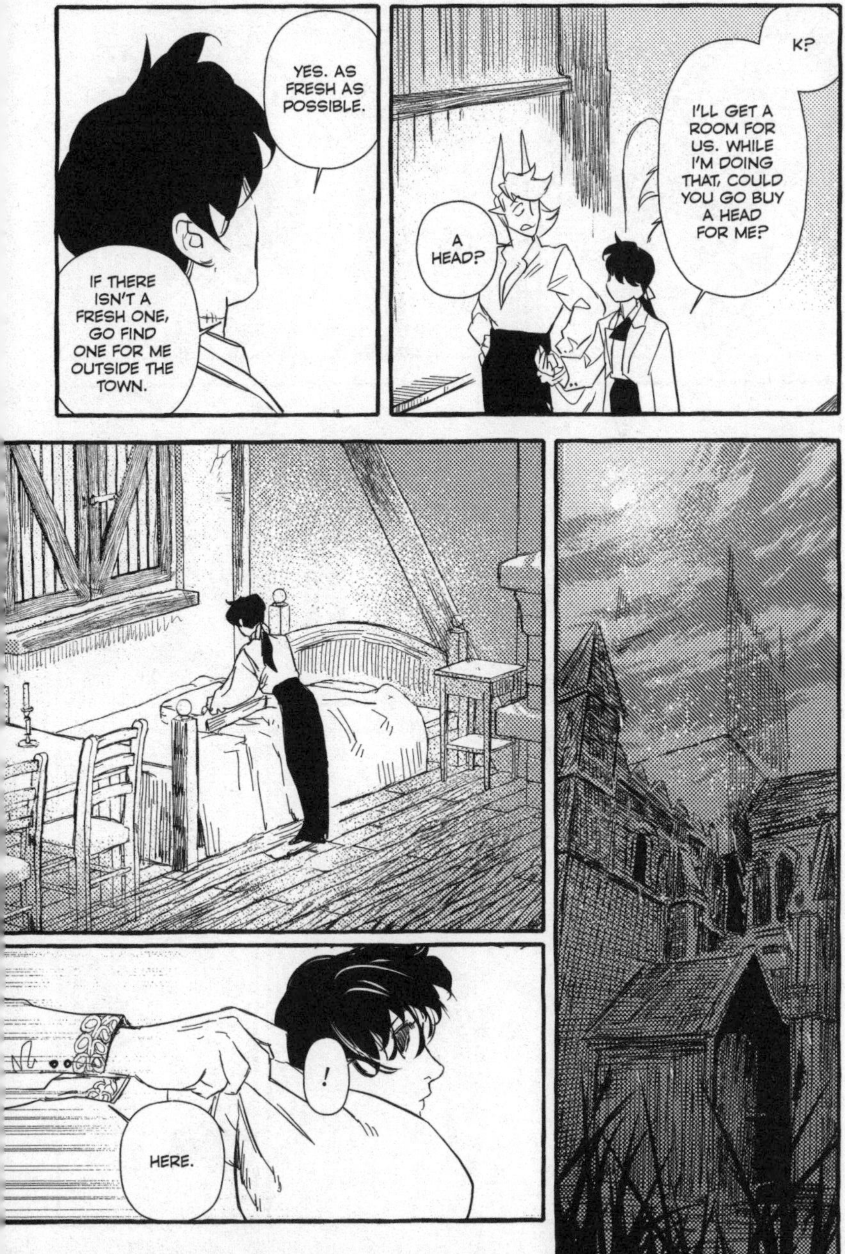
K?
I'LL GET A ROOM FOR US. WHILE I'M DOING THAT, COULD YOU GO BUY A HEAD FOR ME?
A HEAD?
YES. AS FRESH AS POSSIBLE.
IF THERE ISN'T A FRESH ONE, GO FIND ONE FOR ME OUTSIDE THE TOWN.
!
HERE.

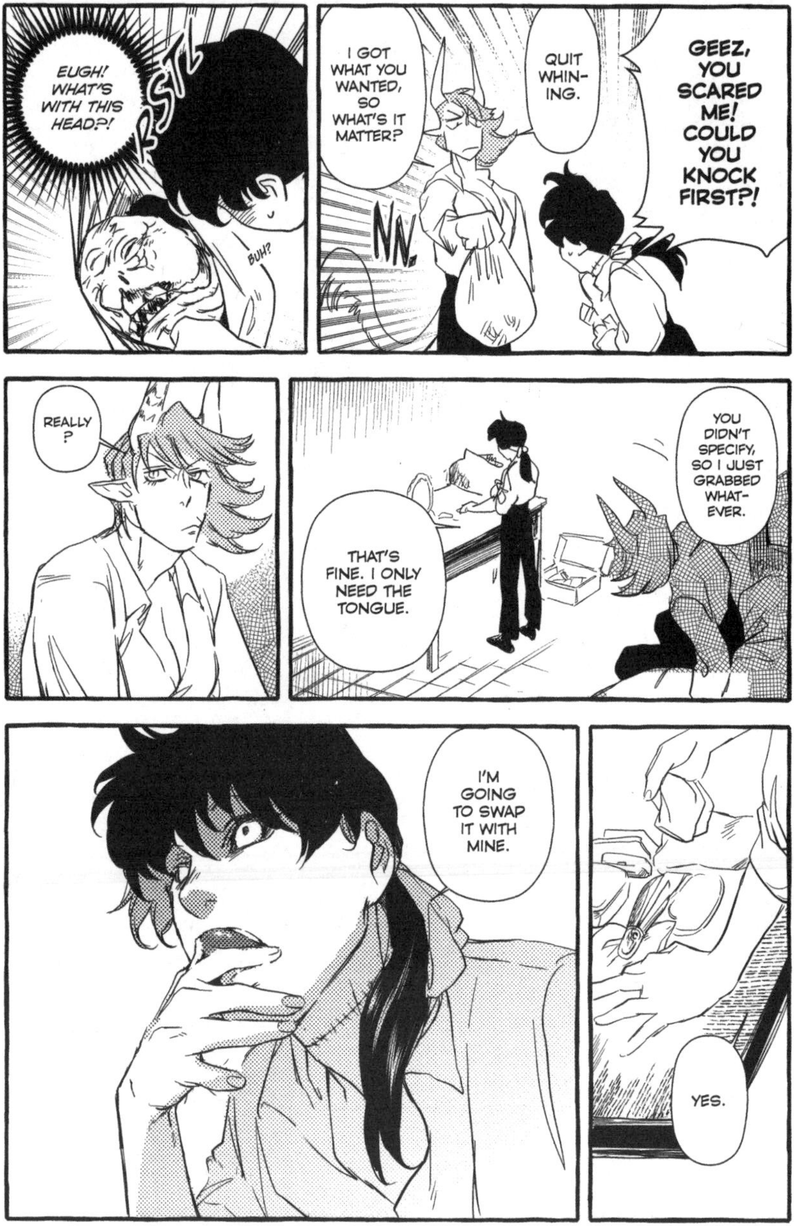
GEEZ, YOU SCARED ME! COULD YOU KNOCK FIRST?!
QUIT WHIN-ING.
I GOT WHAT YOU WANTED, SO WHAT'S IT MATTER?
NN.
RSTL
EUGH! WHAT'S WITH THIS HEAD?!
BUH?
YOU DIDN'T SPECIFY, SO I JUST GRABBED WHAT-EVER.
THAT'S FINE. I ONLY NEED THE TONGUE.
REALLY?
YES.
I'M GOING TO SWAP IT WITH MINE.

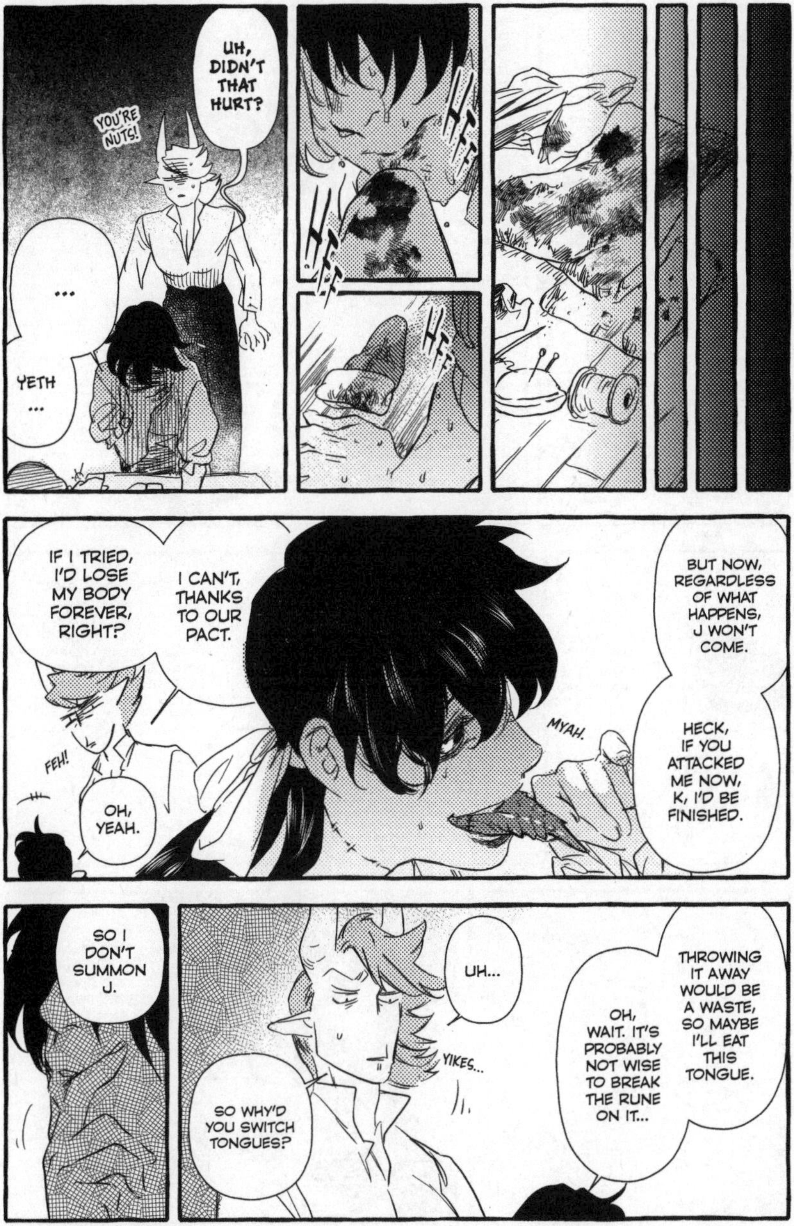
HFF
HFF
HFF
UH, DIDN'T THAT HURT?
YOU'RE NUTS!
...
YETH ...
BUT NOW, REGARDLESS OF WHAT HAPPENS, J WON'T COME.
HECK, IF YOU ATTACKED ME NOW, K, I'D BE FINISHED.
MYAH.
I CAN'T, THANKS TO OUR PACT.
IF I TRIED, I'D LOSE MY BODY FOREVER, RIGHT?
FEH!
OH, YEAH.
THROWING IT AWAY WOULD BE A WASTE, SO MAYBE I'LL EAT THIS TONGUE.
OH, WAIT. IT'S PROBABLY NOT WISE TO BREAK THE RUNE ON IT...
UH...
YIKES...
SO WHY'D YOU SWITCH TONGUES?
SO I DON'T SUMMON J.

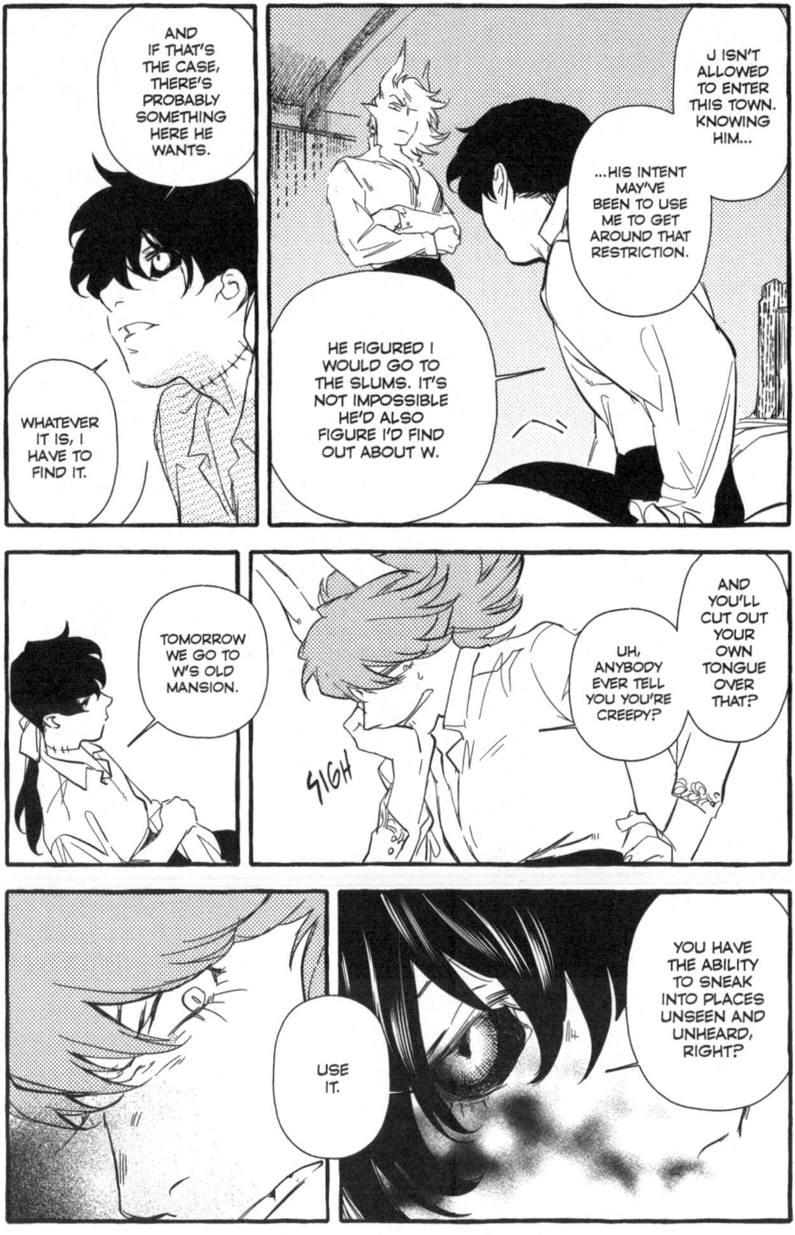
J ISN'T ALLOWED TO ENTER THIS TOWN. KNOWING HIM...
...HIS INTENT MAY'VE BEEN TO USE ME TO GET AROUND THAT RESTRICTION.
HE FIGURED I WOULD GO TO THE SLUMS. IT'S NOT IMPOSSIBLE HE'D ALSO FIGURE I'D FIND OUT ABOUT W.
AND IF THAT'S THE CASE, THERE'S PROBABLY SOMETHING HERE HE WANTS.
WHATEVER IT IS, I HAVE TO FIND IT.
AND YOU'LL CUT OUT YOUR OWN TONGUE OVER THAT?
UH, ANYBODY EVER TELL YOU YOU'RE CREEPY?
SIGH
TOMORROW WE GO TO W'S OLD MANSION.
YOU HAVE THE ABILITY TO SNEAK INTO PLACES UNSEEN AND UNHEARD, RIGHT?
USE IT.

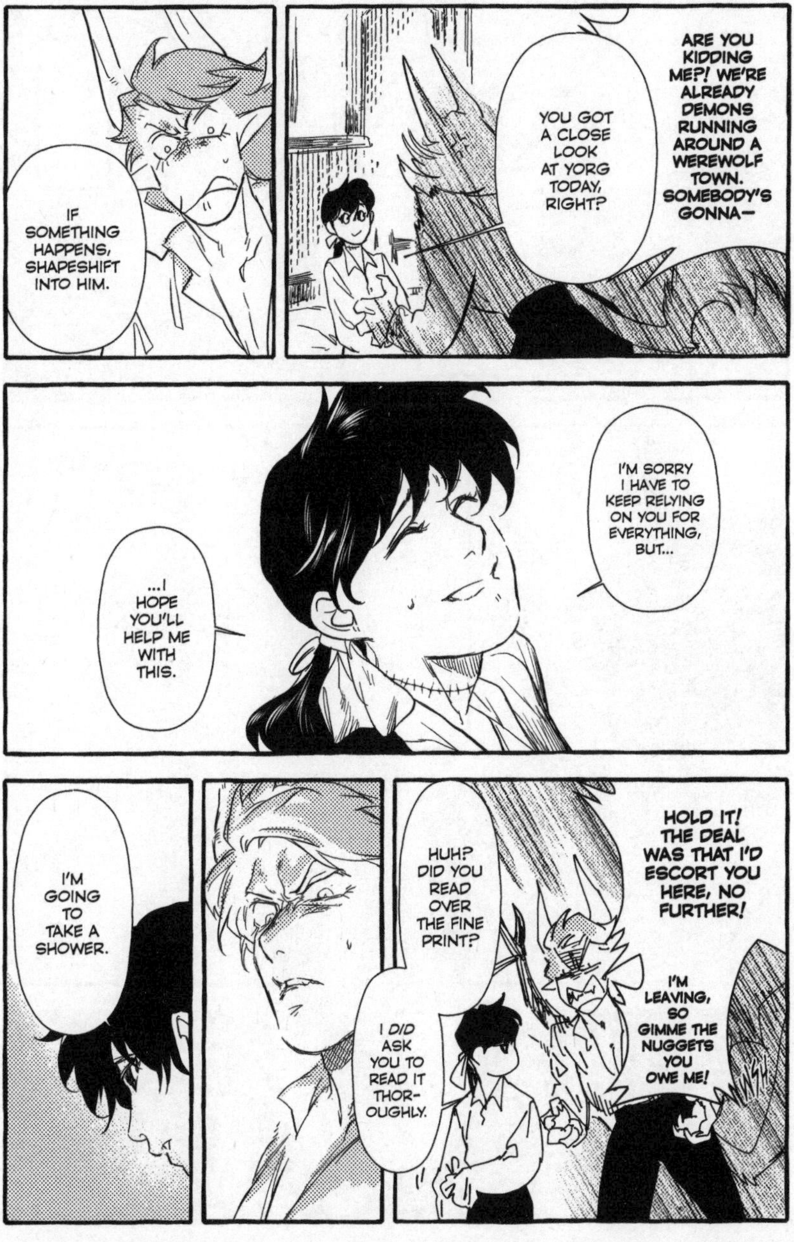
ARE YOU KIDDING ME?! WE'RE ALREADY DEMONS RUNNING AROUND A WEREWOLF TOWN. SOMEBODY'S GONNA—
YOU GOT A CLOSE LOOK AT YORG TODAY, RIGHT?
IF SOMETHING HAPPENS, SHAPESHIFT INTO HIM.
I'M SORRY I HAVE TO KEEP RELYING ON YOU FOR EVERYTHING, BUT...
...I HOPE YOU'LL HELP ME WITH THIS.
HOLD IT! THE DEAL WAS THAT I'D ESCORT YOU HERE, NO FURTHER!
I'M LEAVING, SO GIMME THE NUGGETS YOU OWE ME!
HUH? DID YOU READ OVER THE FINE PRINT?
I *DID* ASK YOU TO READ IT THOROUGHLY.
I'M GOING TO TAKE A SHOWER.

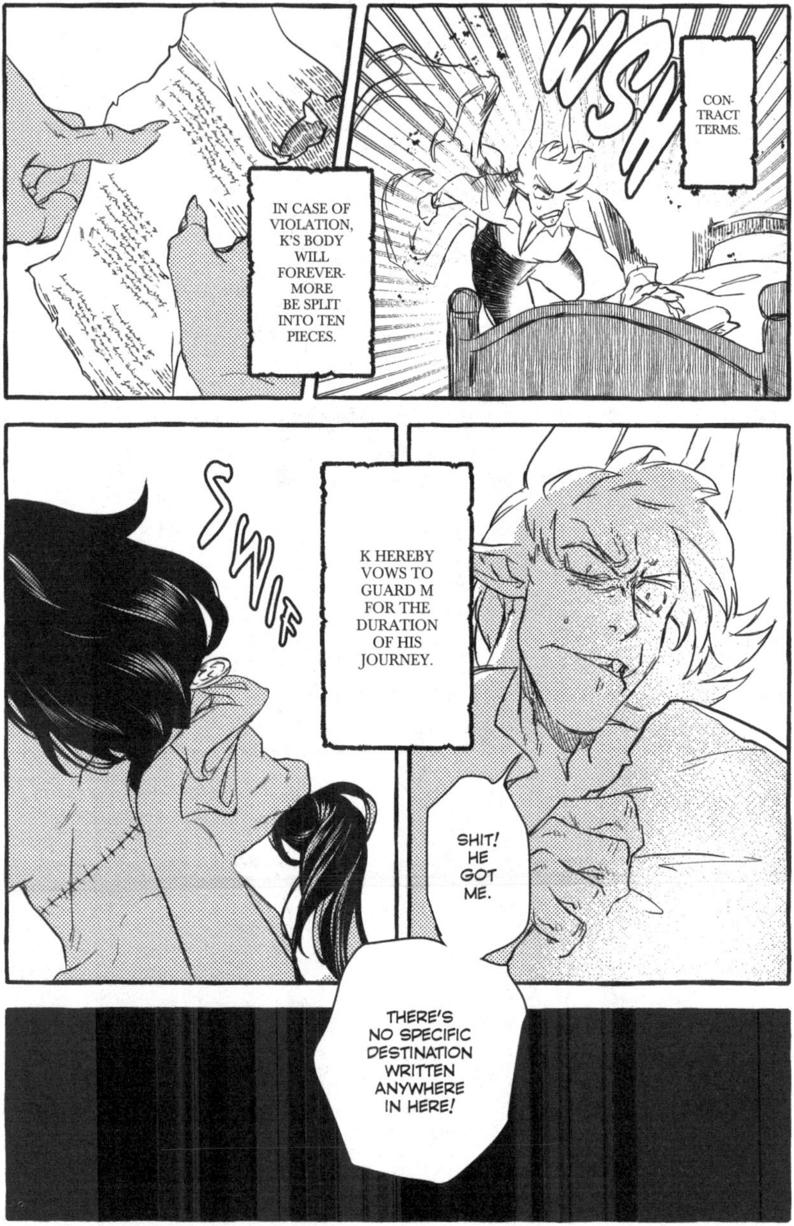
WSH
CON-TRACT TERMS.
IN CASE OF VIOLATION, K'S BODY WILL FOREVER-MORE BE SPLIT INTO TEN PIECES.
K HEREBY VOWS TO GUARD M FOR THE DURATION OF HIS JOURNEY.
SHIT! HE GOT ME.
SWIF
THERE'S NO SPECIFIC DESTINATION WRITTEN ANYWHERE IN HERE!

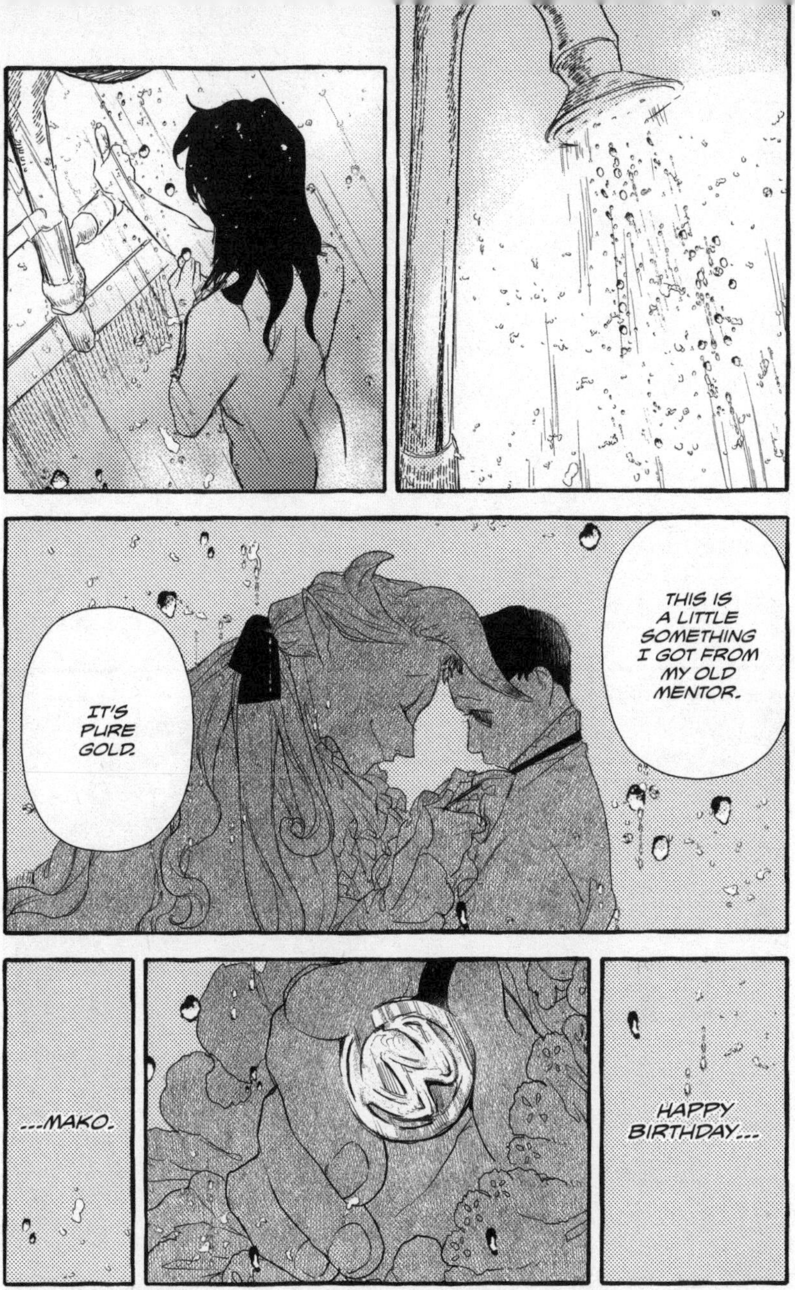
THIS IS A LITTLE SOMETHING I GOT FROM MY OLD MENTOR.
IT'S PURE GOLD.
HAPPY BIRTHDAY...
...MAKO.

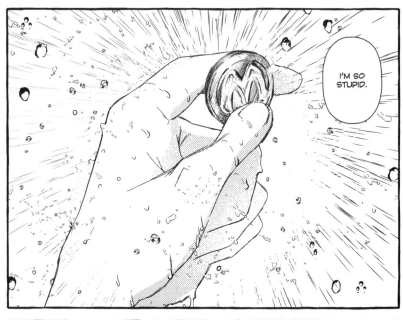

I'M SO STUPID.

GRP

THIS WHOLE TIME...

...I THOUGHT THE GIFT HE GAVE ME WAS MY OWN INITIAL.

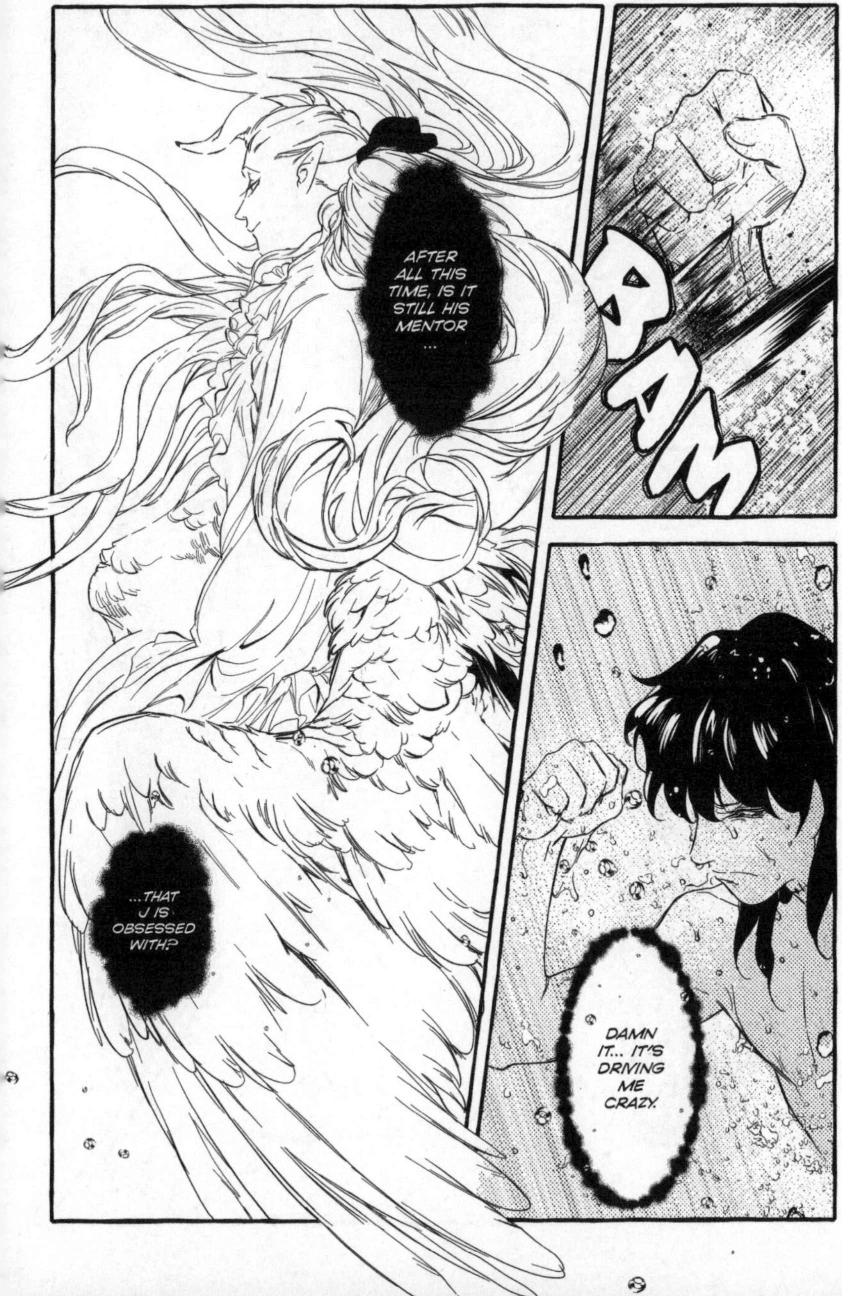
BAM
DAMN IT... IT'S DRIVING ME CRAZY.
AFTER ALL THIS TIME, IS IT STILL HIS MENTOR ...
...THAT J IS OBSESSED WITH?

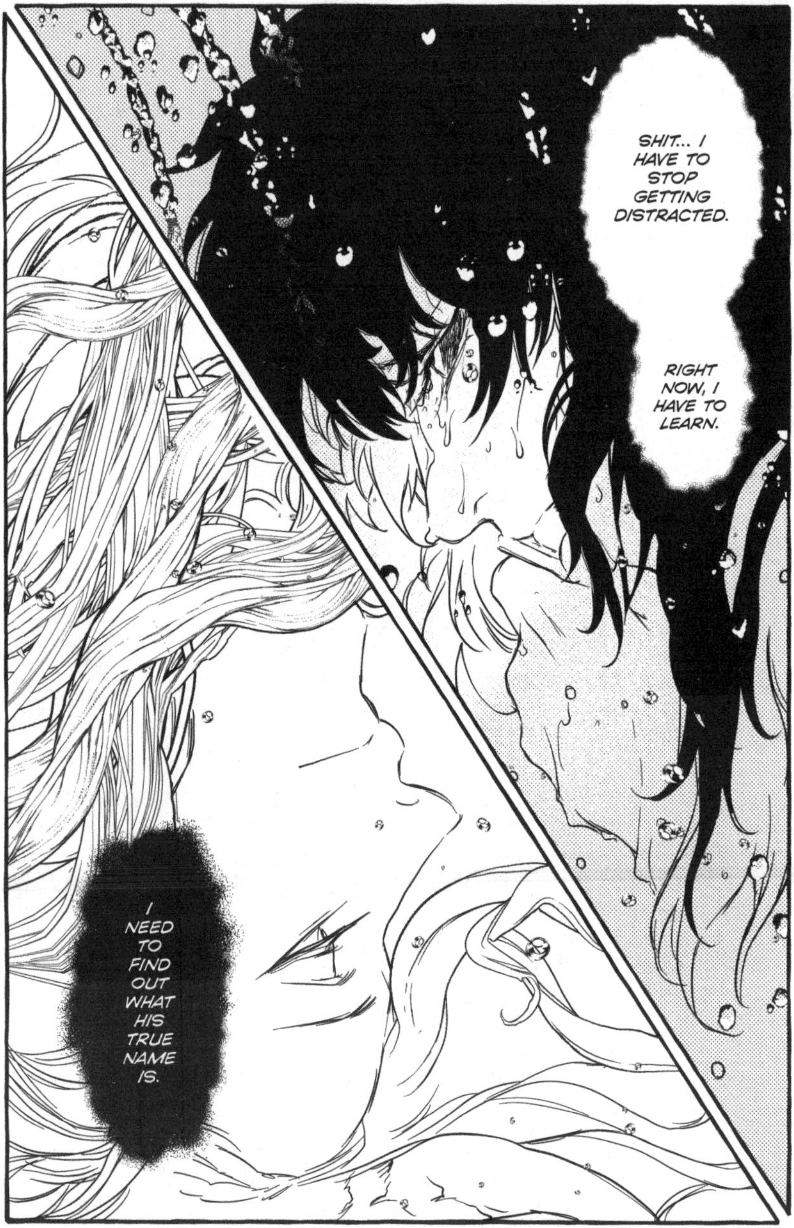
SHIT... I HAVE TO STOP GETTING DISTRACTED.
RIGHT NOW, I HAVE TO LEARN.
I NEED TO FIND OUT WHAT HIS TRUE NAME IS.

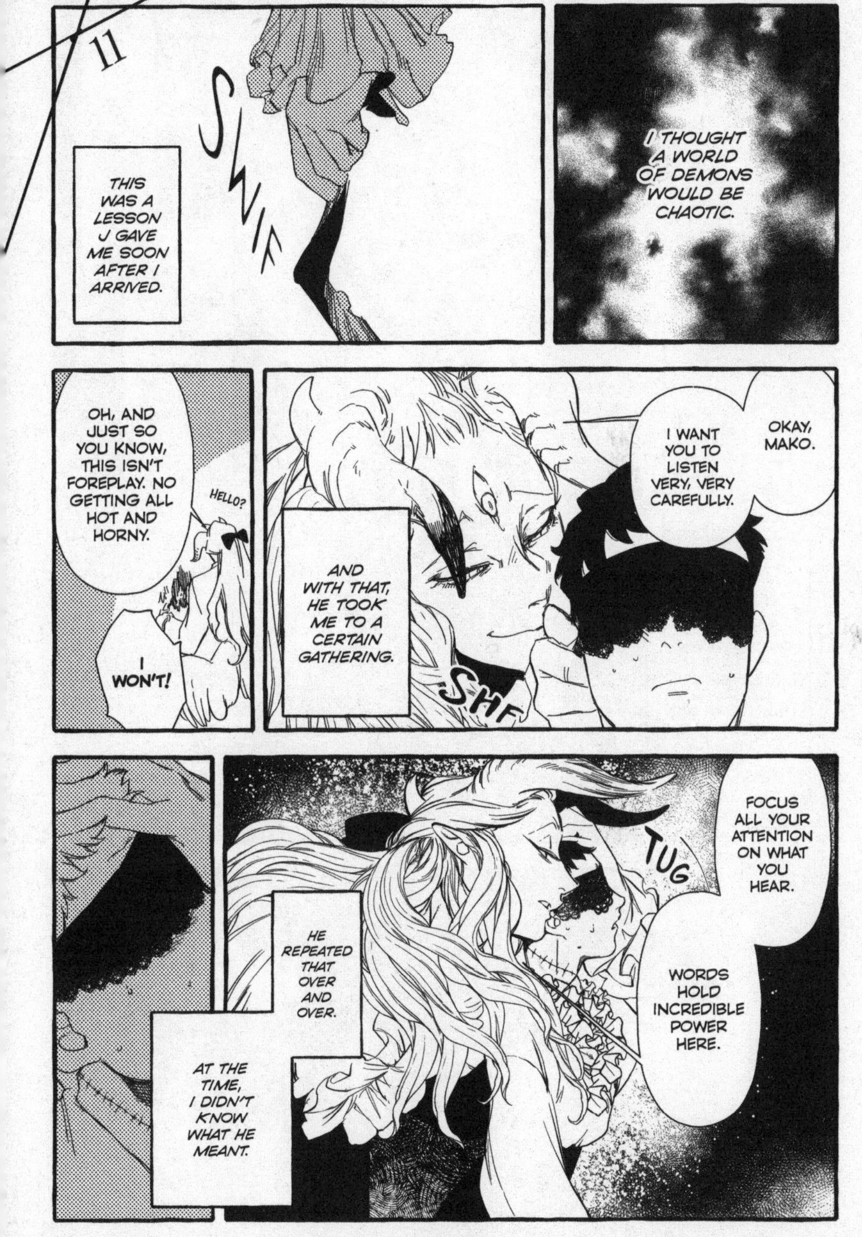
11
I THOUGHT A WORLD OF DEMONS WOULD BE CHAOTIC.
SWIF
THIS WAS A LESSON J GAVE ME SOON AFTER I ARRIVED.
OKAY, MAKO.
I WANT YOU TO LISTEN VERY, VERY CAREFULLY.
AND WITH THAT, HE TOOK ME TO A CERTAIN GATHERING.
SHF
OH, AND JUST SO YOU KNOW, THIS ISN'T FOREPLAY. NO GETTING ALL HOT AND HORNY.
HELLO?
I WON'T!
FOCUS ALL YOUR ATTENTION ON WHAT YOU HEAR.
TUG
WORDS HOLD INCREDIBLE POWER HERE.
HE REPEATED THAT OVER AND OVER.
AT THE TIME, I DIDN'T KNOW WHAT HE MEANT.

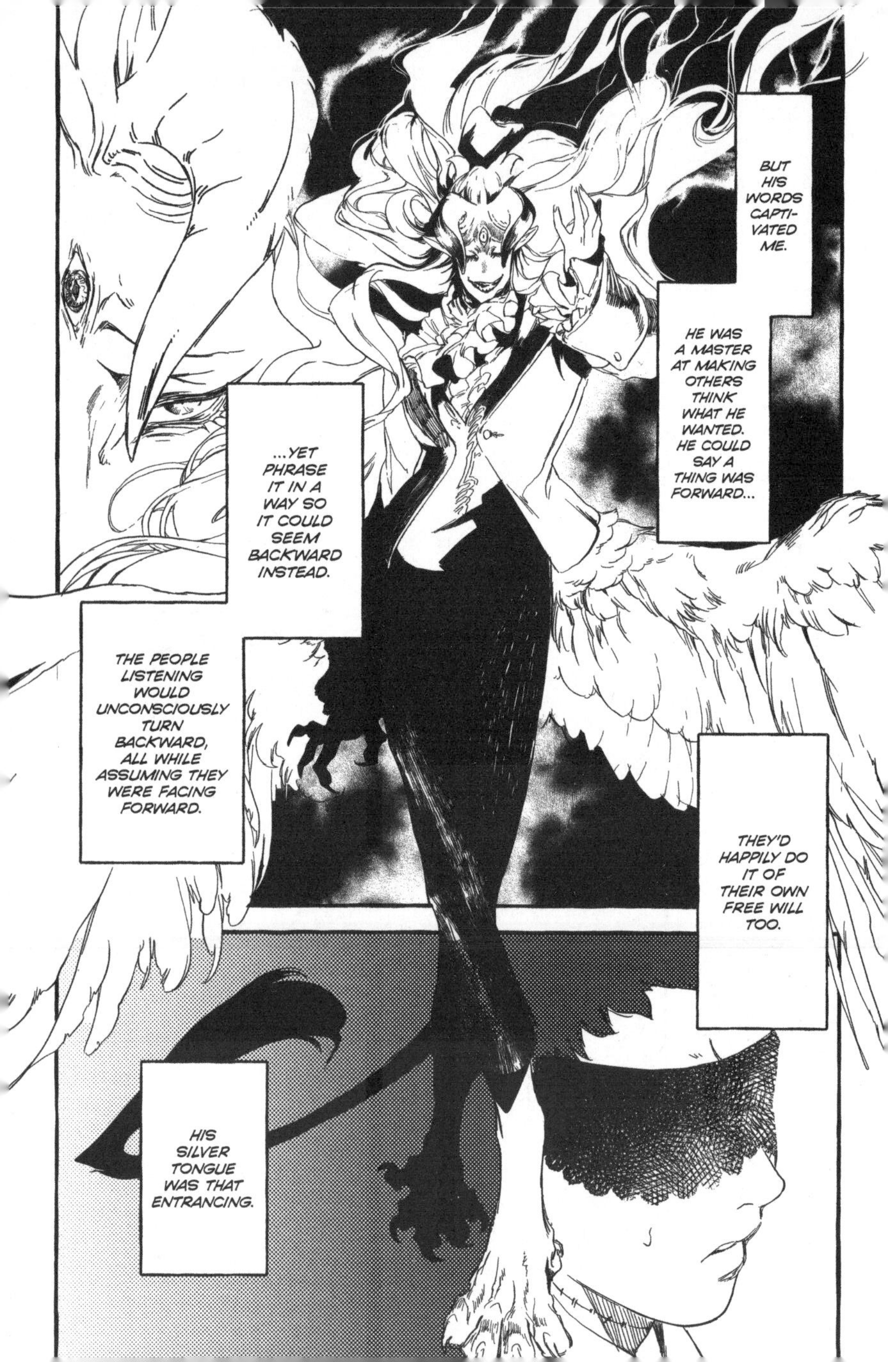
BUT HIS WORDS CAPTIVATED ME.
HE WAS A MASTER AT MAKING OTHERS THINK WHAT HE WANTED. HE COULD SAY A THING WAS FORWARD...
...YET PHRASE IT IN A WAY SO IT COULD SEEM BACKWARD INSTEAD.
THE PEOPLE LISTENING WOULD UNCONSCIOUSLY TURN BACKWARD, ALL WHILE ASSUMING THEY WERE FACING FORWARD.
THEY'D HAPPILY DO IT OF THEIR OWN FREE WILL TOO.
HIS SILVER TONGUE WAS THAT ENTRANCING.

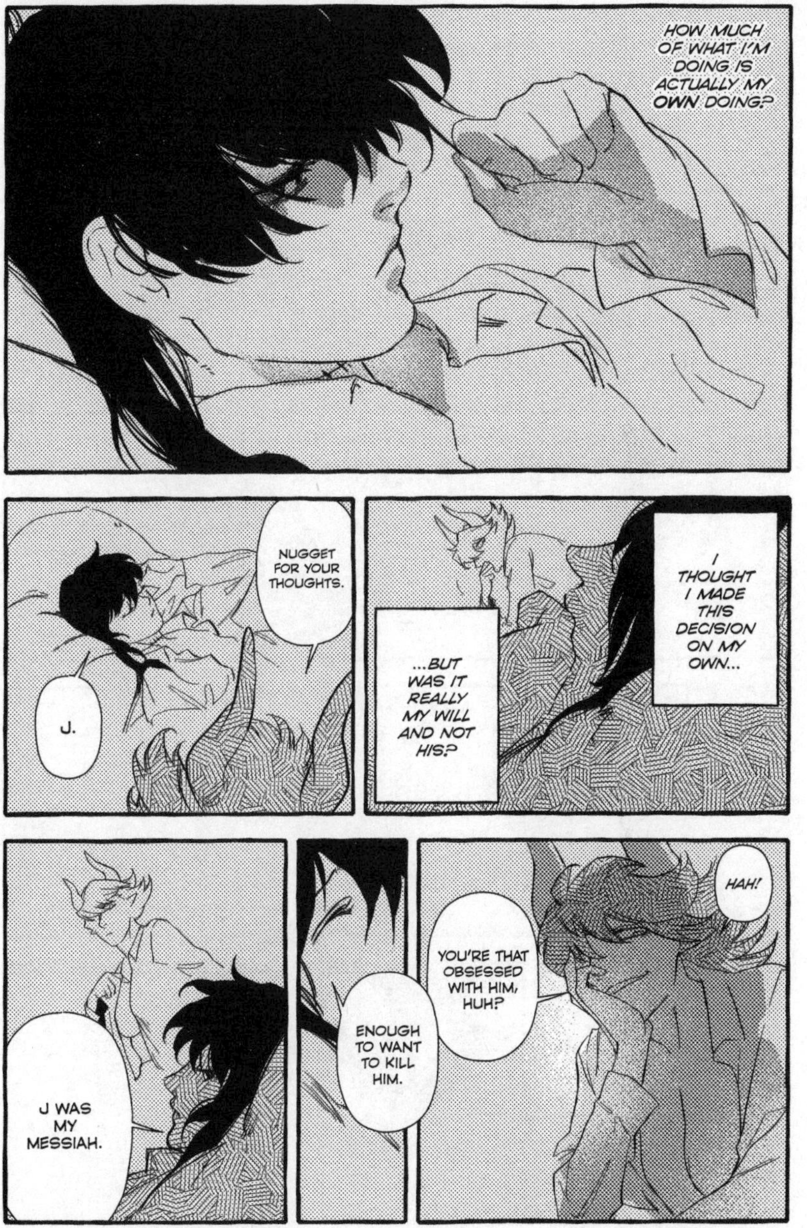
HOW MUCH OF WHAT I'M DOING IS ACTUALLY MY OWN DOING?
I THOUGHT I MADE THIS DECISION ON MY OWN...
...BUT WAS IT REALLY MY WILL AND NOT HIS?
NUGGET FOR YOUR THOUGHTS.
J.
HAH!
YOU'RE THAT OBSESSED WITH HIM, HUH?
ENOUGH TO WANT TO KILL HIM.
J WAS MY MESSIAH.

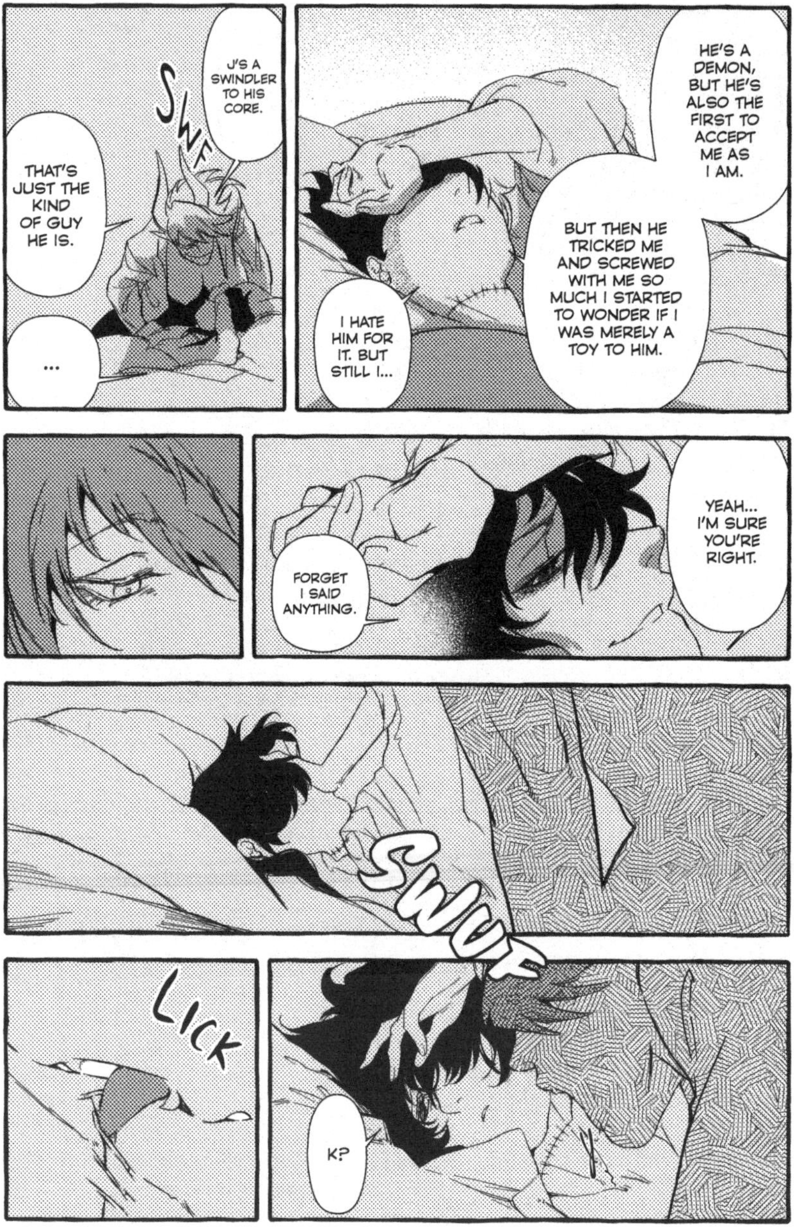
HE'S A DEMON, BUT HE'S ALSO THE FIRST TO ACCEPT ME AS I AM.
BUT THEN HE TRICKED ME AND SCREWED WITH ME SO MUCH I STARTED TO WONDER IF I WAS MERELY A TOY TO HIM.
I HATE HIM FOR IT. BUT STILL I...
J'S A SWINDLER TO HIS CORE.
SWF
THAT'S JUST THE KIND OF GUY HE IS.
...
YEAH... I'M SURE YOU'RE RIGHT.
FORGET I SAID ANYTHING.
SWUF
K?
LICK

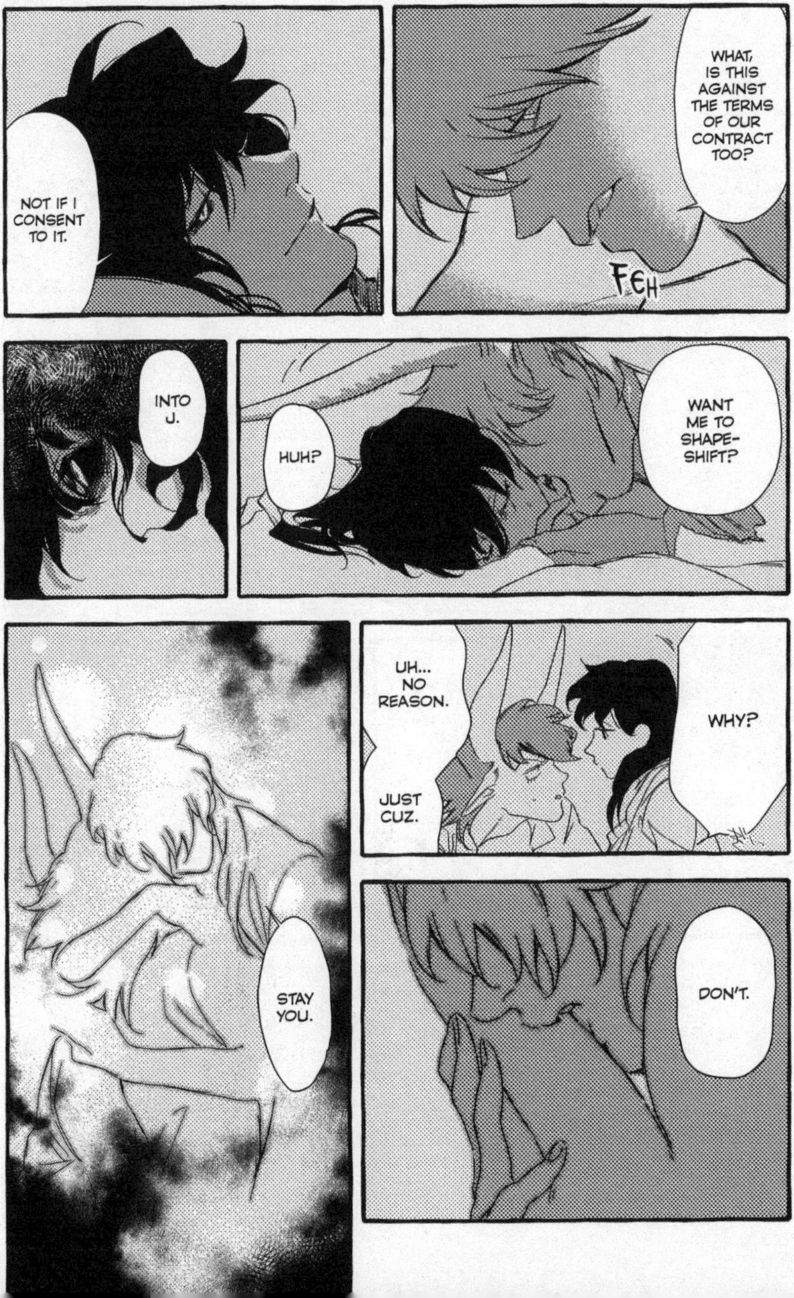
WHAT, IS THIS AGAINST THE TERMS OF OUR CONTRACT TOO?
FEH
NOT IF I CONSENT TO IT.
WANT ME TO SHAPE-SHIFT?
HUH?
INTO J.
WHY?
UH... NO REASON.
JUST CUZ.
DON'T.
STAY YOU.

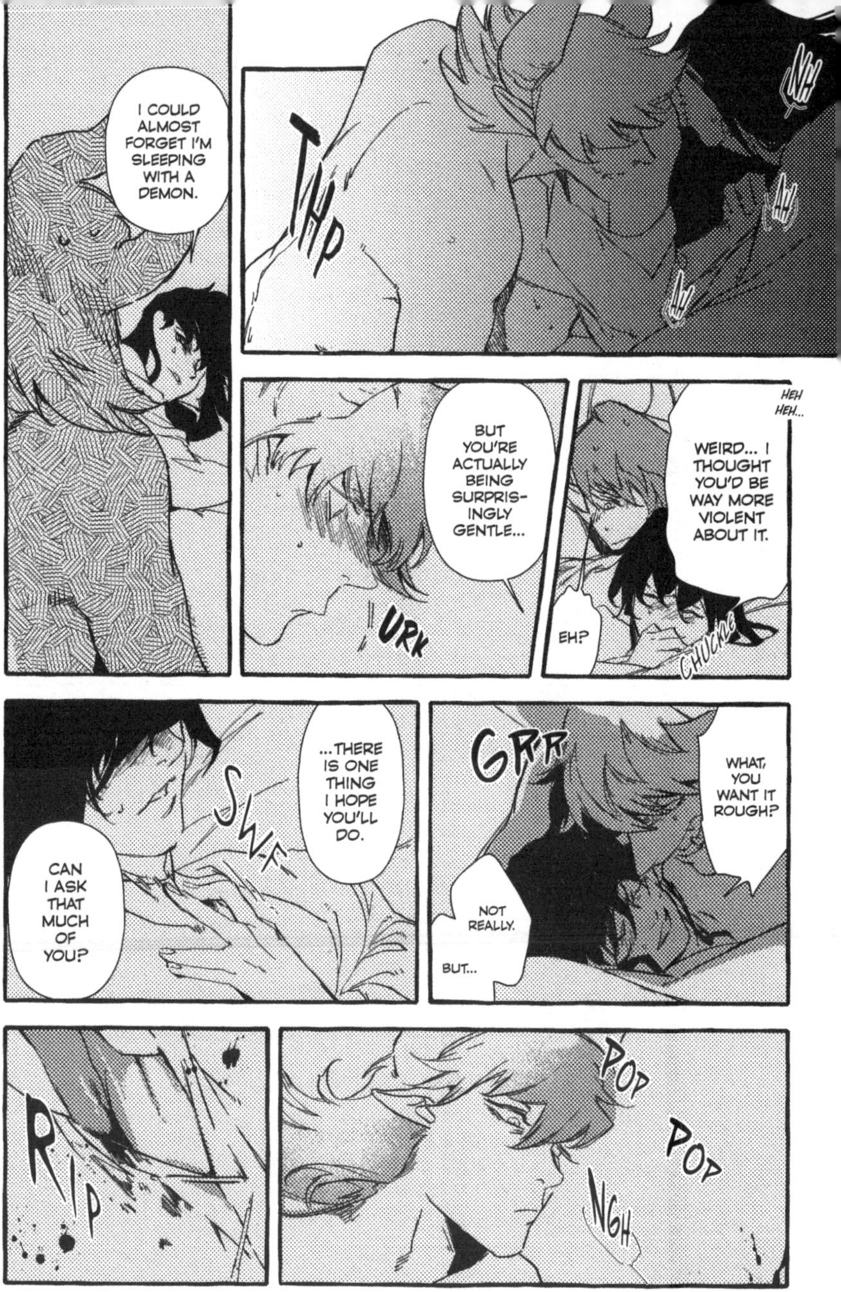
THP
NH
AH
AH
HEH HEH...
WEIRD... I THOUGHT YOU'D BE WAY MORE VIOLENT ABOUT IT.
EH?
CHUCKLE
BUT YOU'RE ACTUALLY BEING SURPRIS-INGLY GENTLE...
URK
I COULD ALMOST FORGET I'M SLEEPING WITH A DEMON.
GRR
WHAT, YOU WANT IT ROUGH?
NOT REALLY.
BUT...
...THERE IS ONE THING I HOPE YOU'LL DO.
SWF
CAN I ASK THAT MUCH OF YOU?
POP
POP
NGH
RIP

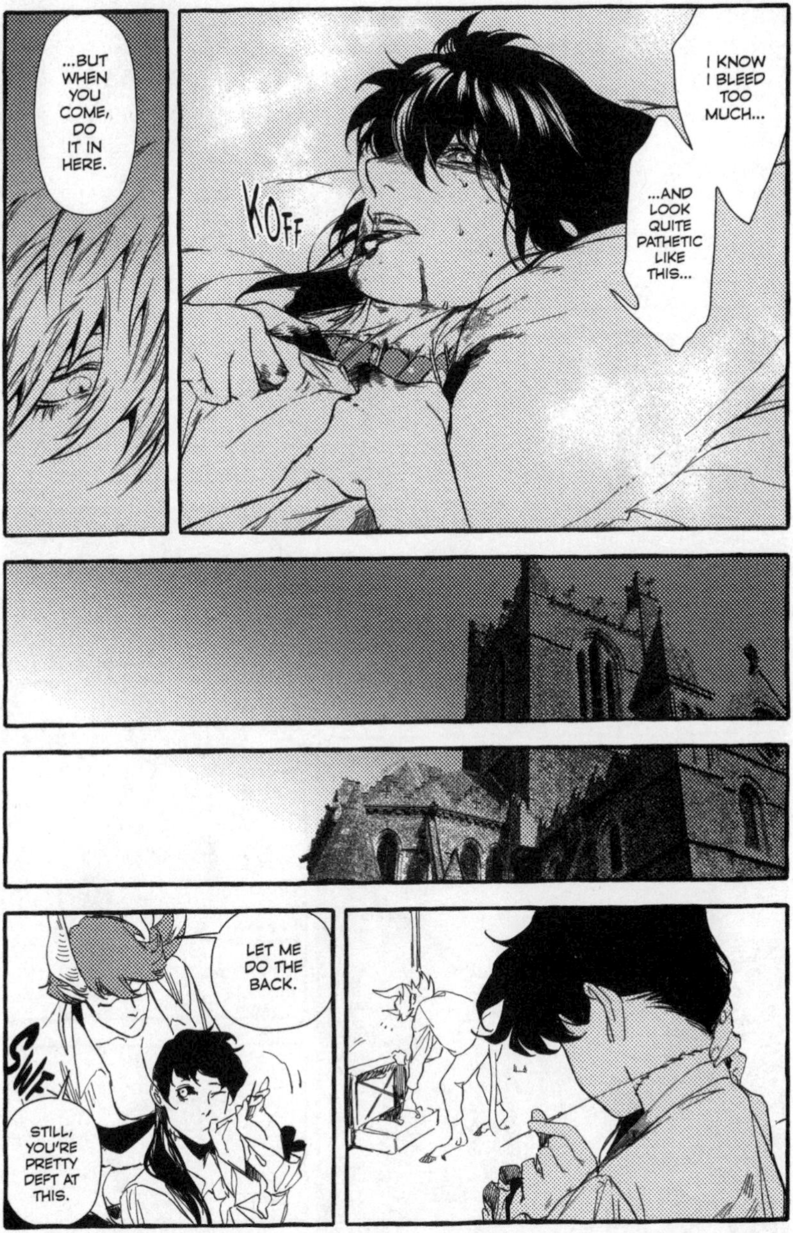
I KNOW I BLEED TOO MUCH...
...AND LOOK QUITE PATHETIC LIKE THIS...
KOFF
...BUT WHEN YOU COME, DO IT IN HERE.
LET ME DO THE BACK.
SWF
STILL, YOU'RE PRETTY DEFT AT THIS.

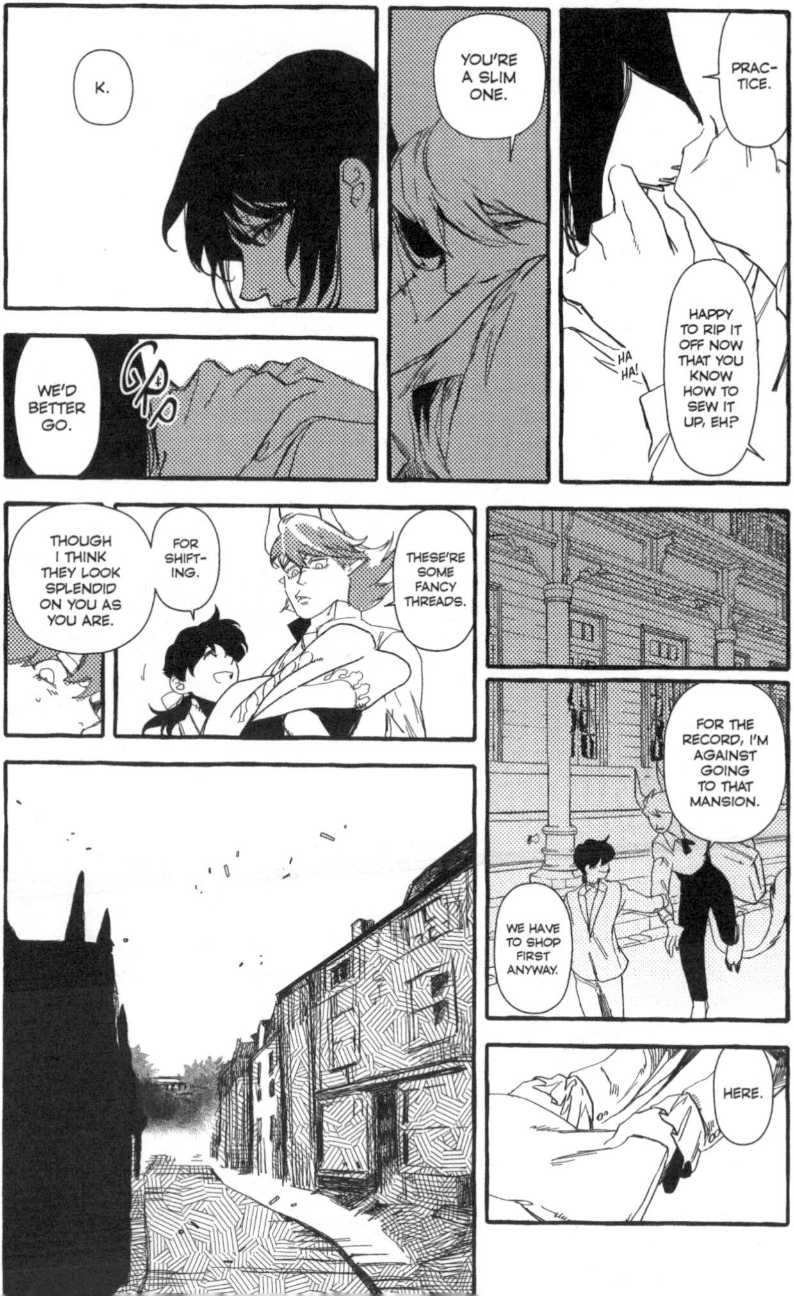
PRAC-TICE.
HA HA!
HAPPY TO RIP IT OFF NOW THAT YOU KNOW HOW TO SEW IT UP, EH?
YOU'RE A SLIM ONE.
K.
GRP
WE'D BETTER GO.
THESE'RE SOME FANCY THREADS.
FOR SHIFT-ING.
THOUGH I THINK THEY LOOK SPLENDID ON YOU AS YOU ARE.
FOR THE RECORD, I'M AGAINST GOING TO THAT MANSION.
WE HAVE TO SHOP FIRST ANYWAY.
HERE.

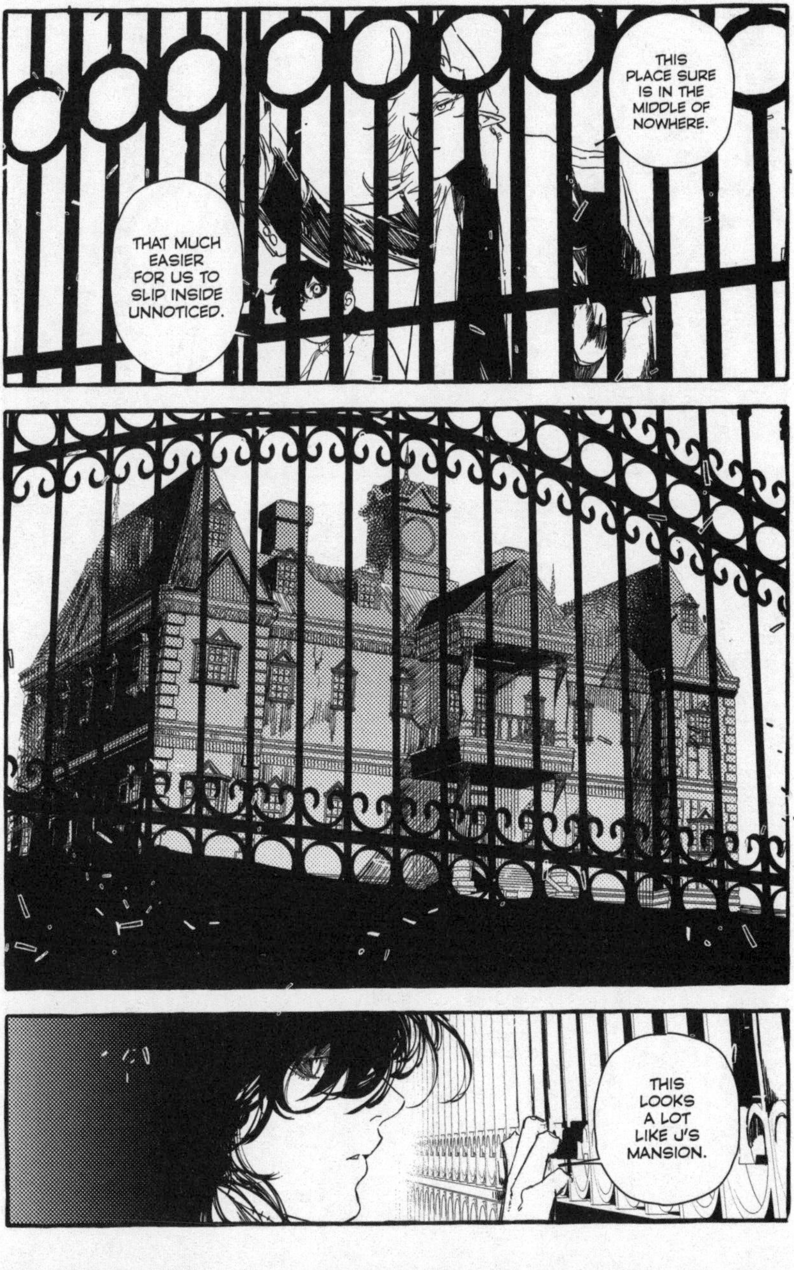
THIS PLACE SURE IS IN THE MIDDLE OF NOWHERE.
THAT MUCH EASIER FOR US TO SLIP INSIDE UNNOTICED.
THIS LOOKS A LOT LIKE J'S MANSION.

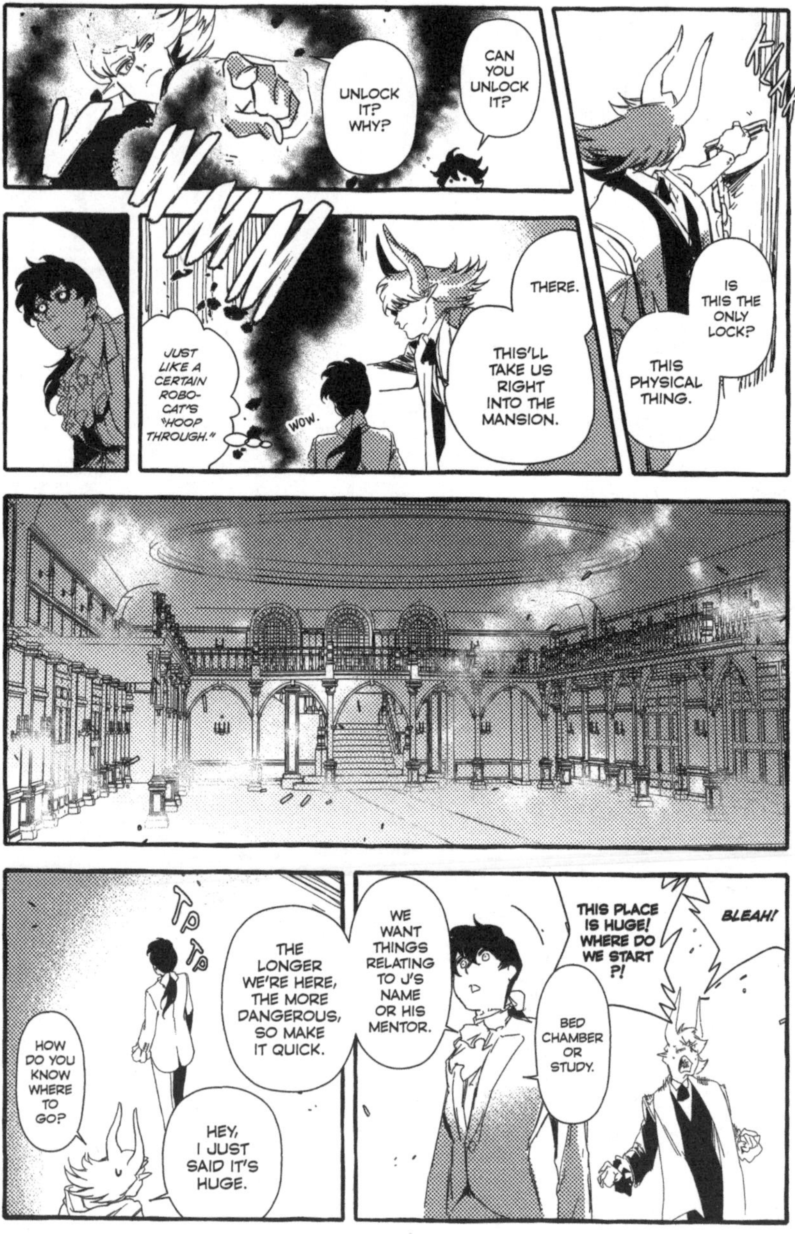
KLAK
IS THIS THE ONLY LOCK?
THIS PHYSICAL THING.
CAN YOU UNLOCK IT?
UNLOCK IT? WHY?
THERE.
THIS'LL TAKE US RIGHT INTO THE MANSION.
WOW.
JUST LIKE A CERTAIN ROBO-CAT'S "HOOP THROUGH."
BLEAH!
THIS PLACE IS HUGE! WHERE DO WE START?!
BED CHAMBER OR STUDY.
WE WANT THINGS RELATING TO J'S NAME OR HIS MENTOR.
TP TP
THE LONGER WE'RE HERE, THE MORE DANGEROUS, SO MAKE IT QUICK.
HOW DO YOU KNOW WHERE TO GO?
HEY, I JUST SAID IT'S HUGE.

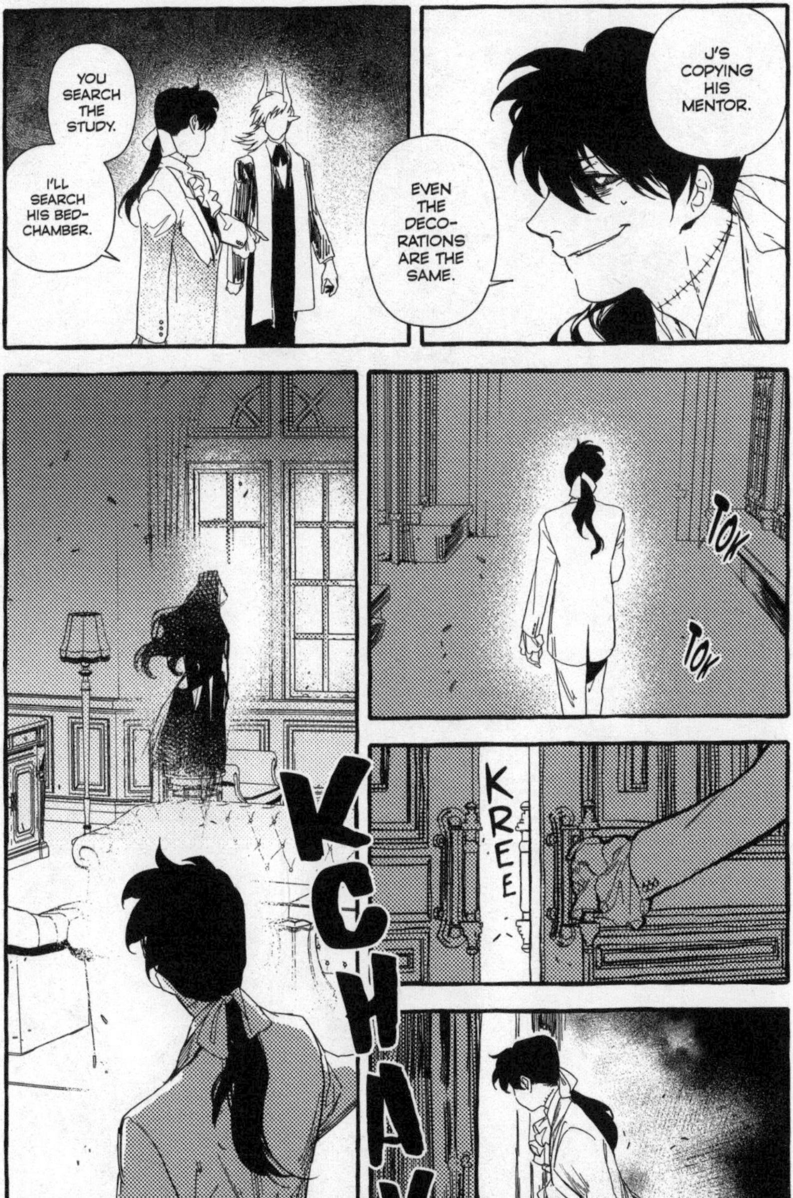
J'S COPYING HIS MENTOR.
EVEN THE DECO-RATIONS ARE THE SAME.
YOU SEARCH THE STUDY.
I'LL SEARCH HIS BED-CHAMBER.
TOK
TOK
KREE
KCHAK

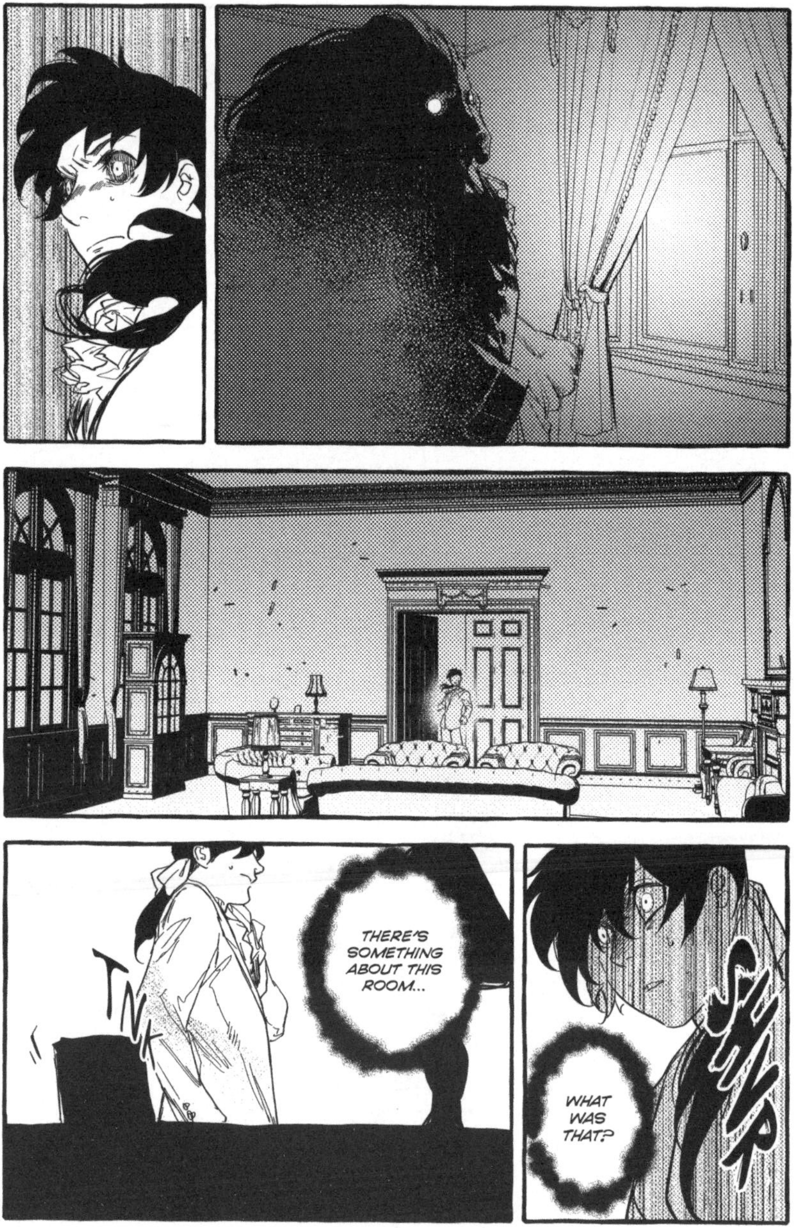
SHIVR
WHAT WAS THAT?
THERE'S SOMETHING ABOUT THIS ROOM...
TNK

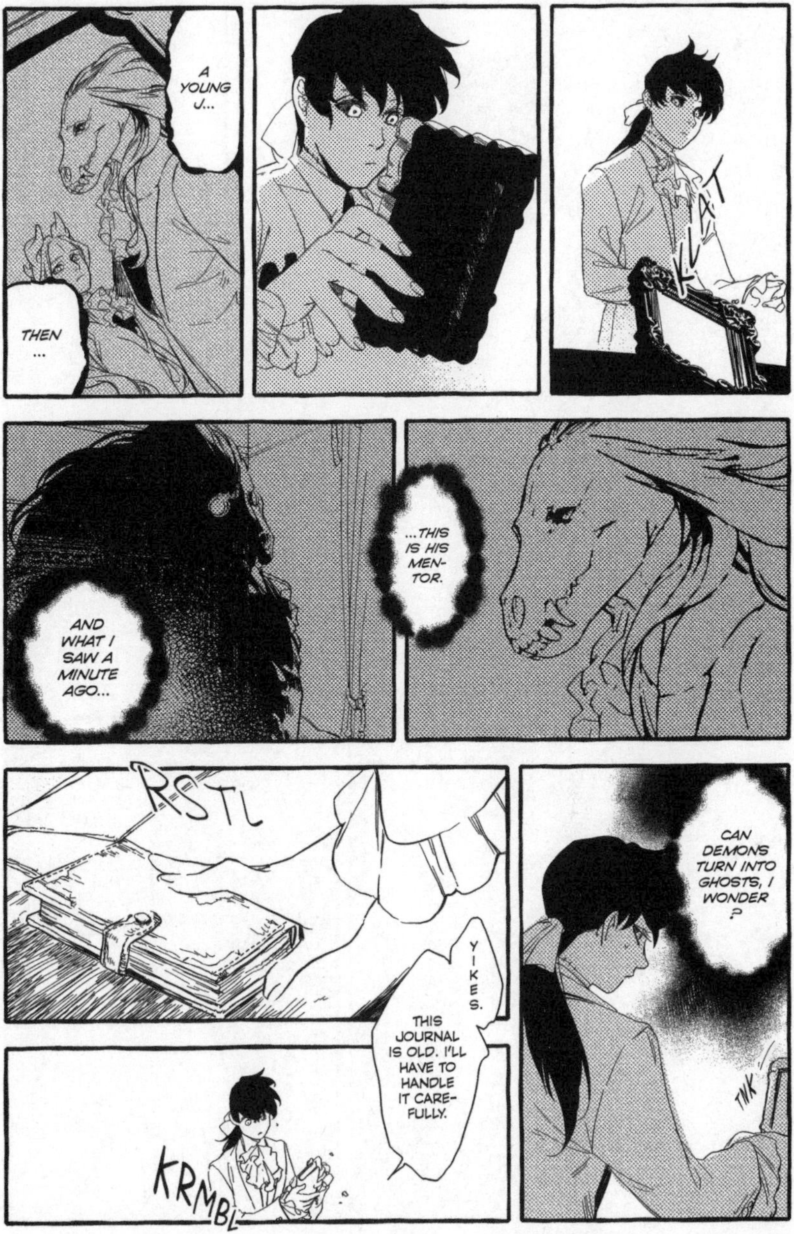
KLAT
A YOUNG J...
THEN ...
...THIS IS HIS MEN-TOR.
AND WHAT I SAW A MINUTE AGO...
CAN DEMONS TURN INTO GHOSTS, I WONDER?
TNK
RSTL
YIKES.
THIS JOURNAL IS OLD. I'LL HAVE TO HANDLE IT CARE-FULLY.
KRMBL

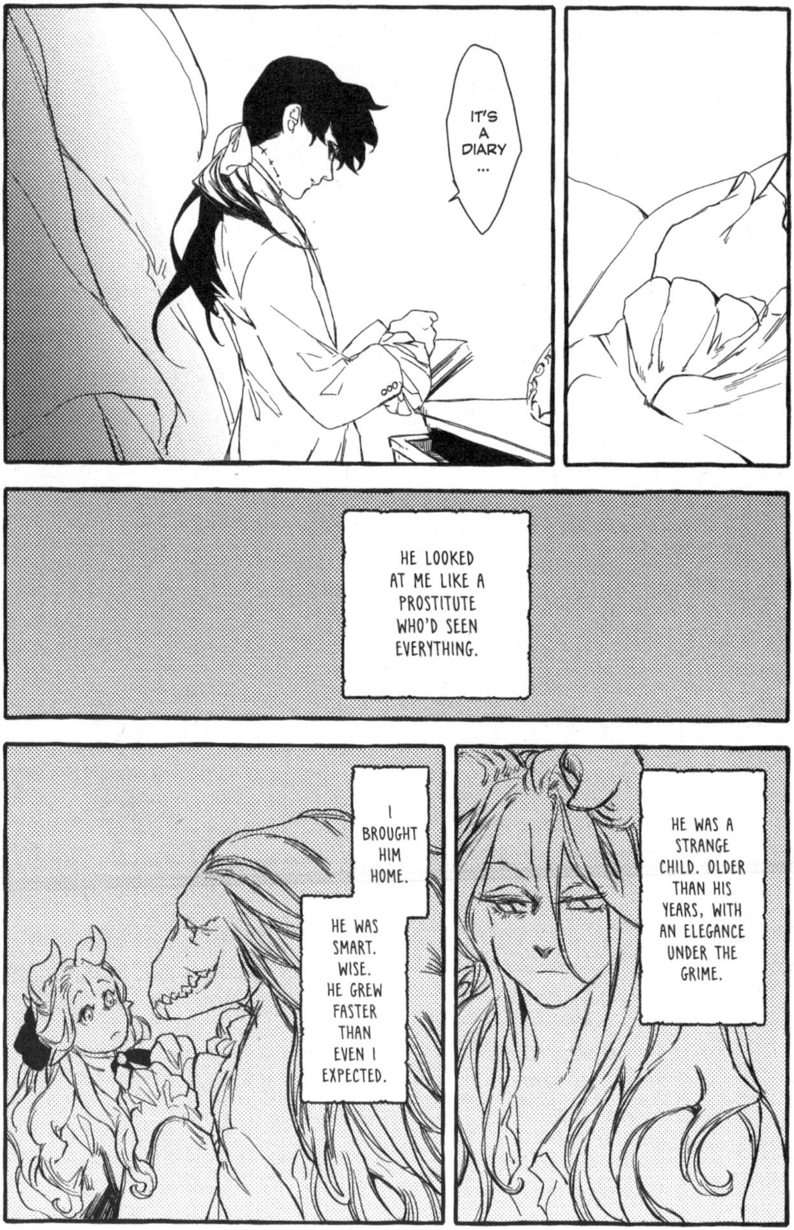
IT'S A DIARY ...
HE LOOKED AT ME LIKE A PROSTITUTE WHO'D SEEN EVERYTHING.
HE WAS A STRANGE CHILD. OLDER THAN HIS YEARS, WITH AN ELEGANCE UNDER THE GRIME.
I BROUGHT HIM HOME.
HE WAS SMART. WISE. HE GREW FASTER THAN EVEN I EXPECTED.

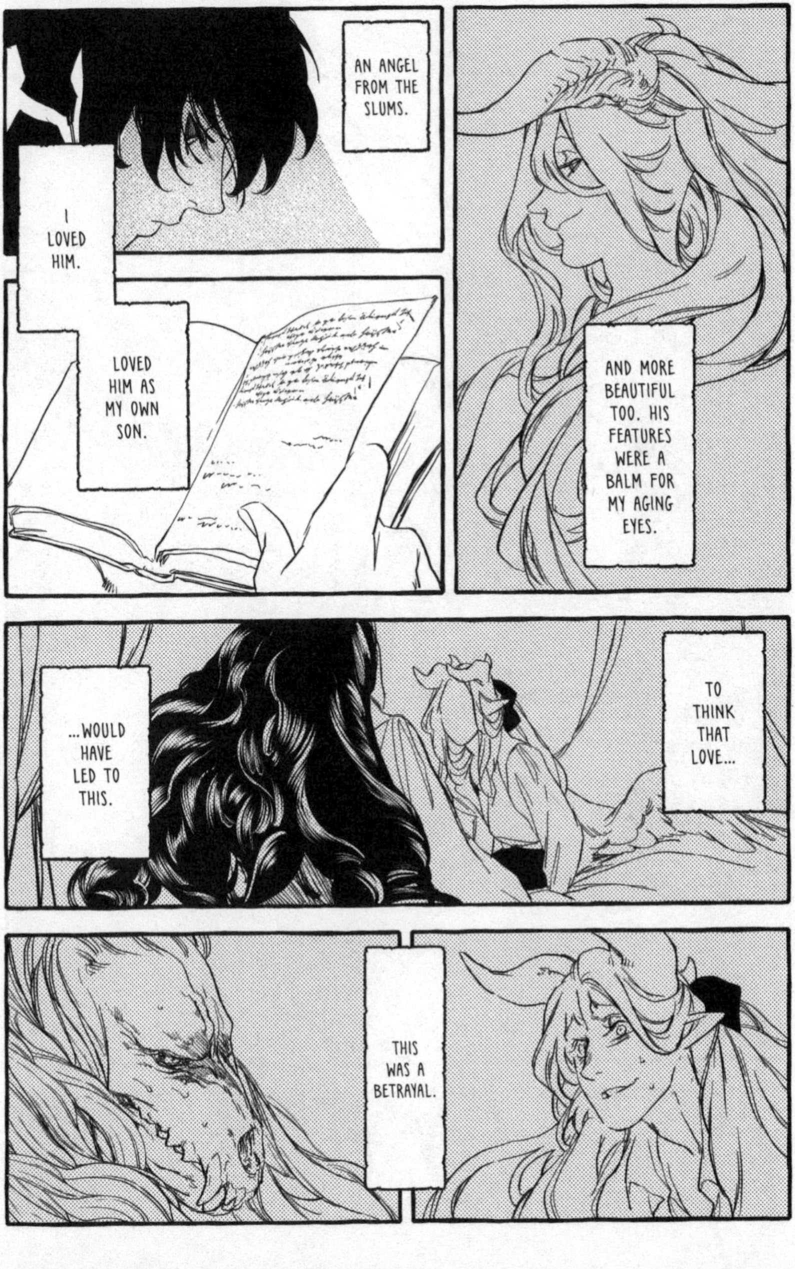
AND MORE BEAUTIFUL TOO. HIS FEATURES WERE A BALM FOR MY AGING EYES.
AN ANGEL FROM THE SLUMS.
I LOVED HIM.
LOVED HIM AS MY OWN SON.
TO THINK THAT LOVE...
...WOULD HAVE LED TO THIS.
THIS WAS A BETRAYAL.

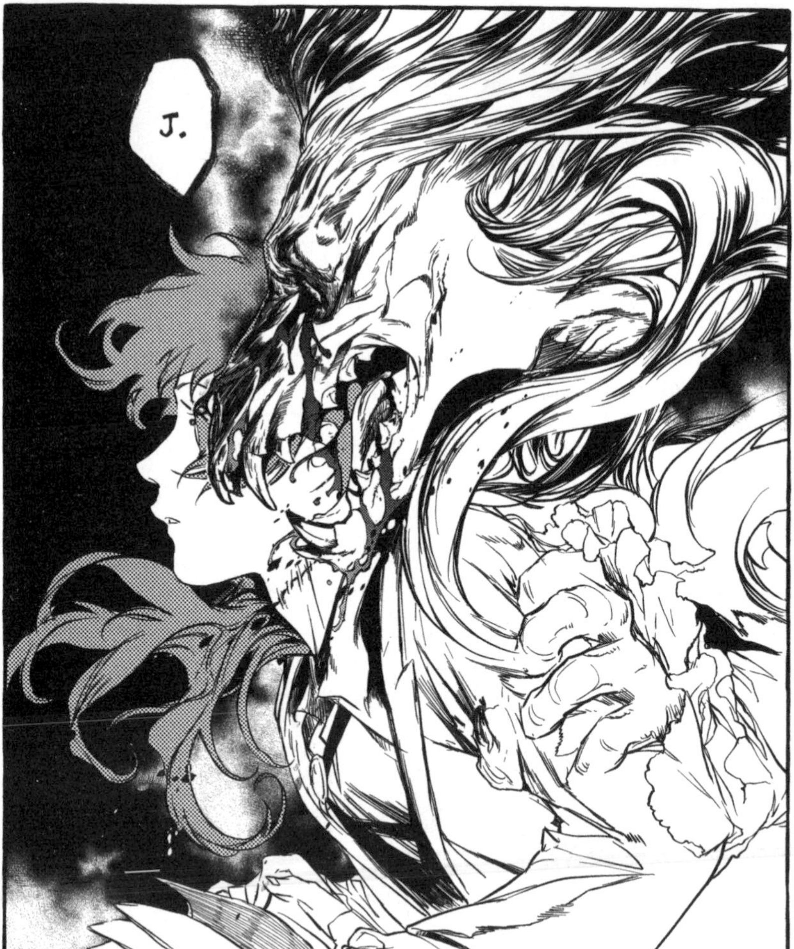
J.

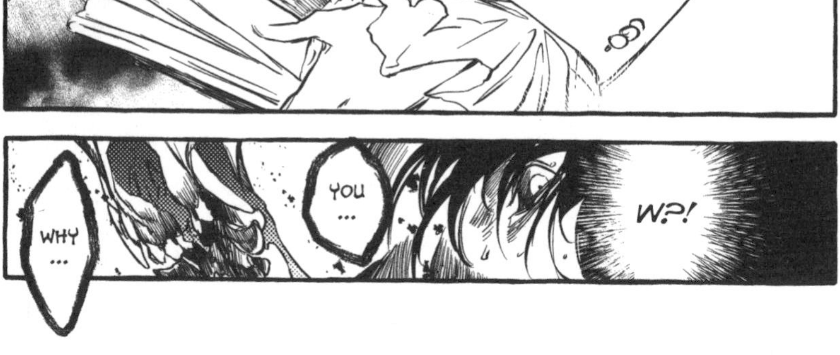
W?!
YOU ...
WHY ...

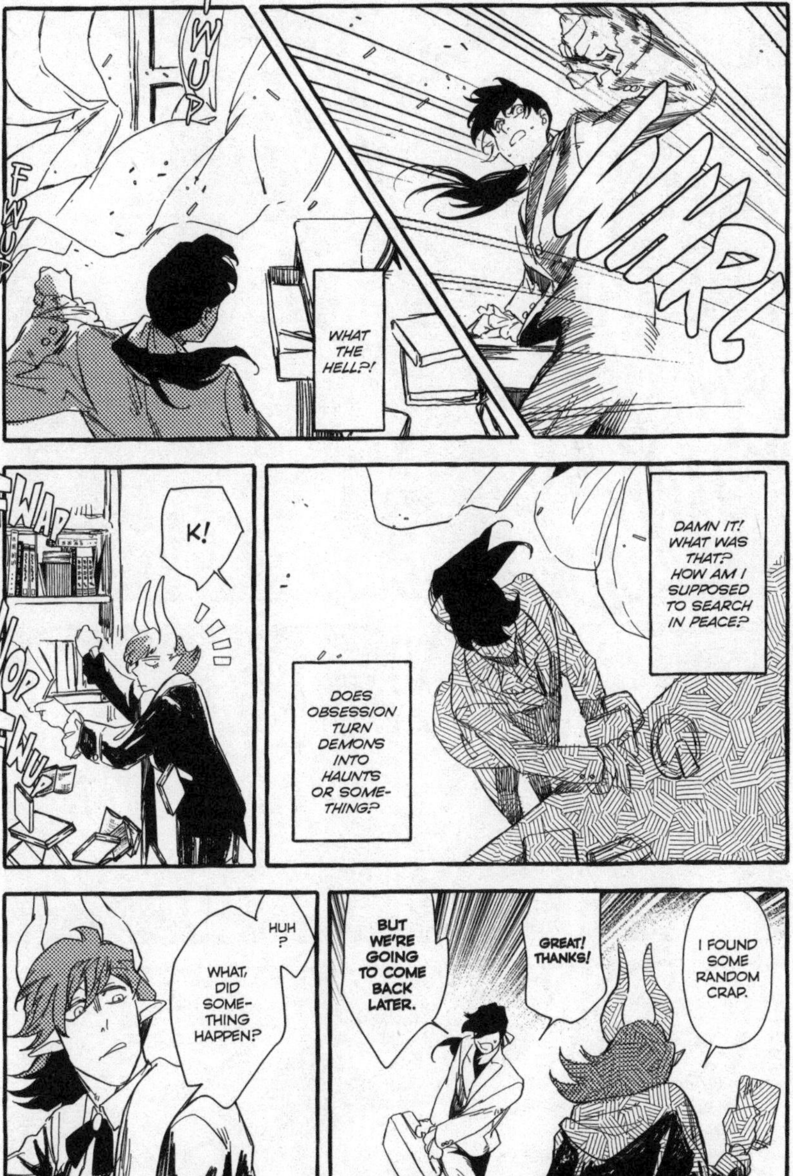
WHIRL
FWUP
WHAT THE HELL?!
FWUP
DAMN IT! WHAT WAS THAT? HOW AM I SUPPOSED TO SEARCH IN PEACE?
DOES OBSESSION TURN DEMONS INTO HAUNTS OR SOME-THING?
K!
FWAP
FWOP
FWUP
I FOUND SOME RANDOM CRAP.
GREAT! THANKS!
BUT WE'RE GOING TO COME BACK LATER.
HUH?
WHAT, DID SOME-THING HAPPEN?

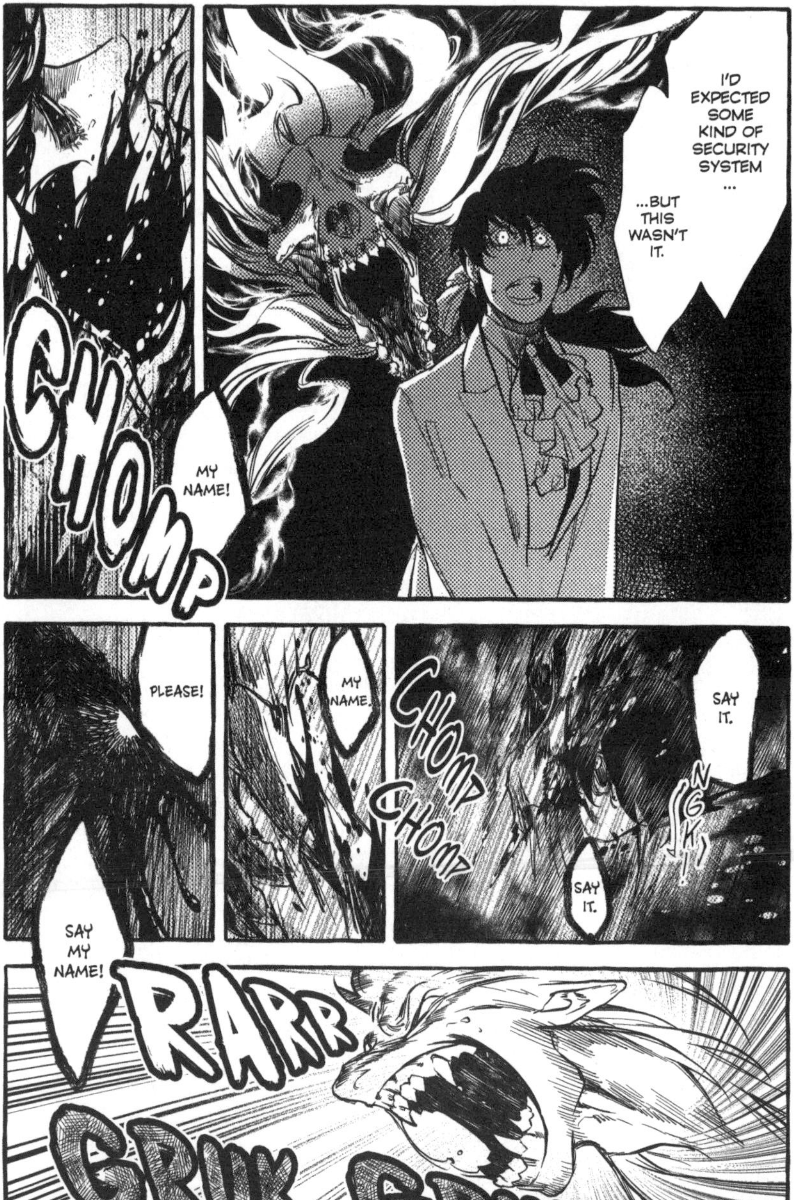
I'D EXPECTED SOME KIND OF SECURITY SYSTEM ...
...BUT THIS WASN'T IT.
MY NAME!
CHOMP
SAY IT.
NGK!
SAY IT.
CHOMP CHOMP
MY NAME.
PLEASE!
SAY MY NAME!
RARR
GRUK GRUK

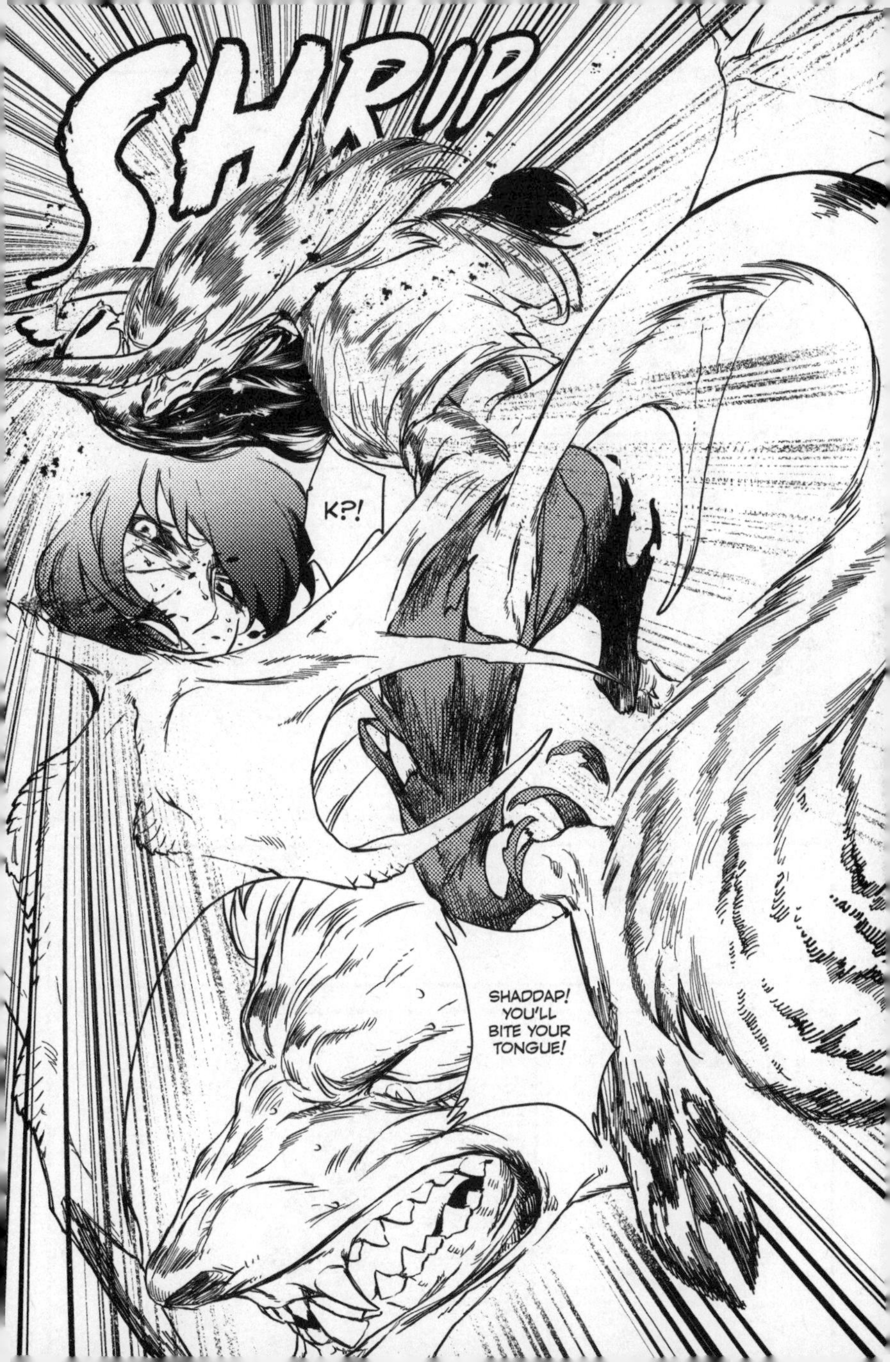
SHRIP
K?!
SHADDAP! YOU'LL BITE YOUR TONGUE!

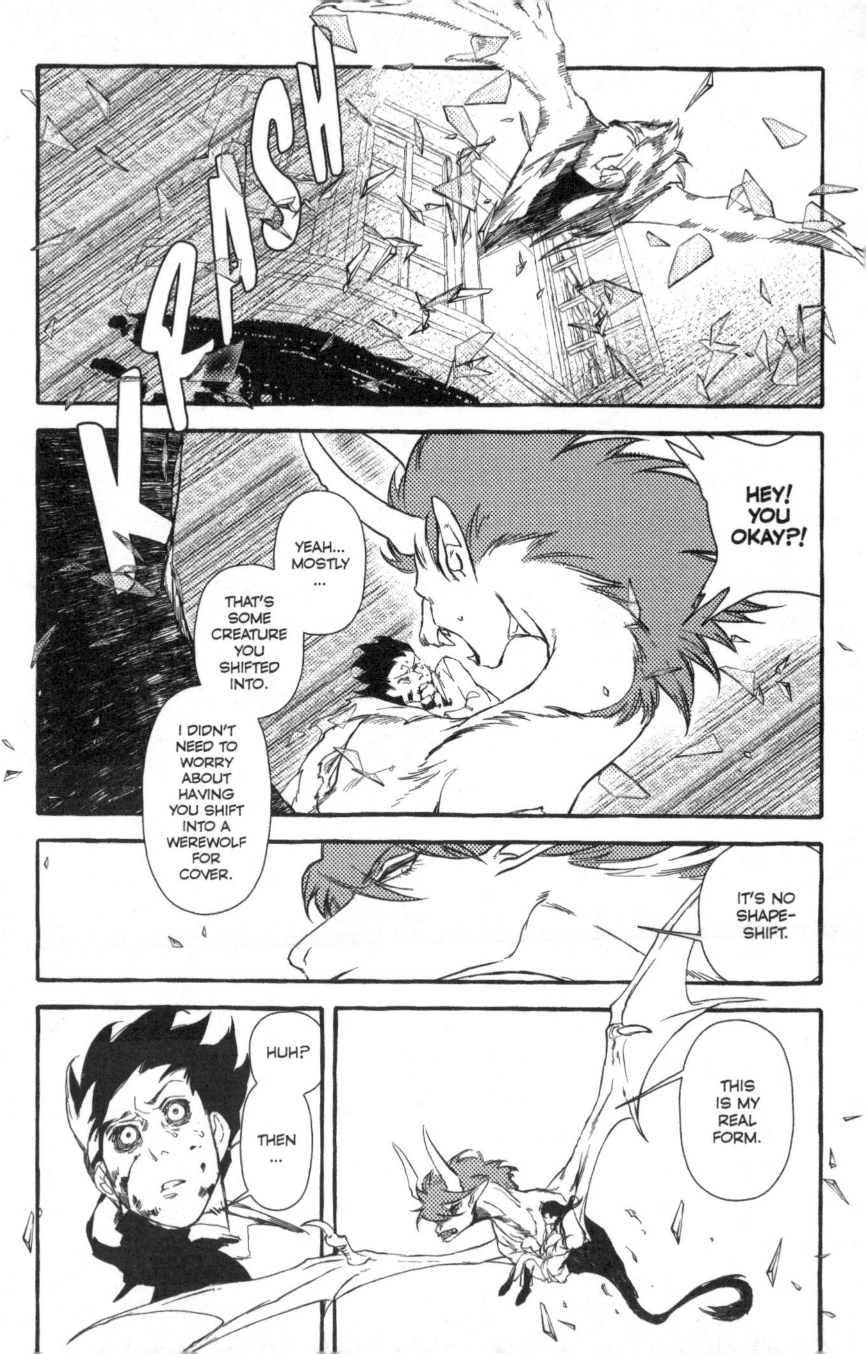

KRASH
HEY! YOU OKAY?!
YEAH... MOSTLY ...
THAT'S SOME CREATURE YOU SHIFTED INTO.
I DIDN'T NEED TO WORRY ABOUT HAVING YOU SHIFT INTO A WEREWOLF FOR COVER.
IT'S NO SHAPE-SHIFT.
THIS IS MY REAL FORM.
HUH?
THEN ...

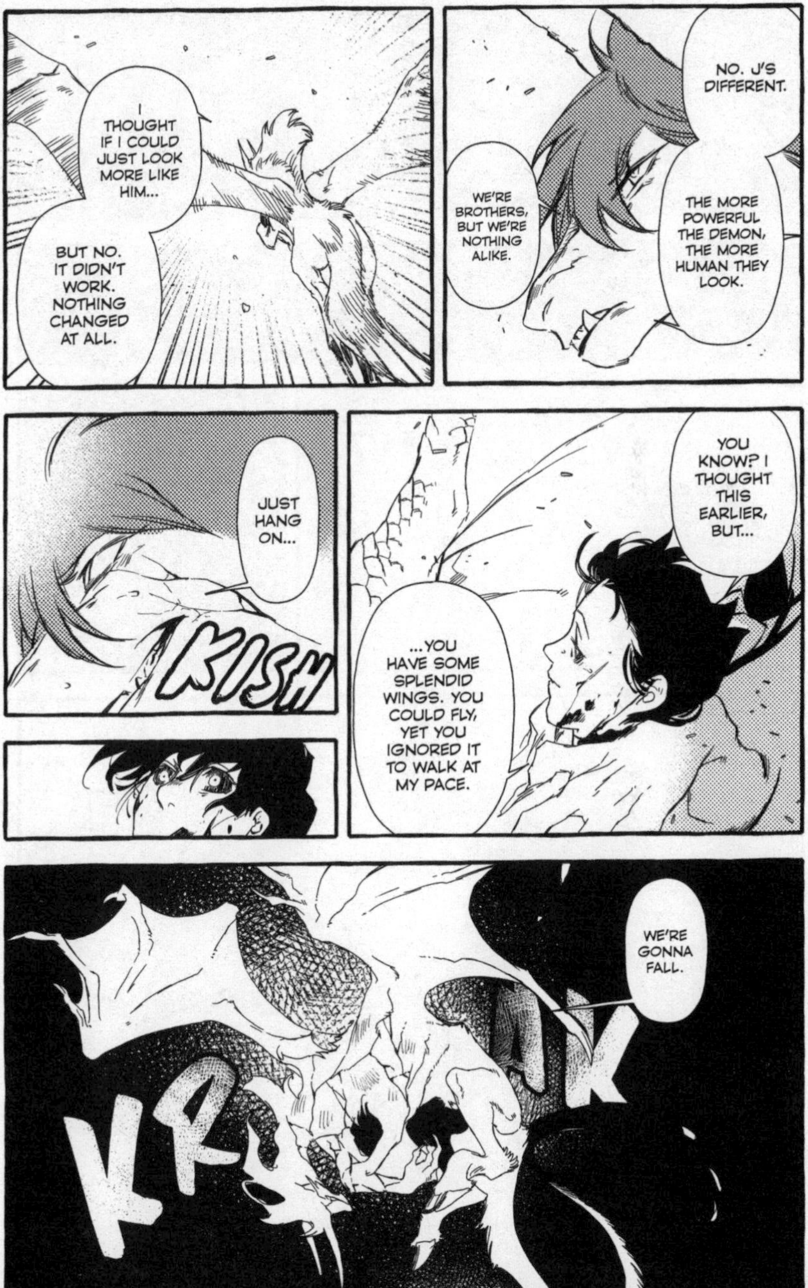
NO. J'S DIFFERENT.
THE MORE POWERFUL THE DEMON, THE MORE HUMAN THEY LOOK.
WE'RE BROTHERS, BUT WE'RE NOTHING ALIKE.
I THOUGHT IF I COULD JUST LOOK MORE LIKE HIM...
BUT NO. IT DIDN'T WORK. NOTHING CHANGED AT ALL.
YOU KNOW? I THOUGHT THIS EARLIER, BUT...
...YOU HAVE SOME SPLENDID WINGS. YOU COULD FLY, YET YOU IGNORED IT TO WALK AT MY PACE.
JUST HANG ON...
KISH
WE'RE GONNA FALL.

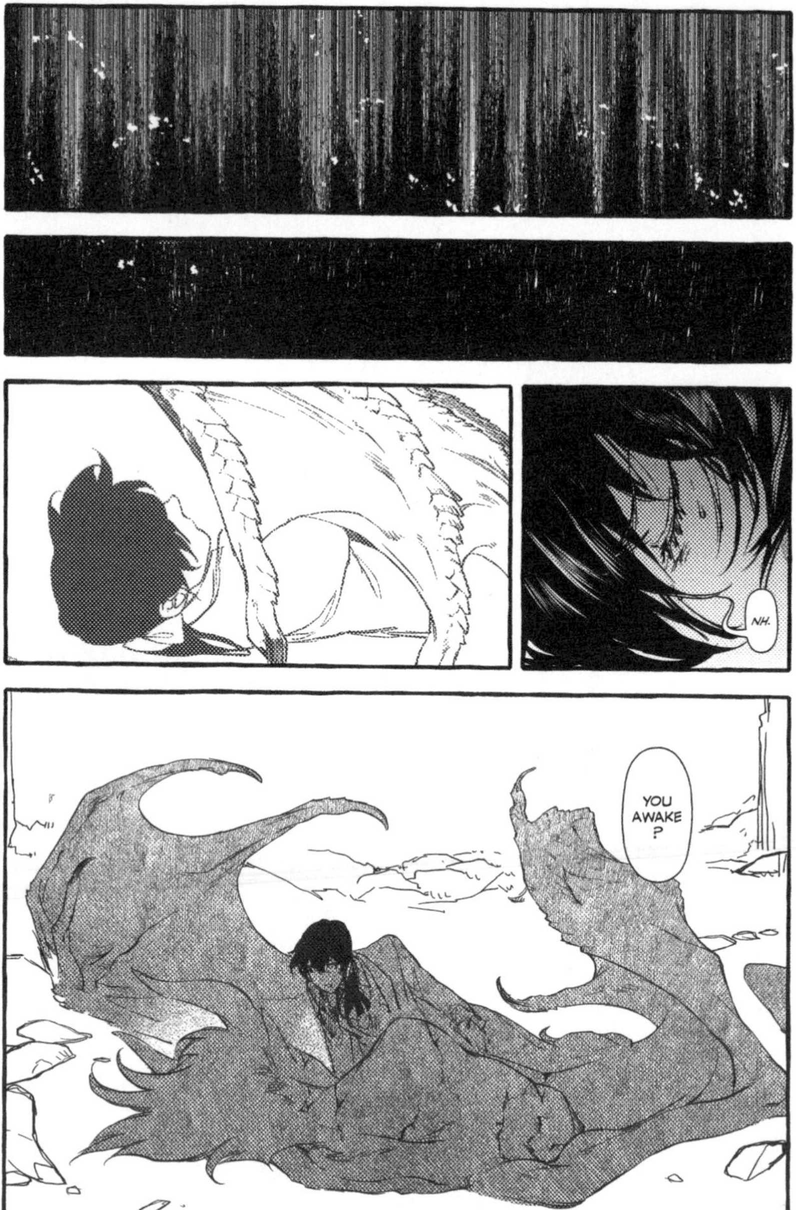
NH.
YOU AWAKE?

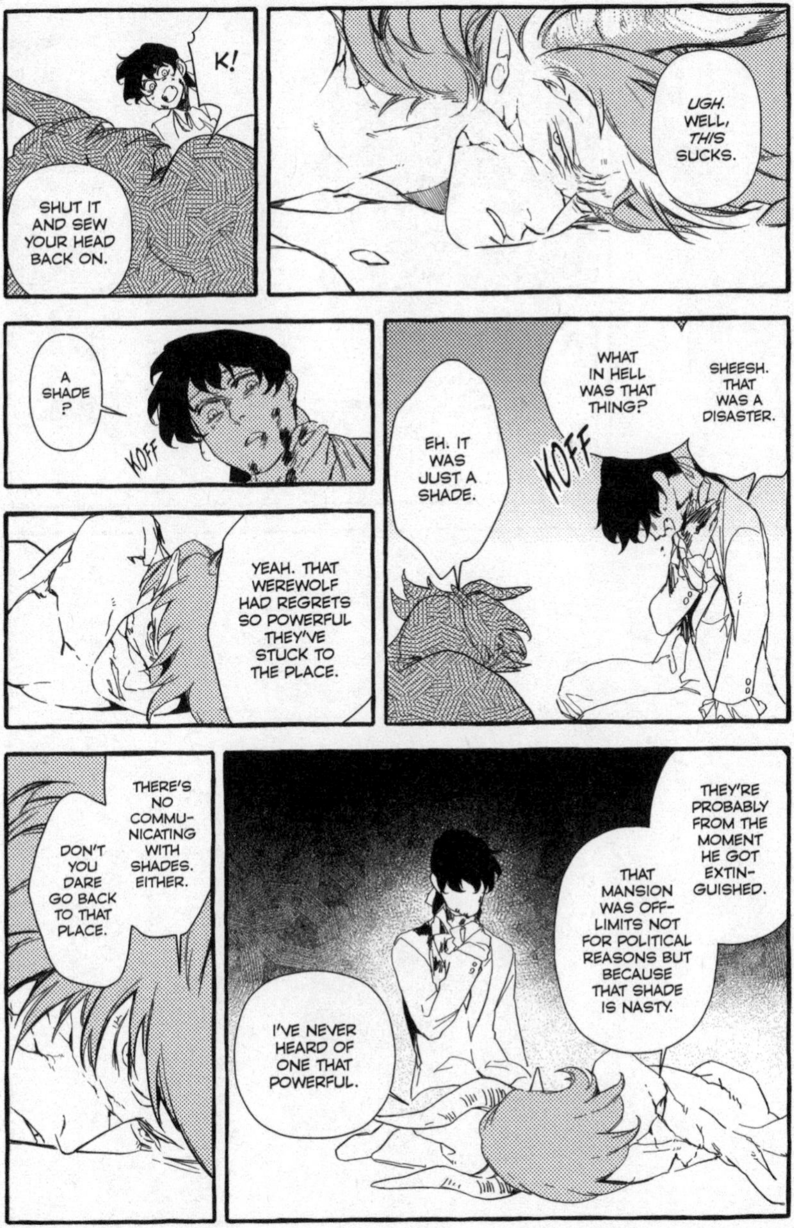
UGH. WELL, *THIS* SUCKS.
K!
SHUT IT AND SEW YOUR HEAD BACK ON.
SHEESH. THAT WAS A DISASTER.
WHAT IN HELL WAS THAT THING?
KOFF
EH. IT WAS JUST A SHADE.
A SHADE?
KOFF
YEAH. THAT WEREWOLF HAD REGRETS SO POWERFUL THEY'VE STUCK TO THE PLACE.
THEY'RE PROBABLY FROM THE MOMENT HE GOT EXTIN-GUISHED.
THAT MANSION WAS OFF-LIMITS NOT FOR POLITICAL REASONS BUT BECAUSE THAT SHADE IS NASTY.
I'VE NEVER HEARD OF ONE THAT POWERFUL.
THERE'S NO COMMU-NICATING WITH SHADES. EITHER.
DON'T YOU DARE GO BACK TO THAT PLACE.

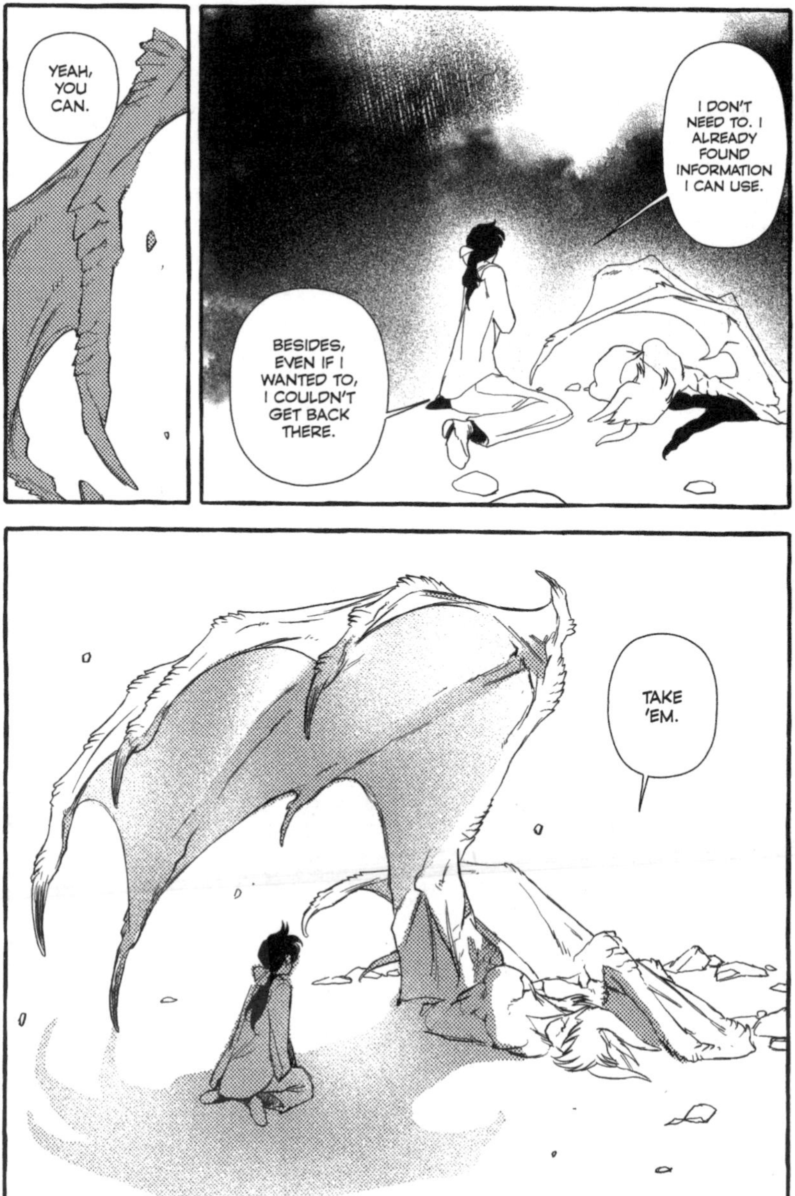
I DON'T NEED TO. I ALREADY FOUND INFORMATION I CAN USE.
BESIDES, EVEN IF I WANTED TO, I COULDN'T GET BACK THERE.
YEAH, YOU CAN.
TAKE 'EM.

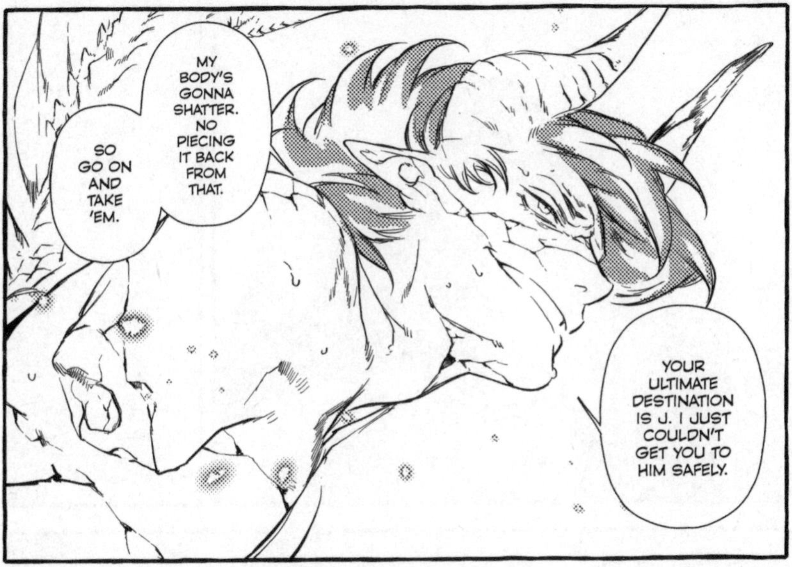
YOUR ULTIMATE DESTINATION IS J. I JUST COULDN'T GET YOU TO HIM SAFELY.
MY BODY'S GONNA SHATTER. NO PIECING IT BACK FROM THAT.
SO GO ON AND TAKE 'EM.

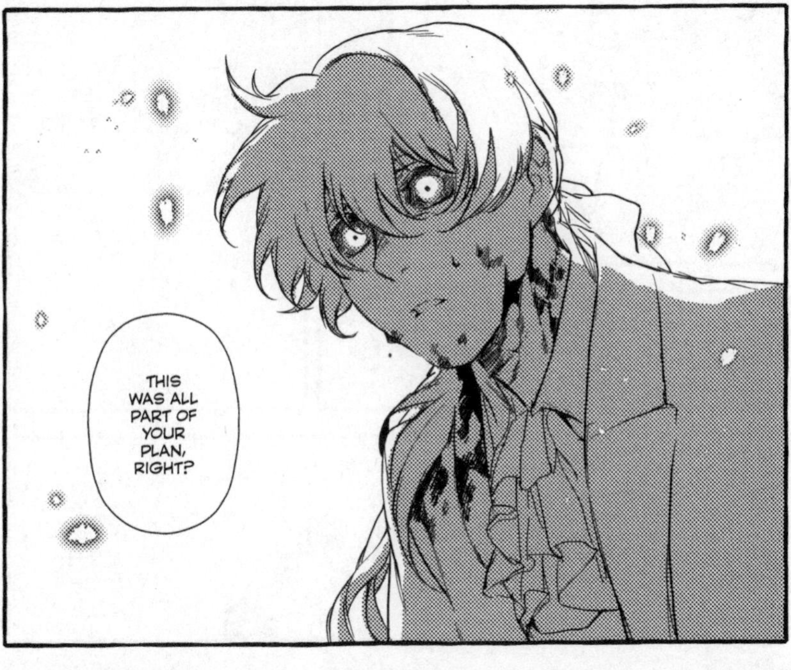
THIS WAS ALL PART OF YOUR PLAN, RIGHT?

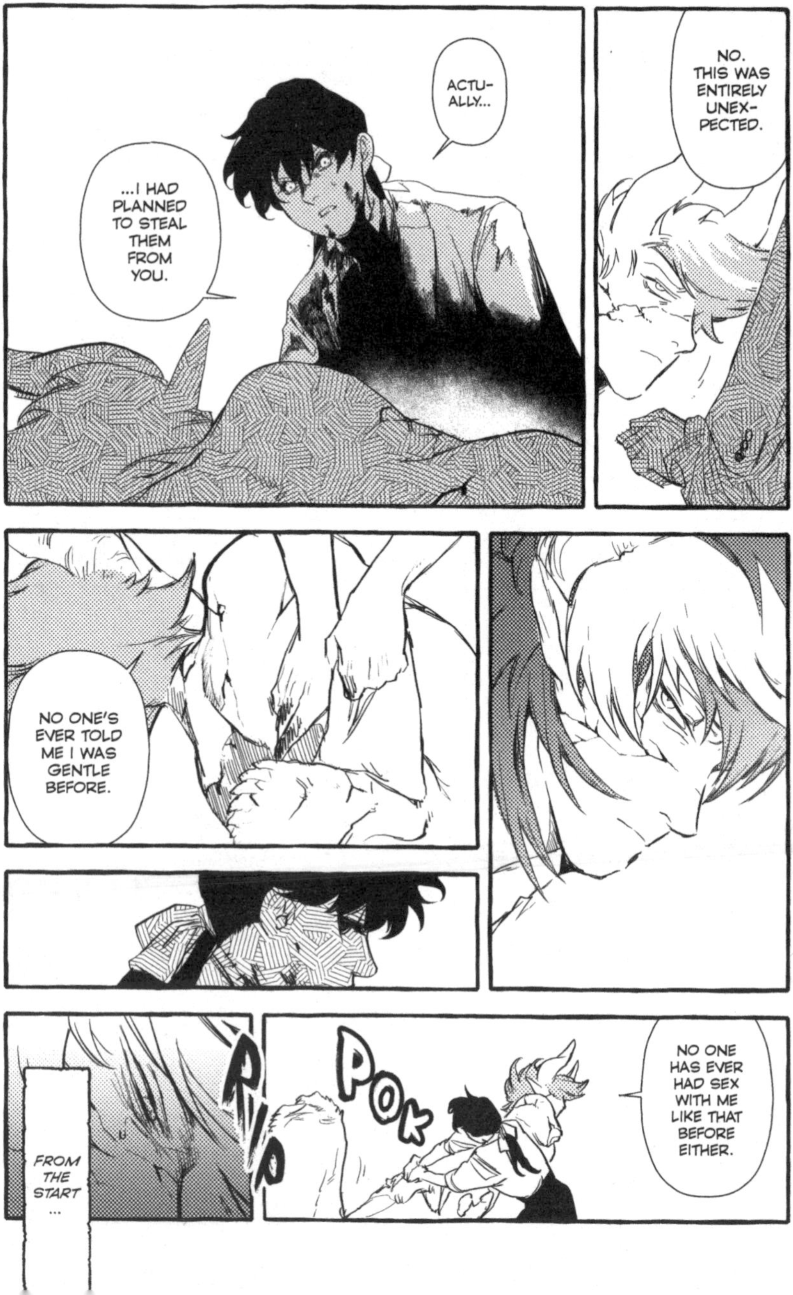
NO. THIS WAS ENTIRELY UNEXPECTED.
ACTUALLY...
...I HAD PLANNED TO STEAL THEM FROM YOU.
NO ONE'S EVER TOLD ME I WAS GENTLE BEFORE.
NO ONE HAS EVER HAD SEX WITH ME LIKE THAT BEFORE EITHER.
POK
RIP
FROM THE START ...

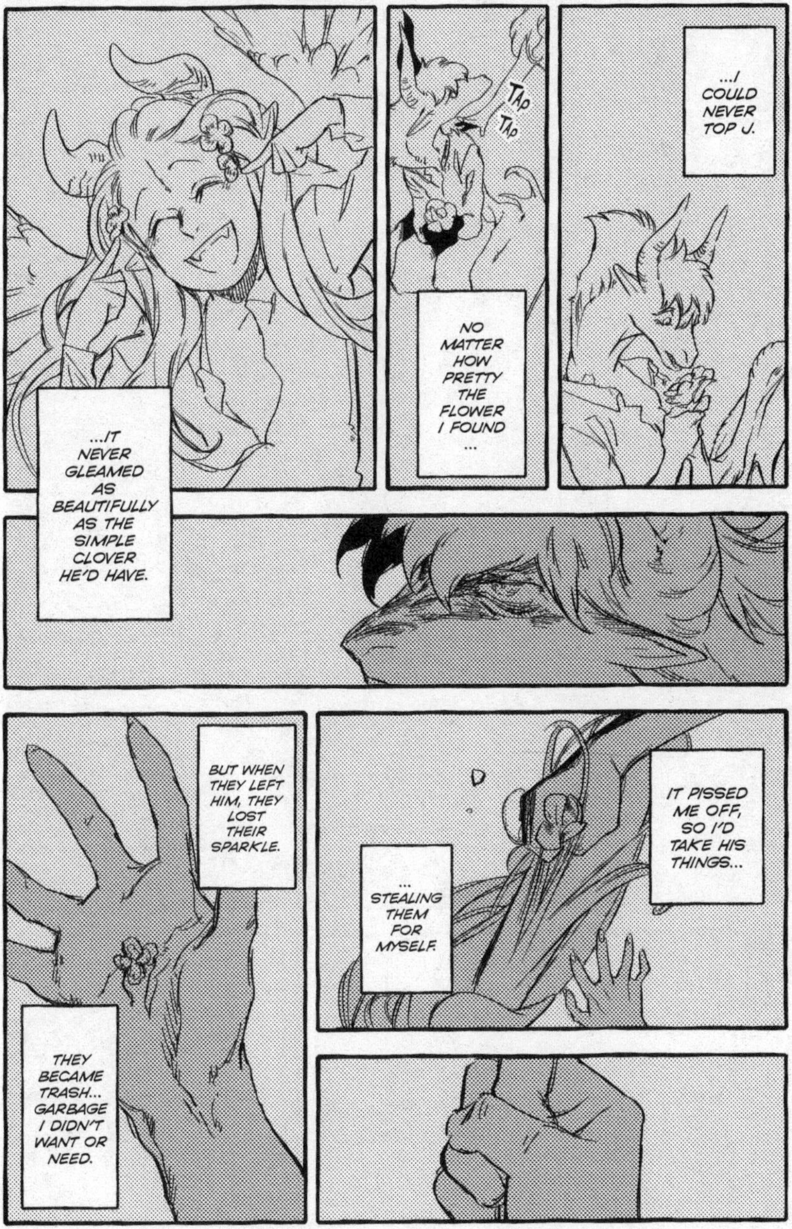
...I COULD NEVER TOP J.
TAP
TAP
NO MATTER HOW PRETTY THE FLOWER I FOUND ...
...IT NEVER GLEAMED AS BEAUTIFULLY AS THE SIMPLE CLOVER HE'D HAVE.
IT PISSED ME OFF, SO I'D TAKE HIS THINGS...
... STEALING THEM FOR MYSELF.
BUT WHEN THEY LEFT HIM, THEY LOST THEIR SPARKLE.
THEY BECAME TRASH... GARBAGE I DIDN'T WANT OR NEED.

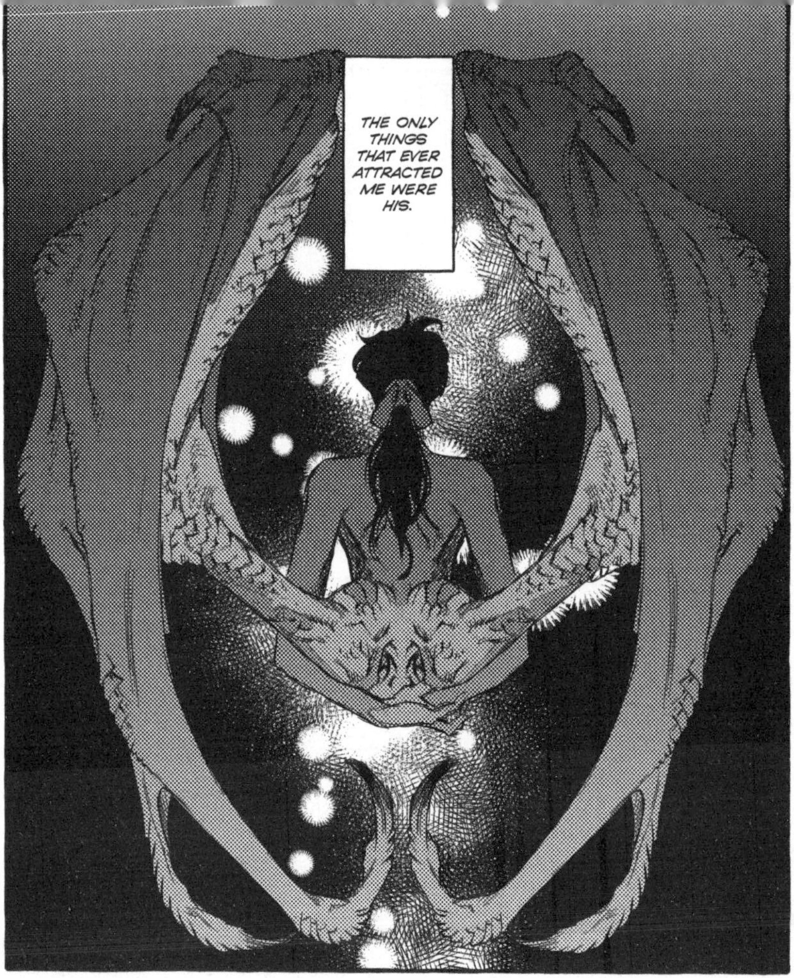
THE ONLY THINGS THAT EVER ATTRACTED ME WERE HIS.

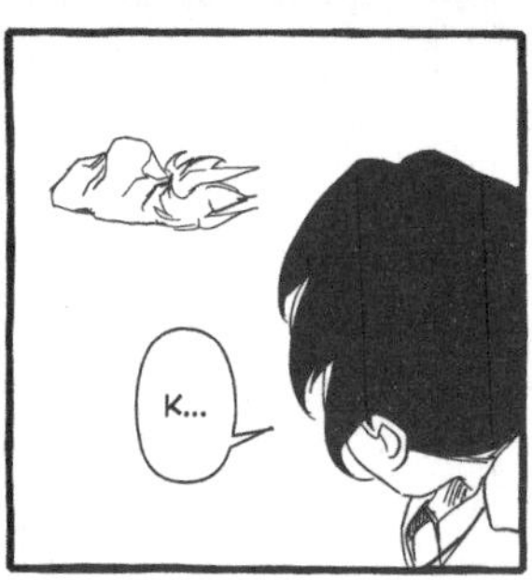
K...

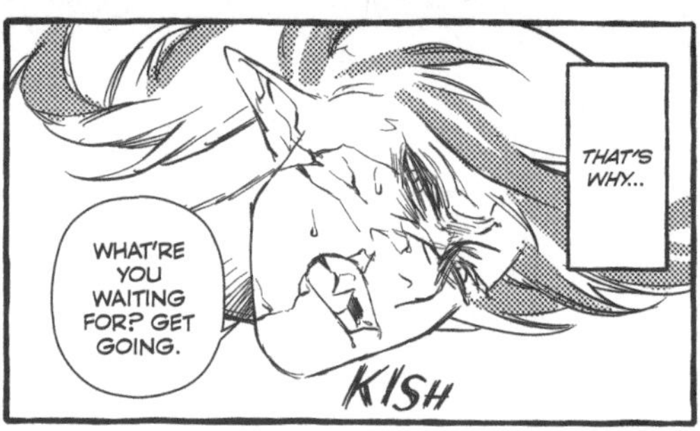
THAT'S WHY...
WHAT'RE YOU WAITING FOR? GET GOING.
KISH

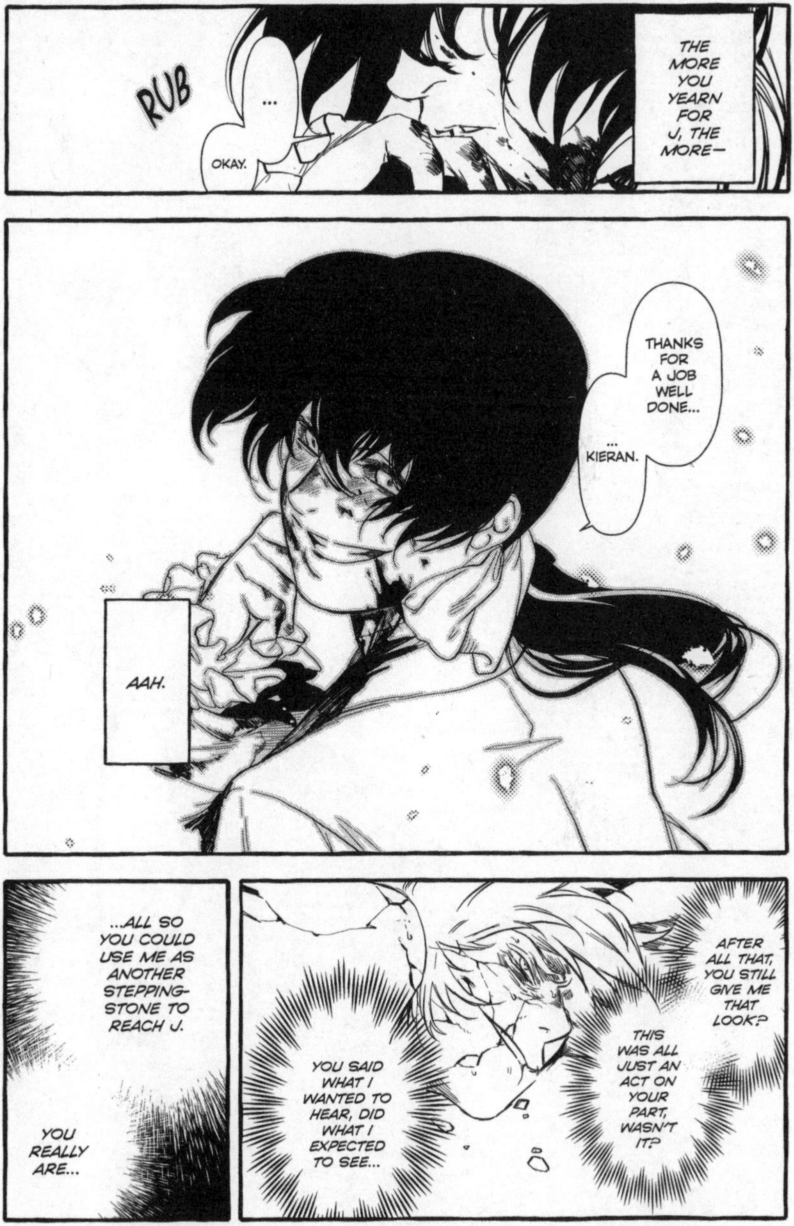
THE MORE YOU YEARN FOR J, THE MORE—
RUB
...
OKAY.
THANKS FOR A JOB WELL DONE...
... KIERAN.
AAH.
AFTER ALL THAT, YOU STILL GIVE ME THAT LOOK?
THIS WAS ALL JUST AN ACT ON YOUR PART, WASN'T IT?
YOU SAID WHAT I WANTED TO HEAR, DID WHAT I EXPECTED TO SEE...
...ALL SO YOU COULD USE ME AS ANOTHER STEPPING-STONE TO REACH J.
YOU REALLY ARE...

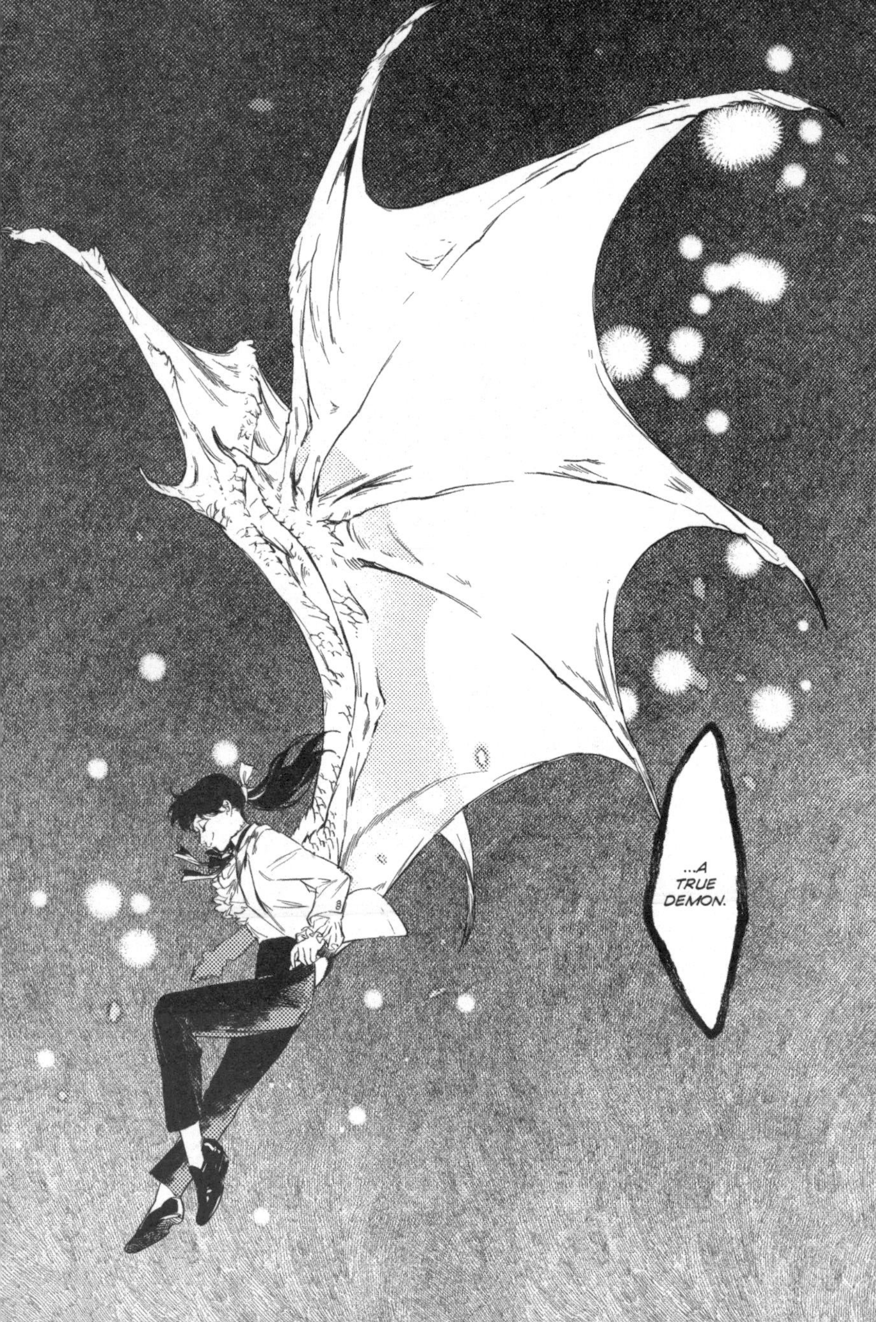
...A TRUE DEMON.

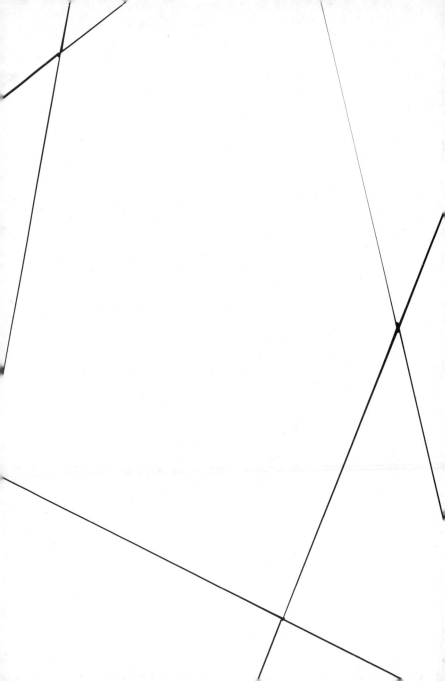

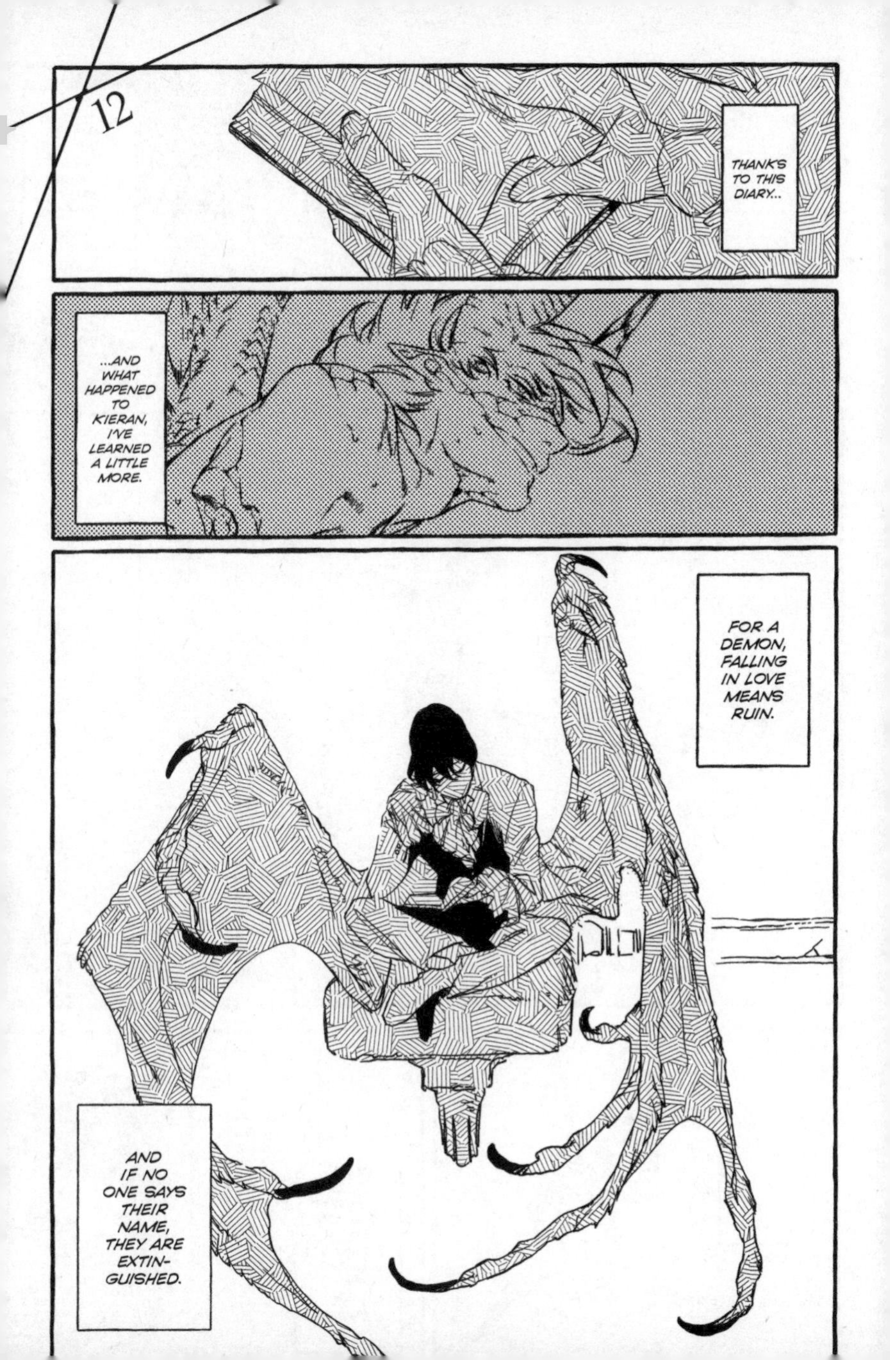
12
THANKS TO THIS DIARY...
...AND WHAT HAPPENED TO KIERAN, I'VE LEARNED A LITTLE MORE.
FOR A DEMON, FALLING IN LOVE MEANS RUIN.
AND IF NO ONE SAYS THEIR NAME, THEY ARE EXTIN-GUISHED.

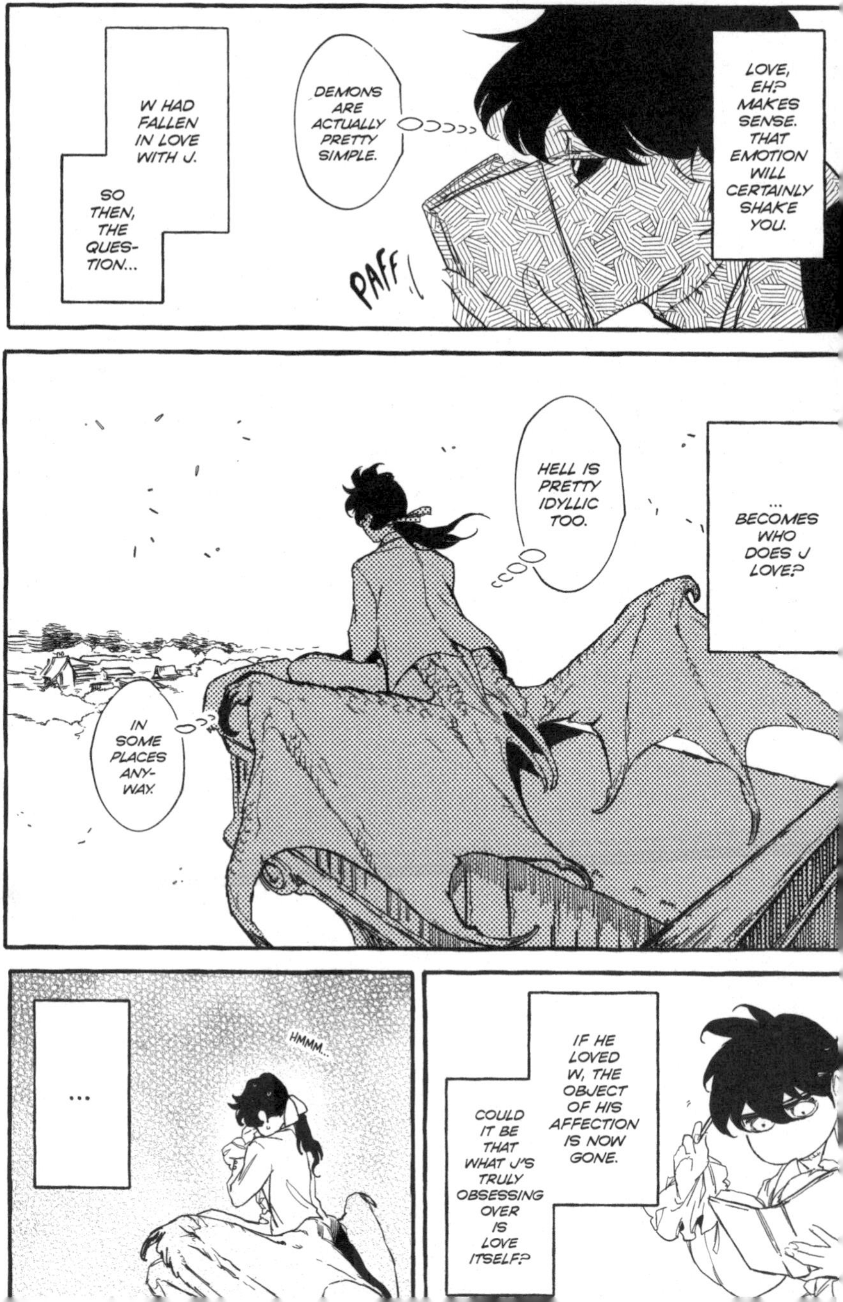
LOVE, EH? MAKES SENSE. THAT EMOTION WILL CERTAINLY SHAKE YOU.
DEMONS ARE ACTUALLY PRETTY SIMPLE.
PAFF
W HAD FALLEN IN LOVE WITH J.
SO THEN, THE QUESTION...
...BECOMES WHO DOES J LOVE?
HELL IS PRETTY IDYLLIC TOO.
IN SOME PLACES ANYWAY.
IF HE LOVED W, THE OBJECT OF HIS AFFECTION IS NOW GONE.
COULD IT BE THAT WHAT J'S TRULY OBSESSING OVER IS LOVE ITSELF?
HMMM...
...

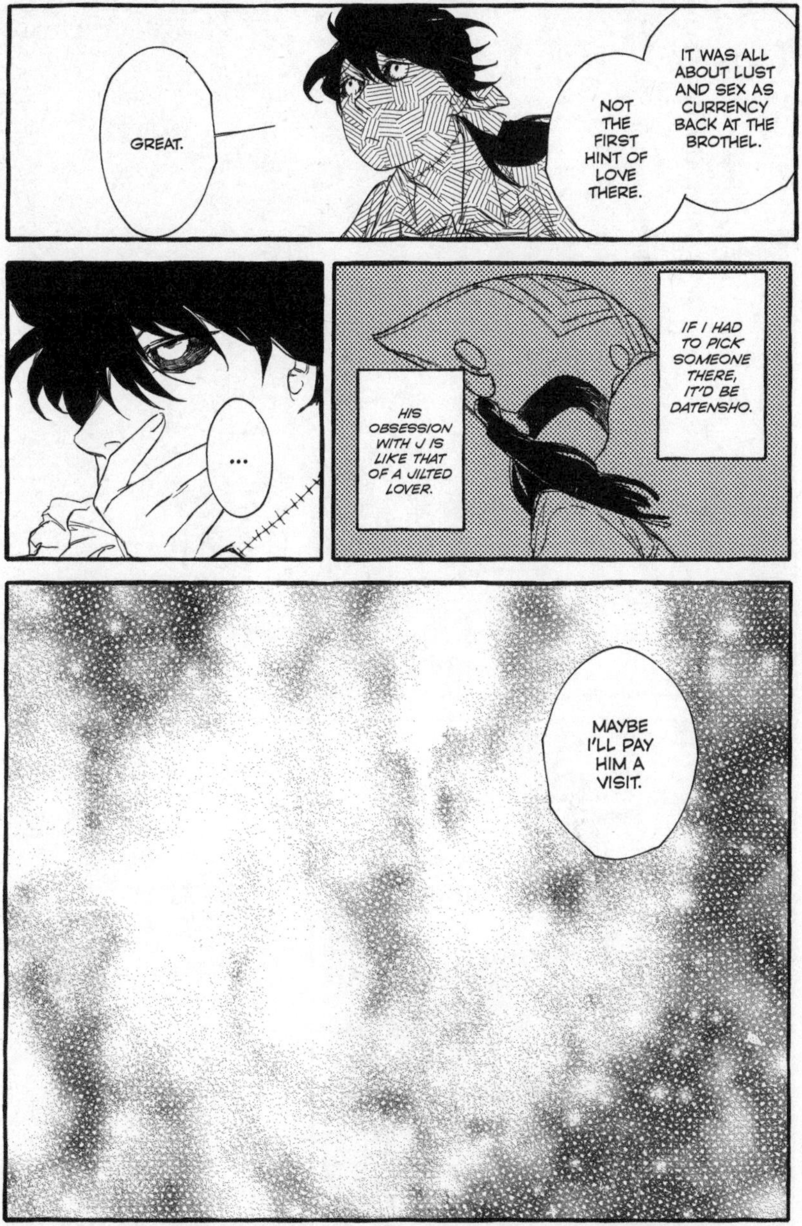
IT WAS ALL ABOUT LUST AND SEX AS CURRENCY BACK AT THE BROTHEL.
NOT THE FIRST HINT OF LOVE THERE.
GREAT.
IF I HAD TO PICK SOMEONE THERE, IT'D BE DATENSHO.
HIS OBSESSION WITH J IS LIKE THAT OF A JILTED LOVER.
...
MAYBE I'LL PAY HIM A VISIT.

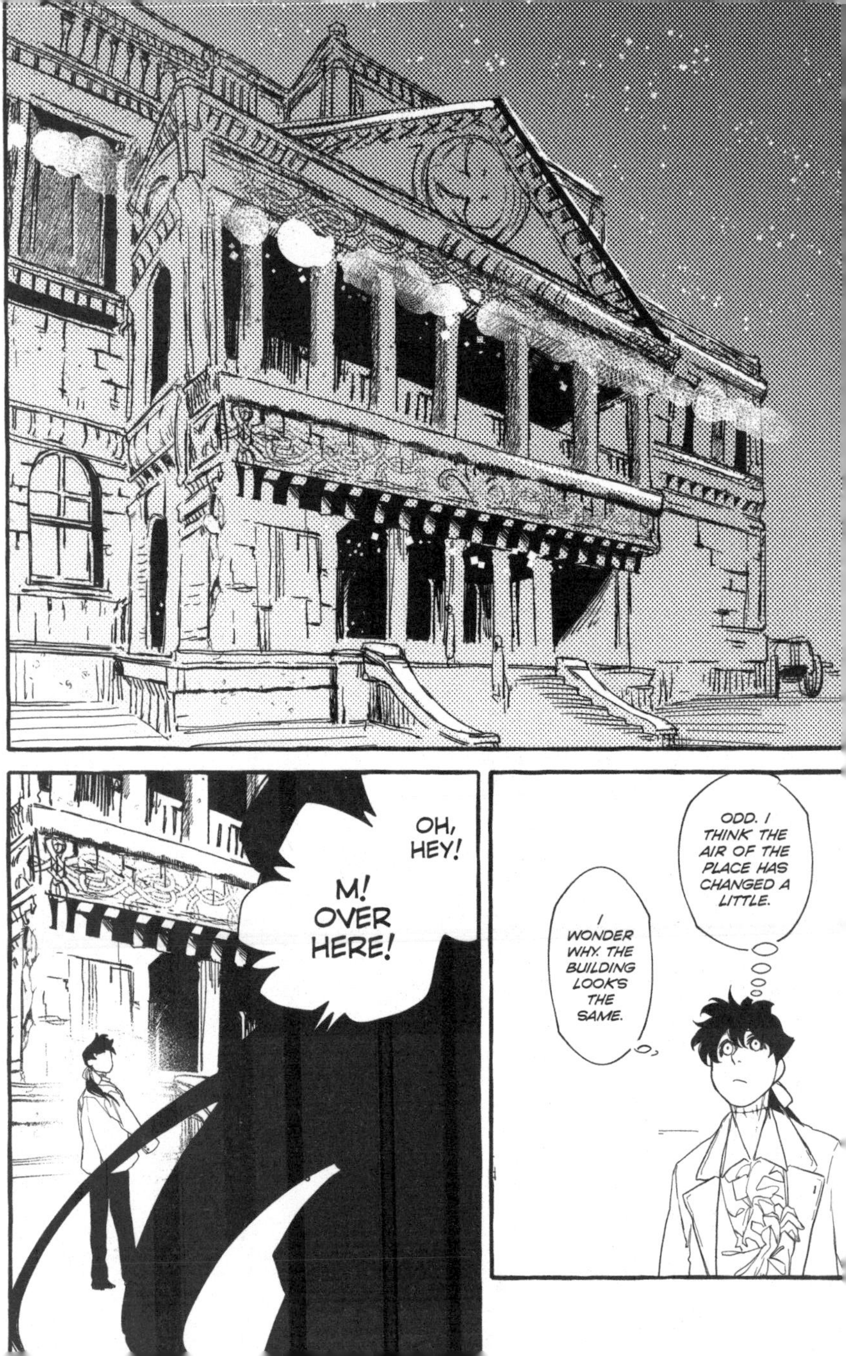
ODD. I THINK THE AIR OF THE PLACE HAS CHANGED A LITTLE.
I WONDER WHY. THE BUILDING LOOKS THE SAME.
OH, HEY!
M! OVER HERE!

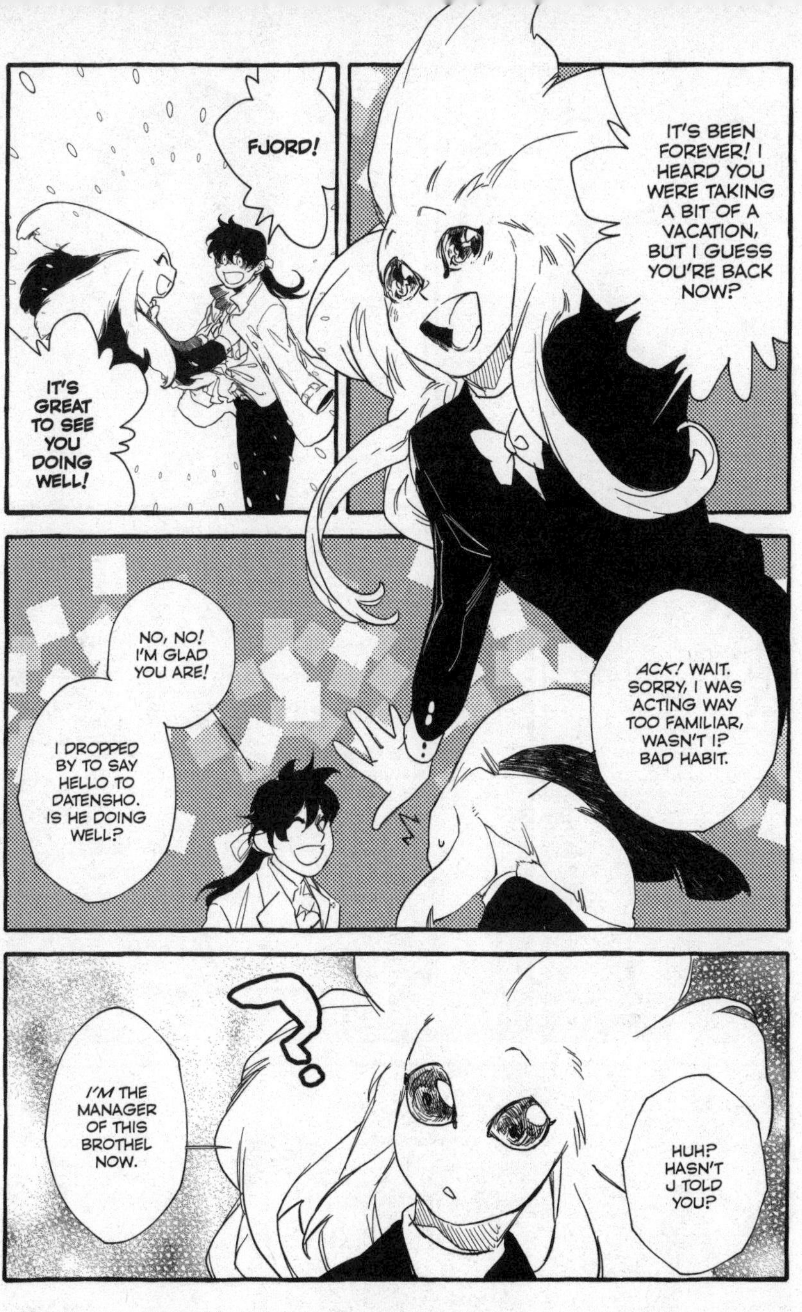
IT'S BEEN FOREVER! I HEARD YOU WERE TAKING A BIT OF A VACATION, BUT I GUESS YOU'RE BACK NOW?
FJORD!
IT'S GREAT TO SEE YOU DOING WELL!
ACK! WAIT. SORRY, I WAS ACTING WAY TOO FAMILIAR, WASN'T I? BAD HABIT.
NO, NO! I'M GLAD YOU ARE!
I DROPPED BY TO SAY HELLO TO DATENSHO. IS HE DOING WELL?
HUH? HASN'T J TOLD YOU?
I'M THE MANAGER OF THIS BROTHEL NOW.

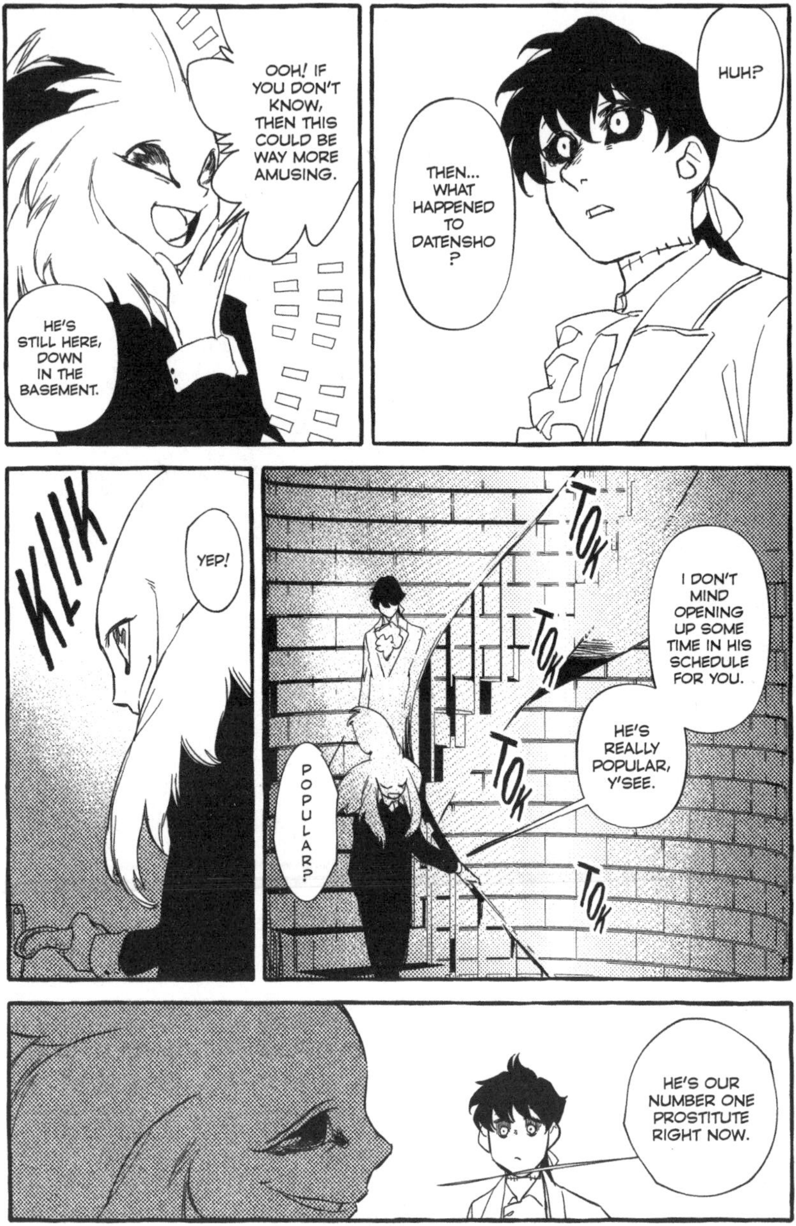
HUH?
THEN... WHAT HAPPENED TO DATENSHO?
OOH! IF YOU DON'T KNOW, THEN THIS COULD BE WAY MORE AMUSING.
HE'S STILL HERE, DOWN IN THE BASEMENT.
TOK
I DON'T MIND OPENING UP SOME TIME IN HIS SCHEDULE FOR YOU.
TOK
HE'S REALLY POPULAR, Y'SEE.
TOK
TOK
POPULAR?
KLIK
YEP!
HE'S OUR NUMBER ONE PROSTITUTE RIGHT NOW.

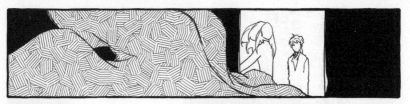

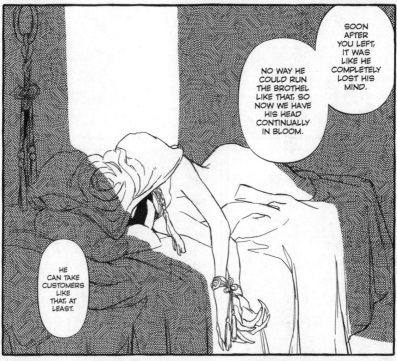

SOON AFTER YOU LEFT, IT WAS LIKE HE COMPLETELY LOST HIS MIND.
NO WAY HE COULD RUN THE BROTHEL LIKE THAT, SO NOW WE HAVE HIS HEAD CONTINUALLY IN BLOOM.
HE CAN TAKE CUSTOMERS LIKE THAT, AT LEAST.
CON-STANTLY IN BLOOM?
WHEN AN INCENSATE'S MINOR RAFFLESIAS ALL DIE, THEY BIRTH MORE.
RAFFLESIAS ARE MONSTERS, SO JUST KILL 'EM AS THEY'RE BORN AND THE INCENSATE'S HEAD WILL KEEP BLOOMING.
DATENSHO'S THE LAST INCENSATE, SO THAT MAKES HIM REALLY POPULAR WITH OUR CLIENTS.

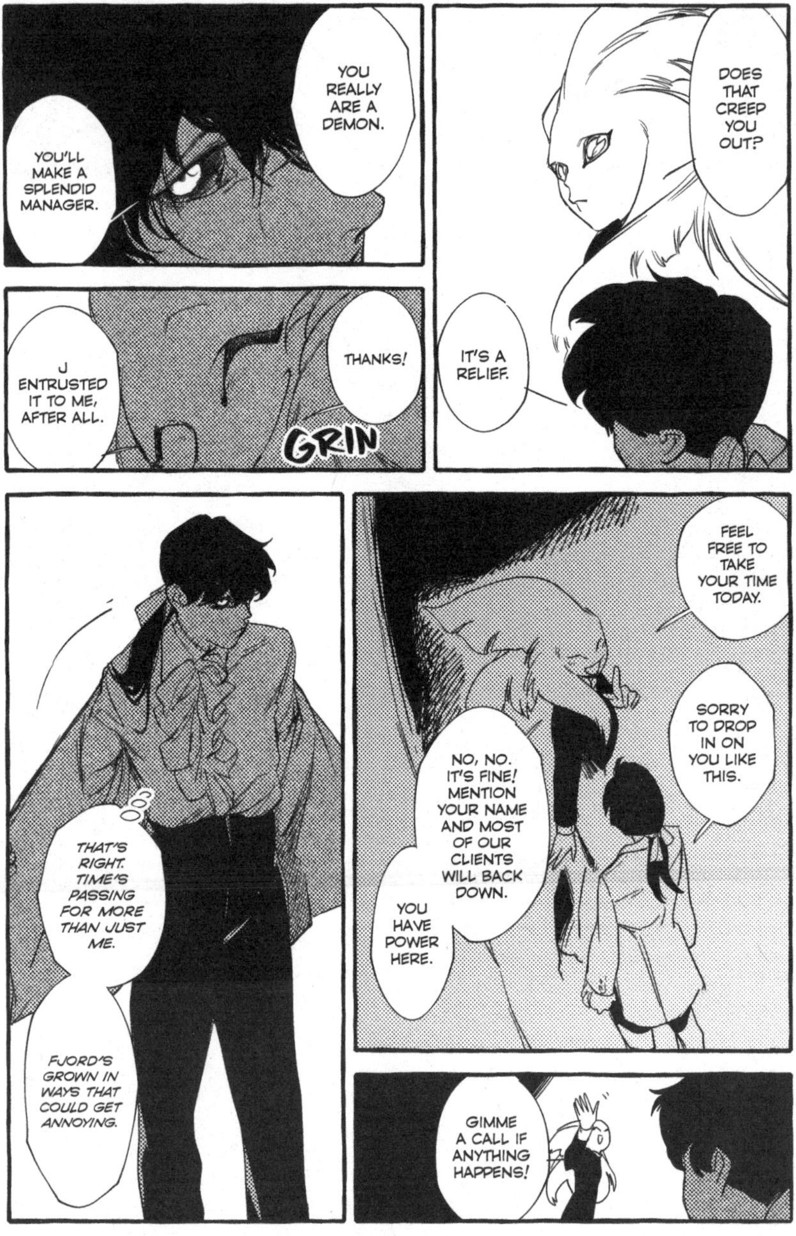

DOES THAT CREEP YOU OUT?
IT'S A RELIEF.
YOU REALLY ARE A DEMON.
YOU'LL MAKE A SPLENDID MANAGER.
THANKS!
J ENTRUSTED IT TO ME, AFTER ALL.
GRIN
FEEL FREE TO TAKE YOUR TIME TODAY.
SORRY TO DROP IN ON YOU LIKE THIS.
NO, NO. IT'S FINE! MENTION YOUR NAME AND MOST OF OUR CLIENTS WILL BACK DOWN.
YOU HAVE POWER HERE.
GIMME A CALL IF ANYTHING HAPPENS!
THAT'S RIGHT. TIME'S PASSING FOR MORE THAN JUST ME.
FJORD'S GROWN IN WAYS THAT COULD GET ANNOYING.

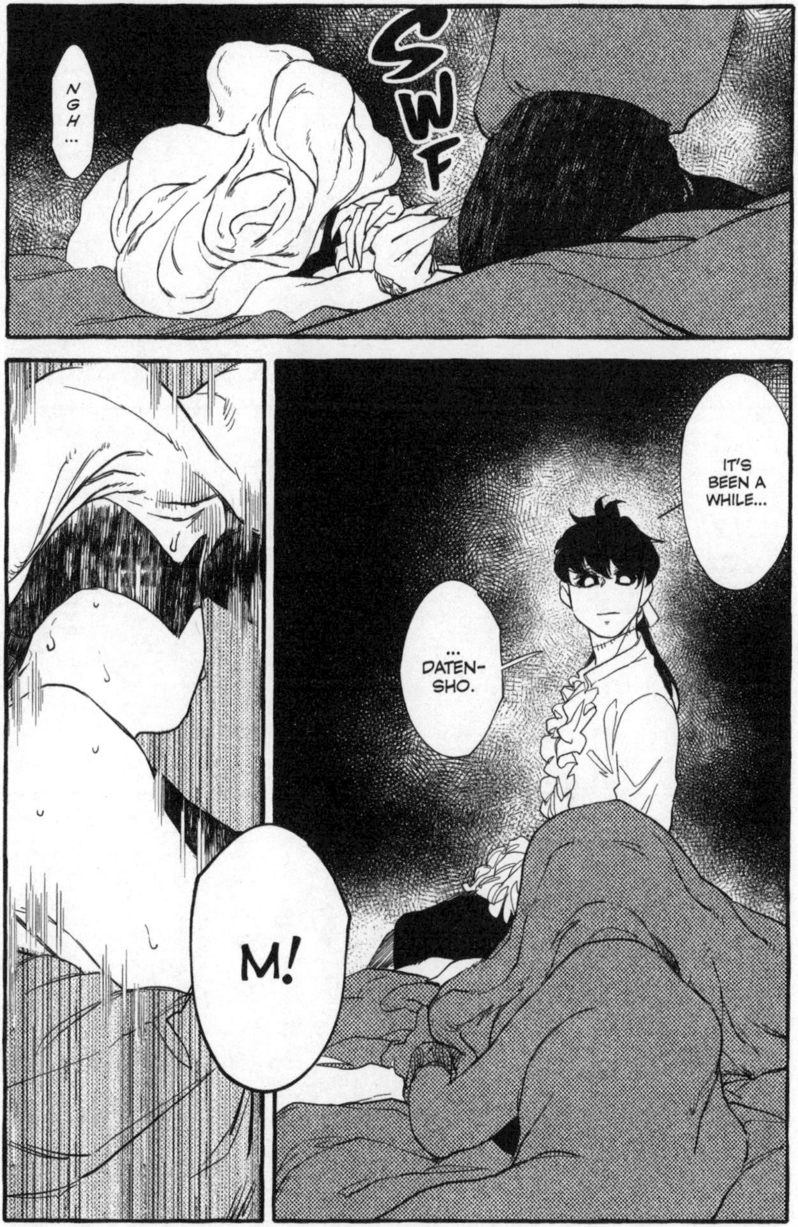
SWF
NGH...
IT'S BEEN A WHILE...
...DATEN-SHO.
M!

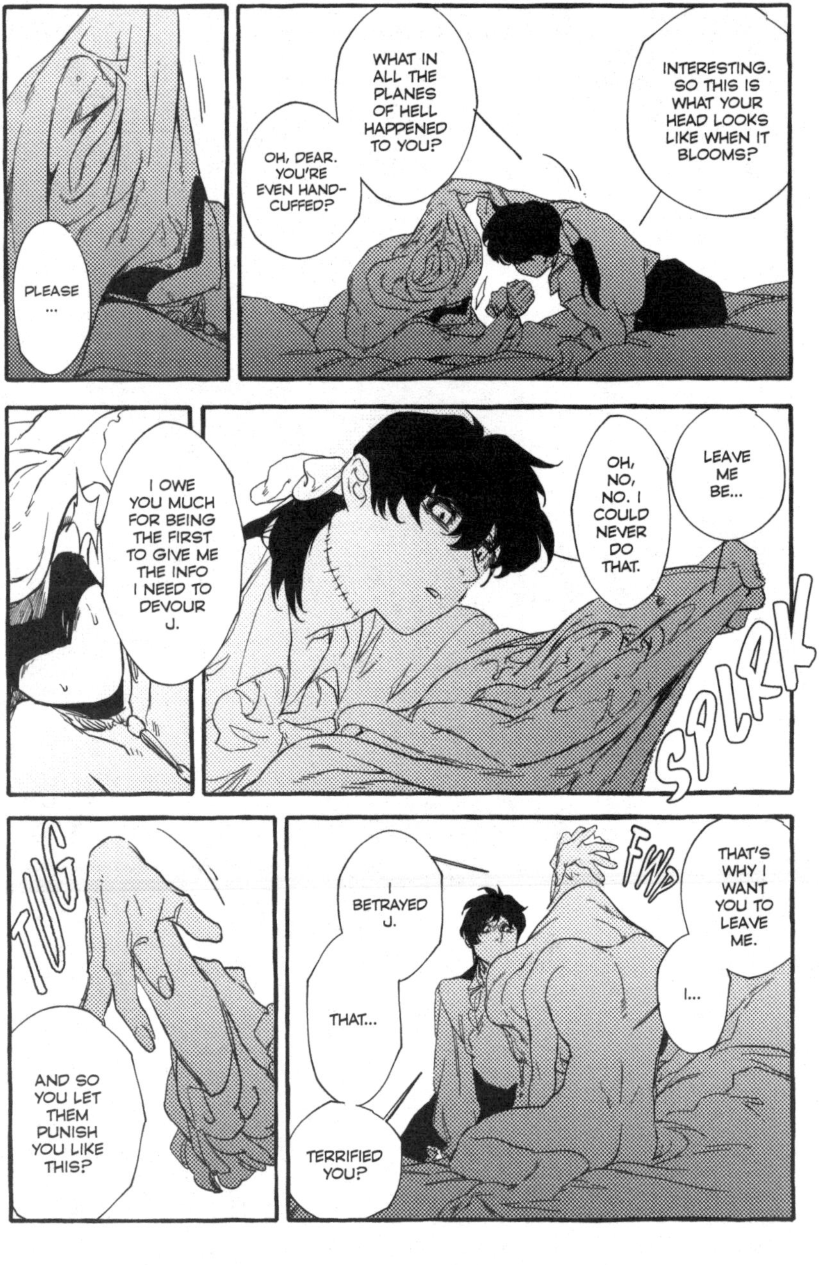
INTERESTING. SO THIS IS WHAT YOUR HEAD LOOKS LIKE WHEN IT BLOOMS?
WHAT IN ALL THE PLANES OF HELL HAPPENED TO YOU?
OH, DEAR. YOU'RE EVEN HAND-CUFFED?
PLEASE ...
LEAVE ME BE...
OH, NO, NO. I COULD NEVER DO THAT.
SPLRK
I OWE YOU MUCH FOR BEING THE FIRST TO GIVE ME THE INFO I NEED TO DEVOUR J.
THAT'S WHY I WANT YOU TO LEAVE ME.
FWP
I...
I BETRAYED J.
THAT...
TERRIFIED YOU?
TUG
AND SO YOU LET THEM PUNISH YOU LIKE THIS?

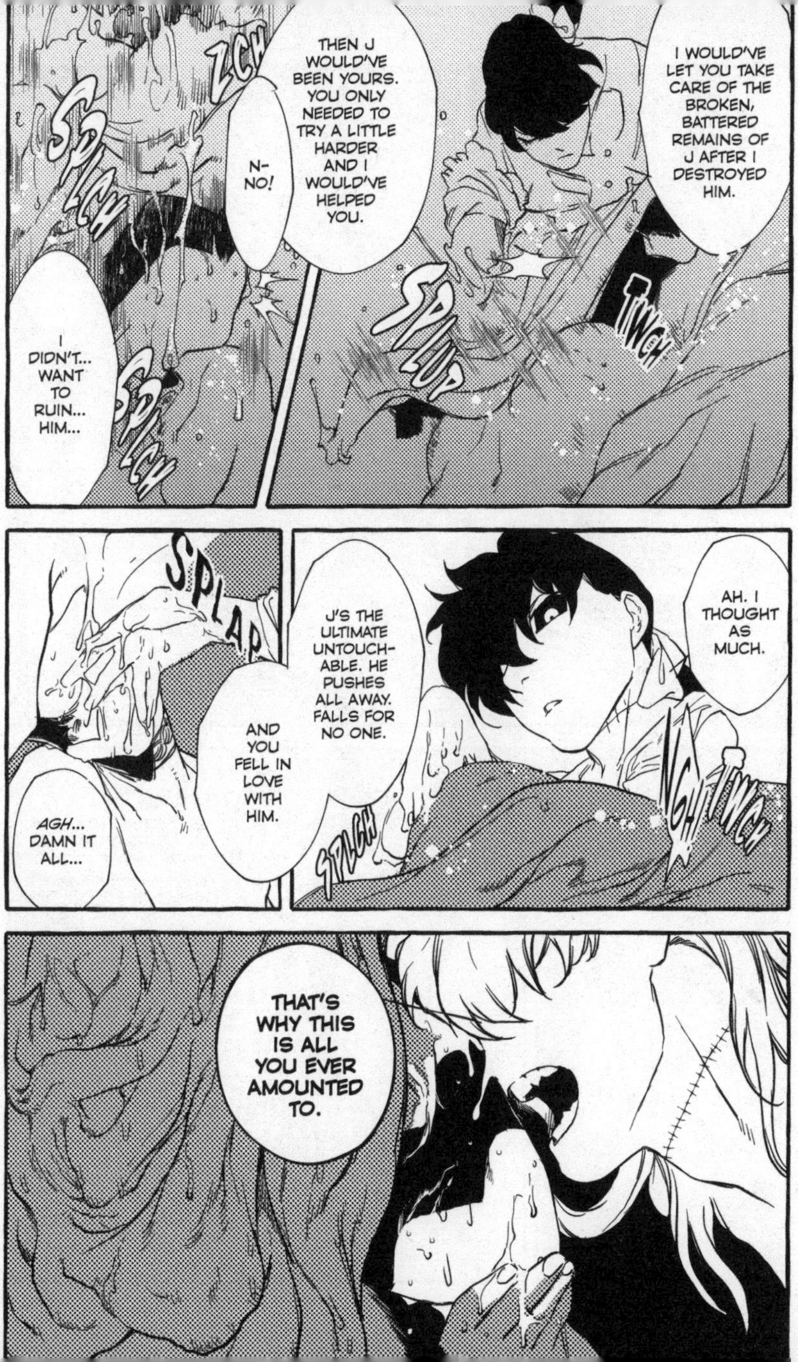
I WOULD'VE LET YOU TAKE CARE OF THE BROKEN, BATTERED REMAINS OF J AFTER I DESTROYED HIM.
THEN J WOULD'VE BEEN YOURS. YOU ONLY NEEDED TO TRY A LITTLE HARDER AND I WOULD'VE HELPED YOU.
TWCH
SPLUP
ZCH
N-NO!
SPLCH
I DIDN'T... WANT TO RUIN... HIM...
SPLCH
AH. I THOUGHT AS MUCH.
J'S THE ULTIMATE UNTOUCH-ABLE. HE PUSHES ALL AWAY. FALLS FOR NO ONE.
AND YOU FELL IN LOVE WITH HIM.
NGH!
TWCH
SPLCH
SPLAP
AGH... DAMN IT ALL...
THAT'S WHY THIS IS ALL YOU EVER AMOUNTED TO.

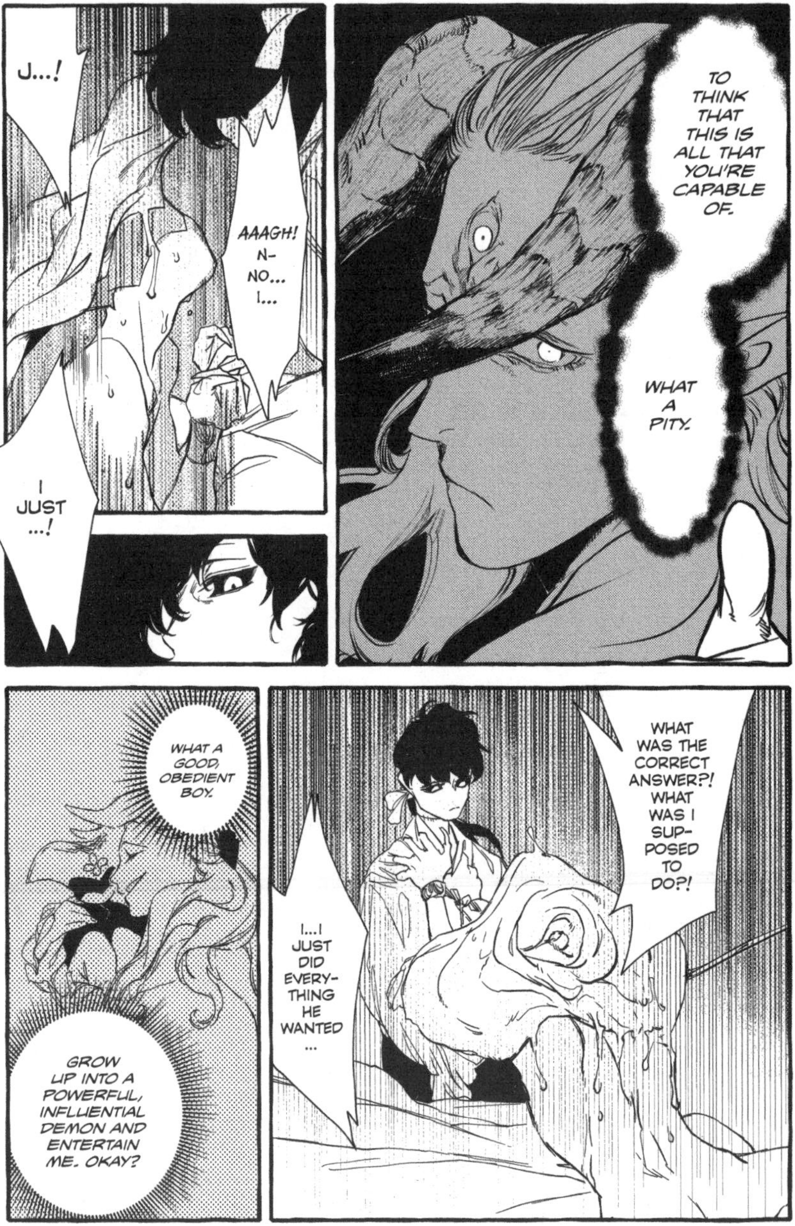
TO THINK THAT THIS IS ALL THAT YOU'RE CAPABLE OF.
WHAT A PITY.
J...!
AAAGH! N-NO... I...
I JUST ...!
WHAT WAS THE CORRECT ANSWER?! WHAT WAS I SUPPOSED TO DO?!
I...I JUST DID EVERYTHING HE WANTED ...
WHAT A GOOD, OBEDIENT BOY.
GROW UP INTO A POWERFUL, INFLUENTIAL DEMON AND ENTERTAIN ME. OKAY?

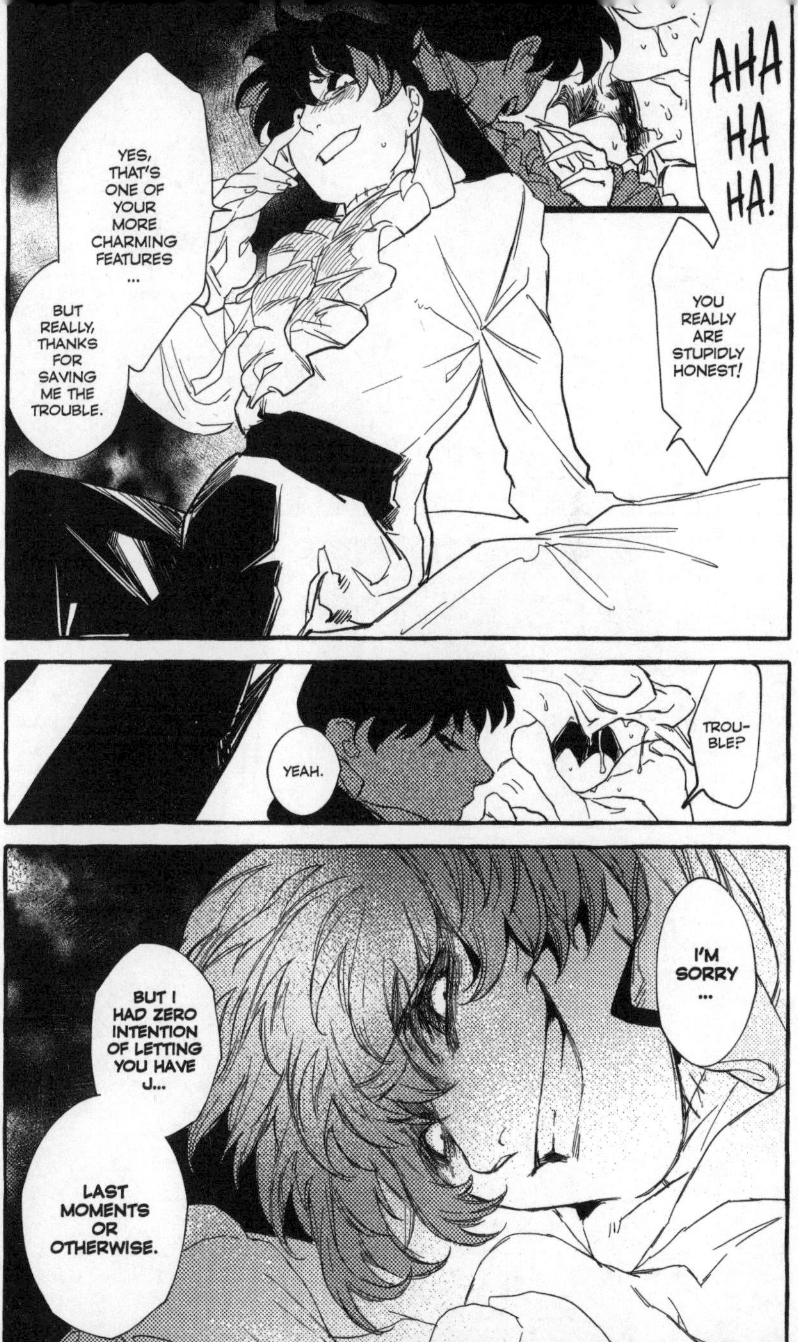
AHA HA HA!
YOU REALLY ARE STUPIDLY HONEST!
YES, THAT'S ONE OF YOUR MORE CHARMING FEATURES ...
BUT REALLY, THANKS FOR SAVING ME THE TROUBLE.
TROU-BLE?
YEAH.
I'M SORRY ...
BUT I HAD ZERO INTENTION OF LETTING YOU HAVE J...
LAST MOMENTS OR OTHERWISE.

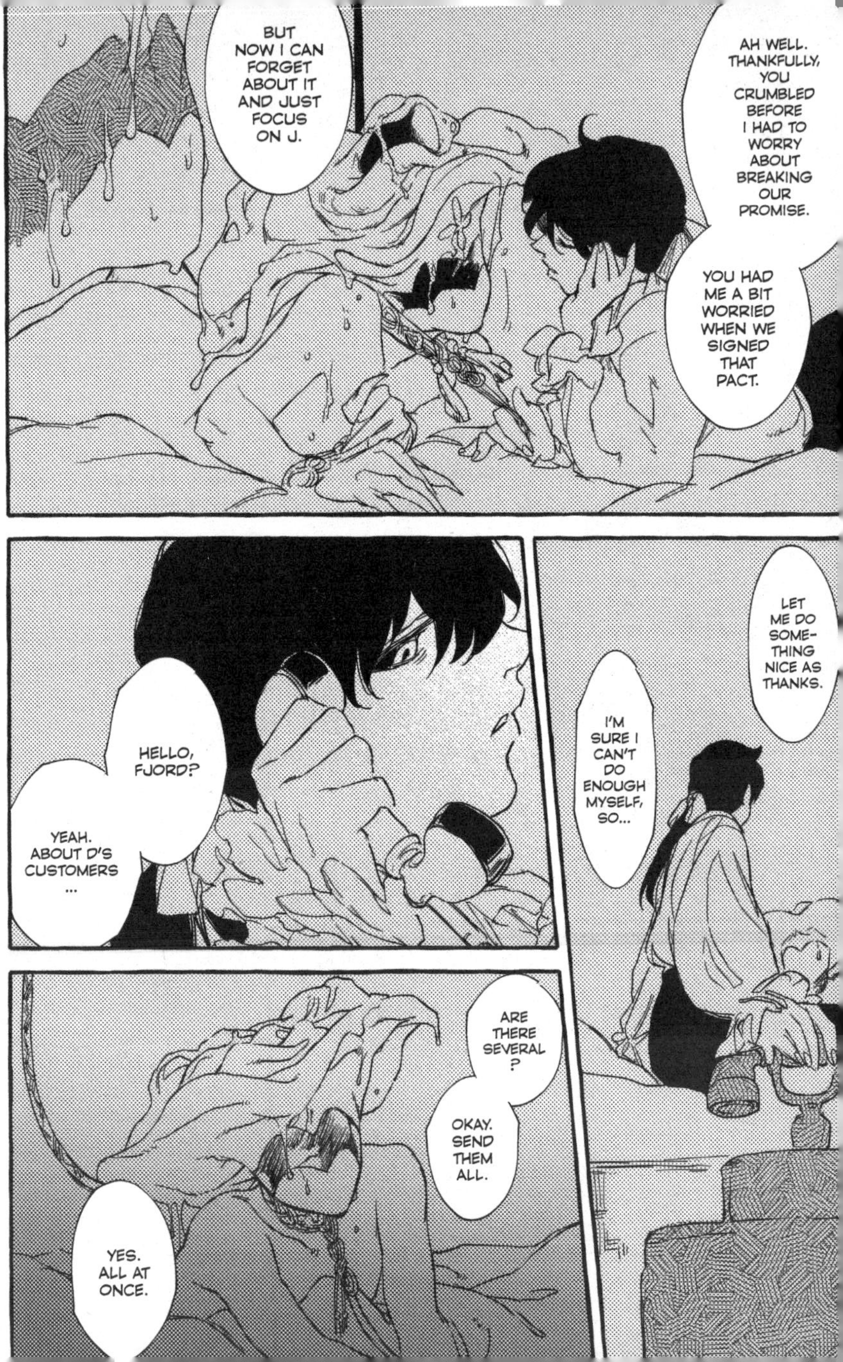
AH WELL. THANKFULLY, YOU CRUMBLED BEFORE I HAD TO WORRY ABOUT BREAKING OUR PROMISE.
YOU HAD ME A BIT WORRIED WHEN WE SIGNED THAT PACT.
BUT NOW I CAN FORGET ABOUT IT AND JUST FOCUS ON J.
LET ME DO SOME-THING NICE AS THANKS.
I'M SURE I CAN'T DO ENOUGH MYSELF, SO...
HELLO, FJORD?
YEAH. ABOUT D'S CUSTOMERS ...
ARE THERE SEVERAL ?
OKAY. SEND THEM ALL.
YES. ALL AT ONCE.

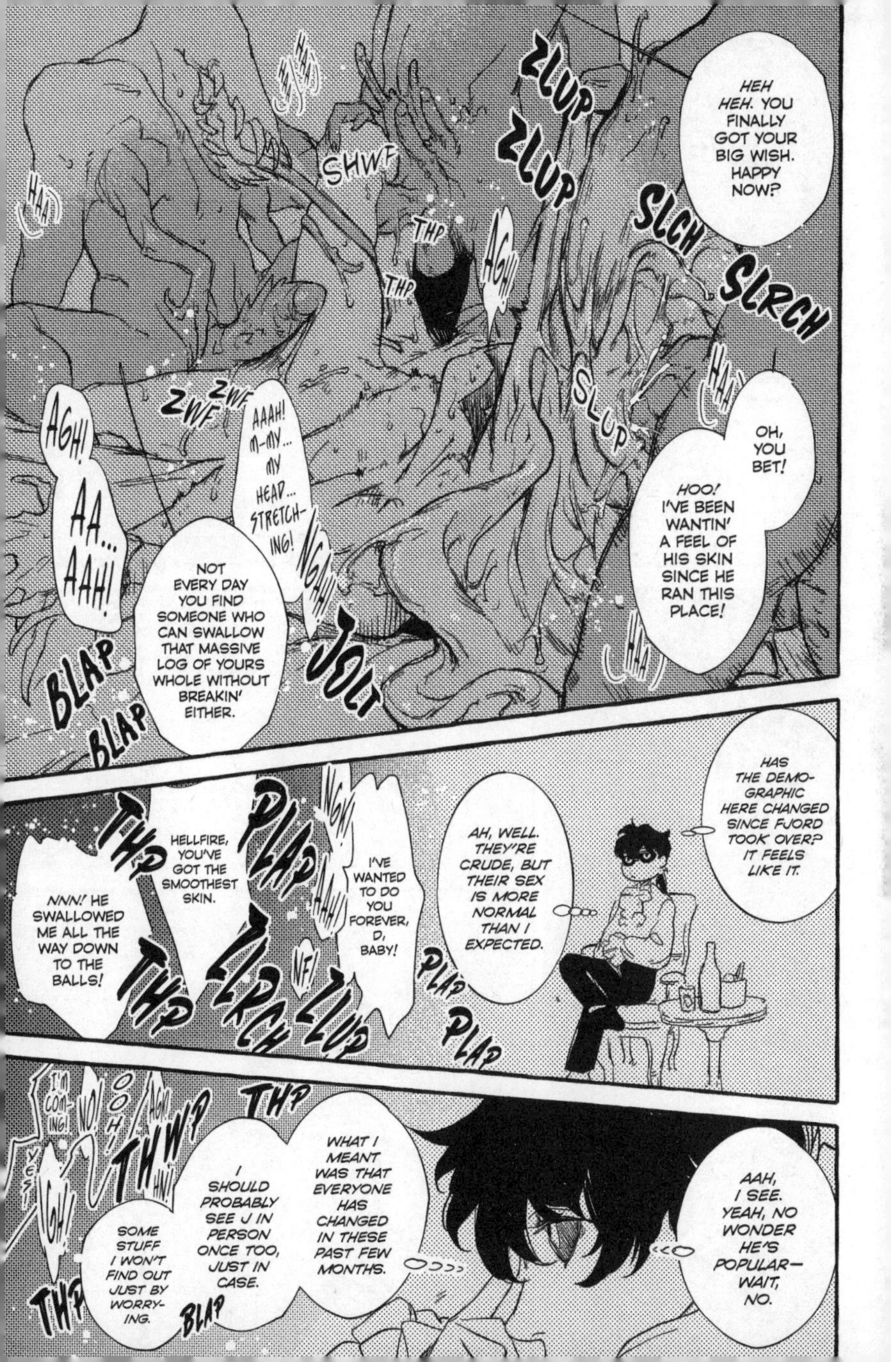
HEH HEH. YOU FINALLY GOT YOUR BIG WISH. HAPPY NOW?
ZLUP ZLUP
SLCH
SLRCH
HAA HAA
OH, YOU BET!
HOO! I'VE BEEN WANTIN' A FEEL OF HIS SKIN SINCE HE RAN THIS PLACE!
HAA
SLUP
AGH!
THP
THP
SHWF
HAA
AAAH! M-MY... MY HEAD... STRETCHING!
ZWF ZWF
NGAH!
JOLT
NOT EVERY DAY YOU FIND SOMEONE WHO CAN SWALLOW THAT MASSIVE LOG OF YOURS WHOLE WITHOUT BREAKIN' EITHER.
AGH! AA... AAH!
HAA
BLAP BLAP
HAS THE DEMOGRAPHIC HERE CHANGED SINCE FJORD TOOK OVER? IT FEELS LIKE IT.
AH, WELL. THEY'RE CRUDE, BUT THEIR SEX IS MORE NORMAL THAN I EXPECTED.
PLAP PLAP
I'VE WANTED TO DO YOU FOREVER, D, BABY!
NGH!
AAH!
NF!
ZLUP
PLAP
HELLFIRE, YOU'VE GOT THE SMOOTHEST SKIN.
ZLRCH
THP THP
NNN! HE SWALLOWED ME ALL THE WAY DOWN TO THE BALLS!
AAH, I SEE. YEAH, NO WONDER HE'S POPULAR—WAIT, NO.
WHAT I MEANT WAS THAT EVERYONE HAS CHANGED IN THESE PAST FEW MONTHS.
I SHOULD PROBABLY SEE J IN PERSON ONCE TOO, JUST IN CASE.
SOME STUFF I WON'T FIND OUT JUST BY WORRYING.
THP
THWP
HN!
AGH!
OOH!
NO!
I'M COMING!
YES!
AGH!
THP
BLAP

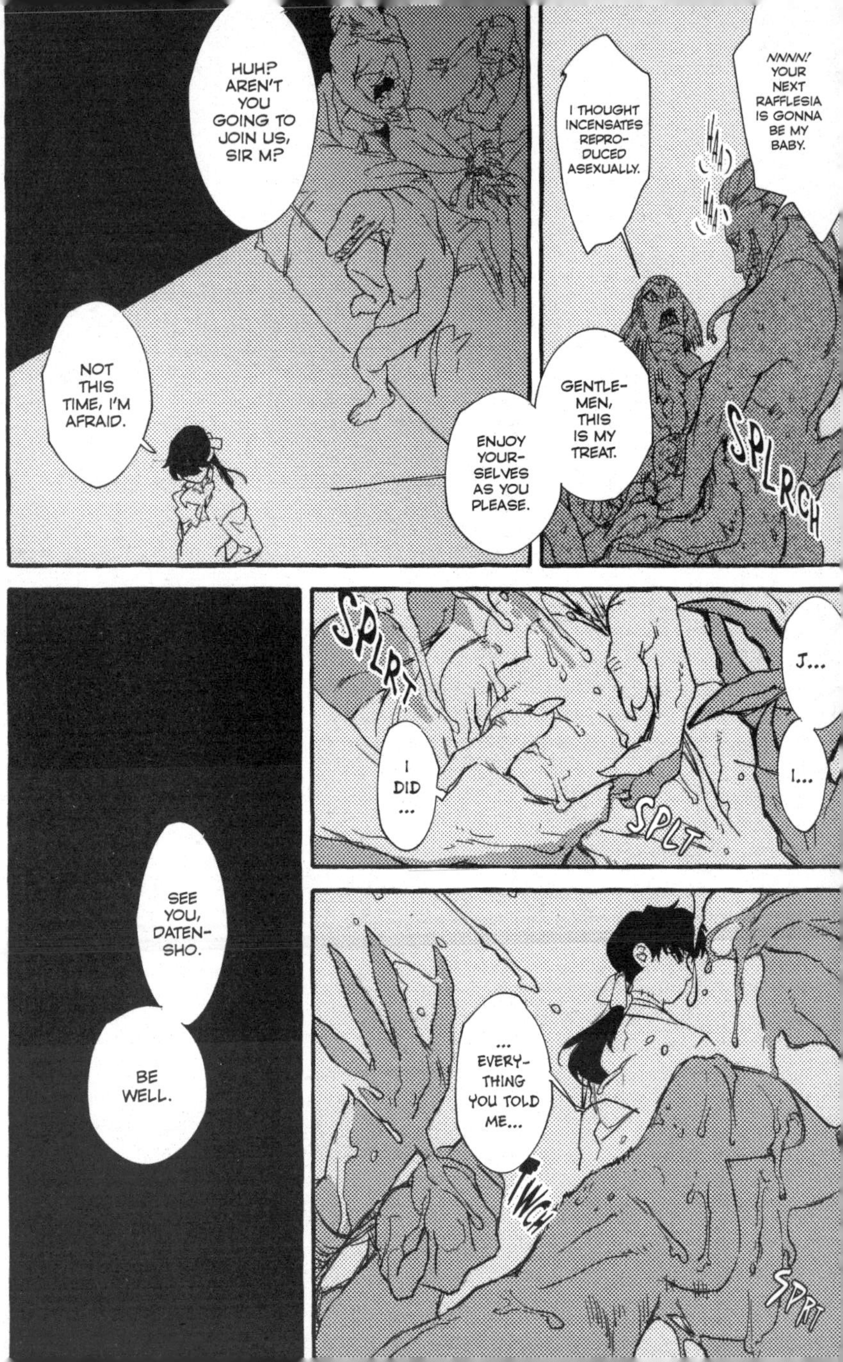
NNNN! YOUR NEXT RAFFLESIA IS GONNA BE MY BABY.
HAA HAA
I THOUGHT INCENSATES REPRODUCED ASEXUALLY.
GENTLEMEN, THIS IS MY TREAT.
SPLRCH
ENJOY YOURSELVES AS YOU PLEASE.
HUH? AREN'T YOU GOING TO JOIN US, SIR M?
NOT THIS TIME, I'M AFRAID.
J...
I...
SPLRT
I DID ...
SPLT
... EVERYTHING YOU TOLD ME...
TWCH
SPRT
SEE YOU, DATENSHO.
BE WELL.

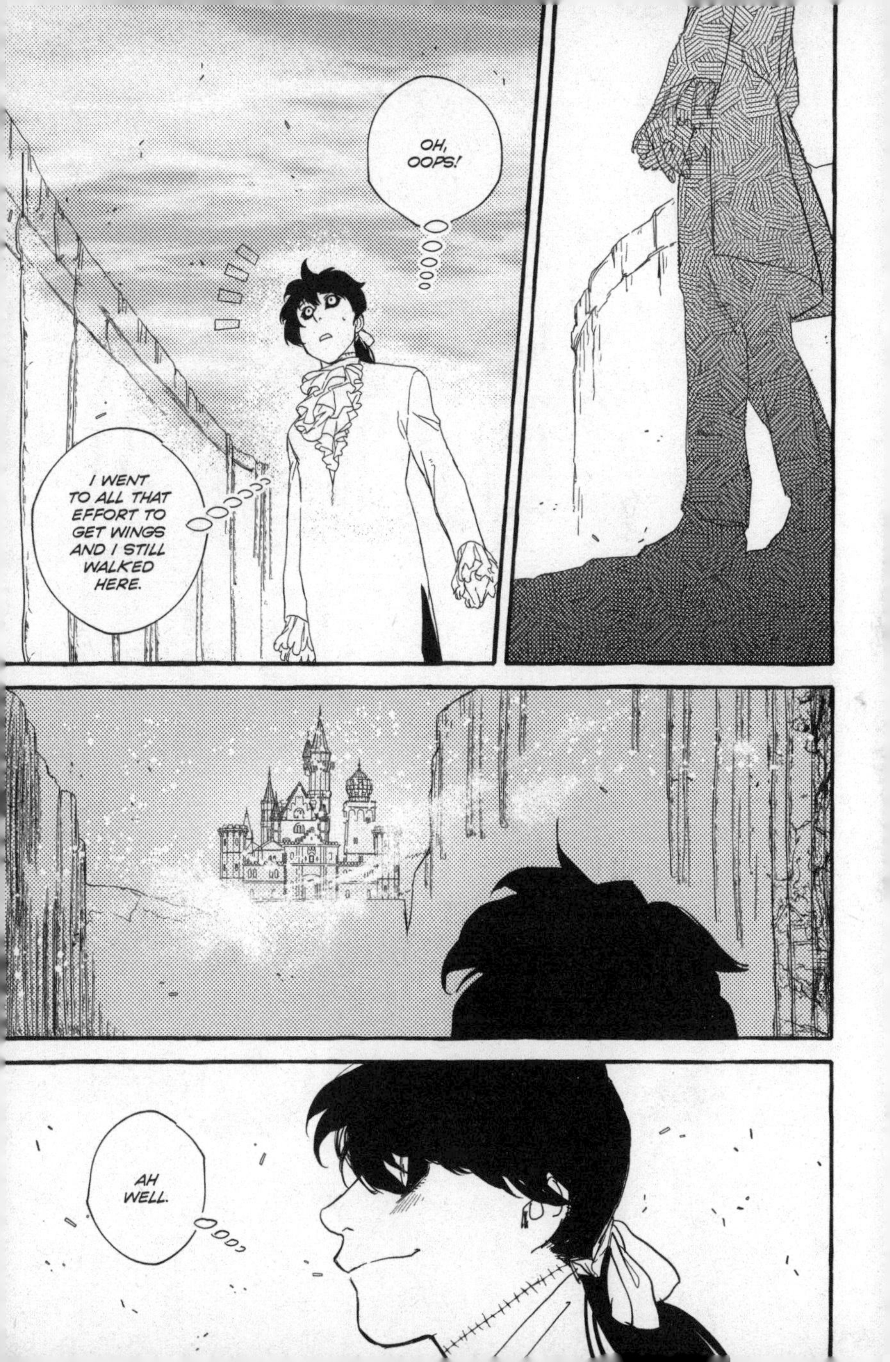
OH, OOPS!
I WENT TO ALL THAT EFFORT TO GET WINGS AND I STILL WALKED HERE.
AH WELL.

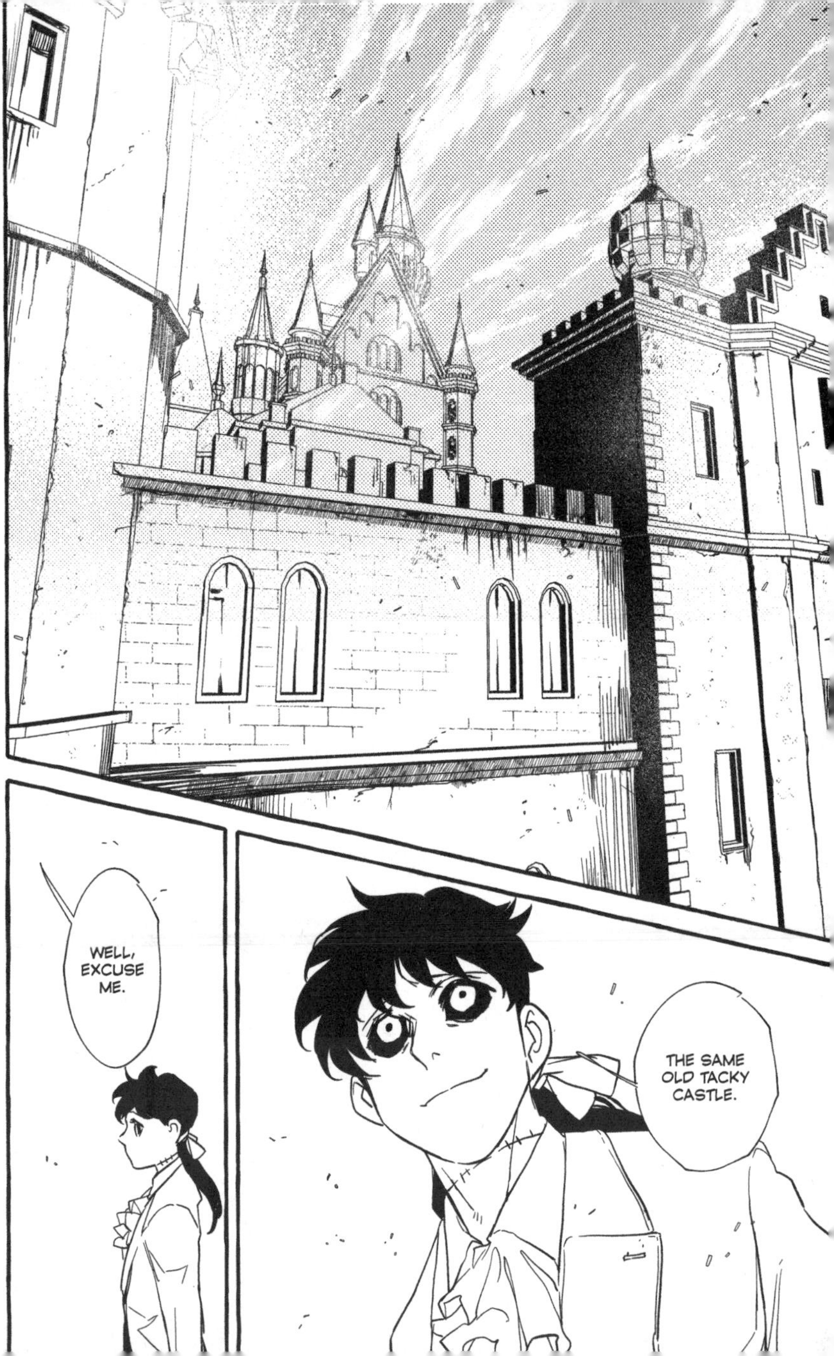
THE SAME OLD TACKY CASTLE.
WELL, EXCUSE ME.

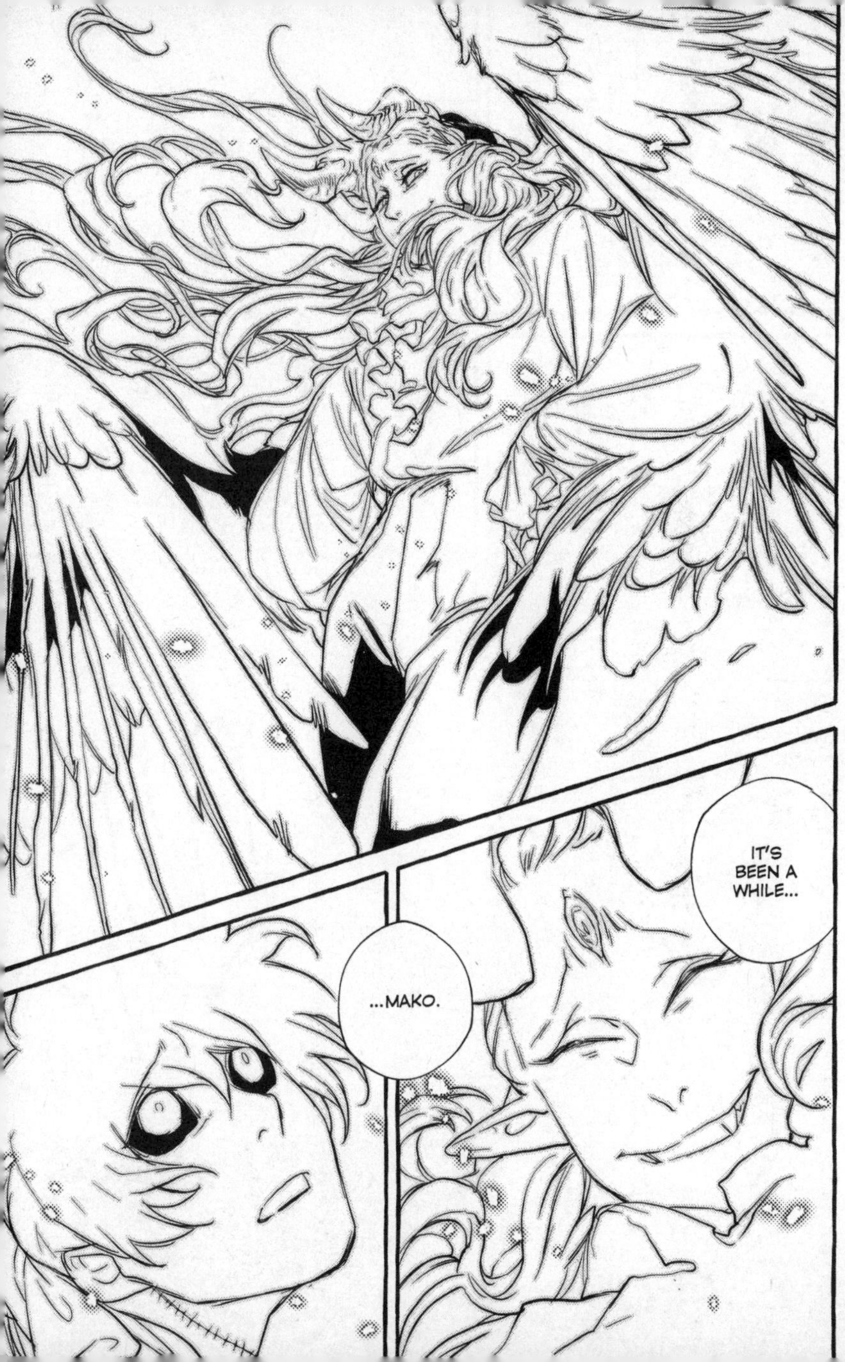
IT'S BEEN A WHILE...
...MAKO.

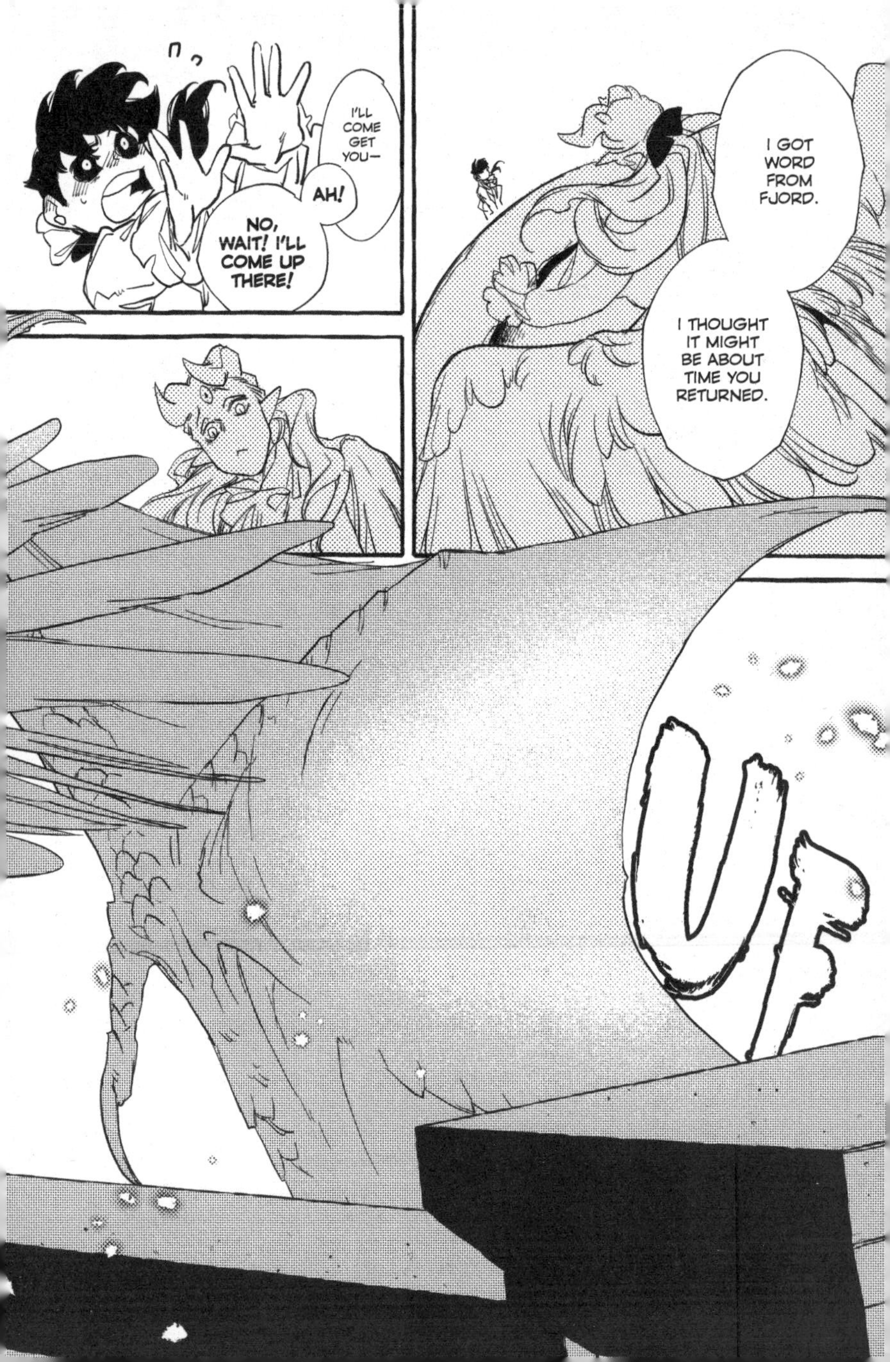
I GOT WORD FROM FJORD.
I THOUGHT IT MIGHT BE ABOUT TIME YOU RETURNED.
I'LL COME GET YOU—
AH!
NO, WAIT! I'LL COME UP THERE!
UP

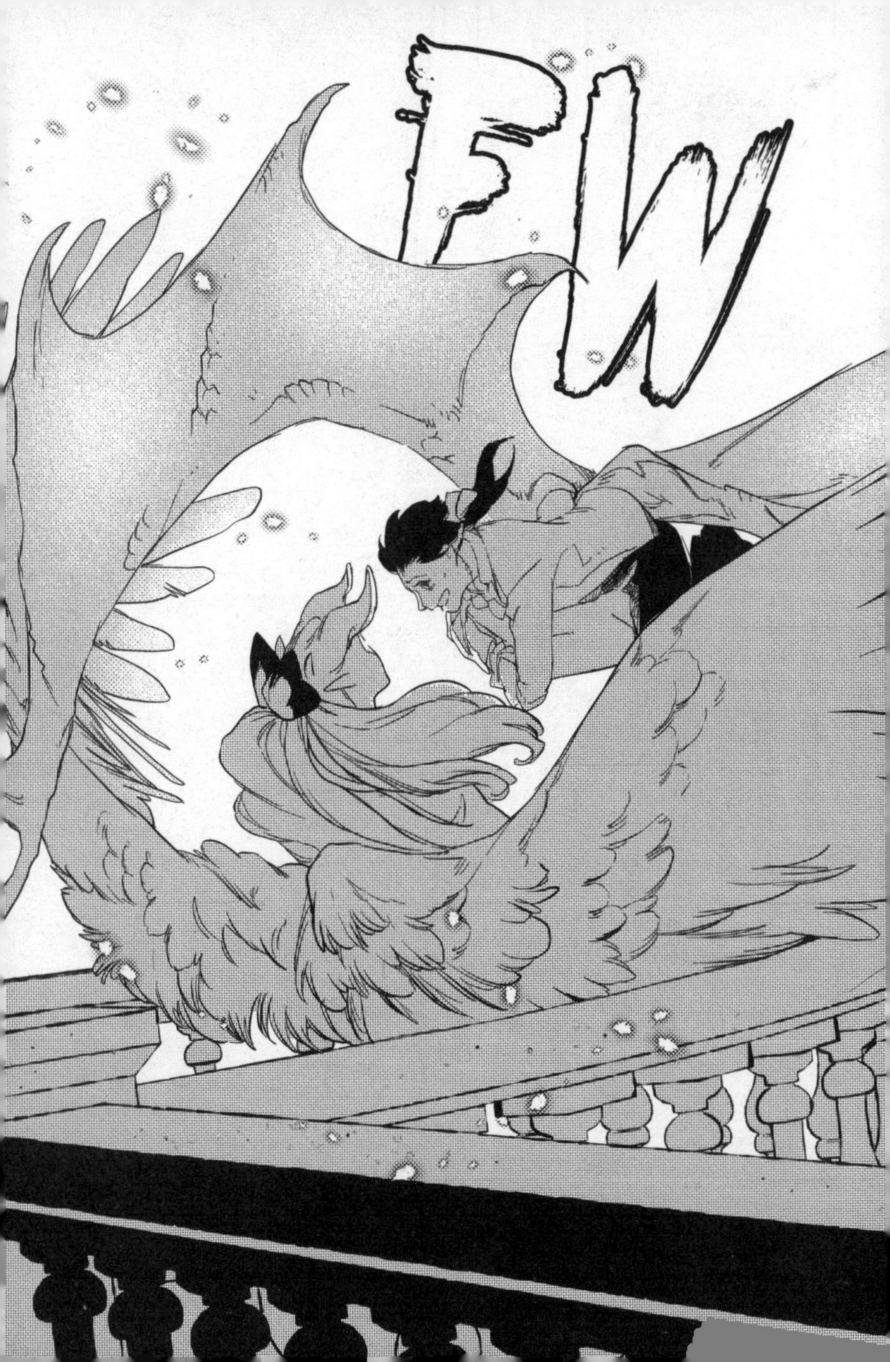
FW

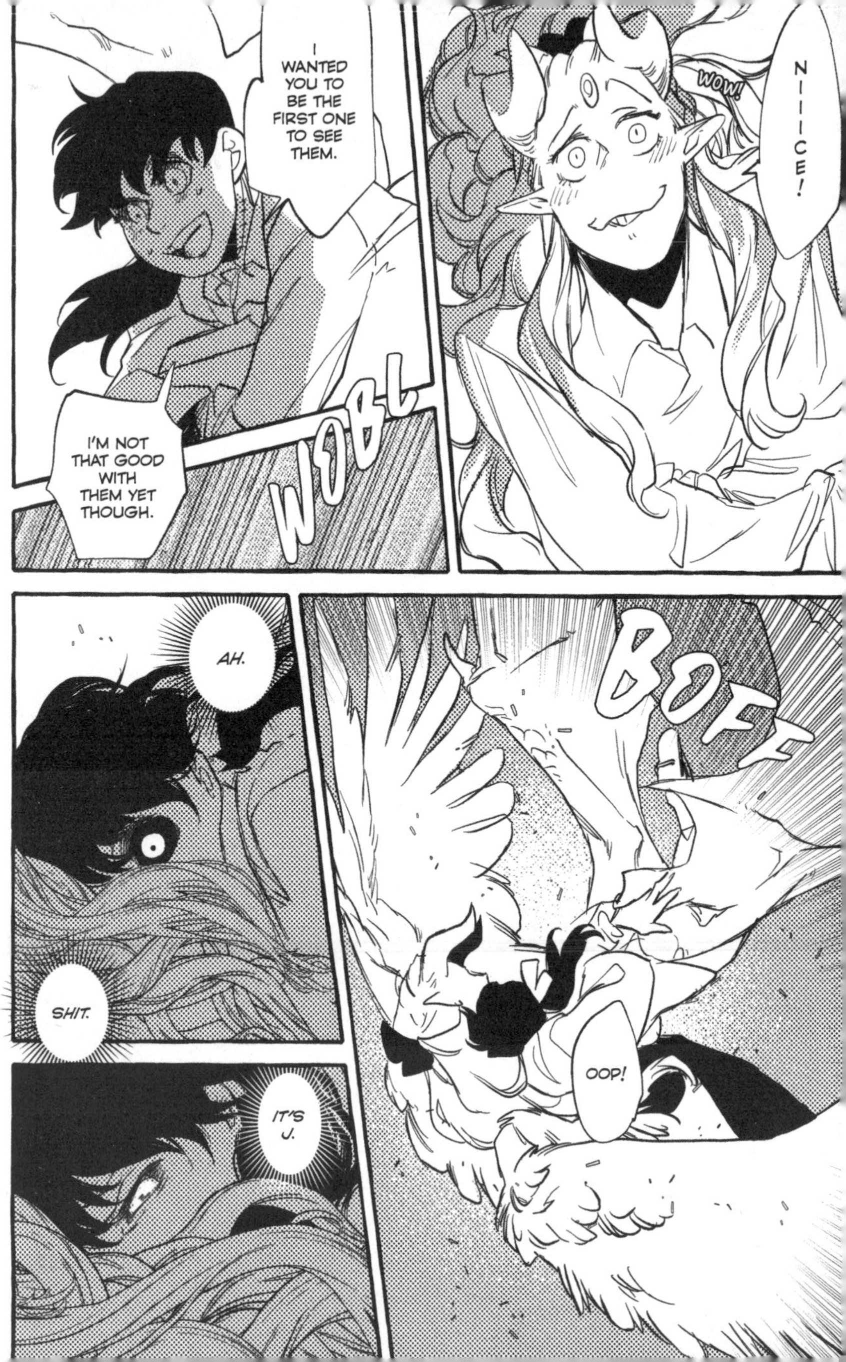
WOW!
NIIICE!
I WANTED YOU TO BE THE FIRST ONE TO SEE THEM.
WOBL
I'M NOT THAT GOOD WITH THEM YET THOUGH.
BOFF
OOP!
AH.
SHIT.
IT'S J.

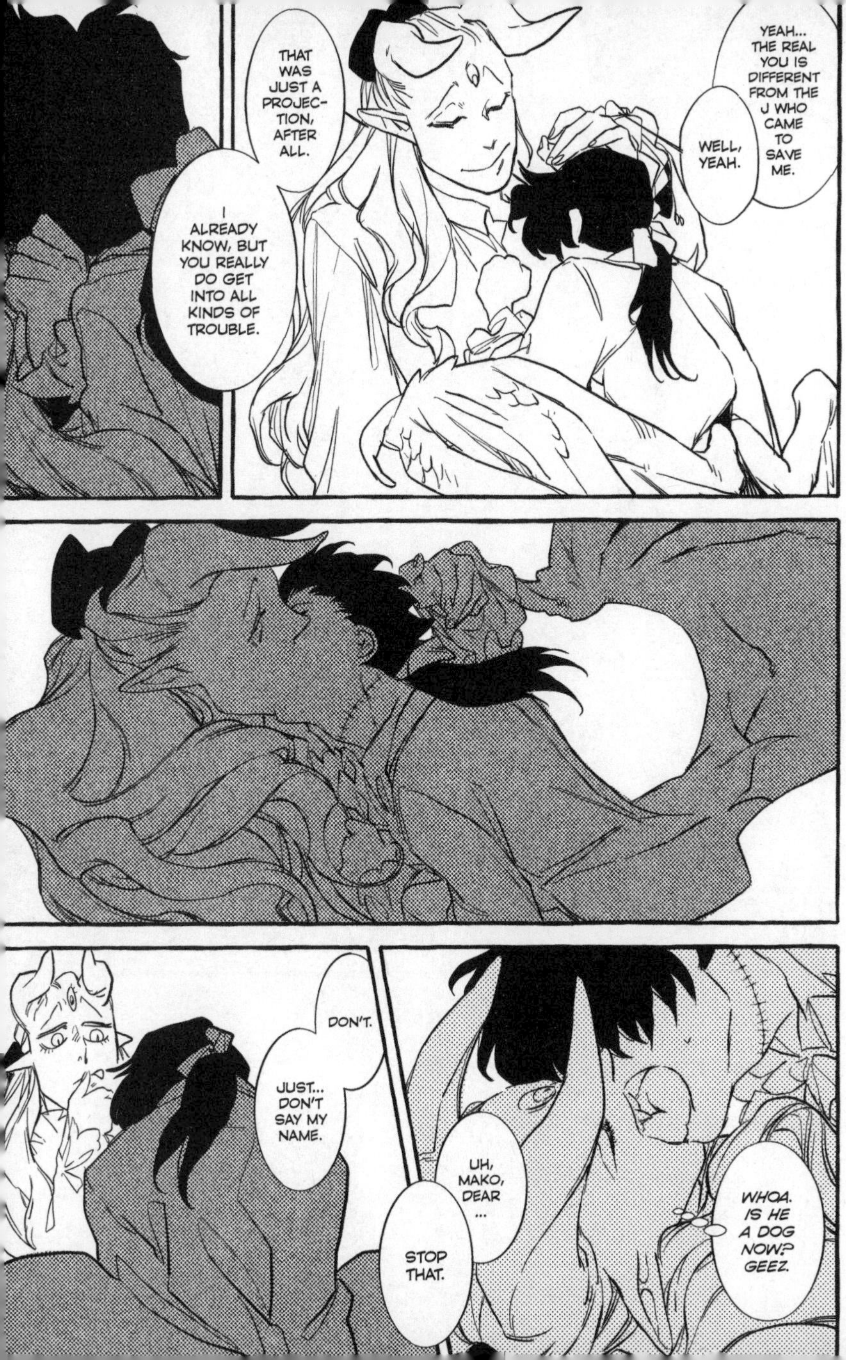
YEAH... THE REAL YOU IS DIFFERENT FROM THE J WHO CAME TO SAVE ME.
WELL, YEAH.
THAT WAS JUST A PROJECTION, AFTER ALL.
I ALREADY KNOW, BUT YOU REALLY DO GET INTO ALL KINDS OF TROUBLE.
WHOA. IS HE A DOG NOW? GEEZ.
UH, MAKO, DEAR...
STOP THAT.
DON'T.
JUST... DON'T SAY MY NAME.

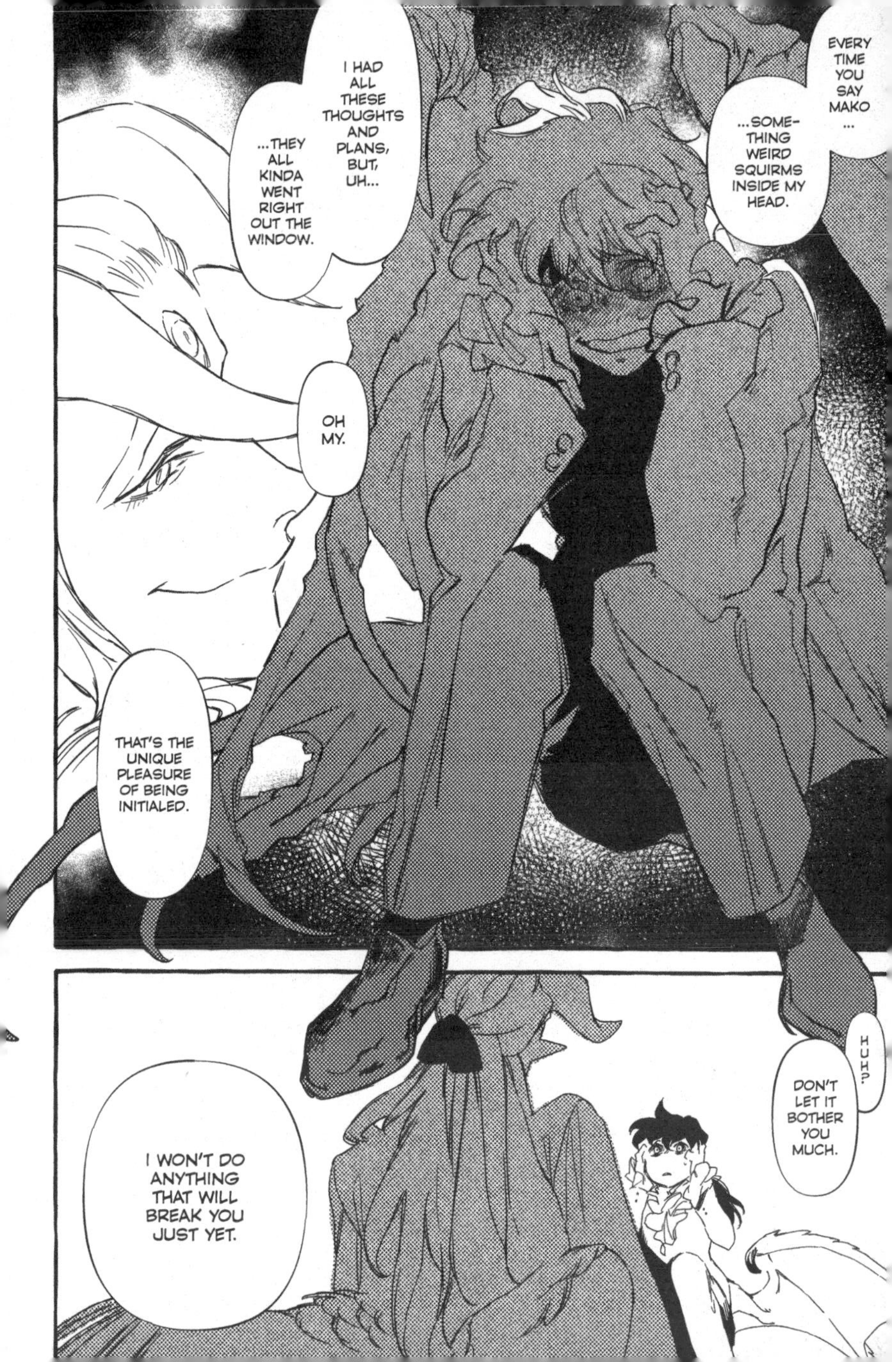
EVERY TIME YOU SAY MAKO...
...SOME-THING WEIRD SQUIRMS INSIDE MY HEAD.
I HAD ALL THESE THOUGHTS AND PLANS, BUT, UH...
...THEY ALL KINDA WENT RIGHT OUT THE WINDOW.
OH MY.
THAT'S THE UNIQUE PLEASURE OF BEING INITIALED.
HUH?
DON'T LET IT BOTHER YOU MUCH.
I WON'T DO ANYTHING THAT WILL BREAK YOU JUST YET.

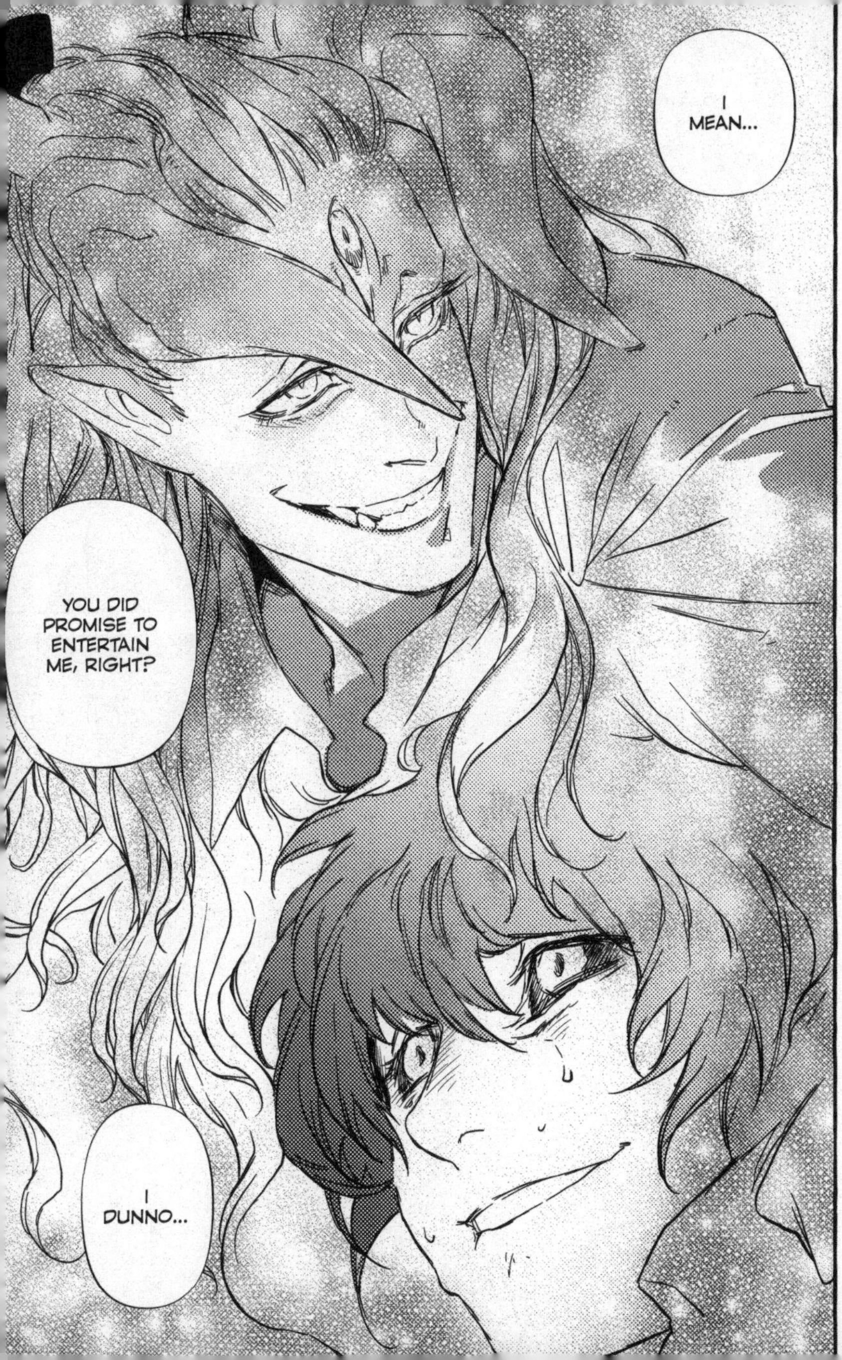
I MEAN...
YOU DID PROMISE TO ENTERTAIN ME, RIGHT?
I DUNNO...

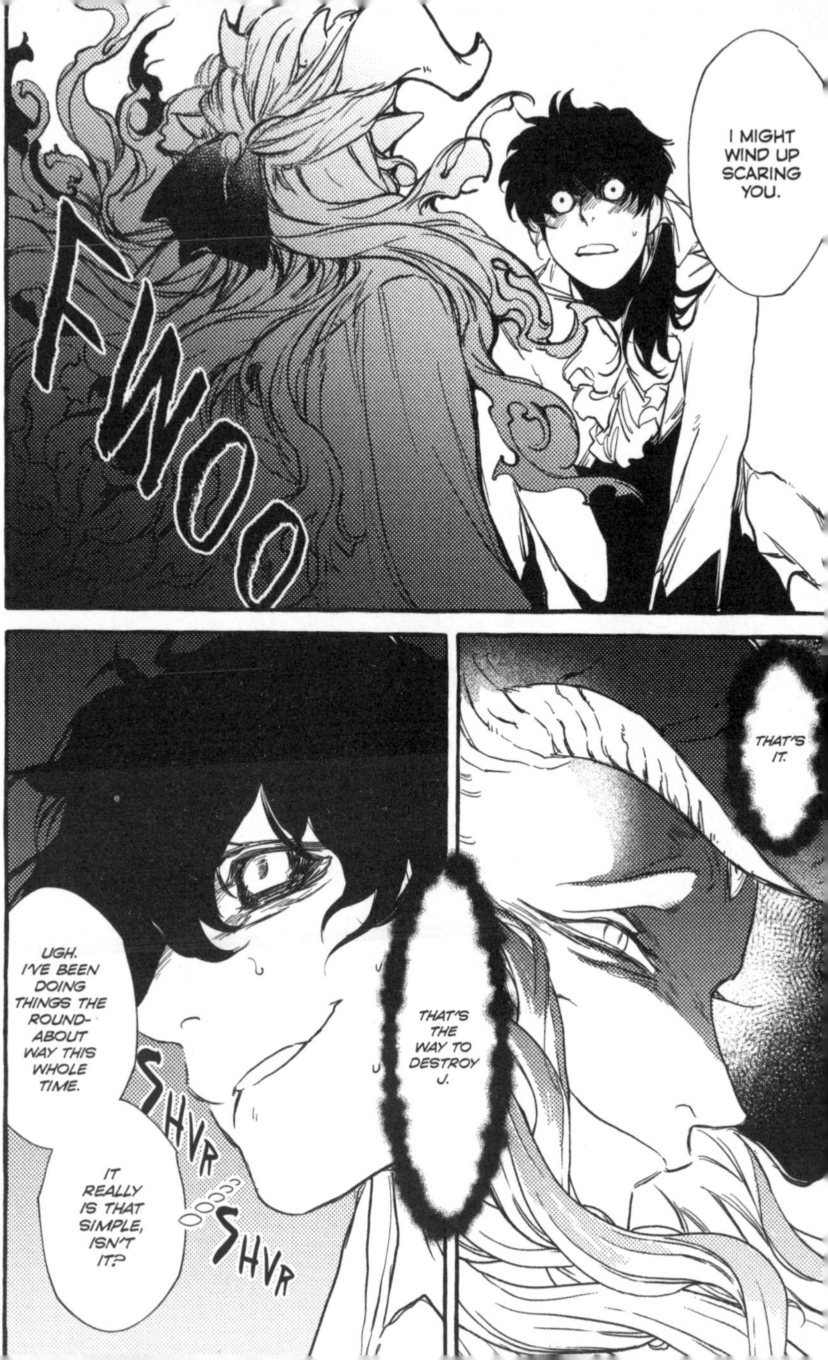
I MIGHT WIND UP SCARING YOU.
FWOO
THAT'S IT.
THAT'S THE WAY TO DESTROY J.
UGH. I'VE BEEN DOING THINGS THE ROUND-ABOUT WAY THIS WHOLE TIME.
SHVR
SHVR
IT REALLY IS THAT SIMPLE, ISN'T IT?
SHVR

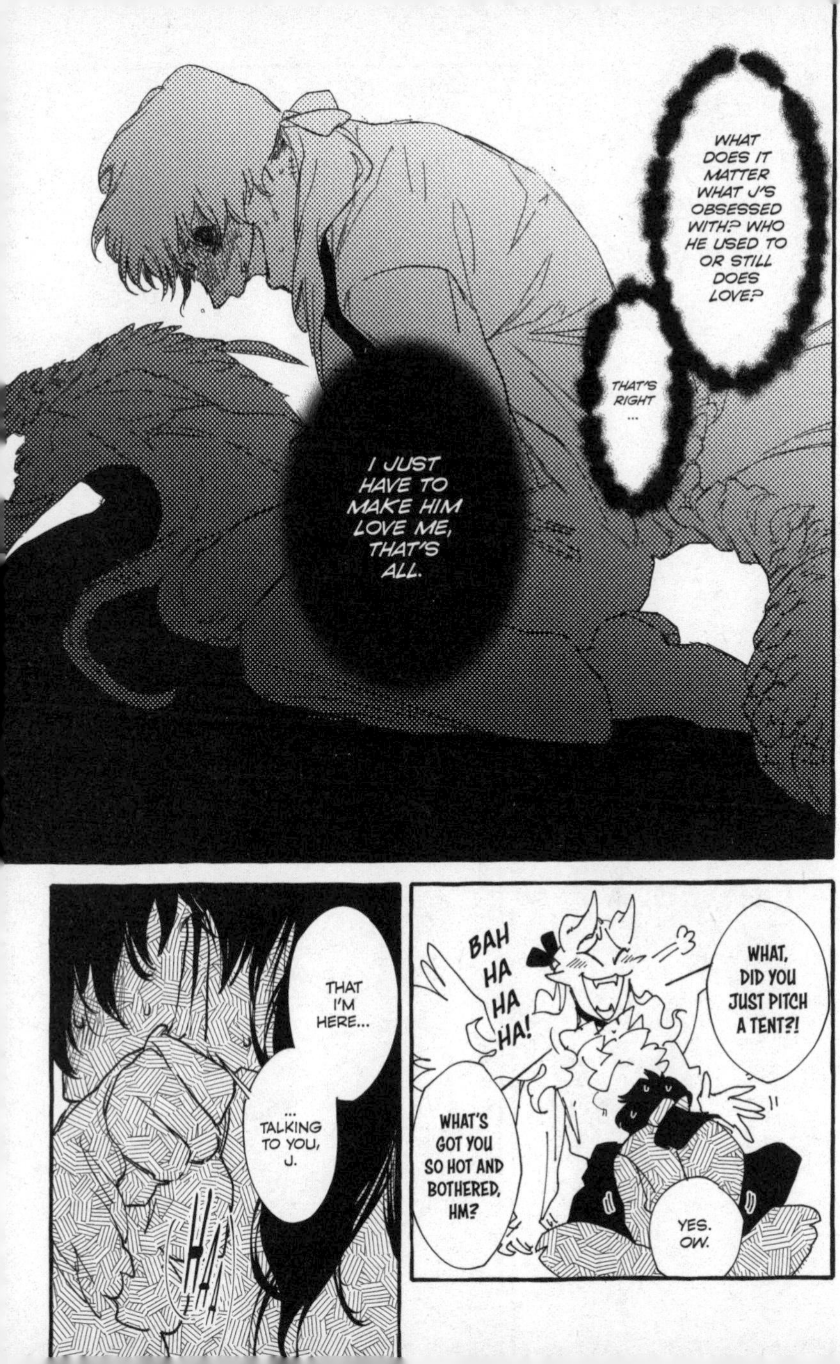
WHAT DOES IT MATTER WHAT J'S OBSESSED WITH? WHO HE USED TO OR STILL DOES LOVE?
THAT'S RIGHT...
I JUST HAVE TO MAKE HIM LOVE ME, THAT'S ALL.
WHAT, DID YOU JUST PITCH A TENT?!
BAH HA HA HA!
WHAT'S GOT YOU SO HOT AND BOTHERED, HM?
YES. OW.
THAT I'M HERE...
...TALKING TO YOU, J.

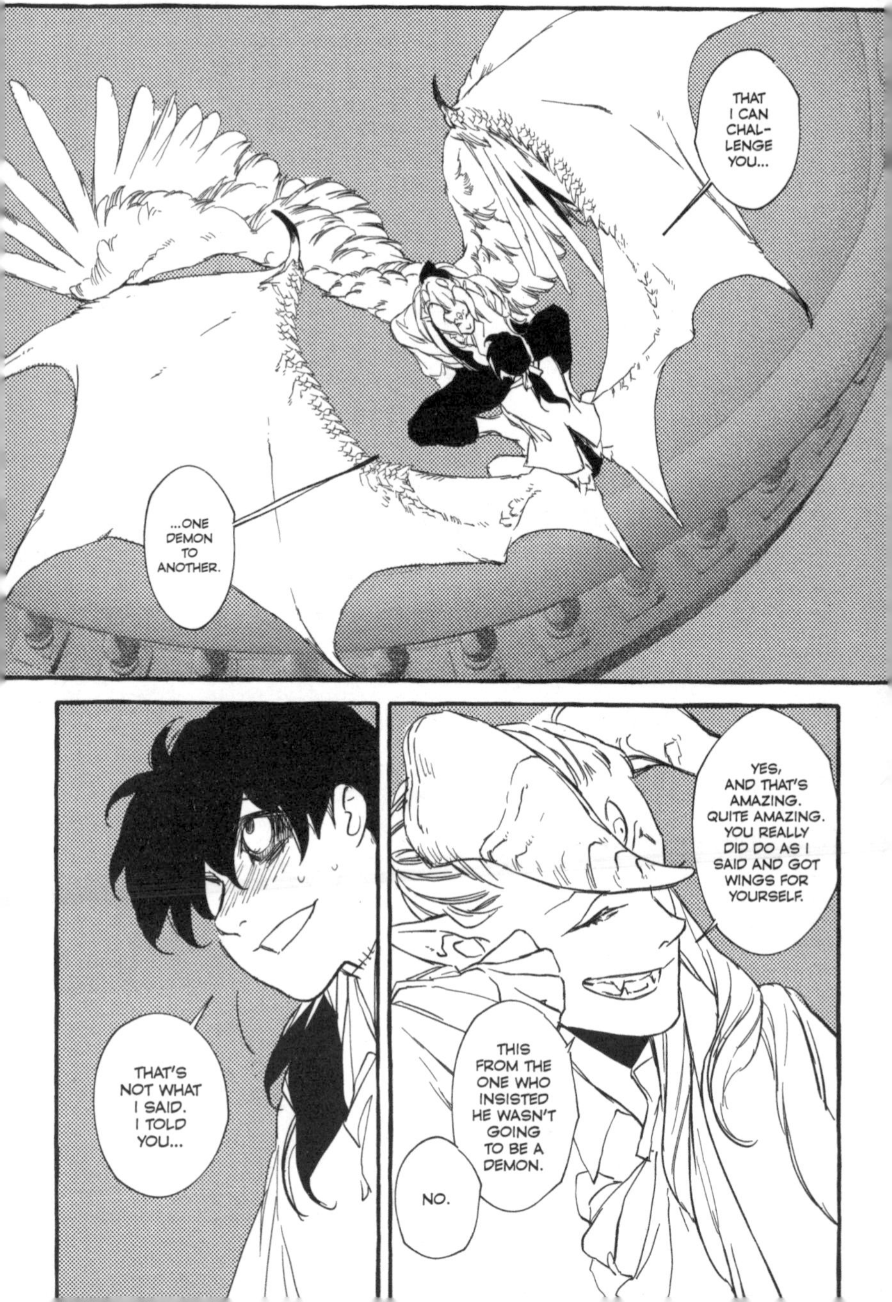
THAT I CAN CHAL-LENGE YOU...
...ONE DEMON TO ANOTHER.
YES, AND THAT'S AMAZING. QUITE AMAZING. YOU REALLY DID DO AS I SAID AND GOT WINGS FOR YOURSELF.
THIS FROM THE ONE WHO INSISTED HE WASN'T GOING TO BE A DEMON.
NO.
THAT'S NOT WHAT I SAID. I TOLD YOU...

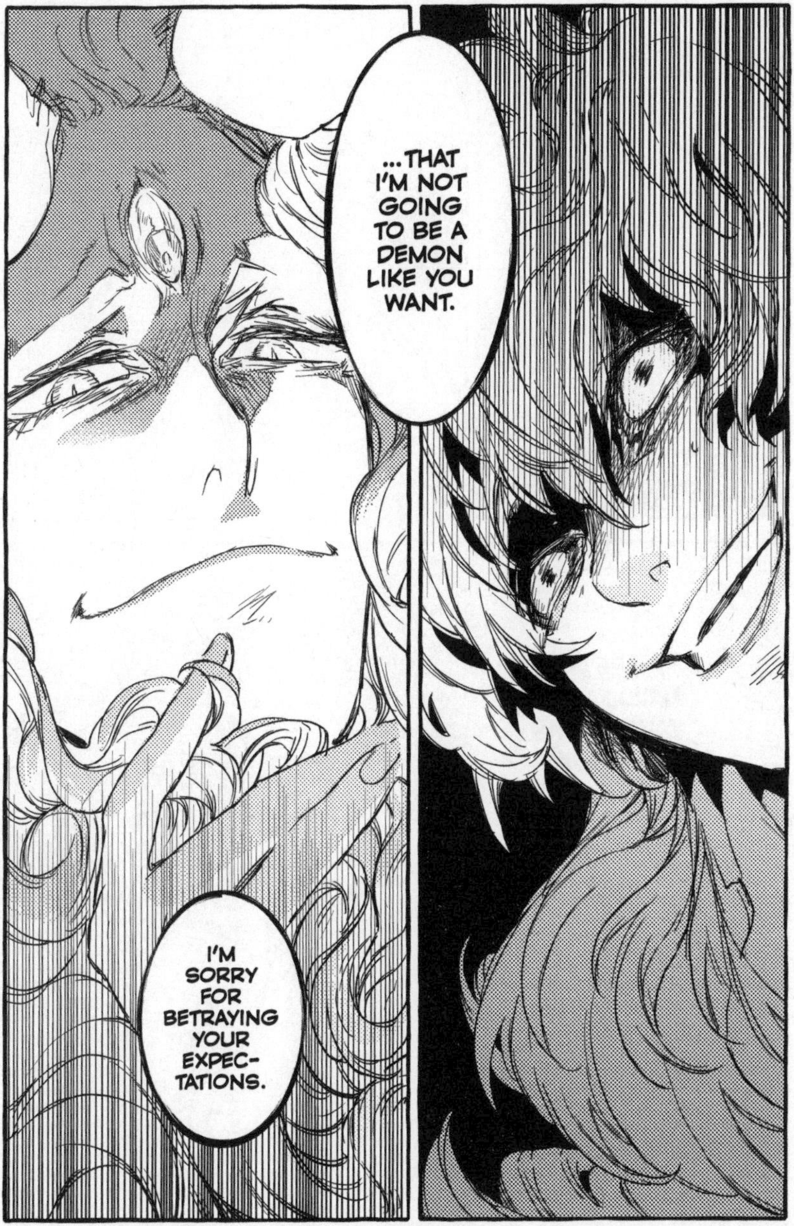
...THAT I'M NOT GOING TO BE A DEMON LIKE YOU WANT.
I'M SORRY FOR BETRAYING YOUR EXPEC-TATIONS.

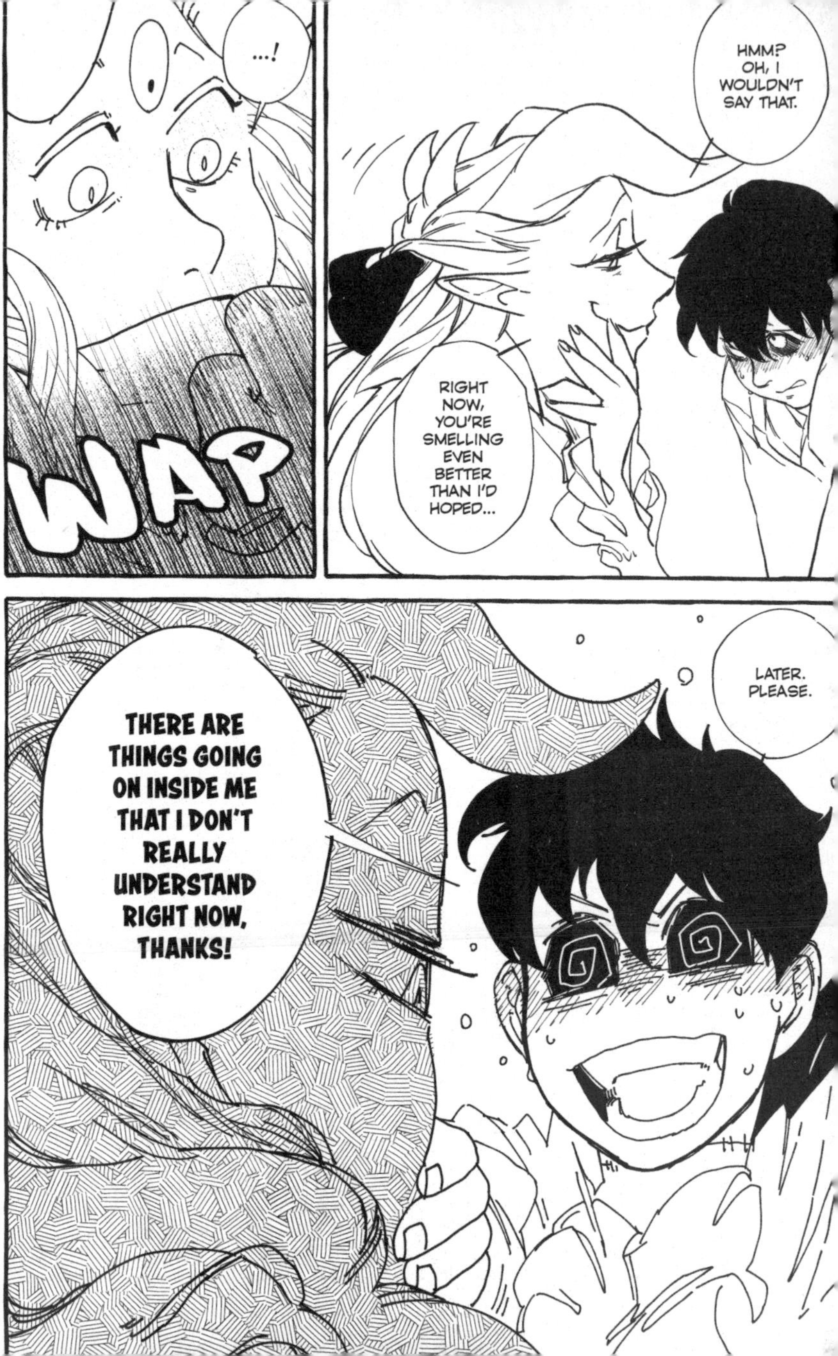
HMM? OH, I WOULDN'T SAY THAT.
RIGHT NOW, YOU'RE SMELLING EVEN BETTER THAN I'D HOPED...
...!
WAP
LATER. PLEASE.
THERE ARE THINGS GOING ON INSIDE ME THAT I DON'T REALLY UNDERSTAND RIGHT NOW, THANKS!

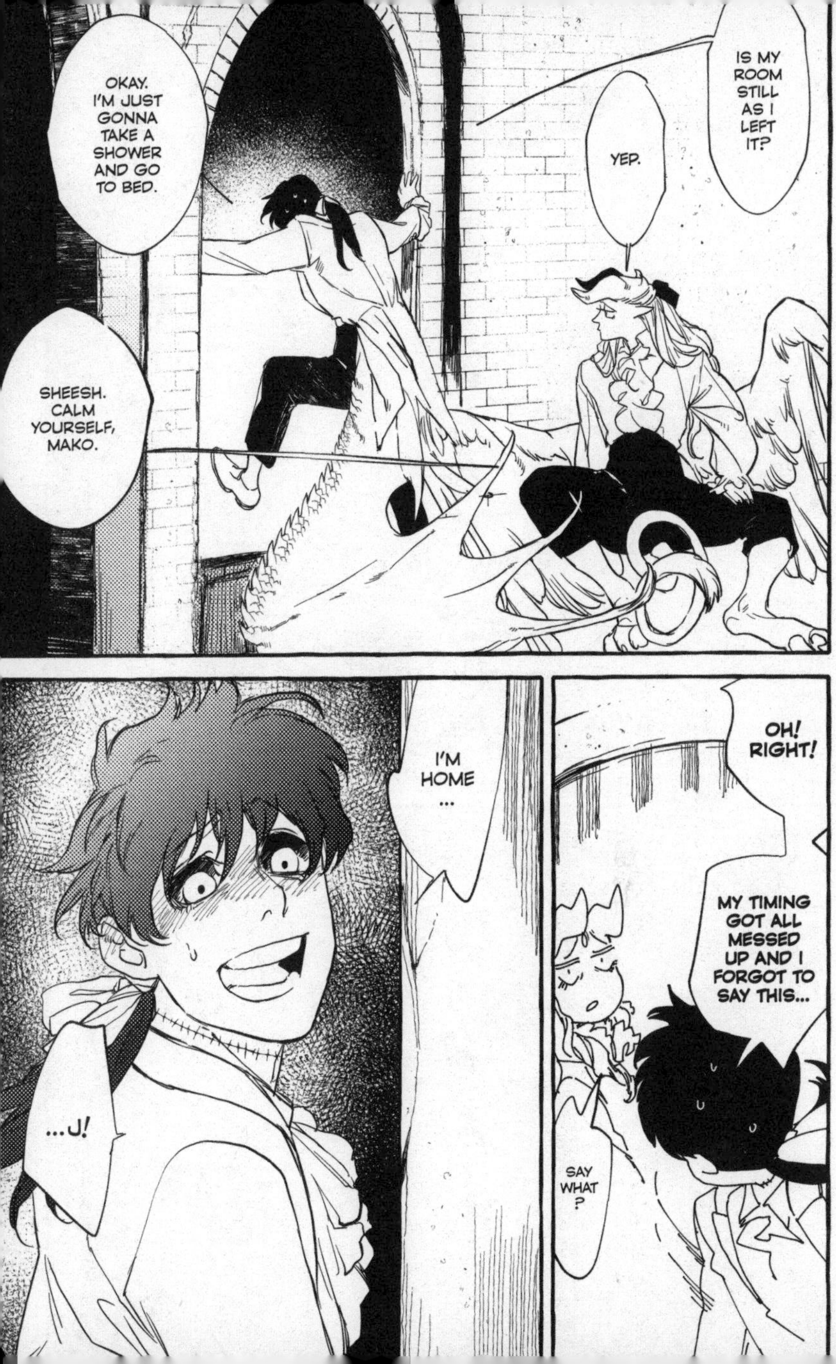
IS MY ROOM STILL AS I LEFT IT?
YEP.
OKAY. I'M JUST GONNA TAKE A SHOWER AND GO TO BED.
SHEESH. CALM YOURSELF, MAKO.
OH! RIGHT!
MY TIMING GOT ALL MESSED UP AND I FORGOT TO SAY THIS...
SAY WHAT?
I'M HOME...
...J!

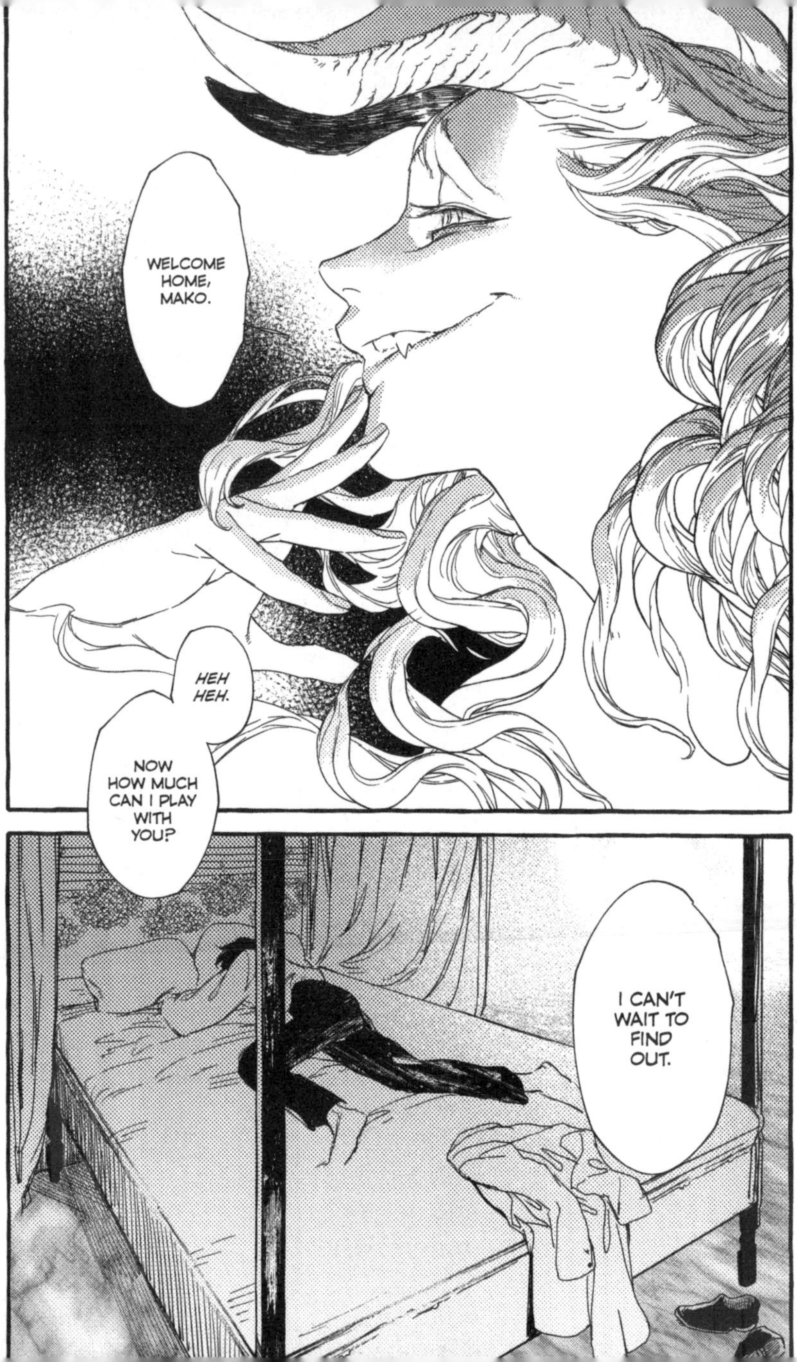
WELCOME HOME, MAKO.
HEH HEH.
NOW HOW MUCH CAN I PLAY WITH YOU?
I CAN'T WAIT TO FIND OUT.

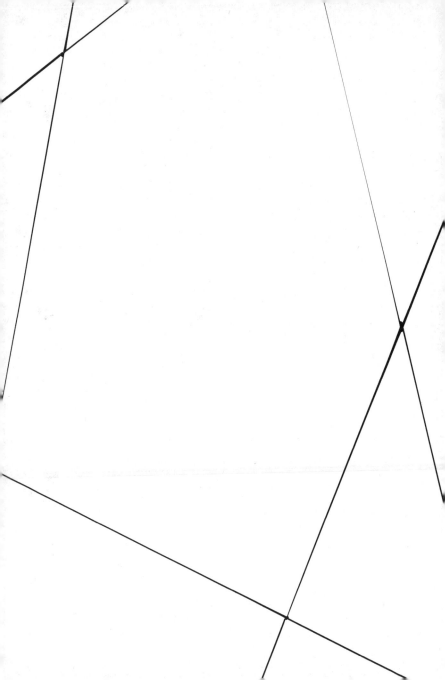

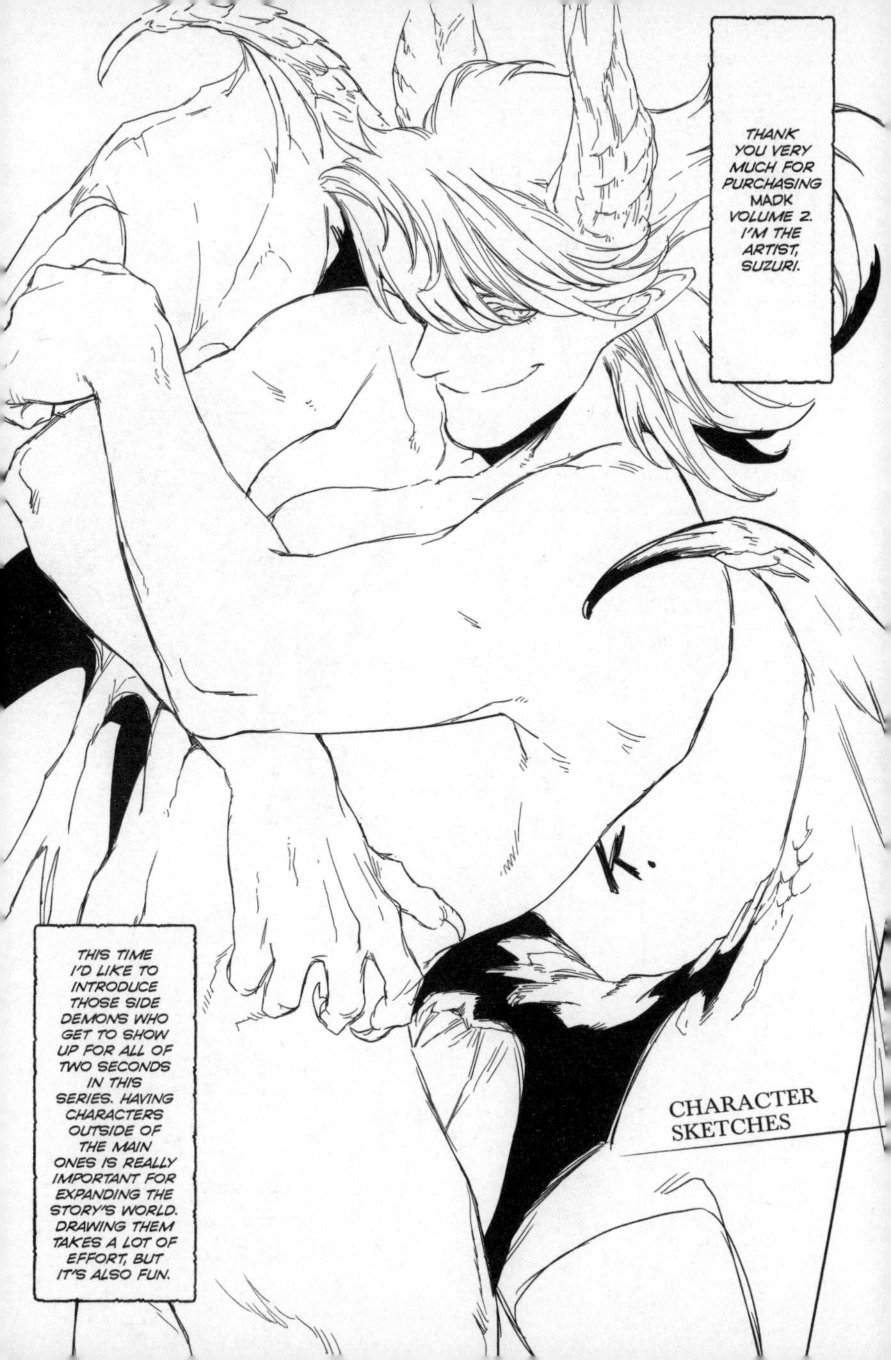
THANK YOU VERY MUCH FOR PURCHASING MADK VOLUME 2. I'M THE ARTIST, SUZURI.
THIS TIME I'D LIKE TO INTRODUCE THOSE SIDE DEMONS WHO GET TO SHOW UP FOR ALL OF TWO SECONDS IN THIS SERIES. HAVING CHARACTERS OUTSIDE OF THE MAIN ONES IS REALLY IMPORTANT FOR EXPANDING THE STORY'S WORLD. DRAWING THEM TAKES A LOT OF EFFORT, BUT IT'S ALSO FUN.
CHARACTER SKETCHES

A YOUNGER DEMON WITH A SPIDER-LIKE FACE, ASVEL IS ONE OF FJORD'S RIVALS. IF A HUMAN MAKES A PACT WITH HIM, HE CAN MAKE THEM RICH QUICKLY NO MATTER THEIR TALENTS. LATER HE REVERSES THOSE FORTUNES JUST AS QUICKLY, COLLECTING THE SHATTERED SOUL AFTERWARD. FRIENDLY AND CHARMING, HE HAS A SOFT SPOT FOR STRONGLY DETERMINED PEOPLE. HE ONCE ALMOST RUINED HIMSELF BY FALLING IN LOVE WITH A HUMAN WOMAN.

CAIN

ABEL

ASVEL

TWIN DEMONS SHARING ONE BODY. CAIN HAS A DEEP, RASPY VOICE, WHILE ABEL'S IS A HIGH, CLEAR TENOR. BOTH OF THEM TEND TO TALK AT ONCE, CONFUSING AND TIRING THE MORTAL THEY'RE TALKING TO. ONCE THAT MORTAL IS THOROUGHLY BEFUDDLED, THEY WILL SUDDENLY SPEAK AS ONE AND STEER THE PACT TO THEIR BENEFIT.

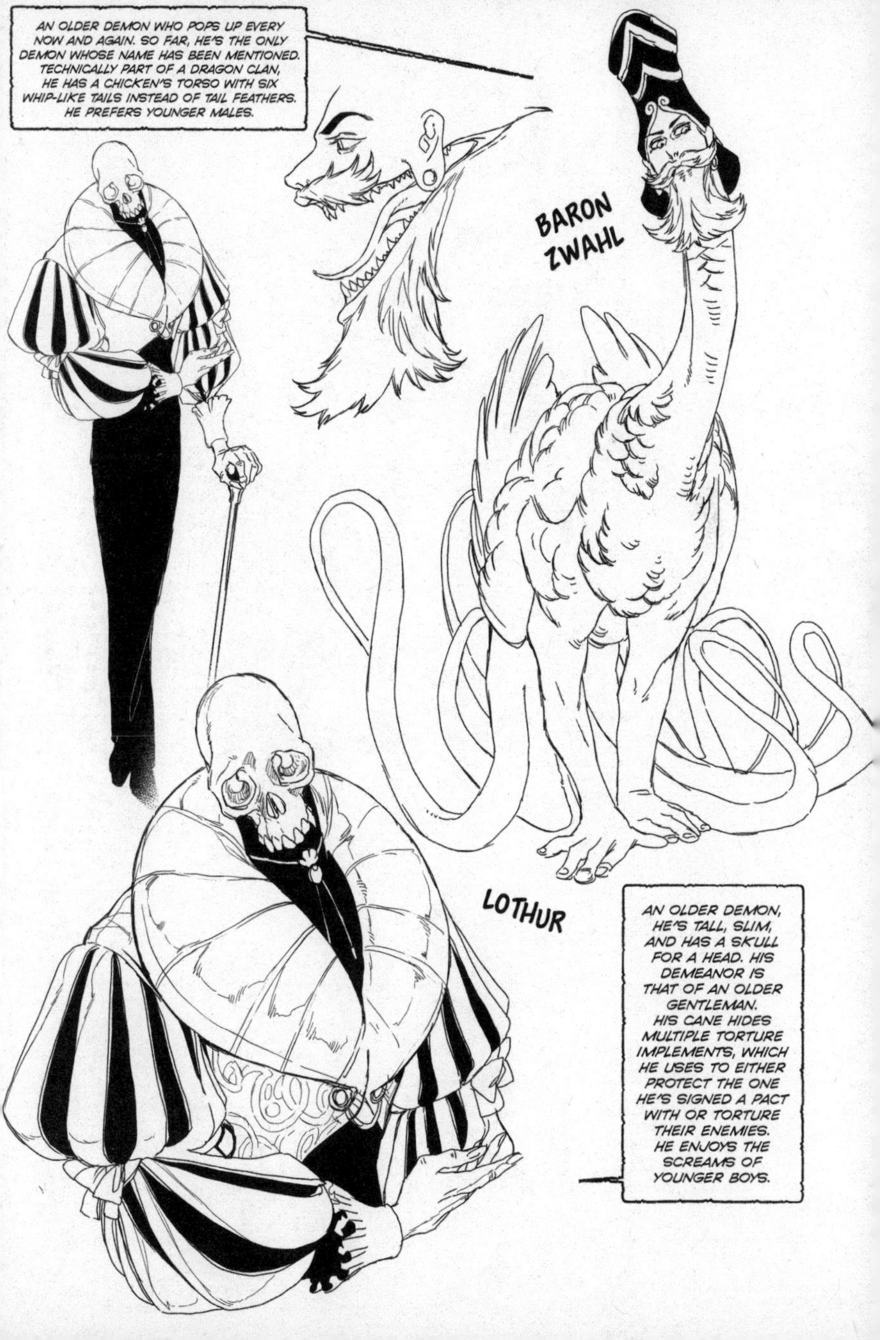
AN OLDER DEMON WHO POPS UP EVERY NOW AND AGAIN. SO FAR, HE'S THE ONLY DEMON WHOSE NAME HAS BEEN MENTIONED. TECHNICALLY PART OF A DRAGON CLAN, HE HAS A CHICKEN'S TORSO WITH SIX WHIP-LIKE TAILS INSTEAD OF TAIL FEATHERS. HE PREFERS YOUNGER MALES.
BARON ZWAHL
LOTHUR
AN OLDER DEMON, HE'S TALL, SLIM, AND HAS A SKULL FOR A HEAD. HIS DEMEANOR IS THAT OF AN OLDER GENTLEMAN. HIS CANE HIDES MULTIPLE TORTURE IMPLEMENTS, WHICH HE USES TO EITHER PROTECT THE ONE HE'S SIGNED A PACT WITH OR TORTURE THEIR ENEMIES. HE ENJOYS THE SCREAMS OF YOUNGER BOYS.

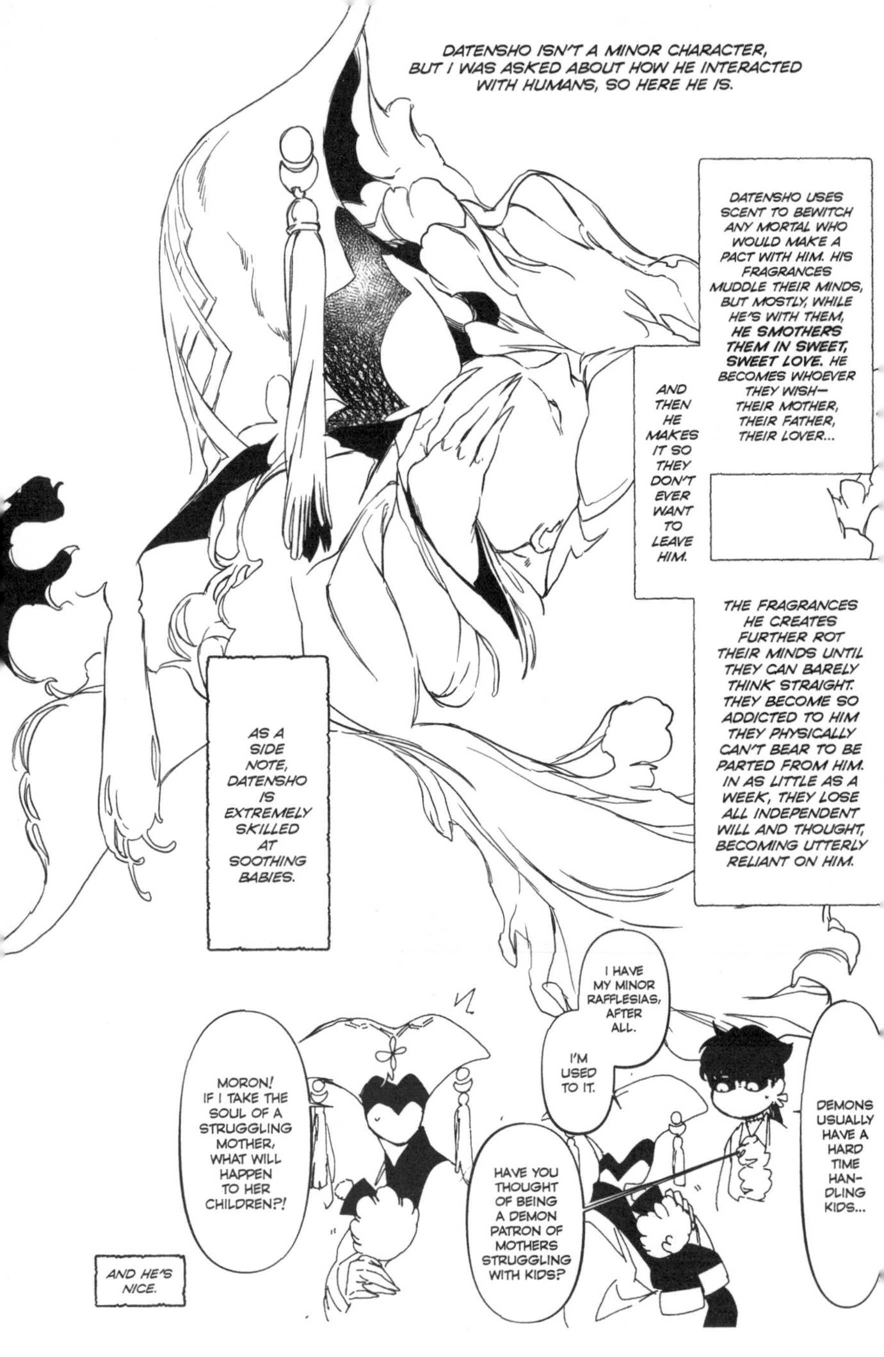
DATENSHO ISN'T A MINOR CHARACTER, BUT I WAS ASKED ABOUT HOW HE INTERACTED WITH HUMANS, SO HERE HE IS.
DATENSHO USES SCENT TO BEWITCH ANY MORTAL WHO WOULD MAKE A PACT WITH HIM. HIS FRAGRANCES MUDDLE THEIR MINDS, BUT MOSTLY, WHILE HE'S WITH THEM, **HE SMOTHERS THEM IN SWEET, SWEET LOVE.** HE BECOMES WHOEVER THEY WISH— THEIR MOTHER, THEIR FATHER, THEIR LOVER...
AND THEN HE MAKES IT SO THEY DON'T EVER WANT TO LEAVE HIM.
THE FRAGRANCES HE CREATES FURTHER ROT THEIR MINDS UNTIL THEY CAN BARELY THINK STRAIGHT. THEY BECOME SO ADDICTED TO HIM THEY PHYSICALLY CAN'T BEAR TO BE PARTED FROM HIM. IN AS LITTLE AS A WEEK, THEY LOSE ALL INDEPENDENT WILL AND THOUGHT, BECOMING UTTERLY RELIANT ON HIM.
AS A SIDE NOTE, DATENSHO IS EXTREMELY SKILLED AT SOOTHING BABIES.
DEMONS USUALLY HAVE A HARD TIME HAN-DLING KIDS...
I HAVE MY MINOR RAFFLESIAS, AFTER ALL.
I'M USED TO IT.
HAVE YOU THOUGHT OF BEING A DEMON PATRON OF MOTHERS STRUGGLING WITH KIDS?
MORON! IF I TAKE THE SOUL OF A STRUGGLING MOTHER, WHAT WILL HAPPEN TO HER CHILDREN?!
AND HE'S NICE.

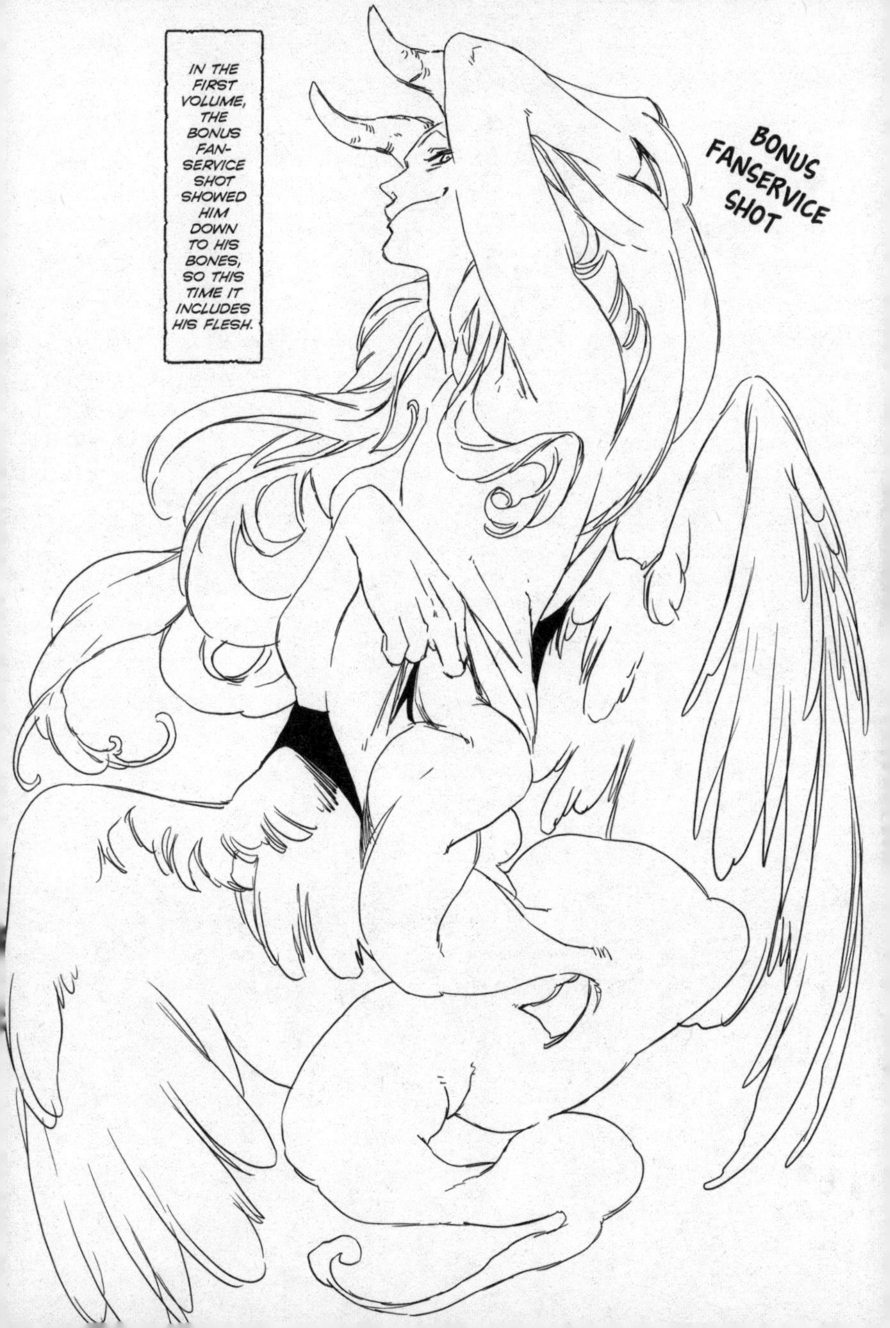
BONUS FANSERVICE SHOT
IN THE FIRST VOLUME, THE BONUS FAN-SERVICE SHOT SHOWED HIM DOWN TO HIS BONES, SO THIS TIME IT INCLUDES HIS FLESH.

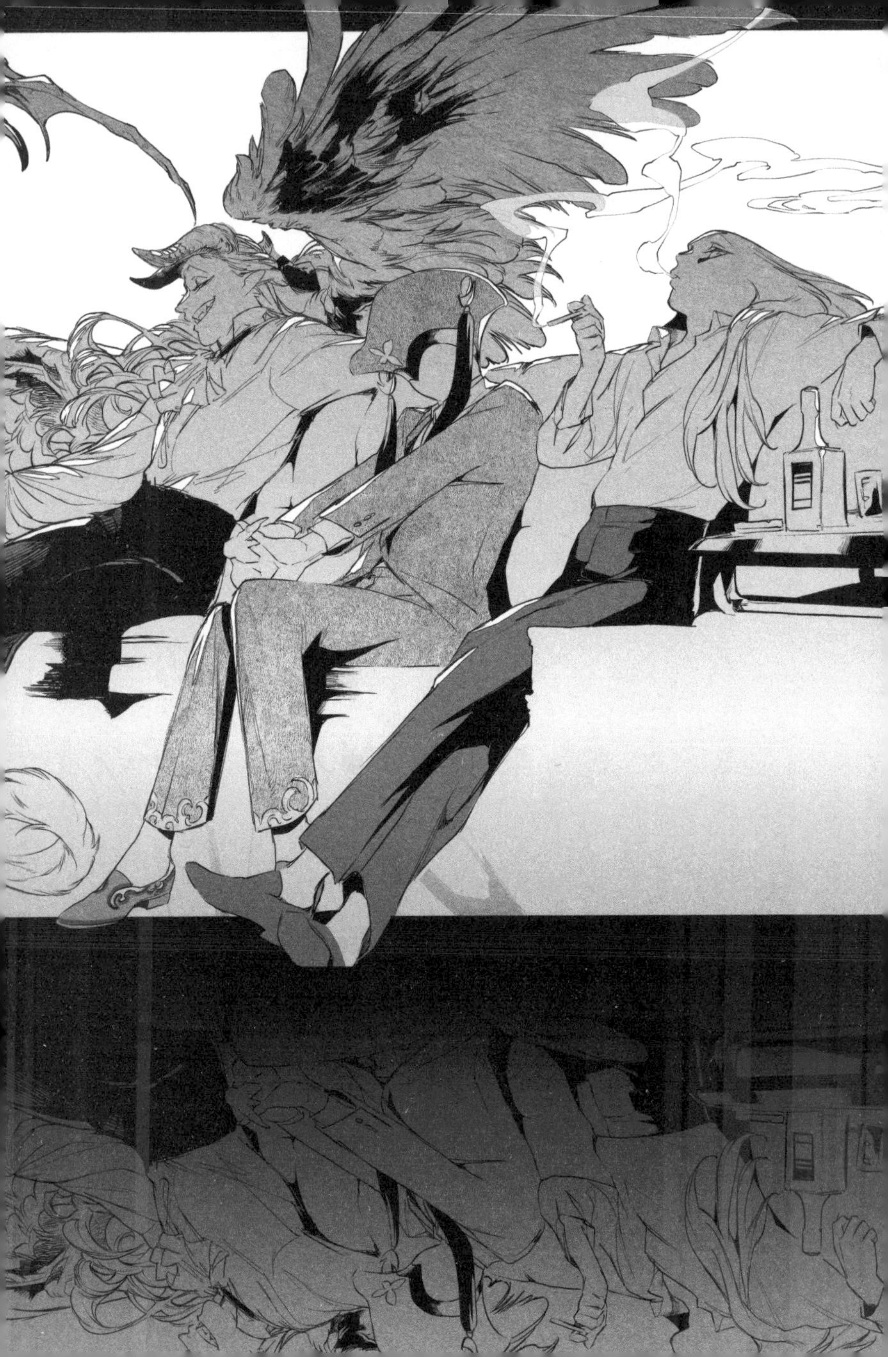

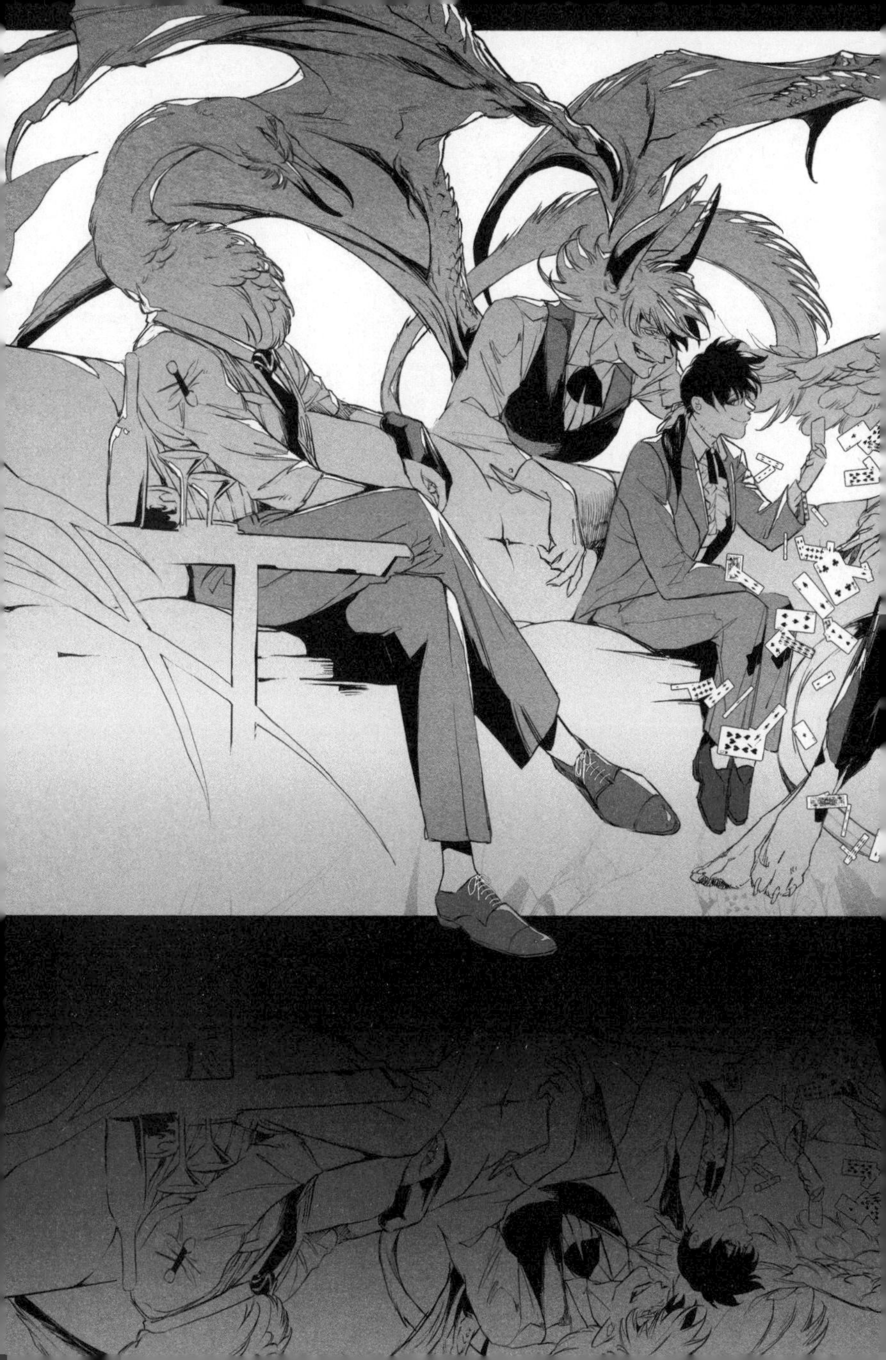

I can't believe it, but here's
volume 2. I'm doing my best
to ensure there's a volume 3.
The fact that I've gotten this
far at all is entirely thanks
to all of you. Thank you!

About the Author

Although *MADK* is the creator's first
English-language release, it was previously
published in French. Prior to becoming
a mangaka, **Ryo Suzuri** worked as a
3D modeler on *Monster Hunter* for the
gaming company Capcom. In addition
to boys' love, the creator has also
released shojo and seinen under the
pen name Ryo Sumiyoshi. You
can find out more about Ryo
Suzuri on Twitter at **@szr_Ryo**.

MADK
Volume 2
SuBLime Manga Edition

Story and Art by **Ryo Suzuri**

Translation—**Adrienne Beck**
Touch-Up Art and Lettering—**Deborah Fisher**
Cover and Graphic Design—**Yukiko Whitley**
Editor—**Jennifer LeBlanc**

Original Japanese edition published by FRANCE SHOIN

This English edition is published by arrangement with FRANCE SHOIN Inc., Tokyo
in care of Tuttle-Mori Agency, Inc., Tokyo.

Canna Comics

Printed in the U.S.A.

Published by SuBLime Manga
P.O. Box 77010
San Francisco, CA 94107

10 9 8 7 6 5 4 3 2
First printing, August 2021
Second printing, May 2022

M MATURE

PARENTAL ADVISORY
MADK is rated M for Mature and is recommended for mature readers. This volume contains graphic imagery and mature themes.

SUBLIME
www.SuBLimeManga.com

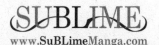

For more information

on all our products, along with the most up-to-date news on releases, series announcements, and contests, please visit us at:

 SuBLimeManga.com

 twitter.com/**SuBLimeManga**

 facebook.com/**SuBLimeManga**

 instagram.com/**SuBLimeManga**

 SuBLimeManga.tumblr.com